ST. MARY'S COLLEGE OF MARYLAND
ST. MARY'S CITY, MARYLAND

THE EUROPEAN UNDERSTANDING OF INDIA

General Editors of the Series

K. A. BALLHATCHET

P. J. MARSHALL

D. F. POCOCK

European attempts to understand India have been pursued in a variety of fields. Many of the books and articles that resulted are still of great historical importance. Not only do they provide valuable information about the India of the time; they are also of significance in the intellectual history of Europe. Each volume in the present series has been edited by a scholar who is concerned to elucidate both its Indian and its European relevance.

Sleeman in Oudh

Portrait of Sleeman by George Duncan Beechey, 1851

050291

SLEEMAN IN OUDH

An Abridgement of W. H. Sleeman's
*A Journey through the Kingdom
of Oude in 1849–50*

*Edited with an Introduction and
Notes by*

P. D. REEVES

Lecturer in History, School of African and Asian Studies,
University of Sussex

CAMBRIDGE

AT THE UNIVERSITY PRESS

1971

Published by the Syndics of the Cambridge University Press
Bentley House, 200 Euston Road, London NW1 2DB
American Branch: 32 East 57th Street, New York, N.Y.10022

Introduction, Notes, Selection

© Cambridge University Press 1971

Library of Congress Catalogue Card Number: 70–134624

ISBN: 0 521 08034 7

Printed in Great Britain
at the University Printing House, Cambridge
(Brooke Crutchley, University Printer)

Contents

Diary of a Tour Through Oude[1]

VOLUME I

[1] The chapters are numbered for this present edition. The original numbering is shown in the Tables of Contents for 1852 and 1858, below pp. 41–8. Note, in particular, that the original chapter X of the 1852 edition (Ch. IV of vol. II in 1858) is omitted entirely from this present edition. The titles, which indicate the sections of the journey covered in the various chapters, have also been added for this edition.

Contents

Map

Plates

Preface

This abridgement of W. H. Sleeman's *Journey Through the Kingdom of Oude* (as it has been previously been called) has two main purposes. The first is to provide a clearer and more manageable text than has hitherto been available of one of the most important of the published documents that we have relating to the history of Oudh. The second is to point up the significance, as I see it, of Sleeman's approach to the study of Indian society.

The importance of Sleeman's *Journey* as source-material for Oudh history hardly requires any emphasis, for it has long been recognised, and used, by those interested in the region. It is perhaps strange that it has not been reprinted before this, but the fact that the material in its two volumes is not particularly well-arranged is probably reason enough. It is certainly the reason for the deletion, in this present edition, of material which, while often fascinating in itself, adds little to the factual record of mid-nineteenth-century Oudh which is contained in Sleeman's diary of his tour and which forms the central (and most valuable) part of the *Journey*. The principles on which these deletions have been made are fully explained in the Introduction; it is sufficient to say here that the basic concern has been to present the text of the diary, as Sleeman originally had it printed, as effectively as possible.

The second of my objectives concerns the history of the study of Indian society. This history is now beginning to be written and, not surprisingly, the work and writings of British officials and administrators figure very prominently in it. One might point here, for example, to Daniel Thorner's critique of Tod's use of the term 'feudalism' in the Indian context; to the discussions by Eric Stokes and Ravinder Kumar of Utilitarian doctrines and their application; to Louis Dumont's study of the concept of the 'village community' in nineteenth-century administrative writings; and to Bernard Cohn's wider-ranging

Preface

'Notes on the history of the study of Indian society and culture.'[1]

That officials should feature so prominently is not really very surprising because until after the Second World War – with a few notable exceptions – the main observers of Indian society at close range were those whose tasks as revenue, judicial or census officials brought them into close touch with it. The results of this predominantly administrative contact were not, of course, an unmixed blessing because the lack of training which they had and the shortness of the time which they had to complete their official tasks meant that officials were, by and large, satisfied with descriptive rather than analytical reporting. Nonetheless, their work is important because it forms a vital part of the background of the modern study of Indian society. The reports, gazetteers, memoranda and memoirs of these men constitute a major source of information for present-day historical and social research concerning India – as the references in most recently-published studies will demonstrate. It is, therefore, of very great importance that the conceptual bases of their approaches to social enquiry and the nature of the categories which they employed in their records should be as fully understood as possible. This edition of Sleeman is a small contribution to this larger task. There are more thorough and more systematic investigators than Sleeman, no doubt, and not until their work has been analysed will that larger task be completed; but Sleeman's work raises many of the main issues which it involves and it is therefore a worthwhile contribution. It certainly seems to me to warrant its place in a series such as the present one which is devoted to attempts to understand India.

This volume has given me great personal satisfaction. I am drawn to the study of Oudh through my own research work which is concerned with the political and agrarian history of nineteenth- and twentieth-century Uttar Pradesh and, in

[1] D. Thorner, 'Feudalism in India' in R. Coulborn (ed.), *Feudalism in History* (Princeton, 1956); E. Stokes, *The English Utilitarians and India* (Oxford, 1959); R. Kumar, *Western India in the Nineteenth Century* (London, 1968); L. Dumont, 'The "village community" from Munro to Maine', *Contributions to Indian Sociology*, no. ix (December 1966); B. S. Cohn in M. Singer and B. S. Cohn (eds), *Structure and Change in Indian Society* (Chicago, 1968).

Preface

particular, the activities and fortunes of the landlords of that state –
the *taluqdars* of Oudh and the *zamindars* of Agra province.
I have greatly appreciated the opportunity, therefore, to act as
Sleeman's editor and I want to thank David Pocock, in particular, for originally suggesting that I might take part in this series.
His encouragement and advice has been a great help throughout.
I would also like to express my gratitude for the help which I
have received from Professor Ballhatchet. In addition to editorial
discussion, he gave me an opportunity to present an earlier
version of the views now expressed in the Introduction to his
seminar at the School of Oriental and African Studies, an
opportunity which was invaluable to me.

Any historian necessarily incurs weighty debts of gratitude to
the people who run the libraries and archives from which he
obtains his material. In my case I am particularly grateful to
those at the Bodleian Library, Oxford, who made it possible for
me to have a complete copy of the 1852 text of the Diary from
which to work; to those at the India Office Library and the
University of Sussex Library who are always ready to help; and
to the Librarian of the University of Canterbury, Christchurch,
New Zealand, who kindly allowed me to borrow his library's
copy of Sleeman's *Journey* which is annotated by its original
owner, Lieutenant Weston, who was Sleeman's assistant and
one of the party on the tour. My thanks are due to Dr Ian
Catanach of the Department of History at the University of
Canterbury, who made this possible and who also gave me other
valuable guidance on source material.

I would also like to thank Brigadier J. C. Sleeman, and Mrs
Sleeman, for their many kindnesses and for permission to repro-
duce as a frontispiece the fine portrait of Sir William Sleeman,
Brigadier Sleeman's great-grandfather, which once hung in the
Residency in Lucknow.

I have many friends at the University of Sussex who have
given much help and encouragement during the preparation of
this volume. Bruce Graham, Anthony Low, Fred Bailey and
Richard Brown and, for the period that he was at the University
as a visiting professor, Tom Metcalf, all listened to, and on
occasions read through, my thoughts on Sleeman. My thanks to

Preface

them all, and my assurance that none of them is responsible for anything that is written here. There is another group to whom I would like to express my appreciation: a small but lively graduate student class at the University of Michigan, Ann Arbor, who made my time there in 1966 such a pleasure and with whom a copy of Sleeman's *Journey* forms a permanent link. Finally, my thanks go to my wife and children who have borne with this typescript longer than they would care to remember.

Sleeman's spelling and transcriptions of vernacular terms has been preserved in the text; but an attempt is made in the notes and in the glossary to provide more acceptable transcriptions where possible. No attempt has been made to indicate phonetic values by diacritical marks and the somewhat haphazard marks given in Butter's list of *chaklas* have been omitted.

P. D. REEVES

Kingston near Lewes,
Sussex
April 1971

Introduction

W. H. Sleeman's *Journey through the kingdom of Oude* is the most detailed account that we have of conditions in pre-annexation Oudh.[1] But, in the form in which the book has been known since it was published in 1858, its utility has been greatly restricted. The chief drawback has been its apparent lack of arrangement: the reader is presented with a jumble of impressions and facts, interspersed with lengthy historical digressions and anecdotes, and other more speculative material, and the lack of an index has made it difficult to use effectively. All too often its anecdotes, which have appealed to later writers because they are illustrations of the exotic and the wayward,[2] have been taken over, while the much more valuable factual record of rural life and administrations has remained largely unutilised. This edition of the *Journey*, it is hoped, will go some way towards remedying this situation by bringing to the fore the factual record.

EDITORIAL PRINCIPLES

There were in fact two printings of the diary which Sleeman kept on his 'journey through the kingdom of Oude': one in 1852 in Lucknow which Sleeman himself supervised; and another in 1858 in London after his death. The background to these two editions is discussed later.[3]

This present edition is based on the 1852 text, which is the only version that Sleeman himself saw. The copy which I have used is that which belonged to Lady Sleeman, now in the Bodleian Library, Oxford; in addition to being one of the

---

[1] More properly Avadh or Awadh, but Oudh is the most common British–Indian spelling. Sleeman's 'Oude' is retained in his text and in quotations from it and other contemporary sources, but elsewhere 'Oudh' is used.

[2] For example, R. Coupland, *India. A Restatement* (Oxford, 1945), pp. 289–90, who gives four extracts to illustrate 'The misgovernment of Oudh'. Also M. Edwardes, *The Orchid House. Splendours and Miseries in the Kingdom of Oudh, 1827–1857* (London, 1960), part II.

[3] See below pp. 13–18.

original copies, this has a number of manuscript corrections by Sleeman which make it especially valuable. Not that there is a great deal of difference between the two versions. Some material which appeared as footnotes in the 1852 version (particularly that which added details through to 1851) was printed in the text in 1858; some portions of the Preface were omitted in 1858;[1] and there was an attempt to add emphasis to one particular sentence;[2] but apart from these items I have not been able to trace any major interference with Sleeman's text.[3]

As printed in the 1850s the *Journey* is a sprawling and untidy work of two volumes and over 700 pages. The core of the book is the diary which Sleeman wrote on his tour over the three months of December 1849 and January and February 1850; but a great deal of additional material was added subsequently while it was being printed. A complete edition of the two-volume work not being practicable (or possibly desirable) at this time, a decision had to be made as to what should be omitted for this edition. The principles that have been followed here are to return as far as possible to the diary of the tour and to focus attention on 'the state of the country and the condition of the people'[4] – which must mean very largely the rural areas and rural society. Material additional to the diary has been retained only if it has seemed relevant to an understanding of Oudh rural society in 1849–50. Thus, material of the following kinds has been omitted whenever possible: purely historical accounts such as the lengthy discussion of Oudh–British relations in the first half of the nineteenth century which appeared in volume two; anecdotes concerning the Court in Lucknow, much of which is already well-known and often retailed; sections which merely catalogue long lists of crimes; and speculative or anecdotal digressions ('wolves nurturing children' or 'Mr Ravenscroft's murder') which, while they are sometimes interesting in themselves, interrupt the flow and purpose of the diary to an un-

[1] See below p. 51.

[2] See below p. 57. In *A Journey through the Kingdom of Oude in 1849–1850* (London, 1858) [hereafter given as *JTKO*] the sentence is at vol. I, pp. 23–4.

[3] References are made to pages in both 'editions' in the extracts printed below because it will be more convenient for readers to be able to consult the 1858 edition which is the only one readily available.

[4] *JTKO*, vol. I, p. 1; see p. 53 below.

Introduction

necessary extent. Where the actions of the court or the officers of government impinge directly on the lives of the people, however, the material remains relevant and is preserved. The result, it is hoped, has been to present as clearly as possible – avoiding a mere collection of snippets – Sleeman's observations of Oudh rural society, its social structure, its agricultural and economic bases, its outlook and its folklore, and the institutions of government which affected it, in the years immediately prior to the British take-over. There is no more detailed, accurate or unbiased an account of Oudh in this period than that which Sleeman presents in his diary and it is, therefore, this which is worth preserving and which will be of interest to the general reader and of value to the student of the history of the societies of northern India.

A diary is not the most coherent way in which to present material on a strange country, of course: information comes in fragments and understanding of the various aspects of a subject develops slowly.[1] The compensation is that one has the opportunity of seeing something of this process of comprehension, that one shares to some extent the journey and its unfolding of information. Certainly this is what one gains by Sleeman's account as a diary and no attempt has been made here to re-arrange the material except in the limited sense that the entries are brought closer together by the omission of extraneous material and that the information on forts and jungles is placed at the end of the text as an appendix. It is hoped that the indications of the route which are given in the titles of the chapters for this edition, together with the map which shows the dates of travel and the districts being traversed in particular chapters will help to give the reader a greater sense of the direction and location during the tour, and that the index will make it possible to bring related sections together; but apart from these aids the diary is left to tell its own story in its own way and to reveal mid-nineteenth-century Oudh – the last Indian-ruled area to come under direct British government – as Sleeman saw and heard and recorded it.

[1] Cf. Arthur Young, *Travels in France During the Years 1787, 1788 and 1789*, ed. C. Maxwell (Cambridge, 1929), pp. 1–3 for Young's consideration of the advantages and disadvantages of the 'diary' or 'essay' form of travel book.

Introduction

Oudh was the last of the Indian principalities to be annexed to British India but it had a long and troubled history of relations with the British power in the sub-continent before it was taken over.[1]

The Mughal province (*suba*) of Oudh, which the Nawab Wazirs Saadat Khan and Safdar Jang controlled formally as *subadars* (governors) and in fact as independent rulers from 1720 to 1754, occupied a strategic position across the Ganges valley and facing on to the territories of the Maratha confederacy and the disintegrating empire (and beyond it of those, like Nadir Shah of Persia, waiting to invade). In this early eighteenth-century period the English East India Company was not in a position to determine the deployment of authority in this area; but with the rise of the Company's power in Bengal in the late 1750s and the 1760s it was brought into direct contact with the 'country powers' and the balance of sub-continental power assumed great importance. This involvement was brought out forcibly by the intervention in the affairs of Bengal of the new Nawab Wazir of Oudh, Shuja-ud-daula, who joined with Mir Kasim, the unseated Nawab of Bengal, in an attack on the Company's forces which led to the defeat of the forces of the allied nawabs at Buxar in 1764 and the subsequent chasing of Shuja-ud-daula to Jajmau (in Cawnpore district) where the Oudh army was defeated again in 1765. So involved were they by this time, indeed, that the servants of the Company tried as a result of these victories to remove Shuja-ud-daula from his territories altogether and to hand Oudh to Shah Alam, the holder

---

[1] For Oudh–British relations see: *Cambridge History of India*, vol. v, *British India, 1497–1858*, chs 12, 16, 21 and 31; P. Basu, *Oudh and the East India Company 1785–1801* (Lucknow, 1943); W. Knighton, *The Private Life of an Eastern King* (Oxford, 1921), ed. with introduction by S. B. Smith; P. Moon, *Warren Hastings and British India* (London, 1947); J. Strachey, *Hastings and the Rohilla War* (Oxford, 1892); P. Marshall, *The Impeachment of Warren Hastings* (Oxford, 1965), ch. 6; C. Srinivasachari, *The Inwardness of British Annexations in India* (Madras, 1951), ch. 8. Also the following papers in the *Proceedings of the Indian History Congress* [*PIHC*]: N. Chatterji, 'Col. Baillie's charges against Lord Hastings', 18 *PIHC* (Calcutta, 1956), pp. 203–8; S. N. Prasad, 'The Oudh Treaty of 1837', 13 *PIHC* (Calcutta, 1952), pp. 297–302; S. K. Singh, 'Minto and the Begums of Oudh', 14 *PIHC* (Calcutta, 1953), pp. 295–301.

of what was left of the Mughal empire. The Court of Directors in London refused, however, to countenance such a wholesale usurpation of the Nawab Wazir and only the territories in the land between the Ganges and the Jamna rivers (the *doab*), which Safdar Jang had wrested from the Nawab of Farrukhabad in 1748, were given to Shah Alam.

By the mid-1770s, the hostilities of Buxar were reformed by the exigencies of north Indian politics. When the Emperor, Shah Alam, switched his allegiance to the Marathas and agreed to cede the lower *doab* territories (which included the strategically vital fort at Allahabad) to Sindhia, Warren Hastings returned the *doab* territories to Shuja-ud-daula and went on to help Oudh absorb the troublesome Rohilla chieftains who had built themselves into a strong local position in 'Rohilkhand' and who were prepared to use this position in alliance with the Marathas against the encroaching British power.

If Hastings involved the Company in north Indian politics still further, he also took steps to safeguard this involvement and to strengthen the British position. His aid to Oudh's expansion in 1773 was accompanied by the appointment of a Resident at the court of the Nawab Wazir and the establishment of sub-sidised British forces in Oudh. He thus began the process of Oudh's subordination to British influence, for both of these moves affected the nature of the relationship between the Company and Oudh. While the frontiers of northern and central India remained open and in question – that is, as long as the Maratha power remained in the field and the fate of the old empire was not fully determined – Oudh held an important position in north Indian strategy, but a position which, as a state, it was largely unable to fulfil. In 1775, the Company took advantage of the death of Shuja-ud-daula to conclude a new treaty at Faizabad which increased the subsidy from Oudh for the use of British troops, diverted the tribute paid by the *zamindar* of Ghazipur to the Company and, most important of all, provided for the Benares region to be ceded to the Company. Later, default on the subsidies for the Company's troops brought reprisals in the form of further exactions of territory: in 1797, the fort at Allahabad; and in 1801, the crescent of districts comprising Rohilkhand, the lower *doab* of the Ganges and Jamna, and Gorakhpur. The loss of these territories reduced Oudh to the position of a state isolated from sub-continental politics by a British perimeter wall; only to the north, where it bordered the hill-state of Nepal, which was itself to fall increasingly under British domination in the first half of the nineteenth century, did Oudh touch on non-British territory. After 1801, therefore, Oudh's significance was what it could offer rather than what it could do. The wealth controlled by its government and the manpower of important social groups within it which were prepared to act as mercenary troops for the Company, drew and kept the two powers, Oudh and the Company's government, together.

The Resident's functions were adapted to these changes. In the late eighteenth century the Residency was primarily a diplomatic post, concerned with the satisfaction of British military and political interests in north India. With the decline of Oudh's strategic importance, however, the Resident assumed increasingly the role of part-guardian of British interests and part-controller of the Nawab Wazirs. The Residents, indeed, increasingly acquired a place in the administration of the state itself in the first half of the nineteenth century, charged as the Company was by several of the Nawabs with the task of superintending the disbursement of pensions and endowments.[1] Whereas, in the eighteenth century, the Resident's position rested on the need for representations to a more-or-less equal ally, in the nineteenth century the Resident was more like a co-manager installed in a business enterprise by one partner. The change was signified by the arrangements that were made after 1819 when the Nawab Wazirs assumed a royal title. As 'Kings of Oudh', the Nawabs ceased to be subordinate to the Kings of Delhi (the last of the Mughals), but the British refused to allow the change to reduce their own status relative to the new Kings. The Resident and the King were to be equals in all formal and ceremonial relations: both, for instance, were to be carried into

[1] C. U. Aitchison, *A Collection of Treaties, Engagements and Sunnuds relating to India and Neighbouring Countries* (Calcutta, 1876), vol. II: *Treaties, etc. relating to the N.W.P., Oudh, Nepal, Bundelcund and Baghelcund*, pp. 132–47.

each other's presence; and the King was required to meet an incoming Resident, in person, outside the walls of the capital.[1] The Resident had an establishment of his own and he had a number of tasks specific to his post: relations with the sepoys who served in the Company's forces, which meant dealing with their petitions for help in local affairs; the disbursement of payments from the treasury attached to the Residency, and the receipt of funds; relations with the Court itself; the management of a range of special institutions in Lucknow; and intelligence operations within the Kingdom.[2] As a result, the Resident and his staff established clear political rights in the Kingdom, and especially in the capital. Dr Fayrer, who was the Surgeon at the Residency from 1853 until 1858, records how Sleeman instructed him in the intricacies of this position when he arrived. Matters of ceremonial and etiquette were of the greatest political importance, Sleeman told him:

native gentlemen should receive only that exact amount of official recognition to which they were entitled, but of which they were constantly trying to obtain more than was their due, with a view to enhancing their importance at the court of the king. He explained that certain observances were due to different grades; that, for example, some native gentlemen were to have chairs, others *morahs* (stools), others were not permitted to sit in the presence of the Resident or of the officers of the Residency, while others were not received as visitors at all. He explained to me that they might try to make my profession a means of gaining a point in this respect, and that on pretence of sickness or fatigue, they might try to obtain interviews and

[1] J. Fayrer, *Recollections of My Life* (Edinburgh, 1900), p. 90, for description of Resident's visit to King. For requirement that the King should meet a new Resident personally, see F. J. Goldsmid, *James Outram. A Biography*, 2 vols (London, 1880), vol. II, p. 101; see pp. 102–4 for a description of Outram's arrival. Cf. L. von Orlich, *Travels in India*, trans. H. Evans Lloyd, 2 vols (London, 1845), vol. II, p. 94, for description of an earlier Resident's reception.

[2] See Fayrer, *Recollections*, pp. 86, 94 for his duties as Residency Surgeon and later Assistant Resident. There has been no thorough study of the Residency system in this period but see U. Low, *Fifty Years with John Company. From the Letters of General Sir John Low of Clatto, Fife, 1822–1858* (London, 1936) which gives some sketchy information on the residency of Low (1831–43). For general studies see: E. Thompson, *The Making of the Indian Princes* (Oxford, 1943); T. G. P. Spear, *Twilight of the Mughals* (Cambridge, 1951); E. Thompson, *The Life of Charles, Lord Metcalfe* (London, 1937); *Selections from the Papers of Lord Metcalfe*, ed. J. W. Kaye (London, 1855); *Selections from the Ochterlony Papers (1818–25)*, ed. N. K. Sinha and A. K. Dasgupta (Calcutta, 1964) and K. N. Panikkar, *British Diplomacy in North India. A study of the Delhi Residency 1803–1857* (New Delhi, 1968).

Introduction

chairs, and that they might attempt to propitiate by fees if they thought they could do so with impunity, though they knew that was treading upon dangerous ground. In short, he warned me that they were a very intriguing set, and that their great desire was to be supposed to be intimate at the Residency and to have influence with the British political officers, and that any such suggestion might be made improper use of.[1]

Nonetheless, the Resident's ability to influence social and economic affairs was limited and Residents could do no more than witness the changes which, during the first half of the nineteenth century, increased disorder and instability in the kingdom. Successive Residents reported that the Kings seemed unable to govern satisfactorily and that disorder and oppression was general, although most saw little outside the immediate environs of the capital and heard little except for the reports of the 'news writers' or what was to be gleaned from their confidants at court. Successive Governors-General remonstrated with the Kings on the basis of these reports and insisted that continued 'misgovernment' would force the British to act; but up until the late 1840s these threats were not carried out. This 'restraint' on the part of the British may have been due, as is sometimes suggested, to the fact that the Kings' continued loyalty made them useful or, more simply, to the fact that continued loyalty made it difficult to justify annexation. There is also the fact that other areas in the sub-continent assumed greater importance, or were more attractive, than Oudh in this period. Certainly it was clear that the net was closing in by the late 1840s: Sind and the Panjab were both annexed in the 1840s; and Oudh's condition caused frequent comment and much speculation. Henry Lawrence, in a perceptive article in the *Calcutta Review* in 1845, called for urgent changes in the government of the Kingdom, and in 1847 the Governor-General, Lord Hardinge, presented the King with an ultimatum which demanded improvement in the government by October 1849, in default of which the British would act. The King did apparently respond to this ultimatum to the extent of submitting a memorandum of

[1] Fayrer, *Recollections*, p. 85. Fayrer later, as Assistant Resident, served as 'Residency Newswriter' and was responsible for gleaning news from the King's newswriters' reports; pp. 94–5. See Sleeman to J. W. Hogg, 28 October 1952, for a description of this means of gaining information; *JTKO*, vol. II, pp. 379–80.

Introduction

proposed reforms through the Resident,[1] but they were not put into effect.

Lord Dalhousie, who became Governor-General in 1848, favoured a further extension of British territory in the sub-continent, and he considered Oudh an area which was most likely to require British control. In September 1848, just nine months after his arrival in India, he foreshadowed changes in Oudh. 'There seems little reason to expect or hope that in October 1849, any amendment whatever will have been effected', he wrote to Sleeman. He went on, therefore, to offer Sleeman the opportunity to oversee the changes which would be necessary in the government of Oudh. 'The reconstruction of the internal administration of a great, rich, and oppressed country, is a noble as well as an arduous task for the officer to whom it is intrusted, and the Government have recourse to one of the best of its servants for that purpose.'[2]

SLEEMAN

Dalhousie knew that in Sleeman he chose an officer well-qualified for the task of recommending administrative changes in a region in which crime and social conflict were widespread. His career gave him experience as a soldier, and administrator, a 'political' agent and – above all perhaps – a skilful and able police officer.[3]

The first phase of William Henry Sleeman's career began in

[1] R. W. Bird, *Dacoitee in Excelsis; or The Spoliation of Oude by the East India Company* (Allahabad, reprint 1924), pp. 81–9.

[2] Dalhousie to Sleeman, 16 September 1848, in *JTKO*, vol. I, pp. xvii–xix. Also in Bird, *Dacoitee in Excelsis*, pp. 91–2 and in W. H. Sleeman, *Rambles and Recollections of an Indian Official*, rev. annotated ed. by V. A. Smith (Oxford, 1915) [hereafter *R and R*], p. xxv. On Dalhousie see *Private Letters of the Marquess of Dalhousie*, ed. J. G. A. Baird (Edinburgh, 1910); W. W. Hunter, *The Marquess of Dalhousie* (Oxford, 1890); S. N. Prasad, *Paramountcy under Dalhousie* (Delhi, 1964); M. A. Rahim, *Lord Dalhousie's Administration of the Conquered and Annexed States* (Delhi, 1963), ch. 9; E. Arnold, *The Marquess of Dalhousie's Administration of British India*, 2 vols (London, 1865), vol. II, ch. 24.

[3] Biographical memoir, *JTKO*, vol. I, pp. xi–xvi; *R and R*, pp. xxi–xxx and also bibliography of Sleeman's writings, pp. xxxi–xxxvii; *DNB*, vol. XVIII, pp. 373–4. Also see the biography by F. Tuker, *The Yellow Scarf. The story of the life of Thuggee Sleeman* (London, 1961), G. Bearce, *British Attitudes Towards India, 1784–1858* (Oxford, 1961), pp. 260–2, looks briefly at Sleeman's writings.

Introduction

1809, his twenty-first year, when he came to India as an infantry
cadet in the East India Company's Bengal Army. He remained
a soldier until 1820, during which time he saw service in the
territories near Oudh. As a young officer he took part in the
campaigns of the Nepal war of 1814–16, marching along the
eastern borders of Oudh; and afterwards he was stationed at
Allahabad and at Pratapgarh, a cantonment within Oudh. In
1820 he went into civil employ as an assistant to the Governor-
General's agent in the newly-acquired Sagar and Narbada
territories in Central India, where his duties were those of a
district officer concerned primarily with the collection of land
revenue and the administration of justice. From 1826 onwards,
however, while still occupied as a district officer, he began –
largely by accident – his connection with the work for which he
is best known, the campaign against the thugs, the highly-
organised and skilful highway robbers who strangled their
victims and then buried the bodies to avoid detection. The
initial campaign against the thugs was the work of a number of
officers in Central India, but Sleeman became the best known of
these because it was he who pressed the government of Lord
William Bentinck into adopting a full-scale operation against
them in the 1830s, involving not only the use of squads of
specially-trained and mounted police, but also judicial methods
with regard to both the admission of evidence and the trial of
prisoners which were unusual (and even irregular) for British
courts.[1] This thuggee work reached a peak in 1835 when Sleeman was appointed Superintendent of the Thuggee Department,
with responsibility for co-ordinating operations throughout
northern and central India. In this capacity Sleeman controlled
the series of campaigns from 1836 to 1839 during which the
thug networks in northern India were broken up. In 1839 the
task of operations against the dacoits – armed robbers who

[1] On thuggee see J. W. Kaye, *The Administration of the East India Company*
(London, 1853; reprint Allahabad, 1966), part III, ch. 2; B. Hjejle, 'The Social
Policy of the East India Company with regard to Sati, Slavery, Thagi and Infanti-
cide' (unpublished D.Phil. thesis, Oxford University, 1958), part III. G. Bruce,
The Stranglers. The Cult of Thuggee and its overthrow in British India (London,
1968), is a popularised account. Also, Meadows Taylor, *Confessions of a Thug*
(London, rev. ed. 1873), which was first published in 1839; and J. Masters, *The
Deceivers* (London, 1952).

Introduction

operated in gangs and some of whom used methods not unlike those of the thugs – was added to the thuggee work, thus rounding out the second and most important phase of Sleeman's career. The third phase began in 1843 when he was appointed Resident at Gwalior, the Court of Sindhia, the most important of the Maratha chiefs of Central India. He had already been offered (in 1841) the Residency at Lucknow, in fact, but he had not been able, for personal reasons, to accept the position at that time.[1] Instead, in 1842, he went to investigate a minor uprising in Bundelkhand and in the next year he took the appointment at Gwalior. He was still there when Dalhousie wrote to him in September 1848 to offer him the position of Resident at Lucknow.

By this time his various appointments had given him considerable knowledge of the social and economic conditions of central and northern India, and he had also acquired wide experience of travel and investigation in this area. The anti-thug campaigns had kept him constantly on the move through the region and he had added to this experience an unofficial journey from Jabalpur to Meerut in 1836 which he recorded in his best-known book, *Rambles and Recollections of an Indian Official*, which was first published in 1844.[2] In this collection of observations, conversations and stories, his knowledge, his far-ranging interests and his skills come through very clearly. Unlike some other well-known nineteenth-century travellers in this part of India – Bishop Heber or Miss Emily Eden,[3] for instance – Sleeman travelled through country that he knew well and could appraise, and he was able to communicate freely and intelligently with the people whom he met. Malcolm Darling's 'rural rides' in twentieth-century Panjab are probably the only

[1] Because of Sir John Low's private financial troubles, Sleeman offered to let him continue: Low, *Fifty Years*, p. 259n.; *DNB*, vol. xviii, p. 373 and *R and R*, biographical memoir, p. xxiv.

[2] First ed. London, 1844 in 2 vols. New ed. by V. A. Smith in 2 vols, London, 1893. Revised ed. Oxford, 1915, in one vol.

[3] R. Heber, *Narrative of a Journey through the Upper Provinces of India from Calcutta to Bombay, 1824–25...* 3 vols (London, 3rd ed. 1828), and see M. A. Laird, *Bishop Heber in Northern India. Selections from Heber's Journal* (Cambridge, 1971); E. Eden, *Up the Country. Letters written to her sister fom the Upper Provinces of India*, introduction and notes by E. Thompson (Oxford, 1937). Edwardes, *The Orchid House* reproduces material from a number of travellers.

travel accounts from north India which bear comparison with Sleeman's journals.

More important in many ways than the *Rambles and Recollections*, however, were the materials derived from the operations against the thugs. In 1836, under the title *Ramaseeana, or a Vocabulary of the Peculiar Language used by the Thugs*[1] he had printed a glossary of the thug argot (*ramasi* as they called it) which he had compiled by interrogation of thug prisoners and informers, and also other papers dealing with thug organisation, methods and lore. *Ramaseeana*, as Vincent Smith later commented, was 'a very roughly compiled and coarsely printed collection of valuable documents'.[2] It is of importance here mainly because it illustrates very well Sleeman's methods in this work, and particularly the careful and systematic methods of analysis which were the essential basis for the successful operations against the thugs who operated in tightly-disciplined bands over considerable distances away from their homes and in a variety of disguises. Their language was in fact their code of commands and the description of the instruments of their trade, as well as the signs and omens upon which they were dependent for the timing of their operations; it was crucial to their ability to mix with their victims and prepare for their strike without arousing suspicion, and the cracking of the code was a major step in Sleeman's success. Once his officers were armed with a systematic account of the signals it was possible to identify thugs and thug operations. He then added to this such things as genealogies of thug families which established the networks within which the 'trade' was practised and this enabled Sleeman's men to mount a series of highly successful campaigns.

It is important to note here also Sleeman's interest in scientific and technical subjects. He was keenly interested throughout his career in agriculture and arboriculture; he was responsible for introducing improved varieties of sugar cane to India from Mauritius and as a district officer he took an interest in the public provision of trees. His Oudh diary itself gives evidence of his scientific interest; in discussing the geology and the

[1] Calcutta, 1836.
[2] *R and R*, p. xxxi.

Introduction

soils of Oudh, for instance, he uses terms which suggest that he was abreast of the scientific discussion of such matters in his own day.[1]

THE TOUR AND THE DIARY

Sleeman arrived in Lucknow in January 1849 and set about the preparation of a report on conditions for Dalhousie. This was ready by September, along with his suggestions for a course of action to be followed by the Government of India.[2] Sleeman saw the basic fault of the situation as the lack of effective central government and the maladministration which followed from it, and he urged Dalhousie to follow a plan (which he drew up in June 1849) under which the King would delegate his powers to a Board of three members chosen from 'the highest and ablest members of the aristocracy present in the capital'[3] who would have full power to deal with the land revenues, the police, the judicial system and the army under British 'guarantees during good conduct'.[4] He believed that such an administration would be able to restore order, and so make it possible for an Indian king to reign, without the system of government having features 'opposed to native usages, feelings and institutions to prevent its being adhered to' – especially by the strongly-armed and entrenched landholders of the countryside.[5]

To supplement this report he determined to make a tour through the countryside to see conditions for himself and to provide more detailed information for Dalhousie.[6] He asked

[1] See below p. 109. The *Oxford Universal Dictionary* (3rd ed. 1944) shows that several of the scientific terms on p. 65 were just coming into use at this time: ulmic (1831), humic (1844), potassa (1843). Cf. Sleeman to Col. Sykes, 12 January 1853, in *JTKO*, vol. ii, p. 395, for his interest in geology. It is not the contention here that his 'science' would be regarded as entirely valid today; all that is intended is to point to the fact that he had an interest in scientific matters and scientific method of an 'up to date' kind in the 1840s.
[2] See the letters from Sleeman to H. M. Elliot, secretary to the government in Calcutta, and Lord Dalhousie, in *JTKO*, vol. i, pp. xlvi–xlviii; lvi–lviii; lx–lxix; lxxv–lxxviii. [3] Sleeman to Elliot, 23 March 1849; *JTKO*, vol. i, lii.
[4] Sleeman to Dalhousie, August 1849; *JTKO*, vol. i, p. lii.
[5] *Ibid.* p. lxvi.
[6] There seems to be no evidence for the claim in the introduction to *JTKO* (p. xvii) that Dalhousie requested him to make the tour. The Oudh Court was annoyed by the request and by his actions on the tour; see Bird, *Dacoitee in Excelsis*, pp. 94–5; and R. M. Martin, *The Indian Empire*, 2 vols (London, n.d. [c. 1858]), vol. i, p. 72.

Introduction

permission for this tour in March 1849 and in November he confirmed his intention; on 1 December 1849 he set out with an entourage of two companies of sepoys, his wife and children, three younger officers (one of whom was also accompanied by his wife) and a number of important Indian officials, chief among whom was Raja Bukhtawar Singh. The tour, which was a circuit of the kingdom, took three full months, and was a unique tour for a Resident and more detailed than any similar journey by a European in Oudh. There had been a number of earlier European visitors to various parts of Oudh but none had spent so long in the countryside or gone into so many parts (particularly in the north).[1]

It can be noted here that there was a claim in the later nineteenth century that Sleeman – despite his acknowledged acuteness – was shepherded around on his tour, that the people to whom he talked were 'tutored' and that he therefore 'saw a good deal through durbar spectacles'. This claim was first put forward by J. F. Macandrew in his Rae Bareli settlement report of 1872 and it was repeated by Harcourt Butler in his pamphlet on 'Oudh Policy' published in 1896.[2] These men were basically concerned, for political reasons, to uphold the 'honour' of the taluqdars and particularly, in this case, those of Rae Bareli to whom, they claimed, Sleeman had been 'unfair'. But, as H. C. Irwin, another Oudh official and one who was no lover of the taluqdars, pointed out, while 'it has been said, probably with some degree of truth' that Sleeman was deceived and 'unconsciously exaggerated the

---

[1] D. Butter, *Outlines of The Topography and Statistics of the Southern Districts of Oud'h and of the Cantonment of Sultanpur-Oud'h* (Calcutta, 1839) is the major published source before Sleeman. The story of Mr Ravenscroft, who absconded from Cawnpore after embezzling Company funds and went to Gonda district, where he was murdered, is told in *JTKO*, vol. I, pp. 112–22 (it is omitted from our text below for reasons of space), and gives some idea of the unusualness of Europeans in the northern districts. The knowledgeable F. J. Shore, the judge at Farrukhabad on the Oudh border, seems to know mainly the south; see his descriptions in *Notes on Indian Affairs*, 2 vols (London, 1837), vol. II, pp. 262–3. [J. W. Kaye] in *North British Review*, vol. xxv, no. L (August 1856), pp. 548–9 cites a report by Capt. E. Laurence of the Bengal Army 'who was then the paymaster of family monies in Oude' and who, he says, 'traversed the whole length and breadth of the country' in c. 1826; but I have not seen this report.

[2] J. F. Macandrew, *Report on the settlement operations of the Rae Bareli district* (Lucknow, 1872), pp. 16–18. S. H. Butler, *Oudh Policy. Considered historically and with reference to the present political situation* (Allahabad, 1896), pp. 24–5.

enormities of the Taluqdars', 'yet there can be no grounds for supposing that the Oudh Government would go out of its way to make the conduct of its own troops or servants more odious or oppressive than it actually was'.[1] It is certainly true that Raja Bukhtawar Singh accompanied Sleeman throughout, and one can suppose that he was there for some purpose, but Sleeman seems well aware of the fact that people would try, and were indeed trying, to 'cover up'.[2] It is, in fact, hard to see how the Diary can be read as markedly favouring either the taluqdars or the administration. Sleeman had some sympathy for the local officials, given the problems that they faced, but he had little praise for either the Oudh government itself or its members at that time. And while he reports adversely on the taluqdars in some areas he does give a good many instances (as Macandrew has to admit) of taluqdars encouraging cultivation and maintaining order in their own domains. There is, in reality, little in this charge against Sleeman other than an indication of the political calculations of later administrators.

The Diary which Sleeman kept during his three-month tour was intended to assist Dalhousie in his assessment of the situation in Oudh. When he returned to Lucknow at the end of February 1850, therefore, he set to work to add further material to the Diary and to prepare it for presentation to Dalhousie and the government. So that it would remain confidential – he was constantly worried about the possibility of correspondence and other papers being exposed at the Court and used improperly[3] – he brought a small printing press, and a compositor to operate it, into the Residency and had the diary printed on his own 'Parlour Press'.[4] By April 1852 he had printed eighteen copies, twelve of which he distributed between the Government of India, the Governor-General, the Court of Directors, the Chairman and Deputy Chairman of the East India Company, one

[1] H. C. Irwin, *The Garden of India; or Chapters in Oudh history and affairs* (London, 1880), pp. 152–3.
[2] See below p. 194 for an example with regard to the feeding of artillery bullocks.
[3] Sleeman to H. M. Elliot, 20 March 1849; *JTKO*, vol. I, pp. l–lii.
[4] Sleeman to J. W. Hogg, 4 April 1852 in *JTKO*, vol. II, p. 357; and Sleeman to Col. Sykes, 12 January 1853 in *JTKO*, vol. II, pp. 393–4.

Introduction

other Director of the Company (Colonel Sykes) and to his
family (his brother and his five children).[1] At this juncture,
Sleeman had no plans to publish the Diary in any other form
than this. He was proud of it[2] and he believed that it presented a
full and valuable picture of the country; but he regarded it as
the Government's property and he was apparently prepared to
let the Government dispose of it as it thought best.[3] As J. W.
Kaye remarked, 'it might have long lain in the dignified ob-
scurity of the Company's Record-office' if it had not been for the
combination of circumstances which followed Sleeman's retirement from the Lucknow Residency.[4]

Ill-health, which had increasingly marked the later years of
his service, forced Sleeman to retire in 1854 and, after some time
in the hill stations of northern India, to set off home early in
1856. On the way, however, he died and was buried at sea off
Ceylon on 10 February 1856 – just four days after the annexation of Oudh. Sleeman had never accepted annexation as a solution to the problem of Oudh. His reply to Dalhousie when
accepting the appointment at Lucknow in 1848 had been critical
of the Governor-General's propensity for annexation and he
never overcame his objections to this policy.[5] He was convinced
that the government of Oudh needed to be changed; but the plan
for a Board to reform the administration under British guarantees, which he formulated in 1849, remained his solution to the
problem and he continued to press it upon Dalhousie (with increasing urgency in 1852, in fact).[6] Dalhousie found it difficult
to take a final decision on the Oudh question,[7] however, and no

[1] For basic list see *JTKO*, vol. II, pp. 393–4; and also p. 387.
[2] Sleeman to J. W. Hogg, 4 April 1852 in *JTKO*, vol. II, p. 358.
[3] See *JTKO*, vol. II, pp. 358, 394; also Prefaces of 1852 and 1858.
[4] [J. W. Kaye,] 'The conquest of Oude' in *Edinburgh Review*, vol. 107 (April
1858), p. 517. The attribution of authors for articles in nineteenth-century journals
is based on W. E. Houghton (ed.), *The Wellesley Index to Victorian Periodicals
1824–1900* (London and Toronto, 1966), vol. I.
[5] Sleeman to Dalhousie, 24 September 1848 in *JTKO*, vol. I, pp. xliii–xlv; also
letters to J. W. Hogg in vol. II, pp. 376–83, 387–90 and 390–3.
[6] Cf. letters to J. W. Hogg, *loc. cit.*, and Sleeman to Dalhousie, in April and
September 1852 and September 1854 in *JTKO*, vol. II, pp. 362–4, 365–73, and 423.
[7] Dalhousie expected Oudh to come under British management within two
years of his taking office (Baird, *Private Letters*, p. 33) but he found himself
thwarted both because the King would not provide him with a clear excuse for such
a drastic step (*ibid.* p. 262) and he was unsure whether the Company would back

action had been taken by the time Sleeman retired. He was succeeded in the Residency by Sir James Outram. Dalhousie asked Outram for a further report and in this Outram also argued against annexation, although he painted (in part from the evidence collected by Sleeman) as dark a picture of conditions as usual. Finally, in 1855, at the end of his governor-generalship, Dalhousie recommended that the Government should get the King to vest control in the Company while still retaining his position and titles. The Court of Directors, however, decided against this and ordered the Governor-General instead to effect the annexation of Oudh and the abolition of the throne of its Kings.[1]

The annexation, which passed off largely without incident,[2] was followed by an outcry from the Court and the King's supporters and a virulent campaign to vindicate the King and to seek his restoration was begun in London.[3] The King's supporters argued that the annexation was a breach of solemn treaty obligations which rested on the British, as well as being both unwarranted and contrary to natural justice. Sleeman figured prominently in this controversy because of his close connection with Oudh during Dalhousie's regime. Captain R. W. Bird,

him in such a move both because annexation was 'unfashionable' and because, in the early 1850s, the renewal of the Charter required an absence of controversy (*ibid.* p. 169). And then his adventuring in Burma distracted him; see Sleeman's complaints on this score to J. W. Hogg in *JTKO*, vol. II, pp. 358, 381, 383 and 388. Nonetheless, when Sleeman retired, Dalhousie saw the state of Oudh was 'critical', with anything being possible (Baird, *Private Letters*, p. 321); but it still took him until the time of his departure (February 1856) to draw up plans and to obtain the Court of Directors' sanction for them. When it came to the point, he in fact did not advise annexation although he included it as one possible course of action; he was nonetheless pleased to follow the Court's directive that the Kingdom should be annexed (*ibid.* p. 363). See also Prasad, *Paramountcy under Dalhousie*, pp. 143–9, for a very brief résumé.

[1] *Parliamentary Papers*, 1857 (session 1), vol. XI, 'Papers relating to Oude'.

[2] Baird, *Private Letters*, p. 370, for report from Dalhousie that there had been an instance of firing on troops who had seized officers for arrears.

[3] See 'Oude, as a kingdom' in *Dublin University Magazine*, vol. 49 (January 1857), p. 128, for a view of the entourage in London. Martin, *Indian Empire*, vol. I, pp. 59–89, discusses the Oudh case and cites a number of contemporary pamphlets and articles. The most important contemporary publications were Bird, *Dacoitee in Excelsis* and M. Mohammad Masihuddin Khan, *Oude: Its Princes and its Government Vindicated* (London, 1857), reprinted with notes by Safi Ahmad (Lucknow, 1964). Masihuddin was the King's 'plenipotentiary' to the British court and parliament.

who had formerly been Sleeman's first assistant at the Residency and who had clashed with Sleeman in that office, identified Sleeman as no more than Dalhousie's henchman in a pre-arranged plot to annex the kingdom in a pamphlet which he published under the extravagant title *Dacoitee in Excelsis; or The Spoliation of Oude*. An 'emissary of a foregone conclusion' Bird called Sleeman, and he said that as Resident Sleeman had consistently misused his position and had helped to manufacture evidence to discredit the regime so as to make the annexation more justifiable.[1] These charges were not well-founded but they were nevertheless serious and when, in 1857, Oudh became the centre of the 'mutiny' and the cause of the deposed King's infant son was promoted as a focal point for rebellion against British authority in Lucknow, concern grew at the apparent folly of the annexation and those who had brought it about. It became necessary then for Sleeman's name to be cleared of the charge that he had worked to procure the early annexation of Oudh. Consequently, a letter of Sleeman's, written sometime in late 1854 or early 1855 and strongly denouncing annexationist policies, was published in *The Times* in November 1857. This had the effect of forcing Bird to retract his charges publicly.[2] Then, to exonerate him completely, Sleeman's Diary, together with letters from before and after the tour, which showed that he had been all along in favour of an Oudh-based reformed government and strongly opposed to annexation, was published in London in early 1858.[3]

THE STATE OF OUDH[4]

The material presented by Sleeman in his Diary has been used by writers on Oudh, from the compilers of the Oudh 'Blue Book' of 1856 onwards, as evidence of the chronic misgovernment and the anarchy which characterised the Kingdom in the mid-nineteenth century. But there has been little or no attempt to use that

---

[1] For some indications of Bird's clash with Sleeman see *JTKO*, vol. i, pp. 106–7 and vol. ii, pp. 332–9; and Sleeman to Dalhousie, 18 March 1852, *ibid.* p. 355.

[2] See copy of letter in *JTKO*, vol. i, pp. xxi–xxii; and p. xxii for Bird's retraction.

[3] *JTKO*, vol. i, pp. xv–xvi.

[4] This section is drawn from Sleeman, unless otherwise specified.

material as a means of explaining those conditions. Sleeman himself did not attempt to summarise his material in this way – which remains one of the drawbacks of the diary format which he employed – but, given his skill in observation and in assessing the country through which he passed, his record can be relied on and can be used to place the misgovernment and anarchy of Oudh in perspective.

It is quite clear that Oudh was politically disturbed by the 1850s and it is equally clear that the basic problem was that central control was weak. The government of the Kingdom, which meant the King and his *durbar*, gave too little attention to the strict control of the business of administration – at least that from which they made no immediate personal gain – and the Court seems to have operated an open market for the sale of office and favours. Not that the central government could by any means be written off entirely: there was a recognised bureaucracy and there were recognised administrative procedures. The problem was rather that these institutions and procedures were being misused and hence were falling into both disrepair and disrepute. The question is, Why? The usual answer is the declining personal quality of the rulers themselves and there may be some foundation for this view. More important, on the whole, however, is the situation in which these Kings were placed by the presence of the British in the territory on all sides of their Kingdom and in their capital and Kingdom itself, for that British presence represented, in a number of ways, an alternative power structure which undermined the effectiveness of their government.

The most important part of the British presence was military: the 'Company troops' placed in the Kingdom under the subsidiary system. These troops diminished the independence of Oudh, of course, but it was their ability to interfere in the affairs of the Kingdom that made them a major problem. They were used, for instance, to support the claims of sepoys serving in the Company's army. There were some 50,000 Oudh men serving with the East India Company (Oudh was in fact the chief recruiting ground for sepoys for the Bengal army in the nineteenth century) and they had the right to appeal to the Resident for the redress of their grievances. Such grievances usually

Introduction

involved land and the result was that the Company's troops were often involved in settling local disputes, sometimes on very inadequate grounds.[1] The result was to set the authority of the King's local officers aside and to unsettle local society, for the confrontation of local forces and the Company's troops was, on the whole, an unequal struggle.

The British presence had also economic aspects. Much more investigation will be needed before the precise effects of these influences can be measured but it is possible to point to several areas in which pressure was possibly brought to bear on the Kingdom. In the first place, the British districts provided a haven for men of Oudh for a variety of reasons: to escape from the King's officers and justice for instance, but also simply as a more secure market for capital to be invested in land or in banking enterprises. Gorakhpur, Cawnpore and Farrukhabad (and even the more distant Benares) seem to have been important centres for bankers, 'agricultural capitalists' (money-lenders) and landholders from Oudh.[2] Secondly, there were important groups of pensioners in Oudh who relied upon the receipt of payments made by the Company in its capacity as trustee for various of the earlier Kings who had loaned money to the Company and had directed that the 'interest' due should be used to pay pensions to certain relatives, servants or institutions.[3] Thirdly, there was an important trade in East India Company bonds, bearing five per cent interest, which were sold daily from the Resident's office. Sleeman claimed that Rs 3 crores (that is, 30 million rupees) had been invested by people in Oudh and that 'a great many middle class families' in Lucknow were entirely dependent on the interest from these bonds. He reported in March 1849 that even during the Panjab wars the demand remained steady – a sign, he commented, that the Lucknow public expected the British to win.[4] And in this comment lies in

[1] See the case of Shaikh Mahboob Allee, below p. 165. Cf. Shore, *Notes on Indian Affairs*, vol. I, pp. 153–4 and vol. II, pp. 271–2, 278–9. Note that Sleeman was responsible for having some of these rights curtailed; Prasad, *Paramountcy under Dalhousie*, pp. 80–1. [2] Cf. Butter, *Southern Oud'h*, pp. 85–6.
[3] See Aitchison, *Treaties*, vol. II, pp. 132–47, for details.
[4] Sleeman to H. M. Elliot, 7 March 1849 in *JTKO*, vol. I, pp. xlviii–l; and to J. W. Hogg, 17 November 1850, vol. II, p. 347. Cf. Shore, *Notes on Indian Affairs*, vol. II, pp. 273–4.

fact the importance of these financial operations; the economic effect was clearly two-edged, with capital going out and interest payments of one kind or another coming back in, but the political effect was to add further weight to the British presence by maintaining various groups who had a 'vested interest' in the British presence and who were necessarily led to look to the Resident for support or guidance in a number of ways. This situation was, in fact, steadily sapping the authority and purpose of the Oudh government over the years. Henry Lawrence pointed to the danger of this 'double government' (namely, 'an irresponsible ruler ridden by a powerless Proconsul') which the British had created: 'At Lucknow for years the residents held public durbars, where the guaranteed attended and pleaded against their own Sovereign or his servants. Thus were the Monarch and his subjects arrayed against each other: thus was the Sovereign degraded in his own capital.'[1]

The results of this weakening of the central government are clear from Sleeman's account. In the short run the effect was to weaken seriously the local administrative authorities. The local officials could get neither sufficient nor efficient troops, nor the supplies and ordnance with which to equip and feed those that they had, nor the funds to pay them. A great deal of the difficulty in this regard could be traced to the nepotism and corruption of the Court, as a result of which officers supposedly in command of regiments were often court favourites, or quite incompetent persons (even children), holding a sinecure. These commanders, and others with influence, then put into the regiments incompetent or even fictitious troops who were there simply to swell the accounts so that, if indeed payments were made at all, claims could be submitted for their remuneration and equipment and the amounts so granted pocketed by those who controlled the places. Moreover, what funds were disbursed by the exchequer for such items as the maintenance of cannon, the feeding of artillery bullocks or the provision of uniforms or ammunition, were diverted into those same private pockets and the regiments

---

[1] H. Lawrence, *Essays on the Indian Army and Oude* (Serampore, 1859), p. 328. The previous quotation is from p. 289. This essay, 'The Kingdom of Oude', was originally published in the *Calcutta Review* in 1845.

went without. The result overall was that if the local officials were to give the troops under their 'command' any pay or provisions, they had to allow them to forage and to plunder. Even the so-called 'auxiliary' (*kumaki*) troops, comprising four regiments which were usually commanded by Europeans who seemed to have slightly more success in getting supplies for military purposes, had to be allowed to forage for personal provisions. As such foraging involved the virtual stripping of a village in order to get food, straw (from the thatched roofs) for use as fodder, and whatever fuel was available, the major threat that the nazims had, as Sleeman put it, was just to camp nearby!

The consequence of this weakening of the local administration was the growth of strong and successful local powers, the 'land-holders', though their essential function was that of political leaders rather than farmers or agricultural magnates. They needed to control land so as to be able to appropriate the agricultural surplus (the major economic resource of the King-dom) and they were thus heavily involved in the agricultural process, but it was their maintenance of military forces which was crucial to their local position. They were able, because of the situation which developed, to defy the government by not paying the land revenue (which was the State's basic income), and to attack their neighbours in an effort to absorb more lands (and hence more surplus and more followers). The only guaran-tee of their position lay in their own military power and hence they built mud-wall forts shielded by thick screens of bamboo and scrub ('jungle') to house both their cannon and their re-tainers. Sleeman reported that there were some 250 forts with 500 cannon;[1] but in the disarming of the province which followed the mutiny of 1857–8, some 1,575 forts or fortified houses were levelled and 720 cannon were confiscated.[2] The taluqdar's re-tainers, Sleeman estimated, numbered over 100,000. They were allowed, indeed often encouraged, to operate as robbers outside their patron's domains so as to relieve him of the burden of paying them; some smaller landholders operated mainly, in fact, as the leaders of such gangs of 'dacoits' and often dismissed or

---

[1] *JTKO*, vol. ii, p. 210.

[2] *Calcutta Review*, vol. 35 (September 1860), pp. 132–3, citing Oudh Adminis-tration Report for 1858–9

deserting soldiers joined them and brought their own knowledge
of firearms as well as their own particular expertise in plundering
to the gang's assistance.

Against these entrenched local rulers, officials with unreliable
or ill-equipped troops could do relatively little. They were able
at times to gain the help of some strong local landholders to
defeat other landholders, particularly when one man had a direct
interest in seeing another's 'estate' reduced or dismantled
(though such a move was dangerous because a man never knew
when he would need help himself), but more often the officials
had little or no chance of effectively reducing their opponents.
Moreover, if they did appear likely to be able to overwhelm the
forces that a landholder had at his disposal or which he could
gather together, they were likely to find that the objects of their
mission had fled to the jungles, having first broken down their
houses (which were always of mud and not of brick for just this
reason) and destroyed whatever they could not take with them,
on the theory that if there was nothing of value left the officials
would have to move on and they would be able to resume their
villages and lands. The way to beat off the government, it was
believed, was to devastate the country so that the government
could not get anything from it and would therefore sue for
'peace' – that is, a return to cultivation – which was the only
way, in most places, by which taxable wealth could be produced.

While they were a major cause of disturbance in the countryside, the landholders also provided the major element of
stability in the Oudh political system at that time. The largest
and strongest were in a position to maintain order in their own
domains and they had an interest in doing so because they stood
to gain directly from the agricultural development of 'their'
lands. Such landholders, Sleeman reported, had the best cultivated areas in the Kingdom and they were active in encouraging
good cultivators to settle in their areas by giving them seeds,
grants to build wells, and bullocks and other aids. Sleeman's
summary of the position of Nawab Allee of Mahmudabad
applied to many of these men:

[he] has always money at command to purchase influence at court when
required; and he has a brave and well-armed force with which to aid the

governor of the district, when he makes it worth his while to do so, in crushing a refractory landholder. These are the sources of his power, and he is not at all scrupulous in the use of it – it is not the fashion to be so in Oude.[1]

While there were a good many local rajas whose clan or family control over the land was of long standing, many of the most prominent landholders of Sleeman's tour were men who had built up their domains themselves by force of arms, or financial or legal manipulation, or by a combination of all of these. There was in fact very considerable political and social mobility at this level in Oudh in the early nineteenth century. But there was also a major element of weakness in the system; for these men could not aspire to take the next, and logical step, which was to attempt, either on their own or in some form of alliance, to displace the Nawabi dynasty and assume supreme control themselves. This they would have done in the period before British power became paramount in the region. But now they were only too well aware that the British would not permit such an attack on their 'allies'. They took care, therefore, to avoid as far as possible involvement with the Company's troops and concentrated their attention on the task of expanding and consolidating their local position in the smaller sphere of inter-necine strife. The dynasty thus remained, but at the price of being a British cypher and of being largely unheeded, at least locally, as the government of the Kingdom. Nor could it ever hope to refurbish its claims to leadership by drawing its 'nobility' together with the promise of an external adventure, for it was surrounded on all sides by the inviolable territories of the Company.

For this situation in which the Kings, and their subjects, were placed, the British presence was largely responsible. The advancing British power, which had reduced the other north Indian kingdoms in turn and which had taken the greater part even of the Nawab of Oudh's territories, had made Oudh a captive political system and the excesses and misgovernment which British observers commented upon were largely the struggles of those caught in its constrictions.

[1] See below pp. 271–2. *JTKO*, vol. ii, p. 220.

Introduction

In 1845, Henry Lawrence had written in much the same vein:

The man, whether King or servant, who has no fears, has no hopes. The man who is not called on for exertion must be almost more than mortal if he bestirs himself. . .Subject states and guaranteed rulers, now as of old, verify the same remark; and no better example can be offered than that of Oude. It has had men of more than average ability, and of at least average worth, as rulers and ministers, who, if left to themselves, would have been compelled in self-defence to shew some consideration for the people they governed. Failing to do so, their exactions would have called into play the rectifying principle of Asiatic monarchies, and the dynasty of Saadut Khan would long since have become extinct. But, protected by British bayonets, the degenerate rulers have felt secure to indulge in all the vices generated by their condition; sacrificing alike the welfare of their subjects and the character of the lord paramount.[1]

Lawrence urged then that the system should be reconstructed with the Resident taking over from the King (though the King would remain in name) and supervising an administration which would be as Indian as possible but which would work under British orders to reduce the elements of disorder (such as the private armies and the forts). In suggesting this remedy he was probably as mistaken as was Sleeman in seeking a solution in a reconstruction of the government at the top with a Board or Council of Regency which would work under British guarantees, for neither of these plans solved the basic problem of the distortions produced within Oudh by the overriding British power which enveloped it. In this sense, annexation was a more satisfactory solution to the problem because it removed the anomalies of the situation in which Oudh was formally free but in fact under constant pressure and a variety of constraints from the British presence. Moreover, by reconstructing the Oudh political system upon a radically different basis, one which provided for economic gain and social and political mobility in ways that did not require (even as they did not permit) the assumption of supreme control, the British were able in fact to satisfy the aspirations of the landholders. (There were 'mistakes' in this regard in the immediate post annexation situation, when the British attempted to largely exclude the landholders from their positions of local power, but

[1] Lawrence, *Essays*, p. 290. For his plans for Oudh administration see pp. 339–41.

Introduction

these were 'corrected' after the revolt of 1857–8.)[1] British rule in Oudh, in its turn, allowed quite novel changes to take place which transformed the position and the rule of the landholders. An examination of these changes lies outside the scope of this present essay, but it may be noted, at least, that there are descendants of a number of taluqdars with whom Sleeman talked, who have adapted themselves to the new political system well enough to be in positions of authority in both the government of the state of Uttar Pradesh (which incorporates the former Oudh) and in the Government of India at New Delhi, in the 1960s.[2]

The annexation of Oudh, then, was not necessarily a praiseworthy act, but there was no satisfactory alternative to it by 1856, short of the (highly unlikely) withdrawal of British power from the Indian sub-continent as a whole. But while that much can be said, it is equally true that the claim that the British had to annex Oudh because Oudh was incapable of governing itself, a claim which was heard then and later, was as hollow as it was vainglorious.

SLEEMAN AND HIS CONTEMPORARIES: THE PROBLEM
OF EXPLAINING INDIA

Those of Sleeman's contemporaries who favoured annexation of Oudh – and they were the majority at the time – believed that they saw in his Diary confirmation of the claim that Oudh had

---

[1] See T. R. Metcalf, *The Aftermath of Revolt: India, 1857–1870* (Princeton, 1964), ch. 4; and Jagdish Raj, *The Mutiny and British Land Policy in North India, 1856–1868* (Bombay, 1965). Also T. R. Metcalf, 'From Raja to Landlord: The Oudh Taluqdars 1850–70' and 'Social Effects of British Land Policy in Oudh' in R. E. Frykenberg (ed.), *Land Control and Social Structure in Indian History* (Madison, Wisconsin, 1969), pp. 123–41, 143–62.

[2] For some view of parts of this adjustment see P. D. Reeves, 'Landlords and Party Politics in the United Provinces, 1934–37' in D. A. Low (ed.), *Soundings in Modern South Asian History* (London, 1968), pp. 261–93; and 'The Politics of Order' in *Journal of Asian Studies*, vol. xxv, no. 2 (February 1966), pp. 261–74. For two detailed studies of 'ex'-taluqdar politicians in the 1960s see P. R. Brass, *Factional Politics in an Indian State* (Berkeley and Los Angeles, California, 1965), ch. 4 (Gonda district) and A. S. Burger, *Opposition in a Dominant-Party System* (Berkeley and Los Angeles, California, 1969), ch. 5 (Pratapgarh district). For a general view see T. R. Metcalf, 'Landlords without Land: The U.P. Zamindars Today', in *Pacific Affairs*, vol. xl, nos. 1 and 2 (1967), pp. 5–18.

to be annexed because it was incapable of being governed by any 'native' government. They took this line even when they recognised that Sleeman himself had not called for annexation; his different conclusions, they believed, derived from his sympathy for 'native rulers'. They did not see that, in fact, he and they represented two very different methods of analysing and explaining India and Indian behaviour. Such a difference did exist, however, and the recognition of it helps to establish why British commentators had so much difficulty in handling the 'Oudh question'. It may, indeed, help to elucidate British attitudes towards a whole range of Indian questions in the nineteenth century. For our present purposes, it gives added point and importance to Sleeman's Diary and the discussion which surrounded it.

Pro-annexationist arguments were often expressed in terms of an idealist view of Indian society, a view in which native society in Oudh – and by extension in India generally – was represented as being essentially incapable of self-government, not because of fortuitous circumstances but because the basic social and political values of Indian culture were opposed to organised and orderly government.

By contrast, Sleeman adopted throughout his work a positivistic mode of explanation which sought explanations for behaviour in terms of causal factors in the social and economic environment. This did not prevent him from being outraged or disgusted by some things which he saw, but it did lead him to seek for rational explanations rather than for explanations deduced from general assumptions about the essentially degenerate character of Indian institutions. Few of his contemporaries were concerned to avoid such assumptions: as an examination of responses to the Diary and to other Sleeman writings in the critical journals of the time will show, most commentators simply assimilated Sleeman's material as a basis for their own assertions and strictures on Indian character, and for the conclusion which they feel able to draw from these views, that India required British government.

Sleeman's approach is apparent in all of his work and throughout the Diary, but an example of his attempt to understand a specific feature of the Indian situation will help to substantiate the point. The example to which we will turn is his attempt to explain the practice of female infanticide among the Rajputs of Oudh.

Sleeman did not condone infanticide; indeed, he was deeply shocked by the thought that such a practice could be generally followed, and freely admitted to, by an entire group within society. Nevertheless, he insisted on the need to understand, and as the Diary proceeds we can discern the process by which he came to see infanticide not simply as some 'gross superstition' or some inherent barbarity in Rajput nature, but as a response by the Rajputs to particular features of their social organisation and one which was 'permitted' by society in general only because of the nature of economic and political power within Oudh society at that time.

The initial point, he perceived, was that the preservation of the hierarchy of clans into which the Rajputs were grouped and which preserved regional and ethnic differences which they regarded as important, depended upon the observance of certain restrictions with regard to marriage. Families in superior clans would not take brides from families in inferior clans without, at least, a very substantial payment by way of 'compensation' (and as a clear proof of the resources of that particular family), nor would they give brides to inferior clans; for either of these exchanges would have the effect of lowering their prestige in the eyes of other clans. Given a general practice of caste endogamy in India, the result of these prescriptions was that families in both superior and inferior clans had a need to rid themselves of daughters for fear that they would suffer the disgrace of not being able to marry them off at all. In addition, superior-clan families had to ensure that they were not disgraced socially and so lowered in the hierarchy, while inferior-clan families had to guard against the need to pay over-extravagant sums as 'dowry'. At the base of the inferior-clans' concern (and ultimately of the superior-clans', which might be lowered in the social scale) lay a desire to protect the family's resources; to limit, that is, the amount of material wealth which passed by way of dowry into other hands. As Rajput predominance in

Introduction

society generally, and any particular Rajput family's pre-dominance in village or local society, depended upon the control of land, this had to be guarded against at all costs. Nor, as Sleeman pointed out, were Rajputs unusual in this:

> The desire to keep the land in the same family has given rise to singular laws and usages in all nations in the early stage of civilisation, when industry is confined almost exclusively to agriculture, and land is almost the only property valued. Among the people of the Himmaleh [*sic*] hills, as in all Sogdiana, it gave rise to polyandry; and among the Israelites and Mahommedans, to the marriage of many brothers in succession to the same woman.[1]

Moreover, being dominant, the Rajputs were able to do as they wished without the interference (although not with the support) of other groups. After a discussion with a Rajput who strongly expounded the argument that duty to one's family was a primary obligation, Sleeman wrote:

> I am satisfied that these notions were honestly expressed, however strange they may appear to others. Habit has brutalised them or rendered them worse than brutes in regard to their female offspring. They derive profit, or save expense and some mortification by destroying them, and readily believe anything that can tend to excuse the atrocity to themselves and to others. The facility with which men and women persuade themselves of a religious sanction for what they wish to do, however cruel and iniquitous is not, unhappily, peculiar to any class or creed. These Rajpoots know that the crime is detestable, not only to the few Christians that they meet, but to all Mahommedans, and to every other class of Hindoos among whom they live and move. But the Rajpoots, among whom alone this crime prevails, are the dominant class in Oude; and they can disregard the feelings and opinions of the people around them with impunity. The greater part of the land is held by them; and in the greater part of the towns and villages their authority is paramount. Industry is confined almost exclusively to agriculture. They have neither merchants nor manu-facturers to form, or aid in forming, a respectable and influential middle class; and the public officers of the state they look upon as their natural and irreconcilable enemies. When the aristocracy of Europe buried their daughters alive in nunneries, the state of society was much the same as it is now in Oude.[2]

And, he went on to point out, there was additional confirmation of the importance of such considerations as causes of infanticide

[1] Below p. 127; see *JTKO*, vol. I, p. 232.
[2] Below pp. 279–80; see *JTKO*, vol. II, p. 250.

in the contrasting unimportance to Rajputs of *suttee* which was also, to European minds, a social crime: 'That suttees were formerly very numerous in Oude is manifest from the very numerous tombs we see in the vicinity of every town and almost every village; but the Rajpoots never felt much interested in them; they were not necessary either to their pride or purse.'[1]

This approach, which tries to find causal explanations for behaviour, informs the Diary as a whole. It marks Sleeman apart from his contemporaries who generally had no hesitation in operating upon a set of stereotyped explanations of Indian institutions and behaviour which were grounded in the assumption that Indian society was degenerate, and from which they drew the simple political point that only British rule would make possible order and justice within (in this case) Oudh.

The one exception whom I have found is A. H. Layard, the archaeologist, who commented on Sleeman's material in the course of an article in the *Quarterly Review* for July 1858. Layard was a Liberal Member of Parliament from 1852 to 1857 and again from 1860 to 1869. He was defeated in the elections of March 1857 and he travelled out to India in late 1857 to investigate the situation arising from the 'mutiny' which had broken out in May of that year. His *Quarterly Review* article, written on his return, was a survey of a number of recently published books and pamphlets dealing with those events in India. His main concern was with the degree to which deteriorating social relations between Europeans and Indians had made possible the situation in which an uprising could take place. In addition, he was led to comment on Sleeman's Diary, which had been recently published but which was not actually included in the list of books under review, because of the importance which he attached to the annexation of Oudh as a contributory cause of the Mutiny. He contested (for political as well as intellectual reasons) the commonly-held view that what Sleeman had reported was evidence of some inherent incapacity of Indians to rule themselves or some basic depravity of Indian character.

The report of Sir W. Sleeman upon the state of Oude has led to the hasty conclusion that Indian landholders are little better than beasts of prey

[1] Below p. 280; see *JTKO*, vol. ii, p. 251.

Introduction

whose sole occupation consists in destroying their neighbour's property, and in reducing to ruin their own. But this social disorganisation could only have occurred during a state of anarchy, such as may have existed at times in Oude as in other parts of India, and for which we ourselves have been too frequently responsible in consequence of the support and countenance we have afforded to native dynasties... In Oude the disgraceful outrages and misery described by Sir W. Sleeman, were the results not of any inherent vice in the talookdar system, but of feeble and demoralized rulers, whose action and authority had been weakened by our interference, who relied upon our support for their persistence in criminal negligence, and who had been induced to commit acts of injustice and oppression to replace the money which we had done them the honour of borrowing, and had not repaid.[1]

Apart from Layard, most other commentators in the journals of the day saw the Diary as providing clear evidence of Indian political incapacity and, hence, of the need for British rule.

The existence of the Diary was known before its publication in 1858: there was an extract from it in the Oudh 'Blue Book' of 1856[2] and there were a number of extensive extracts from it in a preliminary 'review' by J. W. Kaye in the *North British Review* for August 1856. Kaye, who was in the political and secret department of the East India Company's administration in London and so had access to the copy sent to the Company by Sleeman, set the tone for the earliest reviews. The extracts in the Blue Book, Kaye wrote in justifying his own more extensive quotations, afforded 'an inadequate idea of the extent and variety of its illustrations of native misrule'.[3] Not, he pointed out, that Sleeman was himself antagonistic towards the Indian states or their rulers; on the contrary, he was the most tolerant and sympathetic of Indian officers. But the picture which he drew was nonetheless horrifying and went far to explain why Dalhousie had had to annex the kingdom in 1856. 'We do not believe that there is an Englishman so saturated and sodden with

---

[1] [A. H. Layard,] article no. VIII, in *Quarterly Review*, vol. 104, no. 207 (July) 1858, pp. 262–3. Layard's political interest comes from the controversy surrounding Lord Canning's 'Oudh Proclamation' concerning land rights in the province; see Metcalf, *Aftermath of Revolt*, and M. Maclagan, '*Clemency Canning*' (London, 1962).

[2] *P.P.*, 1857 (session 1), vol. XI, 'Papers relating to Oude', pp. 91–4.

[3] [J. W. Kaye,] 'The Annexation of Oude' in *North British Review*, vol. XXV, no. L (Aug. 1856), p. 533.

prejudice, as really to believe that the people of our Oude will not be happier under our rule than under that of their native princes.'[1] The only question was likely to be, why was Oudh not annexed before?

In April 1858, following the publication of the Diary as *A Journey Through the Kingdom of Oude*, Kaye was able to make a much more detailed commentary in the *Edinburgh Review*. The full blast of the Mutiny had been felt by that time, of course, and the enormity of Indian conduct (in British eyes) added piquancy to the picture which Sleeman presented: '...we do not remember to have met with any work which gives so faithful or frightful an account of the effects of Native Indian Government, or which contains so much original information to explain the events that have recently astonished the world'.[2] He continued:

It may be questioned whether the absorption of Oude into the British territories contributed directly to the great mutiny of 1857; but there cannot be the slightest doubt, that indirectly *the condition of Oude, the ferocity of its chiefs, the warlike habits of the people, the fanaticism of its castes, and the hatred which prevails in that province against the restraints of law and government* did promote the insurrection, and served to render Oude the rallying point of the disaffected, and the arena of a protracted resistance. That the tract of country which has been the shortest time under British rule should be that in which the movement against our authority would most nearly resemble a popular outbreak, was assuredly to have been expected. We need not seek for any explanation of the fact beyond the range of the most obvious suggestions of our ordinary experience. If there had been nothing anarchical and exceptional in the social condition of the country, we could still have understood the natural impatience of the people under a newly-imposed yoke. But when we read these recent events by the light thrown upon them by this publication of Colonel Sleeman's official tour in Oude in the years 1849 and 1850, we see at once that it would have been little short of a miracle, if the military revolt in the adjacent provinces had not roused into intense action that spirit of resistance to constituted authority, which had grown with the growth and strengthened with the strength of the great landholders of Oude.[3]

Once again Kaye underlined the fact that Sleeman himself was a sympathetic and tolerant observer, that he sought wherever possible to exonerate the people about whom he reported. But

---

[1] *Ibid.* p. 552.
[2] [J. W. Kaye] 'The Conquest of Oude' in *Edinburgh Review*, vol. 107 (April 1858), p. 513.
[3] *Ibid.* pp. 513–14. Emphasis added.

Introduction

for Kaye himself the conclusions were abundantly clear: when the British annexed Oudh their task 'was not merely to depose a dynasty but to change the whole condition of society'.[1] This task involved breaking down the local powers and establishing law, and to Kaye it was clear that 'no native power could by possibility have been equal to such an undertaking':[2] 'under its native rulers it has not been, *and could never be*, anything more than a vast den of robbers'.[3] The basis of the charge is that Indians were incapable of governing themselves, not simply that the Oudh situation had become an impossible one. There was no thought that political change could have proceeded from within Oudh society, which was the basis of Sleeman's own proposals for the replacement of the Nawab by a Council of Regency. It is not being argued that Sleeman's particular scheme would have been more practicable than annexation – indeed, as already suggested, it would probably merely have compounded the problems of the country – but it is nonetheless important to recognise that the suggestion derived from a very different view of how Indian society functioned.

J. W. Kaye was, however, a moderate commentator when put beside Dr George Trevor, Canon of York and one-time East India Company chaplain at Madras, who reviewed the Diary along with Knighton's titillating *Private Life of an Eastern King* for *Blackwood's Edinburgh Magazine* in May 1858. Notwithstanding the drawback of their somewhat clumsy style and arrangement, Trevor found Sleeman's two volumes 'instructive': 'the work contains deeply interesting revelations of the state of the government and population of Oude, besides curious, and sometimes marvellous, anecdotes of natural and social *phenomena*.'[4] Trevor took from Sleeman one paramount lesson: Indians not only could not govern themselves, they did not want government in the sense of a lawful and ordered state.

Trevor worked from the premiss that Indians were somehow an exceptional people with an exceptional historical culture which precluded the normal features of social and political order.

---

[1] *Ibid.* p. 523.
[2] *Loc. cit.* [3] *Ibid.* p. 540. Emphasis added.
[4] [G. Trevor], 'Oude' in *Blackwood's Edinburgh Magazine*, vol. LXXXIII, no. DXI (May 1858), p. 634. Trevor's italics.

3   33   RSI

Introduction

One thing must be obvious to every reader of Sir W. Sleeman's pages – viz. that the population he describes would resist to the last *any* system of administration which promised to enforce order, equity and humanity. Such ruffians as Maun Singh and his whole fraternity of Rajpoot robbers, will fight to the death for the traditional rights of their 'order'; and the very people who suffer, find the system so agreeable to Hindu tradition and genius, that on the whole they rather like it. Native life in Oude has, in fact, been a lottery glittering with the most splendid prizes, in the contemplation of which the blanks and the fearful cost of the game are overlooked. The European looking at Oude sees justice perverted, humanity outraged, debauchery and villainy everywhere triumphant; the land held by brigands, women imprisoned, dishonoured, scourged, and mutilated; men dragged from their blazing homes by night, beaten with clubs, scalded with boiling oil, hacked to pieces with swords, or left to die lingeringly with their noses cut off to the bone, and their religious pride trampled under the hoof of a brutal robber. Such is the normal condition of the 'garden of India' when regarded from the European point of view. To the Hindu, on the contrary, these are the incidental losses of the game which no one anticipates till they are experienced, and no one pities but the immediate relatives of the loser. On the other hand there is the pleasure of robbing, plundering, and cheating, in such diversified ways that few can be excluded from the chances of participation. There are waiting maids, and worse than that, becoming queens, and dying worth thousands of rupees; men of low birth and station rising to unheard of riches and power; singers and fiddlers ruling a kingdom; footpads and highwaymen growing into barons and earls. Above all, this is the state of things most agreeable to precedent and religious tradition. It is the *Mahabharat* [*sic*] in little – the nearest approach which this *Kali Yug* can supply to the glorious days of Ramchunder. Never believe that all this is surrendered in exchange for the merely ideal advantages of justice, liberty, security and order! No! the gallant Rajpoots (foul murderers of their female babes), and the 'mild and sensible' Brahmins, who discoursed with primitive simplicity at the side of the British Resident's elephant – pretty panthers toying in the sun! – are not the men to exchange all they hold dear in life for European abstractions. It is not so easy as some philanthropists imagine, to govern men for their own good. Human nature is 'very far gone from righteousness'; and in nations as well as in the individual heart, it takes a good battle to subdue it.[1]

---

[1] *Ibid.* pp. 639–40. The *Mahabharata* is the great epic poem of the Hindus which recounts the story of the war between the Pandavas and the Kauravas. *Kali Yug* is the fourth (and present) age of the world. 'Ramchunder' is Ram-chandra, the hero of the epic poem the *Ramayana* who is remembered in Oudh as the god-prince of Kosala, the capital of which was at Ayodhya in Faizabad district, and which was the 'earliest' Oudh. The reference to 'mild and sensible Brahmins' is from Sleeman (below p. 227) and twists his meaning completely.

Introduction

This view is not simply prejudice (although there is enough of that!); rather, it is the notion that Indian – particularly Hindu – society was both inherently and necessarily debased because it was founded upon the wrong principles and that all Indian (or Hindu) behaviour could be explained simply by reference to the fact that it was Indian. This contrasts strikingly with Sleeman's point of view, which is that Indian behaviour, individual and social, is explicable in precisely the same terms as other human behaviour. Men, Sleeman suggests, endowed with the same mental processes, will tend to react in very similar ways if placed in similar economic, social or political situations, whether they are Indian or European, whether they are in Oudh or in England.

This contrast in modes of explanation can be seen in material other than that relating specifically to Oudh. If we look at *Ramaseeana*, Sleeman's collection of papers concerning the thugs, which was published in 1836, and the review of the book which Charles Trevelyan contributed to the *Edinburgh Review* in January 1837, we can see the same contrast underlined very clearly.

Sleeman himself was not without a touch of wonder at the strangeness of thuggee:

India is emphatically the land of superstition and in this land the system of Thuggee, the most extraordinary that has ever been recorded in the history of the human race, had found a congenial soil, and flourished with rank luxuriance for more than two centuries, till its roots had penetrated and spread over almost every district within the limits of our dominions.[1]

But the acceptance of a divine origin for their 'craft', the acceptance that is of superstitious belief, did not make the thugs unique, he argued. 'A Thug considers the persons murdered precisely in the light of victims offered up to the Goddess; and he remembers them, as a Priest of Jupiter remembered the oxen, and a Priest of Saturn the children sacrificed upon their altars.'[2] The religious sanctions which this divine origin provided, were of importance in ensuring a high degree of discipline within the group, of course,[3] but the explanation of the long

---

[1] *Ramaseeana* (Calcutta, 1836), p. 13.
[2] *Ibid.* pp. 7–8.   [3] *Ibid.* p. i.

Introduction

success of the thugs lay even so in mundane considerations. The fact was that circumstances in India were extremely favourable to their operations:[1] the practice of sending consignments of valuables over long distances by relatively unguarded couriers; the way in which people travelled, on foot or on pony, making relatively little contact with townspeople on the way; the existence of tracts of country with long grass or jungle through which the roads had to pass; and the generally slow transport available which made overtaking difficult – all of these circumstances aided the thugs in the execution and concealment of their crimes. They, moreover, were extremely careful in all their operations and skilled in the techniques of it: they operated well away from their own localities; they took care in choosing their victims (they would not kill women or Europeans, for instance); they were careful in disposing of bodies and the goods which they got from their robberies.[2] And they either avoided detection by their fellow-villagers or they took care to be most acceptable neighbours and fellow-villagers: caste divisions which made their business their own concern tended to further ensure that, even if they were thought to be thugs, they were unlikely to be apprehended.[3]

Charles Trevelyan, who served in India from 1826 to 1840 and who published his *On the education of the people of India* in 1838, began his review of the book by disclaiming any intention to moralise;[4] but he finished by elaborating a fierce denunciation of the moral standards of Hindus and Hindu society. He began by setting out Sleeman's own analysis but he refused to accept this as a sufficient explanation. The full explanation lay, he believed, in 'false religion' and in the preparedness of the Indian public to tolerate people like the thugs because they all shared this 'false religion'.

[1] *Ibid.* pp. iv–v; also pp. 4–5.
[2] *Ibid.* pp. iii–iv. On the care that they took not to kill Europeans (or others, like government servants whose death might lead to inquiry) see Hjejle, 'The Social Policy of the East India Company', p. 283. [3] *Ibid.* pp. ii–iii.
[4] [Charles Edward Trevelyan], 'The Thugs; or Secret Murderers of India' in *Edinburgh Review*, vol. 64 (January 1837), p. 358. Trevelyan (1807–86) followed his service in India with 20 years as assistant secretary at the Treasury (1840–59); he returned to India as governor of Madras (1859–60) and, more successfully, as finance member of the Viceroy's council (1863–5).

Introduction

The truth is that the same religious feeling which leads the Thugs to believe that they are performing a laudable action in murdering travellers who are thrown in their way while the auspices are favourable, causes them to be regarded without horror by other Hindus. They are supposed only to be doing their duty in that state of life to which God has called them. All Hindus, as well as the Thugs, believe in Kalee; and regarding them as her followers, they respect them, and dread the consequences of being instrumental in their punishment.[1]

Moreover, Sleeman's point that because of caste restrictions social groups in India were often clearly and effectively kept from a close knowledge of each other's affairs, becomes for Trevelyan the truth that 'in India universal selfishness prevails'.[2] Indeed, he is sure that it is possible to generalise the difference in European and Indian moral standards:

The 'royal law of love' has no prevalence there: nobody thinks of 'doing unto others as he would be done by'. The difference between ourselves and the natives in these respects is a constant theme of admiration to them. Great as our intellectual superiority is, it does not make nearly the same impression upon them as our moral superiority does. In regard to natural powers of the mind, the natives and ourselves may be much on a level. Even in point of intellectual acquirements, the majority of the English in India have not much to boast of; but the superiority of our moral qualities, – our veracity, our trustworthiness, our mutual dependence, our disposition to unite for the attainment of objects of public interest, even though we may not be ourselves immediately concerned, – is fully admitted by them. Europeans, on their first arrival in India, are often surprised, and somewhat disappointed, at hearing such frequent praise of what appear to them the commonplace qualities of veracity and public spirit. He rather expects to hear our eminence in science and the arts, or our proficiency in war or government, made the subject of eulogy. Experience only can teach, that nothing is so truly astonishing to a morally depraved people as the phenomenon of a race of men, in whose word perfect confidence may be placed, and who are often ardent in the pursuit of objects in which their own interest is not directly concerned. The natives are conscious of their inferiority in nothing so much as this. They require to be taught rectitude of conduct much more than literature and science.[3]

On this basis, Trevelyan can round out his charge, for Hinduism is shown up by thuggee to be 'pure unmixed evil'. 'We should merely weaken the effect of such a disclosure as that which we

[1] *Ibid.* p. 393. [2] *Loc. cit.*
[3] *Ibid.* pp. 393–4. For Sleeman's very different estimate of Indian character see *R and R*, ch. 57, 'Veracity'.

have made', he concludes, 'were we to go through the long catalogue of Hindu gods and goddesses, and to mention the vices which are under special patronage of each.'[1]

Trevelyan was by no means incapable of understanding the nature of thug operations or the analysis which Sleeman made of them. Rather, he dismissed Sleeman's explanations because they did not take sufficient account of the fact that the people being discussed were Hindus. There was no possibility, in his view, that thugs were merely aberrant members of Hindu society; rather, they represented the essence of that society, which was evil because it was 'false'. Nor would he allow that there was the possibility of any but the most attenuated comparison possible between Hindu society and European society. 'If any practice at all approaching in atrocity to that of Thuggee, were to be discovered in England, it would be immediately put down by an united effort of the whole people...In India, however, the state of moral feeling is quite different. The Thugs have nothing to fear from public opinion.'[2] It was possible, he felt, to compare Hinduism with other religions, but there was no doubt of the result of such a comparison:

Almost every false religion has paid court to some of the bad passions of mankind. But neither in Greece, in Carthage, nor in Scandanavia, was superstition ever so diametrically opposed to morality as in India, at the present day. If we were to form a graduated scale of religions, that of Christ and that of Kalee would be the opposite extremes.[3]

The corollary of this state of affairs was also, of course, to Trevelyan's mind quite clear:

Occasions like these afford the best illustration of the advantages of our supremacy in India. Even if the requisite public spirit and intelligence were not wanting, the native states are incapable, from mutual jealousy and distrust, of combining together for the accomplishment of any object of general interest. At this point, the supreme power steps in; – explains to subordinate allies the extent of the evil, and the nature of the remedies which ought to be applied; collects for one common effort the resources of the whole of India, and directs that effort by European intelligence, energy and perseverance.[4]

[1] [Trevelyan] in *Edinburgh Review*, p. 394.
[2] *Ibid.* p. 392.   [3] *Ibid.* p. 394.
[4] *Ibid.* p. 368.

Introduction

The justification which J. W. Kaye or Dr Trevor gave twenty years later for the annexation of Oudh was in precisely the same terms.

Sleeman's approach differed in that his handling of his material – whether on the thugs or on Oudh – asserted that Indian society was comprehensible, that it could be analysed in terms of socio-economic, or psychological-cultural, factors in the same way as other (European) societies. This may now seem a commonplace; it was clearly not – on the evidence of views like those of Trevelyan or Trevor or Kaye – a common-held view in the mid-nineteenth century. Nor was the political conclusion that he drew from his observations – that political change was possible within Indian society and that if the British power had any function it was to allow these changes to take place – shared by his mid-nineteenth-century contemporaries.

The contrast of views in mid-century was not a new one, although the Kayes and Trevelyans and Trevors had certainly gained ground by then. In an earlier generation – already active when Sleeman came as a young ensign to India – there had been men who, like him, were to see that while the British might be in a position to command in India, Indian society was not bereft of institutions suited to its needs. 'It is too much regulation that ruins everything', wrote Sir Thomas Munro in 1818. Englishmen, he went on, 'suppose that no country can be saved without English institutions. The natives of this country have enough of their own to answer every useful object of internal administration, and if we maintain and protect them, the country will in a very few months settle itself.'[1] They saw, moreover, that change could not simply be caused by outsiders. 'Great and beneficial alterations in society, to be complete, must be produced within that society itself; they cannot be the mere fabrication of its superiors, or of a few who deem themselves enlightened',[2] wrote Sir John Malcolm – the Agent to the Governor-General in Central India under whom Sleeman had begun his civilian career. Such opinions were by mid-century very largely brushed

[1] G. R. Gleig, *The Life of Major-General Sir Thomas Munro*, 3 vols (London, 1830), vol. III, p. 252.
[2] J. Malcolm, *A Memoir of Central India, including Malwa and Adjoining Provinces*, 2 vols (London, 3rd ed. 1832), vol II, p. 282.

aside: although these men accomplished much themselves, the overall spirit of British government in India proceeded from the principle that innovation – which was taken to mean European institutions – was essential. They were rejected still more forcibly over such questions as the annexation of Oudh and, after the 'mutiny' of 1857, it was to be many years before they were to be able to assert once more that Indians were capable of governing themselves.

The original 'Table of Contents'

[1852: I, i–iv; II, i–vi] [1858: I, vii–x; II, iii–vi]

CONTENTS[a]
OF THE FIRST VOLUME

CHAPTER I

Departure from Lucknow – Gholam Huzrut – Attack on the late Prime Minister, Ameen-od Dowla – A similar attack on the sons of a former Prime Minister, Aga Meer – Gunga Sing and Kulunder Buksh – Gorbuksh Sing, of Bhitolee – Gonda-Bahraetch district – Rughbur Sing – Prethee Put, of Paska – King of Oude and king of the Fairies – Surafraz Mahal.

CHAPTER II

Bahraetch – Shrine of Syud Salar – King of the Fairies and the Fiddlers – Management of Bahraetch district for forty-three years – Murder of Amur Sing, by Hakeem Mehndee – Nefarious transfer of *khalsa* lands to Tallookdars, by local officers – Rajah Dursun Sing – His aggression on the Nepaul territory – Consequences – Intelligence Department – How formed, managed and abused – Rughbur Sing's management of Gonda and Bahraetch for 1846–47 – Its fiscal effects – A gang robber caught and hung by Brahmin villagers – Murder of Syampooree Gosaen – Ramdut Pandee – Fairies and Fiddlers – Ramdut Pandee, the Banker, the Rajahs of Toolseepoor and Bulrampoor – Murder of Mr Ravenscroft, of the Bengal Civil Service, at Bhinga, in 1823.

[a] This table of contents is set out as in the 1852 edition. The portions in italics do not appear in the table of contents of the 1858 edition, although these items are in fact in the text.

The 1858 edition numbers the chapters of volume II from I to VI instead of consecutively as in the 1852 edition. The 1858 edition has these additional items:

volume I: before Chapter I,
  'Biographical sketch of Major-General Sir W. H. Sleeman, K.C.B., page xi; Introduction, page xvii; Private Correspondence preceding the Journey through the Kingdom of Oude, p. xxiii.'

volume II: after Chapter VI,
  'Private Correspondence subsequent to the Journey through the Kingdom of Oude, and relating to the Annexation of Oude to British India, page 332.'

Original Table of Contents

Original Table of Contents

[a] *Sic* = 'presenting'?

Original Table of Contents

CONTENTS
OF THE SECOND VOLUME

CHAPTER VII

a Given incorrectly as 'Passes' in 1858 edition.

Original Table of Contents

CHAPTER VIII

^a Given as 'Pallee' in 1858.
^b For 'taken back', 1858 edition has 'saved'.

Original Table of Contents

---

[a] 1858 edition has 'his'.

Original Table of Contents

---

[a] 1858 edition has 'supports' for 'supporting' at both places in this sentence.
[b] 1858 has 'but'.   [c] 1858 has 'its'.
[d] 1858 omits 'only'.
[e] For 'who always', 1858 edition has 'which'.

Original Table of Contents

DIARY

OF A

TOUR THROUGH OUDE,

IN

DECEMBER 1849, & JANUARY & FEBRUARY, 1850.

BY

THE RESIDENT

Lieutenant=Colonel W. H. Sleeman.

~~~~~~~~~~~~~~~

VOLUME I.

~~~~~~~~~~~~~~~

PRINTED AT LUCKNOW IN A PARLOUR PRESS.

1852.

RSI

The title page of the 1858 edition reads:

A / Journey / through the / Kingdom of Oude, / in 1849–1850; /

By direction of the Right Hon. the Earl of Dalhousie, / Governor-General. /

With Private Correspondence relative / to the Annexation of Oude to British India, &c. /

By Major-General Sir W. H. Sleeman, K.C.B. / Resident at the Court of Lucknow. /

In Two Volumes. / Vol. I. /

London: / Richard Bentley, / Publisher in Ordinary to Her Majesty. / 1858.

[Title page reproduced by courtesy of the Curators of the Bodleian Library, Oxford.]

Preface

My object, in writing this DIARY OF A TOUR THROUGH OUDE, was, to prepare for submission to the Government of India, as fair and full a picture of the real state of the country, condition and feeling of the people of all classes, and character of the government under which they at present live, as the opportunities which the tour afforded me might enable me to draw. In order to facilitate the perusal I have had the DIARY printed at my own expense, in a small parlour press which I purchased, with type, for the purpose.[a]

I may, possibly, be considered to have succeeded in this my object; but I can hardly hope that any one unconnected with the Government of India generally, or with that of Oude in particular, will ever find much to interest or amuse him in the perusal of the DIARY OF A TOUR, without adventures through a country so devoid as Oude is of commerce and manufactures, of works of ornament or utility, and above all of persons places and things associated in the mind of the reader with religious, poetical, or historical recollections.[b]

The DIARY must, for the present, be considered as an official document, which may be perused, but cannot be published wholly or in part without the sanction of Government previously obtained.[c]

W. H. SLEEMAN[d]

[a] In the 1858 edition there are minor punctuation changes in the first sentence of this paragraph, and the second sentence is omitted entirely.

[b] This paragraph is omitted in the 1858 edition.

[c] The 1858 edition adds a footnote to this paragraph: 'This permission was accorded by the Honourable Court of Directors in December last.'

[d] Dateline, 'Lucknow, 1852', is added in 1858 edition.

DIARY OF A
TOUR THROUGH OUDE

CHAPTER I

[From Lucknow to Bahraetch, 1–9 December 1849]

[1852: I, 1–2] [1858: I, 1–3]

December 1, 1849. – I left Lucknow to proceed on a tour through Oude, to see the state of the country and the condition of the people. My wish to do so I communicated to Government, on the 29th of March last, and its sanction was conveyed to me, in a letter from the Secretary, dated the 7th of April. On the 16th of November I reported to Government my intention to proceed, under this sanction, on the 1st December, and on the 19th I sent the same intimation to the king. On the 28th, as soon as the ceremonies of the Mohurrum terminated, His Majesty expressed a wish to see me on the following day; and on the 29th I went at 9 A.M., accompanied by Captain Bird,[a] the first Assistant, and Lieutenant Weston,[b] the Superintendent of the Frontier Police,[c] and took leave of the king, with mutual expression of good will. The minister, Alee Nakee Khan, was present. On the 30th I made over charge of the Treasury to Captain Bird, who has the

[a] The author of *Dacoitee in Excelsis; or the Spoliation of Oude by the East India Company*; cf. above, Introduction, pp. 17–18.

[b] See W. L. Low, *Lieutenant-Colonel Gould Hunter-Weston of Hunterston...One of the defenders of Lucknow during the Indian Mutiny 1857–8. A Biographical Sketch* (Selkirk, 1914). I have to thank Dr Ian Catanach of the University of Canterbury, Christchurch, New Zealand, for bringing this biography to my attention and also for arranging for me to consult Weston's personal and annotated copy of the 1858 edition, which is now in the Library of that University.

[c] A police force designed to protect the Gorakhpur frontier, organised in 1845 and consisting of 560 men: E. Thornton, *A Gazetteer of the Territories under the Government of the East-India Company and of the Native States on the continent of India*, 4 vols (London, 1854), vol. IV, pp. 36–7. See also Low, *Hunter-Weston*, chs 4–6 for some glimpses of the work of the force from Weston's letters.

charge of the department of the Sipahees' Petitions[a] and the
Fyzabad Guaranteed Pensions[b]; and, taking with me all the
office establishments not required in these three departments, proceeded, under the usual salute, to Chenahut, eight
miles.[1]

The Minister, Dewan and Deputy Minister, Ghoolam Ruza,
came out the first stage with me, and our friend Moonuwur-od
Dowla, drove out to see us in the evening.

December 2, 1849. – We proceeded to Nawabgunge, the minister
riding out with me, for some miles, to take leave, as I sat in my
tonjohn. At sunrise I ventured, for the first time since I broke
my left thigh bone on the 4th April, to mount an elephant, the
better to see the country. The land, on both sides of the road,
well cultivated, and studded with groves of mango and other
trees and very fertile.

The two purgunnas of Nawabgunge and Sidhore are under
the charge of Aga Ahmud, the Amil, who has under him two
naibs or deputies, Ghoolam Abbas and Mahummud Ameer. All
three are obliged to connive at the iniquities of a Landholder,
Ghoolam Huzrut, who resides on his small estate of Jhareea-
poora, which he is augmenting, in a manner too common in
Oude, by seizing on the estates of his weaker neighbours. He
wanted to increase the number of his followers, and on the 10th
of November 1849, he sent some men to aid the prisoners in the
great jail at Lucknow to break out. Five of them were killed in
the attempt, seven were wounded, and twenty-five were retaken,
but forty-five escaped, and among them Fuzl Allee, one of the
four assassins, who, in April 1847, cut down the late minister,
Ameen-od Dowla, in the midst of his followers, in one of the

---

[1] My escort consisted of two Companies of Sipahees, from the 10th Regiment
Native Infantry, and my party of Captain Hardwick, Lieutenant Weston, and
Lieutenant and Mrs Willows and my wife and children, with occasional visitors
from Lucknow and elsewhere.

[a] From Sleeman's later discussion of sipahee (sepoy) petitions, this was clearly
a major task of the Residency; cf. above, Introduction, pp. 19–20.

[b] See C. U. Aitchison, *A Collection of Treaties, Engagements and Sunnuds
relating to India and Neighbouring Countries*, 7 vols (Calcutta, 1876), vol. II, *Treaties,
etc. relating to the N.W.P., Oudh, Nepal, Bundelcund and Baghelcund*, pp. 115–47,
for details of pensioners.

Diary of a Tour Through Oude

principal streets of Lucknow, through which the road, leading from the city to Cawnpore, now passes. One of the four, Tuffuzzul Hoseyn, was killed in attempting to escape on the 8th August 1849, and one, Allee Mahomed, was killed in this last attempt. The third, Fuzl Allee, with some of the most atrocious and desperate of his companions, is now with this Ghoolam Huzrut, disturbing the peace of the country. The leader in this attempt was Ghoolam Hyder Khan, who is still in jail at Lucknow...

[1852: I, 18–33] [1858: I, 20–37]

About two years ago this Ghoolam Huzrut took by violence possession of the small estate of Golha, now in the Sidhore purgunnah; and turned out the proprietor, Bhowannee Sing, a Rathore Rajpoot, whose ancestors had held it for several centuries. The poor man was re-established in it by the succeeding contractor[a], Girdhara Sing; but on his losing his contract, Ghoolam Huzrut, on the 23d of September last, again attacked Bhowannee Sing at midnight, at the head of a gang of ruffians; and after killing five of his relatives and servants, and burning down his houses, turned him and his family out, and secured possession of the village, which he still holds. The king's officers were too weak to protect the poor man, and have hitherto acquiesced in the usurpation of the village. Ghoolam Huzrut has removed all the autumn crops to his own village; and cut down and taken away sixty mango trees planted by Bhowannee Sing's ancestors. Miherban Sing, the son of the sufferer, is a sipahee in the 63d Regiment Native Infantry, and he presented a petition through the Resident in behalf of his father. Other petitions have been since presented, and the Court has been strongly urged to afford redress. Ghoolam Huzrut has two forts, to which he retires when pursued, one at *Para*, and one at *Sarai*, and a good many powerful landholders always

[a] An 'ijaradar'. Under the ijara system of revenue collection, the revenue farmer agreed to pay a specified revenue from a tract and was then given a free hand to collect that sum, and to make a profit as he was able. For a discussion of the system (which he gives as *izarah*) see Jagdish Raj, *The Mutiny and British Land Policy in North India, 1856–1868* (Bombay, 1965), ch. 1.

ready to support him against the government, on condition of
being supported by him when necessary.[1]

December 3, 1849. – Kinalee, ten miles over a plain, highly cultivated and well studded with groves, but we could see neither
town, village nor hamlet on the road. A poor brahmin, Gunga
Sing, came along the road with me, to seek redress for injuries
sustained. His grandfather was in the service of our Government,
and killed under Lord Lake, at the first siege of Bhurtpore in
1804.[a] With the little he left the family had set up as agricultural
capitalists[b] in the village of Poorwa Pundit, on the estate of
Kulunder Buksh, of Bhitwal. Here they prospered. The estate

[1] On crossing the river Ghagra, I directed Captain Bunbury, (who commands a
Regiment in the king of Oude's service with six guns, and was to have accompanied
me, and left the main body of his regiment with his guns under his second in
command, Captain Hearsey, at Nawabgunge,) to surprise and capture Ghoolam
Huzrut, if possible, by a sudden march. He had left his fort of Para, on my passing
within a few miles of it, knowing that the minister had been with me, and thinking
that he might have requested my aid for the purpose. Captain Bunbury joined his
main body unperceived, made a forced march during the night, and reached the fort
of Para at day break in the morning, without giving alarm to any one on the road.
In this surprise he was aided by Khoda Buksh, of Dadra, a very respectable and
excellent landholder, who had suffered from Ghoolam Huzrut's depredations.
He had returned to his fort with all his family on my passing, and it contained
but few soldiers, with a vast number of women and children. He saw that it would
be of no use to resist, and surrendered his fort and person to Captain Bunbury, who
sent him a prisoner to Lucknow, under charge of two Companies, commanded by
Captain Hearsey. He is under trial, but he has so many influential friends about the
Court, with whom he has shared his plunder, that his ultimate punishment is
doubtful. Captain Bunbury was praised for his skill and gallantry, and was honored
with a title by the king. [This footnote is included in the text in the 1858 edition;
I, 21–2.]
[a] Gerard, first Viscount Lake of Delhi and Leswarree, (1744–1808); Commander
in Chief, India, July 1801–July 1805 and October 1805–October 1807; raised to
peerage, Septemper 1804. See *Cambridge History of India* [*CHI*], vol. v, p. 374,
for siege of the Jat fortress of Bharatpur in 1804–5; Lake failed to capture the
fortress after four violent assaults and had to make peace with the Raja, leaving
him in possession of the fort. There was further trouble following a disputed
succession in 1823 and the fort was only taken in 1826 after 'desperate resistance'
from its Jat defenders, *ibid.* p. 577.
[b] Cf. Vincent Smith's comment in his edition of Sleeman's *Rambles and Recollections of an India Official* (Oxford, 1915), p. 150, n. 2; '"Agricultural capitalist" is
rather a large phrase for the humble village moneylender, whose transactions are
usually on a very small scale.' Thornton also uses it of 'many small mahajans or
capitalists, who make advances either in money, wares or grain'; *Gazetteer*,
vol. iv, p. 31. Sleeman, however, uses the term to include much larger money-
lenders; see, e.g., the application of the term to Ram Dutt Pande, who dealt in
lakhs of rupees, p. 82 below.

was, as a matter of favor to Kulunder Buksh, transferred from the jurisdiction of the contractor to that of the Hozoor Tehseel.[1] Kulundur Buksh either could not, or would not, pay the government demand; and he employed two of his relatives, Godree and Hoseyn Buksh, to plunder in the estate and the neighbourhood, to reduce government to his own terms. These two persons, with two hundred armed men, attacked the village in the night; and, after plundering the house of this brahmin, Gunga Sing, they seized his wife, who was then pregnant, and made her point out a hidden treasure of one hundred and seven gold mohurs, and two hundred and seventy-seven rupees. She had been wounded in several places before she did this, and when she could point out no more, one of the two brothers cut her down with his sword, and killed her. In all the brahmin lost two thousand seven hundred and fifty-five rupees worth of property; and, on the ground of his grand-father having been killed in the Honorable Company's service, has been ever since urging the Resident to interpose with the Oude government in his behalf.

The estate of Bhitwal has been retransferred to the jurisdiction of the Amil of Byswara, who has restored it to Kulunder Buksh; and his two relatives, Godree and Hoseyn Buksh, are thriving on the booty acquired, and are in high favor with the local authorities. I have requested that measures may be adopted to punish them for the robbery and the cruel murder of the poor woman; but have little hope that they will be so. No government in India is now more weak for purposes of good than that of Oude.[a]

This village of Kinalee is now in the estate of Ramnuggur Dhumeereea, held by Gorbuksh, a large landholder, who has a strong fort, Bhitolee, at the point of the Delta, formed by the Chouka and Ghagra rivers, which here unite. He has taken refuge with some four thousand armed followers in this fort, under the apprehension of being made to pay the full amount of the

---

[1] The term 'Hozoor Tehseel' signifies the collections of the revenue made by the governor himself, whether of a district or a kingdom. The estates of all landholders who pay their land revenues direct to the governor, or to the deputy employed under him to receive such revenues and manage such estates, are said to be in the 'Hozoor Tehseel'. The local authorities of the districts, on which such estates are situated, have nothing whatever to do with them.

[a] This sentence is put into italics in the 1858 edition; vol. I, pp. 23–4.

government demand, and called to account for the rescue of some atrocious offenders from Captain Hearsey, of the Frontier Police, by whom they had been secured. Gorbuksh used to pay two hundred thousand rupees a year for many years for this estate, without murmur or difficulty; but for the last three years he has not paid the rate, to which he has got it reduced, of one hundred and fifty thousand. Out of his rents and the revenues due to government he keeps up a large body of armed followers, to intimidate the government, and seize upon the estates of his weaker neighbours, many of which he has lately appropriated by fraud, violence and collusion. An attempt was this year made to put this estate under the management of government officers; but he was too strong for the government, which was obliged to temporise, and at last to yield. He is said to exact from the landholders the sum of two hundred and fifty thousand rupees a year. He holds also the estate of Bhitolee, at the apex of the delta of the Ghagra and Chouka rivers, in which the fort of Bhitolee is situated. The government demand on this estate is fifty thousand (50,000) rupees a year. His son, Surubjeet Sing is engaged in plunder, and, it is said, with his father's connivance and encouragement, though he pretends to be acting in disobedience of his orders. The object is, to augment their estate, and intimidate the government and its officers by gangs of ruffians, whom they can subsist only by plunder and malversation. The greater part of the lands, comprised in this estate of Ramnuggur Dhumeereea, of which Rajah Gorbuksh is now the local governor, are hereditary possessions which have been held by his family for many generations. A part have been recently seized from weaker neighbours, and added to them. The rest are merely under him as the governor or public officer, entrusted with the collection of the revenue and the management of the police.

December 4, 1849. – Gunesh Gunge, alias Byram-ghat, on the right bank of the river Ghagra, distance about twelve miles. The country well cultivated, and studded with good groves of mango and other trees. We passed through and close to several villages, whose houses are nothing but mud walls, without a thatched or tiled roof to one in twenty. The people say there is no security in them from the king's troops and the Passies, a large class of men in Oude, who are village watchmen but inveterate thieves and robbers, when not employed as such. All refractory landholders hire a body of Passies to fight for them, as they pay themselves out of the plunder, and cost little to their employers. They are all armed with bows and arrows, and are very formidable at night. They and their refractory employers keep the country in a perpetual state of disorder; and, though they do not prevent the cultivation of the land, they prevent the villages and hamlets from being occupied by any body who has any thing to lose, and no strong local ties to restrain him.

The town of Ramnuggur, in which Gorbuksh resides occasionally, is on the road some five miles from the river. It has a good many houses, but all are of the same wretched description, mud walls, with invisible coverings or no coverings at all – no signs of domestic peace or happiness – but nothing can exceed the richness and variety of the crops in and around Ramnuggur. It is a fine garden and would soon be beautiful, were life and property better secured, and some signs of domestic comfort created. The ruined state of the houses in this town and in the villages along the road, is, in part, owing to the system which requires all the king's troops to forage for themselves on the march, and the contractors and other collectors of revenue, to be continually on the move, and to take all their troops with them. The troops, required in the provinces, should be cantoned in five or six places most convenient, with regard to the districts to be controlled, and most healthy for the people; and provided with what they require, as ours are, and sent out to assist the Revenue Collectors and magistrates, only when their services are indispensably necessary. Some Chundele Rajpoot landholders came to me yesterday to say, that Ghoolam Huzrut, with his bands of armed ruffians, seemed determined to seize upon all the estates of his weaker Hindoo neighbours, and they should soon lose theirs, unless the British government interposed to protect them. Gorbuksh has not ventured to come, as he was ordered, to pay his respects to the Resident; but has shut himself up in his fort at Bhitolee, about six miles up the river from our Camp. The Chouka is a small river which there flows into the Ghagra.

He is said to have four or five thousand men with him; and several guns mounted in his fort. The ferry over the Ghagra is close to our tents, and called Byram-ghat.

December 5, 1849. – Crossed the river Ghagra, in boats and encamped at Nawabgunge, on the left bank, where we were met by one of the collectors of the Gonda Bahraetch district. He complained of the difficulties experienced in realizing the just demands of the exchequer, from the number and power of the Tallookdars of the district, who had forts and bands of armed followers, too strong for the king's officers. There were, he said, in the small purgunnah of Gouras –

1. Pretheeput Sing, of Paska, who has a strong fort called Dhunolee, on the right bank of the Ghagra, opposite to Paska and Bumhoree, two strong holds, which he has on the left bank of that river, and he is always ready to resist the government.
2. Murtonjee Buksh, of Shahpoor, who is always ready to do the same; and a great ruffian.
3. Shere Bahader Sing, of Kuneear.
4. Maheput Sing, of Dhunawa.
5. Surnam Sing, of Arta.
6. Maheput Sing, of Paruspoor.

They have each a fort, or strong hold, mounting five or six guns, and trained bands of armed and brave men of five or six hundred, which they augment, as occasion requires, by Gohars, or auxiliary bands from their friends.

Hurdut Sing, of Bondee, alias Bumnootee, held an estate for which he paid one hundred and eighty-two thousand (1,82,000) rupees a year to government; but he was driven out of it in 1846–47, by Rughbur Sing, the contractor, who, by rapacity and outrage, drove off the greater part of the cultivators, and so desolated the estate that it could not now be made to yield thirty thousand (30,000) rupees a year. The Raja has ever since resided with a few followers in an island in the Ghagra. He has never openly resisted or defied the government, but is said to be sullen, and a bad paymaster. He still holds the estate in its desolate condition.

The people of Nawabgunge drink the water of wells, close to the bank of the river, and often the water of the river itself, and say that they never suffer from it; but that a good many people in several villages, along the same bank, have the goitre to a very distressing degree.

December 6, 1849. – Halted at Byram-ghat, in order to enable all our people and things to come up. One of our elephants nearly lost his life yesterday in the quicksands of the river. Capt. Weston rode out yesterday close to Bhitolee, the little fort of Rajah Gorbuksh Sing, who came out in a litter and told him, that he would come to me to-day at noon, and clear himself of the charges brought against him of rescuing and harbouring robbers, and refusing to pay the government demand. He had been suffering severely from fever for fifteen days.

Kuramut Allee complains that his father, Busharut Allee, had been driven out from the purgunnahs of Nawabgunge and Sidhore, by Ghoolam Huzrut and his associates, who had several times attacked and plundered the town of Nawabgunge, our second stage, and a great many other villages around, from which they had driven off all the cultivators and stock, in order to appropriate them to themselves, and augment their landed estates – that they had cut down all the groves of mango trees planted by the rightful proprietors and their ancestors, in order to remove all local ties; and murdered or maimed all cultivators who presumed to till any of the lands without their permission – that Busharut Allee had held the contract for the land revenue of the purgunnah for twenty years, and paid punctually one hundred and thirty-five thousand (1,35,000) rupees a year to the treasury, till about four years ago, when Ghoolam Huzrut commenced this system of spoliation and seizure, since which time the purgunnah had been declining, and could not now yield seventy thousand (70,000) rupees to the treasury – that his family had held many villages in hereditary right for many generations, within the purgunnah, but that all had been or were being seized by this lawless freebooter and his associates.

Seeta Ram, a brahmin zumeendar of Kowaree, in purgunnah Satrick, complains, that he has been driven out of his hereditary estate, by Ghoolam Imam, the zumeendar of Jaggour, and his associate, Ghoolam Huzrut – that his house has been levelled with the ground, and all the trees, planted by his family, have been cut down and burned – that he has been plundered of all he had by them, and is utterly ruined. Many other landholders complain in the same manner of having been robbed by this gang, and deprived of their estates; and still more come in to pray for protection, as the same fate threatens all the smaller proprietors, under a government so weak, and so indifferent to the sufferings of its subjects.

The Nazim of Khyrabad, who is now here engaged in the siege of Bhitolee, has nominally three thousand four hundred fighting men with him; but he cannot muster seventeen hundred. He has with him only the seconds in command of corps, who are men of no authority or influence, the commandants being at Court and the mere creatures of the singers and eunuchs, and other favourites about the palace. They always reside at and about Court, and keep up only half the number of men and officers, for whom they draw pay. All his applications to the minister to have more soldiers sent out to complete the corps, or permission to raise men in their places, remain unanswered and disregarded. The Nazim of Bahraetch has nominally four thousand fighting men; but he cannot muster two thousand, and the greater part of them are good for nothing. The great landholders despise them, but respect the Komukee Corps, under Captains Barlow, Bunbury and Magness, which are complete, and composed of strong and brave men. The despicable state to which the Court favourites have reduced the king's troops, with the exception of these three corps, is lamentable. They are under no discipline, and are formidable only to the peasantry and smaller landholders and proprietors, whose houses they every where deprive of their coverings, as they deprive their cattle of their fodder.

December 7, 1849. – Hissampoor, 12 miles north east, over a plain of fine soil, more scantily tilled than any we saw on the other side of the Ghagra, but well studded with groves and fine single trees, and with excellent crops on the lands actually under tillage. One cause assigned for so much fine land lying waste is, that the Rajpoot tallookdars, above named, of the Chehdewara, have been long engaged in plundering the Syud proprietors of the soil, and seizing upon their lands, in the same manner as the Mahomedan ruffians, on the other side of the river, have been engaged in plundering the small Rajpoot proprietors, and seizing upon their lands. Four of them are now quiet; but two, Prethee Put and Mirtonjee, are always in rebellion. Lately, while the Chuckladar was absent, employed against Jote Sing, of Churda, in the Turae,[a] these two men took a large train of followers, with some guns, attacked the two villages of Aelee and Pursolee, in the estate of Deeksa, in Gonda, killed six persons, plundered all the houses of the inhabitants, and destroyed all their crops, merely because the landholders of these two villages, would not settle a boundary dispute in the way they proposed. The lands of the Hissampoor purgunnah were held in property by the members of a family of Syuds,[b] and had been so for many generations; but neighbouring Rajpoot tallookdars have plundered them of all they had, and seized upon their lands by violence, fraud, or collusion, with public officers. Some they have seized and imprisoned with torture of one kind or another, till they signed deeds of sale, *Bynamahs*; others they have murdered with all their families, to get secure possession of their lands; others they have despoiled by offering the local authorities a higher rate of revenue for their lands than they could possibly pay.

The Nazim has eighteen guns, and ten auxiliary ones sent out on emergency – not one quarter are in a state for service; and for these he has not half the draft-bullocks required, and they are too weak for use; and of ammunition or *stores* he has hardly any at all. Rajah Gorbuksh Sing came yesterday, at sunset, to pay his respects, and promised to pay to the Oude government all that is justly demandable from him. Written engagements to this effect were drawn up, and signed by both the 'high contracting parties'. Having come in on a pledge of personal security, he was, of course, permitted to return from my Camp, to his own

---

[a] The terai or tarai, is a narrow marshy tract running along the foot of the first range of Himalayan hills; see O. H. K. Spate and A. T. A. Learmonth, *India and Pakistan. A general and regional geography* (London, 3rd ed. 1967), under 'terai'.

[b] Cf. below p. 71.

stronghold in safety. In that place he has collected all the loose characters and unemployed soldiers he could gather together, and all that his friends and associates could lend him, to resist the Amil; and to maintain such a host, he will have to pay much more than was required punctually to fulfil his engagements to the State. He calculates, however, that, by yielding to the government, he would entail upon himself a perpetual burthen at an enhanced rate, while, by the temporary expenditure of a few thousands in this way, he may still further reduce the rate he has hitherto paid.

The contract for Gonda and Bahraetch was held by Rughbur Sing, one of the sons of Dursun Sing, for the years 1846 and 1847 A.D. and the district of Sultanpoor was held by his brother, Maun Sing, for 1845–46 and 1847 A.D. Rughbur Sing in 1846–47 is supposed to have seized and sold or destroyed no less than 25,000 plough bullocks in Bhumnootee, the estate of Rajah Hurdut Sing alone. The estate of Hurhurpoor had, up to that time, long paid government sixty thousand (60,000) rupees a year, but last year it would not yield five thousand (5,000) rupees from the ravages of this man, Rughbur Sing. The estate of Rehwa, held by Jeswunt Sing, tallookdar, had paid regularly fifty-five thousand (55,000) rupees a year, but it was so desolated by Rughbur Sing, that it cannot now yield eleven thousand (11,000) rupees. This estate adjoins Bhumnootee, Rajah Hurdut Sing's, which, as above stated, regularly paid one hundred and eighty-two thousand (1,82,000) rupees – it cannot now pay thirty thousand (30,000) rupees. Such are the effects of the oppression of this bad man for so brief a period.

Some tallookdars live within the borders of our district of Goruckpoor, while their lands lie in Oude. By this means they evade the payment of their land revenues; and, with impunity, commit atrocious acts of murder and plunder in Oude. These men maim or murder all who presume to cultivate on the lands which they have deserted, without their permission, or to pay rents to any but themselves; and the king of Oude's officers dare not follow them, and are altogether helpless. Only two months ago, Mohibollah, a zumeendar of Kuttera, was invited by Hoseyn Buksh Khan, one of these tallookdars, to his house, in the Goruckpoor district, to negociate for the ransom of one of his cultivators, a weaver by cast, whom he had seized and taken away. As he was returning in the evening he was way-laid by Hoseyn Buksh Khan, as soon as he had recrossed the Oude borders, and murdered with one of his attendants, who had been sent with him by the Oude Amil. Such atrocities are committed by these refractory tallookdars every day, while they are protected within our bordering districts. Their lands must lie waste or be tilled by men who pay all the rent to them, while they pay nothing to the Oude government. The Oude government has no hope of prosecuting these men to conviction in our Judicial Courts, for specific crimes, which they are known every day to commit, and glory in committing. In no part of India is there such glaring abuse of the privileges of sanctuary, as in some of our districts, bordering on Oude, while the Oude Frontier Police, maintained by the king, at the cost of about one hundred thousand (100,000) rupees a year, and placed under our control, prevents any similar abuse on the part of the Oude people and local authorities. Some remedy for this intolerable evil should be devised.

At present the magistrates of all our conterminous districts require, or expect, that their charges against any offender in Oude, who has committed a crime in their districts, shall be held to be sufficient for their arrest; but some of them, on the other hand, require, that nothing less than some unattainable judicial proof, on the part of the officers of the Oude government, shall be held to be sufficient to justify the arrest of any Oude offender, who takes refuge in our districts. They hold, that the sole object of the Oude authorities is, to get revenue defaulters into their power; and that the charges against them for heinous crimes, are invented solely for that purpose. No doubt this is often the object, and that other charges are sometimes invented for the sole purpose of securing the arrest and surrender of revenue defaulters; but the Oude revenue defaulters, who take refuge in our districts, are, for the most part, the tallookdars, or great landholders, who either before or after they do so, invariably fight with the Oude authorities, and murder and plunder indiscriminately, in order to reduce them to their own terms. The

Honorable the Court of Directors[a] justly require, that requisition for the surrender of offenders by and from British officers and Native States, shall be limited to persons charged with having committed heinous crimes within their respective territories; and, that the obligation to surrender such offenders, shall be strictly reciprocal, unless, in any special case, there be very strong reason for a departure from the rule. See their letter to the Government of India, 27th May 1835. But some magistrates of districts disregard altogether applications made to them by the sovereign of Oude, through the British Resident, for the arrest of subjects of Oude, who have committed the most atrocious robberies and murders in the Oude territory, in open day, and in the sight of hundreds; and allow refugees from Oude, to collect and keep up gangs of robbers within their own districts, and rob and murder within the Oude territory.[b] Happily such magistrates are rare. Government in a letter dated the 25th February 1848, state – 'that, it is the duty of the magistrates of our districts, bordering on Oude, to adopt vigorous measures for preventing the assembling or entertaining of followers by any party, for the purpose of committing acts of violence on the Oude side of the frontier'.

December 8, 1849. – Pukharpoor, a distance of fourteen miles, over a fine plain of good soil, scantily tilled. For some miles the road lay through Raja Hurdut Sing's estate of Bumnootee, which was, with the rest of the district of Bahraetch and Gonda, plundered by Rughbur Sing, during the two years that he held the contract. We passed through no village or hamlet, but saw some at a distance from the road, with their dwellings of naked mud walls, the abode of fear and wretchedness; but the plain is well studded with groves and fine single trees; and the crops are good where there are any on the ground. Under good

[a] The executive body of the East India Company in England; see C. H. Philips, *The East India Company, 1784–1834* (Manchester, 1940, reprint 1961), pp. 4–9, for a general discussion.

[b] Cf. Shore, *Notes on Indian Affairs*, vol. I, pp. 152–3, for a discussion of connections across the Oudh-British India boundary which was, as Shore pointed out, 'a mere arbitrary line drawn through a tract of country which was formerly under the same government' and with people on either side who were connected by kinship and other ties.

management, the country would be exceedingly beautiful, and was so until within the last four years.

In the evening I had a long talk with the people of the village, who had assembled round our tents. Many of them had the goitre, but they told me, that in this and all the villages, within twenty miles, the disease had, of later years, diminished – that hardly one quarter of the number, that used to suffer from it, had now the disease – that the quality of the water must have improved, though they knew not why, as they still drank from the same wells. These wells must penetrate into some bed of mineral or other substance, which produces this disease of the glands, and may, in time, exhaust it. But it is probable, that the number who suffer from this disease has diminished merely with the rest of the population; and that the proportion which the goitered bear to the ungoitered, may be still the same. They told me, that they had been plundered of all their stock and moveable property, by the terrible scourge, Rughber Sing, during his reign of two years, and could not hope to recover from their present state of poverty for many more, – that their lands were scantily tilled, and the crops had so failed for many years, since this miscreant's rule, that the district which used to supply Lucknow with grain, was obliged to draw grain from it, and even from Cawnpore. This is true, and grain has, in consequence, been increasing in price ever since we left Lucknow. It is now here almost double the price than[a] it is at Lucknow, while it is usually twice as cheap here.

December 9, 1849. – Bahraetch, ten miles north east. We encamped on a fine sward, on the left bank of the Surjoo river, a beautiful clear stream. The cultivation very scanty, but the soil good, with water every where, within a few feet of the surface. Groves and single trees less numerous; and of villages and hamlets we saw none. Under good government, the whole country might, in a few years, be made a beautiful garden. The river Surjoo is like a winding stream in a park; and its banks might, everywhere, be cultivated to the water's edge. No ravines, jungle or steep embankments. It is lamentable to see so fine a country in so wretched a state.

---

[a] 1858 edition, vol. i, p. 36, has 'that' for 'than'.

The Turae forest begins a few miles to the north of Bahraetch, and some of the Great Baronial Landholders have their residence and strong holds within it. The Rajah of Toolseepoor is one of them. He is a kind-hearted old man, and a good landlord and subject; but he has lately been driven out by his young and reprobate son, at the instigation and encouragement of a Court favorite. The Rajah had discharged an agent, employed by him at Court, for advocating the cause of his son, while in rebellion against his father. The agent then made common cause with the son, and secured the interest of two powerful men at Court, Balkrishen Dewan and Gholam Ruza, the deputy minister, who has charge of the estates in the Hozoor Tehsel. The jurisdiction over the estate had been transferred from the local authorities to the Hozoor Tehsel; and, by orders from Court, the father's friends – the Bulrampoor and other Rajahs of the clan – were prevented from continuing the aid they had afforded, to support the father's authority. The father unwilling to have the estate devastated by a contest with the band of ruffians, whom his son had collected, retired, and allowed him to take possession. The son seized upon all the property the father had left, and now employs it in maintaining this band, and rewarding the services of Court favorites. The Nazim of the district is not permitted to interfere, to restore rights or preserve order in the estate, nor would he, perhaps, do either, if so permitted, for he has been brought up in a bad school, and is not a good man. The pretext at Court is, that the father is deranged; but though not wise he is learned, and no man can be more sober than he is, or better disposed towards his sovereign and tenants. That he is capable of managing his estate, is shown by the excellent condition in which he left it...

[*December 10, 1849.* There is no entry for this date. There is a further entry dated *December 9, 1849*[a] but it is an account of happenings at the Court in Lucknow and has no information derived from the tour.]

[a] 1852: vol. I, pp. 38–42; 1858: vol. I, pp. 43–7.

CHAPTER II

[Gonda-Bahraetch 'district', 11–14 December 1849]

[1852: i, 42] [1858: i, 48–9]

Bahraetch is celebrated for the shrine of Syud Salar,[a] a *martyr*, who is supposed to have been killed here in the beginning of the eleventh century, when fighting against the Hindoos, under the auspices of Mahmood Shah, of Ghuznee,[b] his mother's brother. Strange to say, Hindoos as well as Mahommedans make offerings to this shrine, and implore the favors of this military ruffian, whose only recorded merit consists of having sent a great many Hindoos to hell, in a wanton and unprovoked invasion of their territory. They say, that he did what he did against Hindoos, in the conscientious discharge of his duties; and could not have done it without God's permission – that God must then have been angry with them for their transgressions, and used this man, and all the other Mahommedan invaders of their country, as instruments of His vengeance, and means to bring about His purposes. That is, the thinking portion of the Hindoos say this. The mass think, that the old man must still have a good deal of interest in Heaven, which he may be induced to exercise in their favor, by suitable offerings and personal applications to his shrine...

[1852: i, 43] [1858: i, 49]

December 11, 1849. – Left Bahraetch and came south east to Imaleea, on the road to Gonda, over a plain in the Pyagpoor estate, almost entirely waste – few groves or single trees to be

---

[a] Ghazi Miyan Salar Mas'ud, killed in battle in 1033 when he was about 19 years of age, and buried at Bahraich. Ghazi is an honorific title for a hero, a warrior, one who fights in the cause of Islam. *The Encyclopaedia of Religion and Ethics*, ed. J. Hastings, 13 vols (Edinburgh, 1920), vol. xi, p. 72, records that it is believed that he 'performed prodigies of valour in conflicts with the Hindus'. See also below, pp. 288–9.

[b] Mahmud of Ghazni (967–1030); from 998–1030 he descended more or less regularly to raid the rich plains of the Ganges.

seen – scarcely a field tilled or house occupied – all the work of the same atrocious governor, Rughbur Sing. No oppressor ever wrote a more legible hand. . . [Note that a long revenue history of the Bahraetch district is omitted at this point.]

[1852: I, 85–90] [1858: I, 96–102]

Almost all the khalsa lands of the Hissampoor purgunnah belonged to the different branches of a very ancient and respectable

Tallookdars of Bahraetch – Government Land Revenue according to the estimate of this year.

Names of Villages.	Govt. demand.	Present Condition.
Bandee	65,000	Almost waste.
Ruhooa	20,000	Ditto.
Nanpara	1,50,000	Falling off.
Gungwal	26,000	Much out of tillage.
Pyagpoor	59,000	Ditto.
Ekona	1,80,000	Ditto.
Bulrampoor	1,50,000	Well tilled.
Toolseepoor	1,05,000	Ditto.
Atrola	80,000	Much out of tillage.
Munkapoor	35,000	Ditto.
Bahmanee Paer	12,000	Ditto.
Gowras alias Chehdwara		
Paruspoor	14,000	Well tilled.
Aruta	18,000	Ditto.
Shahpoor	30,000	Ditto.
Dhunawa	42,000	Ditto.
Paska	20,000	Ditto.
Kumeear	48,000	Ditto.
Churda	62,000	Falling off.
Gonda Pergunnah.	*Govt. demand.*	*Present Condition.*
Desumberpoor	95,000	Rajah Davey Buksh, in good order.
Bhinga	64,000	Recovering.
Akkerpoor	46,015	In good order under Ramdut Pandee.
Sagha Chunda	1,20,729	Ramdut Pande, in good order.
Birwa	24,000	A little out of tillage.

Diary of a Tour Through Oude

family of Syuds. Their lands have, as already stated,[a] been almost all transferred to powerful Tallookdars, and absorbed by them in their estates, by the usual process. It is said – and I believe truly – that Hadee Allee Khan tried to induce the head of the Syud family, to take his daughter in marriage for his eldest son, as he was also a Syud (lineal descendant of the prophet). The old Syud was too proud to consent to this; and he and all his relations and connexion were ruined in consequence. The son – to whom Hadee Allee wished to unite his daughter – still lives on his lands, but in poverty and fear. The people say that family pride is more inveterate among the aristocracy of the country than that of the city; and had the old man lived at Lucknow, he would probably have given his son, and saved his family and estate.

Captain Hardwick, while out shooting on the 10th, saw a dead man hanging by the heels in a mango tree, close to the road. He was one of a gang of notorious robbers who had attacked a neighbouring village belonging to some Brahmins. They killed two, and caught a third member of the gang, and hung him up by the heels to die. He was the brother-in-law of the leader of the gang, Nunda Pandee. There he still hangs, and the greater part of my camp took a look at him in passing.

December 12, 1849. – Gungwal, thirteen miles. The road lay through the estate of Pyagpoor to within a mile of Gungwal. Little cultivation was to be seen the whole way; and what we could see was bad. Little variety of crops, and the tillage slovenly, and without manure or irrigation. The Tallookdar was ruined by Rughbur Sing, and is not on terms with the present Nazim, and he did not appear. The estate of Gungwal is not better cultivated than that of Pyagpoor; nor better peopled – both may be considered as mere wastes, and their assessments as merely nominal. The Tallookdar did not appear. Both were ruined by the rapacious Nazim and his atrocious agents, Goureeshunker, Beharee Lal, Kurum Hoseyn and others.

The Rajah of Toolseepoor, Dirgraj Sing, has an only son, Sahibjee, now 17 years of age. The Rajah's old servants, thinking

[a] See above p. 63.

71

they could make more out of the boy than out of the prudent father, first incited him to go off, with all the property he could collect, to Goruckpoor, where he spent it in ten months of revelry. The father invited him back two months ago, on condition, that he should come alone. When he got within six miles of Toolseepoor, however, the father found, that three thousand armed followers had there been assembled by his agents to aid him in seizing upon him and the estate. Fearing that his estate might be desolated, and he himself confined, and, perhaps put to death, the Rajah ran off to his friend, the Rajah of Bulrampore, for protection.

December 13, 1849. – Purenda, eleven miles. The first half of the way, through the lands of Gungwal, showed few signs of tillage or population – the latter half through those of Purenda and other villages of Gonda, held by Ramdut Pandee, showed more of both. Some nice villages, on each side, at a small distance, and some nice groves of mango trees. On the road this morning, Omrow Pooree, a non-commissioned officer of the Gwalior Contingent,[a] whose family resided in a neighbouring village, came up to me as I passed along, and prayed me to have the murderer of his father seized and punished. He described the circumstances of the case, and on reaching camp, I requested Captain Weston to take the depositions of the witnesses, and adopt measures for the arrest of the offenders. Syampooree[b] was the name of the father of the complainant. He resided in a small hamlet, near the road, called after himself, as the founder, 'Syampooree ka Poorwa', or Syampooree's Hamlet. He had four sons, all fine, stout men. The eldest, Omrow Pooree, a corporal in the Gwalior Contingent, Bhurut Pooree, a private in

[a] One of the special forces, dating from the time of Wellesley (Governor-General, 1798–1805), which were maintained in the principal Indian States at the expense of the ruler to 'enable' them to co-operate effectively with the British when required and to maintain order in their own territories. See T. H. Thornton, *General Sir Richard Meade and the Feudatory States of Central and Southern India* (London, 1898), p. 10. Gwalior was ruled by Sindhia, the most important of the remaining Maratha rulers.

[b] Lt. Weston notes at the foot of vol. I, p. 99 in his own copy of *A Journey through the Kingdom of Oude* [*JTKO*] that 'The story of Syampoorie [*sic*] was abstracted from my report to the Resident'. See above, p. 53, n. 6 for details of Weston's copy of *JTKO*.

1   Palanquin, by an unknown artist, *circa* 1817–32

2   Cultivators irrigating their fields, Lucknow artist, *circa* 1830

3 Durbar scene, Wajid Ali Shah greets Lord Hardinge, by an unknown
artist, *circa* 1847

Captain Barlow's Regiment, Ramchurun and Ramadeen, the two youngest, still at home, assisting their father in the management of their little estate, which the family had held for many generations. One day in the beginning of December 1848, a short, thick-set man passed through the hamlet, accosted Syampooree and his two sons, as they sat at the door, and asked for some tobacco, and entered into conversation with them. He pretended that his cart had been seized by the Nazim's soldiers; and, after chatting with them for a short time, departed.

The second morning after this, before day light, Ramadeen, the youngest son, was warming himself at a fire on a small terrace in front of the door, when he saw a party of armed men approaching. He called out and asked who they were and what they wanted. They told him, that they were government servants, had traced a thief to the village, and come to seize him. Four of the party, who carried torches, now approached the fire and lighted them. Syampooree and his other son, Ramchurun, hearing the noise came out, and placed themselves by the side of Ramadeen. By the light of the torches they now recognised the short, thick-set man, with whom they had been talking two days before, at the head of a gang of fifteen men, carrying fire arms with matches lighted, and five more armed with swords and shields. The short thick-set man was Nunda Pandee, the most notorious robber in the district. He ordered his gang to search the house – on the father and sons remonstrating, he drew his sword and cut down Ramchurun. The father and Ramadeen having left their swords in the house rushed back to secure them; but Nunda Pandee, calling out to one of his followers, Bhowanee-deen, to despatch the son, overtook the father, and at one cut severed his right arm from his body. He inflicted several other cuts upon him before the old man could secure his sword with his left arm. Having got it he placed the scabbard under his foot, drew forth the blade, and cut Nunda Pandee across his sword arm which placed him hors de combat; and rushing out among the assailants he cut down two more, when he was shot dead by a third and noted robber, Goberae. Bhowaneedeen and others of the gang had cut down Ramadeen, and inflicted several wounds upon him as he lay on the ground. The gang then plundered the

73

house, and made off with property to the value of one thousand and fifty rupees, leaving the father and both sons on the ground. The brave old father died soon after day break; but before he expired he named his assailants.

The two youngest sons were too severely wounded to admit of their pursuing the murderers of their father, but their brother, Bhurut Pooree, got leave of absence, returned home; and traced the leader of the gang, Nunda Pandee, to the house of one of his relatives in the village of Kurroura, in Pyagpoor, where he had had his wound sewn up and dressed, and lay concealed. The family then tried, in vain, to get redress from all the local authorities, none of whom considered it to be their duty to look after murderers and robbers of this kind. On the road from Bahraetch to Gungwal we saw very few groves or fine single trees on either side. The water is close to the surface, and the soil good, but for the most part flooded during the rains, and fit only for rice cultivation. To fit it for the culture of other autumn crops would require a great outlay in drainage; and this no one will incur without better security for the returns than the present government can afford. Ramdut Pandee is the greatest agricultural capitalist in these parts...

[1852: I, 96–9] [1858: I, 108–12]

December 14, 1849. – Came on twelve miles to Gonda. The country well studded with groves and fine single trees – the soil naturally fertile, and water near the surface. Cultivation good about Gonda, and about some of the villages along the road it is not bad; but there is no where any sugar cane to be seen beyond a small garden patch. The country is so wretchedly stocked with cattle, that little manure is available for tillage.

The Bulrampore Rajah, a lively, sensible and active young man, joined me this morning, and rode along by the side of my elephant, with the capitalist, Ramdut Pandee, the Nazim, Mahommed Hussan, and old Bukhtawar Sing, the brother of the late Dursun Sing, whom I have often mentioned in this Diary. Rajah Bukhtawar Sing is the king's Mohtamin, or Quarter Master General of the Resident's camp. The Rajah of Toolseepore also, who has been ousted by his son from his estate, joined me last night; but he was not well enough to ride with me. Dogs, hawks and panthers attend for sport,[a] but they afford little or no amusement. Hawking is a very dull and very cruel sport. A person must become insensible to the sufferings of the most beautiful and most inoffensive of the brute creation, before he can feel any enjoyment in it. The cruelty lies chiefly in the mode of feeding the hawks. I have ordered all these hunting animals to return to Lucknow.

Although the personal character of the Toolseepoor Rajah is not respected, that of his son is much worse; and the Bulrampoor Rajah and other large landholders in the neighbourhood, would unite and restore him to the possession of his estate; but the Nazim is held responsible for their not moving in the matter, in order that the influential persons about the Court may have the plucking of it at their leisure. The better to insure this, two companies of one of the king's Regiments have been lately sent out with two guns, to see that the son is not molested in the possession. The Toolseepoor estate extends along from east to west for about one hundred miles, in a belt of from nine to twelve miles wide, upon the southern border of that part of the Oude Tarae forest, which we took from Nepaul in 1815, and made over to the Oude government by the treaty of the 11th May 1816, in lieu of the one crore of rupees which our Government borrowed from Oude for the conduct of that war.[b] The rent roll of Toolseepoor is now from two to three lacks of rupees a year; but it pays to the Oude government a revenue of only one lack and five thousand, over and above gratuities to influential officers. The estate comprises that of Bankee, which was held by a Rajah Kunsa. Dan Bahader, the father of the present Rajah of Toolseepoor, attacked him one night in 1832, put him and some two hundred and fifty of his followers and family to death, and absorbed the estate. Mahngoo, the brother of Kunsa, escaped

[a] Cf. Abul Fazl Allami, *The Ain-i-Akbari* trans. by H. Blochmann, vol. I (Calcutta, 1873), pp. 282–96 for background on Mughal hunting and hawking. Also S. M. Edwardes and H. L. O. Garrett, *Mughal Rule in India* (Oxford, 1930), pp. 282–4 for general discussion. See *R and R*, pp. 115n. and 236–7 for some further details of panthers (*Felis jubata*) kept for hunting. Knighton, *The Private Life of an Eastern King*, ch. 3; 'The hunting party'.

[b] Aitchison, *Treaties*, vol. II, pp. 130–2; the treaty is dated 1st May 1816 but was ratified on 11 May 1816.

and sought redress from the Oude Durbar, but he had no money and could get no redress; and, in despair, he went off to seek employment in Nepaul, and died soon after. Dan Bahader, enriched by the pillage of Bankee, came to Lucknow, and purchased permission to incorporate Bankee with his old estate of Toolseepoor.

Khyreeghur and Kunchunpoor, on the western border of that forest, were made over by us to Oude at the same time, as part of the cession. They had been ceded to our Government, by the treaty of 1801,[a] at an estimated value of two hundred and ten thousand; but up to 1816, they had never yielded to us fifty thousand rupees a year. They had, however, formerly yielded from two to three lakhs of rupees a year to the Oude government; and, under good management, may do so again; but, at present, Oude draws from them a revenue of only sixteen thousand, and that with difficulty. The rent roll, however, exceeds two hundred thousand; and may, in a few years, amount to double that sum, as population and tillage are rapidly extending.

The holders of Khyreegur and Kunchunpoor are always in a state of resistance against the Oude government, and cannot be coerced into the payment of more than their sixteen thousand rupees a year; and hundreds of lives have been sacrificed in the collection of this sum. The climate is so bad, that no people from the open country can venture into it for more than four months in the year – from the beginning of December to the end of March. The Oude government occasionally sends in a body of troops to enforce the payment of an increased demand during these four months. The landholders and cultivators retire before them, and they are sure to be driven out by the pestilence, with great loss of life, in a few months; and the landholders refuse to pay anything for some years after, on the ground, that all their harvests were destroyed by the troops. The rest of the Tarae lands ceded had little of tillage or population at that time, and no government could be less calculated than that of Oude, to make the most of its capabilities. It had, therefore, in a fiscal

[a] Treaty between Saadat Ali Khan and the East India Company, ceding territories in commutation of subsidy payable; Aitchison, *Treaties*, vol. II, pp. 100–3.

point of view, but a poor equivalent for its crore of rupees; but it gained a great political advantage, in confining the Nepaulese to the hills on its border. Before this arrangement took place there used to be frequent disputes, and occasionally serious collisions between the local authorities about boundaries, which were apt to excite the angry feelings of the sovereigns of both States, and to render the interposition of the paramount power indispensible...

CHAPTER III

[Sultanpur 'district', 15–21 December 1849]

[1852: I, 109] [1858: I, 123–4]

December 15, 1849. – Wuzeergunge. On the way this morning, we passed Koorassa, which is said once to have been the capital of a formidable Rajah, the head of the Kulhuns tribe of Rajpoots. The villages which we see along the road seem better and better peopled and provided with cattle. The soil not naturally very fertile, but yields fine returns under good culture, manure and irrigation. Water every where very near the surface. The place is called after the then *Nawab Wuzeer,* Asuf-od Dowlah,[a] who built a country seat here with all appurtenances of mosque, courts, dwelling houses, &c. &c., on the verge of a fine lake, formed in the old bed of the Ghagra river, with tillage and verdure extending down to the water's edge. The garden wall, which surrounds a large space of ground, well provided with fruit and ornamental trees, is built of burnt bricks, and still entire. The late minister, Amen-od Dowlah, persuaded his master, Amjad Allee Shah,[b] to give this garden and the lands around, with which it had been endowed, to his moonshee, Baker Allee Khan, who now resides at Fyzabad, and subsists upon the rents which he derives from them, and which are said to be about twelve hundred rupees a year.

The Bulrampoor Rajah, Ramdut Pandee, the banker, and Rajah Bukhtawar Sing, rode with me this morning. The Rajah of Bulrampoor is an intelligent and pleasing young man...

[1852: I, 111–24] [1858: I, 125–41]

The Rajahs of Toolseepoor and Bulrampoor, and all the merchants and respectable landholders in these parts assure me,

---

[a] Asaf-ud-Daula, reigned 1775–97.
[b] Amjad Ali Shah, reigned 1842–47.

78

that all the large colonies of Bhuduks,[a] or gang robbers by hereditary profession, who had, for so many generations, up to A.D. 1840, been located in the Oude Tarae forest, have entirely disappeared under the operation of the 'Special Police' of the Thuggee and Dacoitee Department,[b] aided and supported by the Oude government; and that not one family of them can now be found any where in Oude. They have not been driven out as formerly, to return as soon as the temporary pressure ceased, but hunted down and punished or made to blend with the rest of society in service or at honest labour.

December 16, 1849. – Nawabgunge, eight miles, over a plain of the same good soil, but not much better cultivated. The people tell me, that garden tillage is now almost unknown in these districts; first, because kachies or gardeners (here called moraes) having been robbed, ruined, and driven into exile by Rughbur Sing, cannot be induced to return to and reside in places, where they would have so little chance of reaping the fruits of their labour; and, secondly, because there are no people left, who can afford to purchase their garden produce. They tell me also, that the best classes of ordinary cultivators, the Koormies and Lodhees, have been almost all driven out of the district from the same cause. The facts are manifest – there are no gardeners, and but few Koormies and Lodhees left; and, there is, in consequence, little good tillage of any kind, and still less of garden cultivation.

The Rajah of Bulrampoor and Ramdut Pandee, the banker, rode with me, and related the popular tradition regarding the

[a] Literally, 'murderers'; they were robbers of a particular 'tribe' who associated with thugs and, like the thugs, murdered those whom they robbed. They resided chiefly on the borders of Oudh but they carried out their operations at a distance. See glossary, below. Also W. H. Sleeman, *Report on Budhuk alias Bagree Decoits [sic] and other Gang Robbers by Hereditary Profession and on the Measures adopted by the Government of India for their Suppression* (Calcutta, 1849).

[b] The forerunner of the Criminal Intelligence Department, the Department was organised in 1835 under Sleeman and was not wound up until 1905. In 1835 Sleeman's appointment was to be 'Superintendent of the operations for the Suppression of Thuggee'; it was not until 1839 that Dacoity operations were added to this. See *CHI*, vol. VI, pp. 33, 373; Kaye, *The Administration of the East India Company*, part III, ch. 2; and B. Hjejle, 'The Social Policy of the East India Company with regard to Sati, Thagi, Dakaiti and Infanticide' (unpublished D.Phil. thesis, University of Oxford, 1958), ch. 15.

head of the Kulhuns family of Rajpoots, Achul Sing, who, about a century and a quarter ago, reigned over the district, intervening between Gonda and Wuzeer Gunge, and resided at his capital of Koorassa. The Rajah had a dispute with one of his landholders, whom he could not get into his power. He requested Rutun Pandee, the banker, to mediate a reconciliation, and invite the landholder to an amicable adjustment of accounts, on a pledge of personal security. The banker consented, but made the Rajah swear by the *River Sarjoo*, which flowed near the town, that he should be received with courtesy, and escorted back safely. The landholder relied on the banker's pledge and came; but the Rajah no sooner got him into his power, than he caused him to be put to death. The banker could not consent to live under the dishonor of a violated pledge; and, abstaining from food, died in twenty-one days, invoking the vengeance of the *River Sarjoo*, on the head of the perfidious Prince. In his last hours the banker was visited by one of the Rajah's wives, who was then pregnant and implored him to desist from his purpose in mercy to the child in her womb; but she was told by the dying man, that he could not consent to survive the dishonor brought upon him by her perjured husband; and that she had better quit the place and save herself and child, since the incensed river Sarjoo would certainly not spare any one who remained with the Rajah. She did so. The banker died, and his death was followed by a sudden rise of the river and tempest. The town was submerged, and the Rajah with all who remained with him perished. The ruins of the old town are said to be occasionally still visible, though at a great depth under the water in the old bed of the Sarjoo which forms a fine lake, near the present village of Koorassa, midway between Gonda and Wuzeer Gunge.

The pregnant wife fled, and gave birth to a son, whose descendant is now the head of the Kulhuns Rajpoots, and the Rajah of Bahmanee Paer, a district on the eastern border of Oude towards Goruckpoor. But, it is a remarkable fact, that the male descendants have been all blind from their birth, or, at least, the reigning portion of them, and the present Rajah is said to have two blind sons. This is popularly considered to be one of the effects of the Rajah's violated pledge to the banker. A handmaid of the Rajah, Achul Sing, is said to have fled at the same time, and given birth to a son, from whom are descended the Kulhuns Tallookdars of the Chehdwara, or Gowaris district, already noticed. The descendants of Rutun Pandee are said still to hold rent free lands, under Achul Sing's descendant, in Bahmanee Paer; and the Pandee is worshipped throughout the districts as a saint or martyr. He has a shrine in every village, at which offerings are made on all occasions of marriage, and blessings invoked for the bride and bridegroom, from the spirit of one who set so much value on his plighted faith while on earth. The two branches of the Kulhuns family, above mentioned, propitiate the spirit of the deceased Pandee by offerings; but there is a branch of the same family at Mohlee, in the Goruckpoor district, who do not. Though Hindoos, they adopt some musulman customs, and make offerings to the old musulman saint, at Bahraetch, in order to counteract the influence of the Pandee's spirit.

Such popular traditions, arising from singular coincidences of circumstances, have often a salutary effect on society, and seem to be created by its wants and wishes; but rivers have, of late years, become so much less prompt in the vindication of their honor, that little reliance is placed upon the oaths taken in their names by the Prince, his officers or his landholders in Oude.

Nawabgunge, Munkapoor and Bahmanee Paer, were transferred to the British Government, with the other lands, under the treaty of 1801; and retransferred to Oude, by the treaty of the 11th of May 1816, in exchange for Handeea, alias Kewae, a slip of land extending along the left bank of the Ganges, between Allahabad and Benares.

	Rent Roll.	Nankur.	Govt. demand.
Nawabgunge, Wuzeergunge, Mahadewa	1,08,000	32,000	76,000
Munkapoor	40,000	12,000	28,000
Bahmanee Paer	12,000	3,000	9,000

The landholders and cultivators complain sadly of the change of sovereigns; and the tillage and population have greatly diminished under the Oude government since 1816, but more especially, since the monster, Rughbur Sing, got the government. Here Ramdut Pandee, the Rajah of Bulrampoor, and the Nazim of the district, have taken leave of me, this being my last stage in their district. Ramdut Pandee holds two estates in this district, for which he pays an annual revenue to government of 1,66,744 13 3, as below.

The estate of Ramdut Pandee, for this year, 1849, comprises—

Sirgha, Chunda, &c.	1,20,729	11	0
Akberpoor, &c.	46,015	2	3
Total	1,66,744	13	3

He holds, at the same time, a small estate in our district of Goruckpoor, where he resides and keeps his family, till he obtains solemn written pledges, confirmed on oath, for their security, not only from the local authority of the day, but from all the commandants of corps and establishments, comprising the military force employed under him. These pledges include all his clients, who may have occasion to visit or travel with him, as the Rajah of Bulrampoor is now doing. These pledges require to be renewed on every change in the local authorities and in the military officers employed under them. He is one of the most substantial and respectable of the agricultural capitalists of Oude, and the highest of his rank and class in this district. He every year stands security for the punctual payment of the revenues due, according to existing engagements, by the principal landholders of the district, to the extent of from six to eight lakhs of rupees; and for this he gets a certain percentage, varying with the character and capability of the landholders. Some are of doubtful ability, others of doubtful character, and he rates his risks and per centage accordingly. He does much good, and is more generally esteemed than any other man in the district; but he has, no doubt, enlarged his own landed possessions occasionally, by taking advantage of the necessities of his clients, and his influence over the local authorities of government. The lands he does get, however, he improves by protecting and aiding his tenants, and inviting and fostering a better class of cultivators. He is looked up to with respect and confidence by almost all the large landholders of the district, for his pledge for the punctual payment of the revenues, saves their estates from the terrible effects of a visit from the Nazim and his disorderly and licentious troops; and this pledge they can always obtain, when necessary, by a fair assurance of adherence to their engagements.

December 17, 1849. – Five miles to the left bank of the Ghagra, whence we crossed over to Fyzabad, on platformed boats, prepared for the purpose by the Oude authorities. Our tents are in one of the large mango groves, which are numerous on the right bank of the river, but scanty on the opposite bank. From the time we crossed this river at Byram ghaut on the 5th, till we recrossed it this morning, we were moving in the jurisdiction of the Nazim of the Gonda and Bahraetch district. After recrossing the Ghagra, we came within that of the Nazim of Sultanpoor, Aga Allee, who was appointed to it this year, not as a contractor, but manager, under the Durbar. The districts, under contractors, are called *ijara*, or farmed districts; those under the management of non-contracting servants of government, are called *amanee*, or districts under the *amanut*, or trust of government officers. The morning was fine, the sky clear, and the ground covered with hoar frost. It was pleasing to see so large a camp, passing without noise, inconvenience or disorder of any kind in so large a river.

The platformed boats were numerous, and so were the peer-heads prepared on both sides, for the convenience of embarking and landing. Carriages, horses, palankeens, camels and troops, all passed without the slightest difficulty. The elephants were preparing to cross, some in boats and some by swimming, as might seem to them best. Some refuse to swim and others to enter boats, and some refuse to do either; but the fault is generally with their drivers. On the present occasion, two or three remained behind, one plunged into the stream from his boat, in the middle of the river with his driver on his back, and both disappeared for a time, but neither was hurt. Those that remained on the left bank, got tired of their solitude, and were, at last, *coaxed* over, either in boats or in the water.

The Sarjoo rejoins the Ghagra a little above Fyzabad, and the united stream takes the old name of the Sarjoo. This is the name the river bears, till it emerges from the Tarae forest, when the large body takes that of the Ghagra, and the small stream, which it throws off, or which perhaps flows in the old bed, retains that of the Sarjoo. The large branch absorbs the Kooreeala, Chouka and other small streams, on its way to rejoin the smaller. Some distance below Fyzabad, the river takes the name of *Dewa*; and uniting, afterwards, with the Gunduck, flows into the Ganges. Fyzabad is three miles above Ajoodheea, on the same bank of the river. It was founded by the first rulers of the reigning family, and called for sometime *Bungalow*, from a bungalow which they built on the verge of the stream. Asuf-od Dowlah disliked living near his mother, after he came to the throne, and he settled at Lucknow, then a small village on the right bank of the Goomtee river. This village, in the course of eighty years, grown into a city, containing nearly a million of souls. Fyzabad has declined almost in the same proportion.

The Nazim has six Regiments, and part of a seventh, on duty under him, making, nominally, six thousand fighting men, but that he cannot, he tells me, muster two thousand; and out of the two thousand, not five hundred would, he says, be ready to fight on emergency. All the commandants of corps reside at Court, knowing nothing, whatever, of their duties, and never seeing their Regiments. They are mere children, or Court favourites, worse than children. He has, nominally, forty-two guns, of various calibre; but he, with great difficulty, collected bullocks enough to draw the three small guns he brought with him from Sultanpoor, to salute the Resident, on his entering his district. I looked at them in the evening. They were seventy-four in number, but none of them were in a serviceable condition, and the greater part were small, merely skin and bone. He was obliged to purchase powder in the bazar for the salutes; and said, that when he entered his charge two months ago, the usual salute of seven guns, for himself, could not be fired for want of powder, and he was obliged to send to the bazar to purchase what was required. The bazar powder used by the Oude troops, is about one third of the strength of the powder used by our troops. His authority is despised by all the Tallookdars of the district, many of whom refuse to pay any rent, defy the government, and plunder the country, as all their rents are insufficient to pay the armed bands, which they keep up. All his numerous applications to Court, for more and better troops and establishments, are disregarded, and he is helpless. He cannot collect the revenue or coerce the refractory landholders and robbers, who prey upon the country.

He says that the two companies and two guns, which were sent out at the Resident's urgent recommendation, to take possession of Shahgunge, and prevent the two brothers, Maun Sing and Rughbur Sing, from disturbing the peace of the country, in their contests with each other, joined Maun Sing, as partisan to oppose his brother; and that Maun Sing has taken for himself all the *bynamah* lands, from which his brother, Rughbur Sing, has been ousted, under the favor of the minister. He tells me also, that Beebee Sogura, the lady who holds the estate of Muneearpoor, and pays fifty thousand rupees a year to the government, was seized by Wajid Allee, his predecessor, before he made over charge of the district to him, and made over to a body of troops, on condition, that she should enter into engagement to pay to them the ten months arrears of pay due to them, out of the rents of the ensuing year; and that they should give him receipts for the full amount of these arrears of pay at once, to be forwarded to the Durbar, that he might get credit for the amount in his accounts for last year – that she has paid them fifteen thousand rupees, but can collect no more from her tenants, as the crops are all being cut or destroyed by the troops, and she is in close confinement, and treated with cruel indignity. The rent roll of her estate is, it is said, equal to one hundred thousand rupees a year.

This was a common practice among governors of districts at the close of last year; and thus they got credit, in account, for large sums, pretended to have been paid out of the revenues of last year; but, in reality, to be paid out of the revenues of the ensuing year. But the collections are left to be made by the troops, for whose arrears of pay the revenue has been assigned, and they generally destroy or extort double what they are entitled to, from their unhappy debtors. This practice of assigning revenues due, or to be due, by landholders, for the arrears of pay, due to the troops, is the source of much evil; and is had recourse to only when contractors and other collectors of revenue are unable to enforce payment in any other way; or require to make it appear, that they have collected more than they really have; and to saddle the revenue of the ensuing year with the burthens properly incident upon those of the past. The commandant of the troops commonly takes possession of the lands, upon the rents, or revenues, of which the payments have been assigned, and appropriates the whole produce to himself and his soldiers, without regard to the rights of landholders, farmers, cultivators, capitalists, or any other class of persons, who may have invested their capital and labor in the lands, or depend upon the crops for their subsistence. The troops, too, are rendered unfit for service by such arrangements, since all their time is taken up in the more congenial duty of looking after the estate, till they have desolated it. The officers and soldiers are converted into manorial under-stewards of the worst possible description. They are available for no other duty till they have paid themselves all that may have been due or may become due to them during the time of their stay; and credit to government but a small portion of what they exact from the landholders and cultivators, or consume or destroy as food, fodder and fuel.

This system, injurious alike to the sovereign, the troops, and the people, is becoming, every season, more and more common in Oude; and must, in a few years, embrace nearly the whole of the land revenue of the country. It is denominated *kubz*, or contract, and is of two kinds, the '*lakulame kubz*', or pledge to collect and pay a certain sum, for which the estate is held to be liable; and '*wusolee kubz*', or pledge to pay to the collector or troops, the precise sum which the commandant may be able to collect from the estate put under him. In the first, the commandant, who takes the *kubz*, must pay to the government collector or the troops the full sum, for which the estate is held to be liable, whether he be able to collect it or not, and his *kubz* is valid at the Treasury, as so much money paid to the troops. In the second, it is valid only as a pledge, to collect as much as he can; and to pay, what he collects, to the government collector, or the troops he commands. The collector, however, commonly understands, that he has shifted off the burthen of payment to the troops – to the extent of the sum named – from his own shoulders to those of the commandant of the troops; and the troops understand, that unless they collect this sum they will never get it, or be obliged to screw it out of their commandant; and they go to the work *con amore*. If they can't collect it from the sale of all the crops of the season, they seize and sell all the stock and property of all kinds, to be found on the estate; and, if this will not suffice, they will not scruple to seize and sell the women and children. The collector, whose tenure of office seldom extends beyond the season, cares little as to the mode, as long as he gets the money; and feels quite sure, that the sovereign and his Court will care just as little, and ask no questions, should the troops sell every living thing to be found on the estate. . .

[*December 18, 1849*. No entry under this date.]

[1852: I, 131–2] [1858: I, 149–50]

December 19, 1849. – Shahgunge, distance twelve miles. This town is surrounded by a mud wall, forty feet thick, and a ditch three miles round, built thirty years ago, and now much out of repair. It belongs to the family of Rajah Bukhtawar Sing. The wall, thirty feet high, was built of the mud taken from the ditch, in which there is now some six or seven feet of water. The wall has twenty-four bastions for guns, but there is no platform, or road for guns, round it on the inside. A number of respectable merchants and tradesmen reside in this town, where they are better protected than in any other town in Oude. It contains a population of between twenty and thirty thousand persons. They put thatch over the mud walls during the rains to preserve them. The fortifications and dwelling houses together are said to have cost the family above ten lakhs of rupees. There are some fourteen old guns in the fort. Though it would be difficult to shell a garrison out of a fort of this extent, it would not be difficult to take it. No garrison, sufficient to defend all parts of so extended a wall, could be maintained by the holder; and it would be easy to fill the ditch and scale the walls. Besides, the family is so very unpopular among the military classes around, whose lands they have seized upon, that thousands would come to the aid of any government force brought to crush them, and overwhelm the garrison. They keep their position only by the purchase of Court favor, and have the respect and attachment of only the better sort of cultivators, who are not of the military classes, and could be of little use to them in a collision with their sovereign. The family, by which it is held, has long been a very influential one at Court, where it has been represented by Bukhtawar Sing, whose brother, Dursun Sing, was the most powerful subject that Oude has had since the time of Almas Allee Khan. They live, however, in the midst of hundreds of sturdy Rajpoots, whom they have deprived of their lands, and who would, as I have said, rise against them, were they to be, at any time, opposed to the government. The country, over which we have passed this morning, is well studded with groves, and well cultivated; and the peasantry seemed contented and prosperous. The greater part of the road lay through the lands acquired, as already described, by this family. Though they have acquired the property in the land by abuse of authority, collusion and violence, from its righful owners, they keep their faith with the cultivators, effectively protect them from thieves, robbers, the violence of their neighbours, and, above all, from the ravages of the king's troops; and they encourage the settlement of the better or more skilful and industrious classes of cultivators in their villages, such as Kachies, Koormies, and Lodhies. They came out from numerous villages, and in considerable bodies to salute me, and expressed themselves well satisfied with their condition, and the security they enjoyed under their present landholders. We came through the village of Puleea, and Rajah Bukhtawar Sing seemed to have great pleasure in showing me the house in which he was born, seventy-five years ago, under a fine tamarind tree, that is still in vigour...

[1852: i, 144–55] [1858: i, 162–74]

December 20, 1849. – Saleepoor, ten miles. The country, on both sides of the road, well studded with trees, hamlets and villages, and well cultivated and peopled. The landholders and peasantry seem all happy and secure, under their present masters, the brother and son of the late Dursun Sing. They are, by them, protected from thieves and robbers, the attacks of refractory barons, and, above all, from the ravages of the king's troops; and the whole face of the country, at this season, is like that of a rich garden. The whole is under cultivation, and covered with the greatest possible variety of crops. The people showed us, as we passed, six kinds of sugar cane, and told us, that they had many more, one soil agreeing best with one kind, and another with another. The main fault in the cultivation of sugar cane is here, as in every other part of India, that I have seen, the want of room, and the disregard of cleanliness. They crowd the cane too much, and never remove the decayed leaves, and sufficient air is never admitted.

Bucktawar Sing has always been considered as the head of the family, to whom Shahgunge belongs, but he has always remained at Court, and left the local management of the estate and the government of the districts, placed under their charge, in contract or in trust, to his brothers and nephews. Bukhtawar Sing has no child of his own, but he has adopted Maun Sing, the youngest son of his brother, Dursun Sing, and he leaves all local duties and responsibilities to him. He is a small, slight man, but shrewd, active, and energetic, and as unscrupulous as a man can be. Indeed old Bucktawar Sing himself is the only member of the family that was ever troubled with scruples of any kind whatever; for he is the only one whose boyhood was not passed in the society of men, in the every day habit of committing, with impunity, all kinds of cruelties, atrocities, and outrages. There is, perhaps, no school in the world better adapted for training thorough-bred ruffians – men without any scruple of conscience, sense of honor, or feeling of humanity – than the camp of a revenue contractor in Oude – it has been the same for the last thirty years that I have known it, and must continue to be the same as long as we maintain, in absolute sway over the people, a sovereign who never bestows a thought upon them, has no feeling in common with them, and can never be persuaded, that his high office imposes upon him the obligation, to labour to promote their good, or even to protect them against the outrage and oppression of his own soldiers and civil officers. All Rajah Bukhtawar Sing's brothers and nephews were bred up in such camps, and are thorough-bred ruffians.

They have got the lands which they hold by much fraud and violence, no doubt, but they have done much good to them. They have invited and established, in comfort, great numbers of the best classes of cultivators from other districts, in which they had ceased to feel secure; and they have protected and encouraged those whom they found on the land. To establish a new cultivator of the better class, they require to give him about twenty five rupees for a pair of bullocks; for subsistence for himself and family till his crops ripen, thirty-six more; for a house, wells, &c. &c., thirty more, or about ninety rupees, which he pays back with or without interest, by degrees. Every village and hamlet is now surrounded by fine garden cultivation, conducted by the cultivators of the gardener cast, whom the family has thus established.

The greatest benefit conferred upon the lands, which they hold, has been in the suppression of the fearful contests, which used to be perpetual between the small proprietors of the military classes, among whom the lands had become minutely subdivided by the law of inheritance, about boundaries and rights to water for irrigation. Many persons used to be killed every year in these contests; and their widows and orphans had to be maintained by the survivors. Now no such dispute leads to any serious conflict. They are all settled at once by arbitrators, who are guided, in their decisions, by the accounts of the Putwaries of villages, and Canoongoes of districts. These men have the detailed accounts of every tenement for the last hundred years; and, with their assistance, village traditions, and the advice of their elders, all such boundary disputes and misunderstandings about rights to water, are quickly and amicably adjusted; and the landlords are strong, and able to enforce whatever decision is pronounced. They are wealthy and pay the government demand punctually; and have influence at Court, to prevent any attempt at oppression on the part of government officers on themselves or their tenants. Not a thief or a robber can live or depredate among their tenants. The hamlets are, in consequence, numerous and peopled by peasantry, who seem to live without fear. They adhere strictly to the terms of their engagements with their tenants of all grades; and their tenants all pay their rents punctually, unless calamities of season deprive them of the means, when due consideration is made by landlords, who live among them, and know what they suffer and require.

The climate must be good, for the people are strong and well made, and without any appearance of disease. Hardly a beggar of any kind is to be seen along the road. The residence of religious mendicants seems to be especially discouraged, and we see no others. It is very pleasing to pass over such lands after going through such districts as Bahraetch and Gonda, where the signs of the effects of bad air and water upon men, women and children, are so sad and numerous; and those of the abuse of power and the neglect of duty on the part of the government and its officers, are still more so.

Last evening, I sent for the two men, above named, who had been confined for six or seven years, and were said to have been so, because they would not sign the *bynamahs* required from them by Maun Sing. Their names are Soorujbulee Sing and Rugonath Sing. They came with the king's wakeel, accompanied by their cousin, Hunooman Sing, on whose charge they were declared to have been confined. I found that the village of Tendooa had been held by their family, in proprietary right, for many generations; and that they were Chouhan Rajpoots by cast. When Dursun Sing was securing to himself the lands of the district, those of Tendooa were held in three equal shares by

1. Soorujbulee and his brothers, Narind and Rugonath.
2. Hunooman Sing, their cousin.
3. Seoruttun, their cousin.

Maun Sing took advantage of a desperate quarrel between them, and secured Soorujbulee and Rugonath. Narind escaped and joined a refractory Tallookdar, and Seoruttun and Hunooman did the same. Hunooman Sing was, however, invited back, and entrusted, by Maun Sing, with the management of the whole estate, on favorable terms. In revenge for his giving in to the terms of Maun Sing, and serving him, the absconded co-sharers attacked his house several times, killed three of his brothers, and many other persons of his family, and robbed him of almost all he had. This was four years ago. He complained, and the two brothers were kept more strictly confined than ever, to save him and the village. Hunooman Sing looked upon the two prisoners as the murderers of his brothers, though they were in confinement when they were killed, and had been so for more than two years, and was very violent against them in my presence. They were no less violent against him, as the cause of their continued confinement. They protested to me, that they had no communication, whatever, with Seoruttun or Narind Sing, but thought it very likely, that they really did lead the gangs in the attacks upon the village, to recover their rights. They offered to give security for their future good behaviour if released; but declared, that they would rather die than consent to sign a *bynamah*, or deed of sale, or any relinquishment, whatever, of their hereditary rights, as landholders.

Bukhtawar and Maun Sing said,

that the people of the village would not be safe, for a moment, if these two brothers were released, which they would be, on the first occasion of thanksgiving, if sent to Lucknow, – that people who ventured to seize a thief or robber in Oude, must keep him, if they wished to save themselves from his future depredations, as the government authorities would have nothing to do with them.

I ordered the king's wakeel to take these two brothers to the Chuckladar, and request him to see them released on their furnishing sufficient security for their future good behavior, which they promised to produce. They were all fine looking men, with limbs that would do honor to any climate in the world. These are the families from which our Native Regiments are recruited; and hardly a young recruit offers himself for enlistment, on whose body marks will not be found of wounds received in these contests, between landlords themselves, and between them and the officers and troops of the sovereign. I have never seen enmity more strong and deadly than that exhibited by contending co-sharers and landholders of all kinds in Oude. The Rajah of Bulrampoor mentioned a curious instance of this spirit in a village, now called the *Kolowar* village, in the Gonda district, held in copartnership by a family of the Buchulgotee tribe of Rajpoots. One of them said he should plant sugar cane in one of his fields. All consented to this. But when he pointed out the place where he should have his mill, the community became divided. A contest ensued, in which all the able bodied men were killed, though not a single cane had been planted. The widows and children survived, and still hold the village, but have been so subdued by poverty, that they are the quietest village community in the district. The village, from that time, has gone by the name of *Kolowar* village, from Koloo, the sugar mill, though no sugar mill was ever worked in the village he believed. He says, the villagers cherish the recollection of this *fight*; and get very angry when their neighbours *twit* them with the folly of it.

In our own districts in Upper India, they often kill each other in such contests; but more frequently ruin each other in litigation in our Civil Courts, to the benefit of the native attorneys and law officers, who fatten on the misery they create or produce. In Oude they always decide such questions by recourse to arms, and the loss of life is, no doubt, fearful. Still the people generally, or a great part of them, would prefer to reside in Oude, under all the risks to which these contests expose them, than in our own districts, under the evils the people are exposed to from the uncertainties of our law, the multiplicity and formality of our Courts, the pride and negligence of those who preside over them, and the corruption and insolence of those who must be employed, to prosecute or defend a cause in them, and enforce the fulfilment of a decree, when passed.

The members of the landed aristocracy of Oude always speak, with respect, of the administration in our territories, but generally end with remarking on the cost and uncertainty of the law in civil cases, and the gradual decay, under its operation, of all the ancient families. A less and less proportion of the annual produce of their lands is left to them in our periodical settlements of the land revenue, while family pride makes them expend the same sums in the marriage of their children, in religious and other festivals, personal servants, and hereditary retainers. They fall into balance, incur heavy debts, and estate after estate is put up to auction, and the proprietors are reduced to poverty. They say, that four times more of these families have gone to decay in the half of the territory made over to us in 1801, than in the half reserved by the Oude sovereign; and this is, I fear, true. They name the families – I cannot remember them.

In Oude, the law of primogeniture prevails among all the Tallookdars, or principal landholders; and, to a certain extent, among the middle class of landholders, of the Rajpoot or any other military class. If one co-sharer of this class has several sons, his eldest often inherits all the share he leaves, with all the obligations incident upon it, of maintaining the rest of the family.[a]

The brothers of Soorujbulee, above named, do not pretend to have any right of inheritance in the share of the lands he holds; but they have a prescriptive right to support from him, for themselves and families, when they require it. This rule of primogeniture is, however, often broken through during the life time of the father, who, having more of natural affection than family pride, divides the lands between his sons. After his death they submit to this division, and take their respective shares, to descend to their children, by the law of primogeniture, or be again subdivided as may seem to them best; or they fight it out among themselves, till the strongest gets all. Among landholders of the smallest class, whether Hindoos or Mahomedans, the lands are subdivided, according to the ordinary law of inheritance.

Our army and other public establishments, form a great 'safety valve' for Oude, and save it from a vast deal of fighting for shares in land, and the disorders that always attend it. Younger brothers enlist in our Regiments, or find employment in our civil establishments, and leave their wives and children under the protection of the elder brother, who manages the family estate for the common good. They send the greater part

[a] The nature of this 'primogeniture' was explained by a writer (probably W. C. Benett) in the *Express* (Lucknow) in 1881: 'the usual principle, even in the case of a Raj, was to divide the emoluments among all the male descendants. In many cases this was deliberately abandoned, and the maintenance of the family dignity was provided for by determining that for the future the bulk of the Raj should descend to the eldest son, the younger sons receiving only just enough for their support.' *Landlord and Tenant in Oudh: Four articles reprinted from the 'Express' newspaper* (Lucknow, 1881).

of their pay to him for their subsistence, and feel assured, that he will see that they are provided for, should they lose their lives in our service. From the single district of Byswara, in Oude, sixteen thousand men were, it is said, found to be so serving in our army and other establishments; and from Bunoda, which adjoins it to the east, fifteen thousand, on an inquiry ordered to be made by Ghazee-od Deen Hyder[a] some twenty-five years ago.

The family of Dursun Sing, like good landholders in all parts of Oude, assign small patches of land to substantial cultivators, merchants, shopkeepers, and others, whom it is useful to retain in their estates, for the purpose of planting small groves of mango and other trees, as local ties. They prepare the well and plant the trees, and then make over the land to a gardener or other good cultivator, to be tilled for his own profit, on condition, that he water the trees, and take care to preserve them from frost during the cold season, and from rats, white ants, and other enemies; and form terraces round them, where the water lies much on the surface during the rains, so that it may not reach and injure the bark. The land yields crops till the trees grow large and cover it with their shade, by which time they are independant of irrigation, and begin to bear fruit. The crops do not thrive under the shade of the trees, and the lands they cover cease to be of any value for tillage. The stems and foliage of the trees, no doubt, deprive the crops of the moisture, carbonic acid gas and ammonia, they require from the atmosphere. They are, generally, watered from six to ten years. These groves form a valuable local tie for the cultivators and other useful tenants. No man dares to molest them or their descendants, in the possession of their well and grove, without incurring, at least, the odium of society; and, according to their notion, the anger of their gods.

The cultivators always point out to them, in asserting their rights to the lands they hold; and reside and cultivate in the village, under circumstances, that would drive them away, had they no such ties to retain them. They feel a great pride in them, and all good landlords feel the same in having their villages filled with tenants who have such ties.

[a] Ghazi-ud-din Haidar, reigned 1814–27; the first King of Oudh.

95

Diary of a Tour Through Oude

December 21, 1849. – Bhurteepoor, ten miles, almost all the way through the estate of Maun Sing. No lands could be better cultivated than they are all the way, or better studded with groves and beautiful single trees. The villages and hamlets along the road are numerous, and filled with cultivators of the gardener and other good classes, who seem happy and contented. The season has been favorable, and the crops are all fine, and of great variety. Sugar cane abounds, but no mills are, as yet, at work. We passed through, and by three or four villages, that have been lately taken from Maun Sing, and made over to farmers, by the local authorities, under instructions from Court; but they are not so well cultivated as those which he retains. The cultivators and inhabitants generally do not appear to enjoy the same protection, or security in the engagements they make. The soil is, every where, good, the water near the surface, and the climate excellent. The soil is here called doomuteea, and adapted to all kinds of tillage.

I should mention, with regard to the subdivision of landed property, that the Rajahs and Tallookdars, among whom the law of primogeniture prevails, consider their estate as principalities, or *reeasuts*. When any Rajah, or Tallookdar, during his life time, assigns portions of the land to his sons, brothers, or other members of the family, they are separated from the *reeasut*, or principality, and are subdivided as they descend from generation to generation, by the ordinary Hindoo or Mahomedan law of inheritance. This is the case with portions of the estate of the Rajah of Korwar, in the Sultanpoor district, one of the oldest Hindoo principalities in Oude, which are now held by his cousins, nephews, &c. &c. near this place, Bhurteepoor.[1]

Dooneeaput succeeded to the *reeasut* on the death of his uncle, the Rajah, who died without issue; and he bestowed portions of the estate on his brothers, Burear and Zubur Sing, which their descendants enjoy, but which do not go to the eldest son, by the

---

[1] Sunkur Sing, of Korwar, had four sons; first, Dooneeaput dies without issue; second, Sookraj Sing, whose grandson, Madhoo Persaud, is now the Rajah; third, Bureear Sing, who got from his brother, lands yielding forty thousand rupees a year, out of the principality. They are now held by his son, Jydut; fourth, Zubar Sing, who got from his brother, lands yielding nineteen thousand rupees a year, which are now held by his son Moheser Persaud. Sunkur Sing was the second brother, but his elder brother died without issue.

law of primogeniture. He was succeeded by his brother, Sookraj, whose grandson, Madhoo Persaud, now reigns as Rajah, and has the undivided possession of the lands belonging to this branch. All the descendants of his grandfather, Sookraj, and their widows and orphans, have a right to protection and support from him, and to nothing more. Jydut, who now holds the lands, yielding forty thousand rupees a year, called upon me, this morning, and gave me this history of his family. The Rajah himself is in camp, and to visit me this afternoon.

It is interesting and pleasing to see a large, well-controlled camp, moving, in a long line, through a narrow road, or path way, over plains, covered with so rich a variety of crops, and studded with such magnificent ever-green trees. The solitary mango tree, in a field of corn, seems to exult in its position – to grow taller and spread wider its branches and rich foliage, in situations where they can be seen to so much advantage. The peepul and bargut trees, which, when entire, are still more ornamental, are, every where, torn to pieces, and disfigured by the camels and elephants, buffaloes and bullocks, that feed upon their foliage and tender branches. There are a great many mhowa, tamarind and other fine trees, upon which they do not feed, to assist the mango in giving beauty to the landscape.

The Korwar Rajah, Madhoo Persaud, a young man, of about twenty-two years of age, came in the evening, and confirmed, what his relative, Jydut, had told me of the rule which required, that his lands should remain undivided with his eldest son, while those which are held by Jydut and his other relatives, should be subdivided among all the sons of the holder. This rule is more necessary in Oude than elsewhere, to preserve a family and its estate from the grasp of its neighbours and government officers. When there happens to be no heir left to the portion of the estate, which has been cut off, it is reannexed to the estate; and the head of the family frequently anticipates the event, by murdering or imprisoning, the heir or incumbent, and seizing upon the lands. Another Rajah, of the same name, Madhoo Persaud, of Amethee, in Salone, has lately seized upon the estate of Shahgur, worth twenty thousand rupees a year, which had been cut off from the Amethee estate, and enjoyed by a collateral branch of the family for several generations. He holds the proprietor, Bulwunt Sing, in prison, in irons, and would soon make away with him were the Oude government to think it worth while to inquire after him. He has seized upon another portion, Ramgur, held by another branch of the family, worth six thousand rupees a year, and crushed all the proprietors. This is the way in which estates, once broken up, are reconsolidated in Oude, under energetic and unscrupulous men. Of course when they think it worth while to do so, they purchase the collusion of the local authorities of the day, by promising to pay the revenues, which the old proprietors paid, during their tenure of office. The other barons do not interfere, unless they happen to be connected, by marriage, with the ousted proprietors, or otherwise specially bound, by interest and honor, to defend them against the grasp of the head of their family. Many struggles, of this kind, are taking place every season in Oude.

CHAPTER IV

[Sultanpur and Partabgarh 'districts', 22–8 December 1849]

[1852: I, 156–85] [1858: I, 175–208]

December 22, 1849. – Sultanpoor, eight miles. Recrossed the Goomtee river, close under the Cantonments, over a bridge of boats, prepared for the purpose; and encamped on the parade ground. The country, over which we came, fertile and well cultivated. For some days we have seen and heard a good many religious mendicants – both Mahomedans and Hindoos – but still very few lame, blind and otherwise helpless persons, asking charity. The most numerous and distressing class of beggars, that importune me, are those who beg redress for their wrongs, and a remedy for their grievances, – 'their name, indeed, is *Legion*', and their wrongs and grievances are, altogether, without remedy, under the present government, and inveterately vicious system of administration. It is painful, to listen to all these complaints, and to have to refer the sufferers, for redress, to authorities who want both the power and the will to afford it; especially, when one knows, that a remedy, for almost every evil, is hoped for from a visit, such as the poor people are now receiving from the Resident. He is expected 'to wipe the tears from off all faces'; and feels, that he can wipe them from hardly any. The reckless disregard shown by the depredators of all classes and degrees, to the sufferings of their victims, whatever be the cause of discontent or object of pursuit, is lamentable. I have, every day, scores of petitions delivered to me 'with quivering lip and tearful eye', by persons who have been plundered of all they possessed, had their dearest relatives murdered or tortured to death, and their habitations burnt to the ground by gangs of ruffians, under landlords of high birth and pretensions, whom they had never wronged or offended. Some, merely because they happened to have property, which the ruffians wished to take; others, because they presumed, to live and labour upon lands which they coveted, or deserted, and wished to have left waste. In these attacks, neither age, nor sex, nor condition, are spared. The greater part of the leaders of these gangs of ruffians are Rajpoot landholders, boasting descent from the *sun* and *moon*,[a] or from the demi-gods, who figure in the Hindoo religious fictions of the Poorans.[b] There are, however, a great many mahomedans at the head of similar gangs. A landholder, of whatever degree, who is opposed to his government, from whatever cause, considers himself in a state of *war*; and he considers a state of war, to authorise his doing all those things which he is forbidden to do, in a state of peace.

Unless the sufferer happens to be a native officer or sipahee of our army, who enjoys the privilege of urging his claims through the Resident, it is a cruel mockery to refer him, for redress, to any existing local authority – one not only feels, that it is so, but sees, that the sufferer thinks that he must know it to be so. No such authority considers it to be any part of his duty, to arrest evil doers, and inquire into and redress wrongs suffered by individuals, or families, or village communities. Should he arrest such people, he would have to subsist and accommodate them at his own cost, or to send them to Lucknow, with the assurance, that they would, in a few days, or a few weeks, purchase their way out again, in spite of the clearest proofs of the murders, robberies, torturings, dishonorings, house burning, &c., which they have committed. No sentence, which any one local authority could pass on such offenders, would be recognised, by any other authority in the State, as valid, or sufficient, to justify him in receiving and holding them in confinement for a single day. The local authorities, therefore, either leave the wrong

[a] Rajput descent is traced through two main lines, Chandravansi ('moon-race') and Suryavansi ('sun-race'), and also through Agnikula ('fire-born'). From these sources there derive 36 'royal races' or clans, of varying status. Clearly, these represent attempts to provide 'origin myths' which would accommodate various groups becoming, or being absorbed as, Rajputs over time.

[b] Puranas, lit. 'old'; ancient legends or stories which follow after the epics (*Ramayana* and *Mahabharata*) and differ from them in that they deal with the activities of gods rather than heroes. They are in verse form. See J. Dowson, *A Classical Dictionary of Hindu Mythology and Religion, Geography, History and Literature* (London, 9th ed. 1957), pp. 245–7.

doers unmolested, with the understanding, that they are to abstain from doing any such wrong, within their jurisdictions, as may endanger, or impede, the *collection of revenues*, during their period of office; or release them with that understanding, after they have squeezed all they can out of them. The wrong doers can so abstain, and still be able to *murder, rob, torture, dishonor, and burn,* upon a pretty large scale; and where they are so numerous, and so ready to unite for purposes, 'offensive and defensive', and the local authorities so generally connive at, or quietly acquiesce in, their misdeeds, any attempt on the part of an honest or overzealous individual, to put them down, would be sure to result in his speedy and utter ruin!

To refer such sufferers to the authorities at Lucknow, would be a still more cruel mockery. The present sovereign[a] never hears a complaint, or reads a petition, or report of any kind. He is entirely taken up in the pursuit of his personal gratifications. He has no desire to be thought to take any interest, whatever, in public affairs; and is altogether regardless of the duties and responsibilities of his high office. He lives, exclusively, in the society of fiddlers, eunuchs, and women – he has done so since his childhood, and is likely to do so to the last. His disrelish for any other society has become inveterate – he cannot keep awake in any other. In spite of average natural capacity, and more than average facility in the cultivation of light literature, or at least '*de faire des petits vers de sa facon*', his understanding has become so emasculated, that he is altogether unfit for the conduct of his domestic much less his public affairs. He sees, occasionally, his prime minister, who takes care to persuade him, that he does all that a king ought to do; and nothing whatever of any other minister. He holds no communication, whatever with brothers, uncles, cousins, or any of the native gentlemen at Lucknow, or the landed or official aristocracy of the country. He sometimes admits a few poets or poetasters, to hear and praise his verses, and commands the unwilling attendance of some of his relations, to witness and applaud the acting of some of his own silly comedies, on the penalty of forfeiting their stipends; but any one who presumes to approach him – even in his rides or drives –

[a] Wajid Ali Shah, reigned 1847–56.

with a petition for justice, is instantly clapped into prison, or, otherwise, severely punished.

His father[a] and grand father,[b] while on the throne, used to see the members of the royal family and aristocracy of the city in Durbar, once a day, or three or four times a week, and have all petitions and reports read over in their own presence. They dictated the orders, and their seal was affixed to them in their own presence, bearing the inscription *molahiza shud* 'it has been seen'. The seal was then replaced in the casket, which was kept by one confidential servant, Muzd-od Dowlah, while the key was confided to another. Documents were thus read and orders passed upon them twice a day – once in the morning, and once again in the evening; and, on such occasions all heads of departments were present. The present king continued this system for a short time, but he soon got tired of it, and made over seal and all to the minister, to do what he liked with them; and discontinued altogether the short Durbar, or Levees, which his father, grand father, and all former sovereigns had held – before they entered on the business of the day, with the heads of departments and secretaries – and, at which, all the members of the royal family and aristocracy of the city attended, to pay their respects to their sovereign; and soon ceased altogether, to see the heads of departments and secretaries, to hear orders read, and to ask questions about state affairs.

The minister has become, by degrees, almost as inaccessible as his sovereign, to all but his deputies, heads of departments, secretaries, and Court favorites, whom it is his interest to conciliate. Though the minister has his own confidential deputies and secretaries, the same heads of departments are in office, as under the present king's father and grand father; and, though no longer permitted to attend upon or see the king, they are still supposed to submit to the minister, for orders, all reports from local authorities, intelligence writers, &c. &c., and all petitions from sufferers; but, in reality, he sees and hears read very few, and passes orders upon still less. Any head of department, deputy, secretary, or favorite, may receive petitions, to be

[a] Amjad Ali Shah, reigned 1842–47.
[b] Muhammad Ali Shah, reigned 1837–42.

submitted to the minister for orders; but it is the *special duty* of no one to receive them, nor is any one held responsible for submitting them for orders. Those only who are in the special confidence of the minister, or of those about Court, from whom he has something to hope or something to fear, venture to receive and submit petitions; and they drive a profitable trade in doing so. A large portion of those submitted, are thrown aside, without any orders at all – a portion have orders so written as to show, that they are never intended to be carried into effect – a third portion receive orders, that are really intended to be acted upon. But they are taken to one of the minister's deputies, with whose views or interests some of them may not square well; and he may detain them for weeks, months, or years, till the petitioners are worn out with 'hope deferred', or utterly ruined, in vain efforts, to purchase the attention they require. Nothing is more common than for a peremptory order to be passed, for the immediate payment of the arrears of pension, due to a stipendiary member of the royal family, and for the payment to be deferred for either, ten and twelve months, till he or she consents to give from ten to twenty per cent – according to his or her necessities – to the deputy, who has to see the order carried out. A sufferer often, instead of getting his petition smuggled on to the minister, in the mode above described, bribes a news writer to insert his case in his report, to be submitted through the head of the department.

At present the head of the intelligence department assumes the same latitude, in submitting reports, for orders, to the minister, that his subordinates, in distant districts, assume, in framing and sending them to him – that is, he submits only such as it may suit his views and interests to submit! Where grave charges are sent to him against substantial men, or men high in office, he comes to an understanding with their representatives in Lucknow, and submits the report to the minister only as a *derniere resort*, when such representatives cannot be brought to submit to his terms. If found out, at any time, and threatened, he has his feed *patrons* or *patronesses* 'behind the throne, and greater than the throne itself', to protect him.

The unmeaning orders, passed by the minister, on reports

and petitions, are commonly, that *so and so* is to inquire into the matter complained of – to see that the offenders are seized and punished – that the stolen property and usurped lands be restored – that *razeenamas*, or acquittances, be sent in by the friends of persons who have been murdered by the king's officers – that the men, women and children, confined and tortured by king's officers, or by robbers and ruffians, be set at liberty and satisfied – the said *so and so*, being the infant commander-in-chief – the king's chamberlain, foot man, coach man, chief fiddler, eunuch, barber, or person uppermost in his thoughts at the time. Similar orders are passed, in his name, by his deputies, secretaries, and favorites, upon all the other numerous petititions and reports, which he sends to them unperused. Not, perhaps, upon one in five does the minister himself pass any order; and of the orders passed by him, not one in five, perhaps, intended to be taken notice of. His deputies and favorites carry on a profitable trade in all such reports and petitions – they extort money, alike, from the wrong doer and the wrong sufferer; and from all local authorities, or their representatives, for all neglect of duty or abuses of authority, charged against them.

As to any investigation into the real merits of any case, described in these reports, from the news writers and local authorities, no such thing has been heard of for several reigns. The real merits of all such cases are, however, well and generally known to the people of the districts in which they occur, and freely discussed by them with suitable remarks on the 'darkness which prevails under the lamp of royalty', and no less suitable execrations against the intolerable system, that deprives the king of all feeling of interest in the well being of his subjects – all sense of duty towards them – all feeling of responsibility to any higher power, for the manner in which he discharges his high trust, over the millions, committed to his care.

As I have said, the king never sees any petitition or report – he hardly ever sees even official notes addressed to him by the British Resident, and the replies to almost all are written without his knowledge. The minister never puts either his seal or signature to any order that passes, or any document whatsoever, with his own hand; he merely puts in the date – as the 1st, 5th, or 10th, – the month, year, and the order itself, are inserted by the deputies, secretaries or favorites, to whom the duty is confided. The reports and petitions, submitted for orders, often accumulate so fast in times of great festivity or ceremony, that the minister has them tied up in bundles, without any orders, whatever, having been passed on them, and sent to his deputies, for such as they may think proper to pass, merely inserting his figure 1, 5, or 10, to indicate the date, on the outermost document of each bundle. If any orders are inserted by his deputies, on the rest, they have only to insert the same date. There is nothing but the *figure*, to attest the authenticity of the order; and it would be often impossible for the minister himself to say, whether the figure was inserted by himself or by any other person. These deputies are the men who adjust all the nuzuranas, or unauthorised gratuities, to be paid to the minister.

They share, largely, in all that he gets; and take a great deal, for which they render him no account. Knowing all that he takes *and ought not to take*, he dares not punish them for their transgressions, and knowing this, sufferers are afraid to complain against them. In ordinary times, or under ordinary sovereigns, the sums paid by revenue authorities in *nazuranas*, or gratuities, before they were permitted to enter on their charges, amounted to, perhaps, ten or fifteen per cent – under the present sovereign they amount to more than twenty-five per cent upon the revenue they are to collect, I believe. Of these the minister and his deputies take the largest part. A portion is paid in advance, and good bonds are taken for the rest, to be paid within the year. Of the money collected, more than twenty-five per cent, on an average, is appropriated by those entrusted with the disbursements, and by their patrons and patronesses. The sovereign gets, perhaps, three-fourths of what is collected; and of what is collected, perhaps, two-thirds, on an average, reaches its legitimate destination; so that one-half of the revenues of Oude, may be considered as taken by officers and Court favorites, in unauthorised gratuities and perquisites. The pay of the troops and establishments, on duty with the revenue collectors, is deducted by them, and the surplus only is sent to the Treasury at

Lucknow. In his accounts he receives credit for all sums paid to the troops and establishments, on duty under him. Though the artillery bullocks[a] get none of the grain, for which he pays and charges government, a greater portion of the whole of what he pays and charges in his accounts, reaches its legitimate destination, perhaps, than of the whole of what is paid from the Treasury at the Capital. On an average, however, I do not think, that more than two-thirds of what is paid and charged to government, reaches that destination.

I may instance the two Regiments, under Thakur Sing, Tirbaydee, which are always on duty at the palace. It is known that the officers and sipahees of those Regiments do not get more than one-half of the pay, which is issued for them every month, from the Treasury. The other half is absorbed by the commandant and his patrons at Court. On every thing sold in the palace, the vender is obliged to add one-third to the price, to be paid to the person, through whom it is passed in. Without this, nothing can be sold in the palace, by European or native. Not a single animal, in the king's establishments, gets one-third of the food allowed for it, and charged for – not a building is erected or repaired at less than three times the actual outlay – two-thirds, at least, of the money charged, going to the superintendent and his patrons.

December 23, 1849. – Halted at Sultanpoor, which is one of the healthiest stations in India, on the right bank of the Goomtee river, upon a dry soil, among deep ravines, which drain off the water rapidly. The bungalows are on the verge, looking down into the river, upon the level patches of land, dividing the ravines. The water, in the wells, is some fifty feet below the surface, on a level with the stream below. There are no groves within a mile of the cantonments; and no lakes, marshes, or jungles, within a

---

[a] See W. H. Sleeman to Dalhousie, 10 April 1852, enclosed memorandum on artillery bullock requirements: 'The complement of bullocks for a battery of six guns, 6 waggons, and 2 store carts, is 106. The number yoked to each gun and waggon is 6, and to each cart 4, leaving a surplus of 26 for accidents...These bullocks are taken care of by 4 sirdars and 59 drivers; and an European sergeant of artillery is appointed as bullock-sergeant to each battery, to superintend the feeding, cleaning, &c. &c.' *JTKO*, vol. ii, p. 365.

great many; and the single trees, in and near the cantonments, are few. The gardens are small and few; and the water is sparingly used in irrigating them, as the expence of drawing it is very great.

There is another good site for a cantonment at Chandour, some twelve miles up the river, on the opposite bank, and looking down upon the stream, from the verge, in the same manner. Chandour was chosen, for his cantonments, by Rajah Dursun Sing, when he had the contract for the district; and it would be the best place for the head-quarters of any establishments, that any new arrangements might require for the administration of the Sultanpoor and surrounding districts. Secrora would be the best position for the head-quarters of those required for the administration of the Gonda-Bahraetch, and other surrounding districts. It is central, and has always been considered one of the healthiest places in Oude. It was long a cantonment for one of our Regiments of Infantry and some guns, which were, in 1835, withdrawn and sent to increase the force at Lucknow, from two to three Regiments of Infantry. The Regiment and guns at Sultanpoor, were taken away in 1837. Secrora was, for some years, after our Regiment and guns had been withdrawn, occupied by a Regiment and guns under Captain Barlow, one of the king of Oude's officers; but it is now altogether deserted. Sultanpoor[a] has been, ever since 1837, occupied by one of the two Regiments of Oude Local Infantry, without any guns, or cavalry, of any kind. There was, also, a Regiment of our regular Infantry at Pertabghur, three marches from Sultanpoor, on the road to Allahabad, with a Regiment of our Light Cavalry. The latter was withdrawn in 1815, for the Nepaul war, and employed again under us during the Mahratta war, in 1817 and 1818. It was sent back again in 1820; but soon after, in 1821, withdrawn altogether; and we have since had no Cavalry of any kind in Oude. Seetapoor was, also, occupied by one of our regular Regiments of Infantry and some guns, till 1837, when they were withdrawn, and their place supplied by the second

[a] For an outline of the cantonment see Butter, *Outlines of the Topography and Statistics of the Southern Districts of Oud'h and of the Cantonment of Sultanpur-Oud'h*, pp. 177–83.

Regiment of Oude Local Infantry. Our Government now pays the two Regiments of Oude Local Infantry, stationed at Sultanpoor and Seetapoor; but the places of those stationed at Secrora and Pertabghur, have never been supplied. One additional Regiment of Infantry is kept at Lucknow, so that our force, in Oude, has only been diminished by one Regiment of Infantry, one of Cavalry, and eight guns, with a Company and half of Artillery. To do our duty, *honestly*, by Oude, we ought to restore the Regiment of Infantry; and, in the place of the Corps of Light, send one of Irregular Cavalry.[a] We ought, also, to restore the Company and half of Artillery, and eight guns, which have been withdrawn. We draw, annually, from the lands, ceded to us, in 1801 – for the protection, which we promised to the king and his people, from 'all internal and external enemies' – no less than two crores and twelve lakhs of rupees, or two millions sterling a year, while the Oude government draws, from the half of its territories, which it reserved, only one half that sum, or one crore of rupees.

Maun Sing is to leave my camp to-day, and to return Shahgunge. Of the fraud and violence, abuse of power, and collusion with local authorities, by which he and his father seized upon the lands of so many hundreds of old proprietors, there can be no doubt; but to attempt to make the family restore them now, under such a government, would create great disorder, drive off all the better classes of cultivators, and desolate the face of the country, which they have rendered so beautiful, by an efficient system of administration. Many of the most powerful of the landed aristocracy of Oude have acquired, or augmented, their

[a] Thornton, *Gazetteer*, vol. IV, p. 37, states that force maintained in Oude by the Company in 1849 amounted to 5,600, of whom 2,000 were local infantry. The remainder were the Company's regular troops, chiefly infantry but with a small body of artillery. Butter, *Southern Districts of Oud'h*, pp. 102–4 has details of local corps organisation from a slightly earlier period; see also *CHI*, vol. VI, pp. 164–5.

'Irregular' troops were those who had to 'find themselves in everything except ammunition and medical stores', as H. T. Lambrick puts it. He gives a detailed account of how the system worked in one particular instance, the Scinde Irregular Horse, in his *John Jacob of Jacobabad* (London, 1960), esp. ch. 13, 'The Indian Ironsides'. Such a system, he points out, required men of substance to join the regiments and it is interesting therefore to note that in September 1848, there were 1600 men in the service, of whom over 1500 came from the Delhi districts and Oudh, most of them being Muslims; pp. 178–9.

estates, in the same manner, and within the same time; and the same difficulty would attend the attempt, to restore the old proprietors in all parts. A strong and honest government might overcome all these difficulties, and restore to every rightful proprietor the land unjustly taken from him, within a limited period; but it should not attempt to enforce any adjustment of the accounts of receipts and disbursements for the intervening period. The old proprietor would receive back his land in an improved condition, and the usurper might fairly be considered, to have reimbursed himself for all his outlay. The old proprietor should be required to pledge himself to respect the rights of all new tenants.

December 24, 1849. – Meranpoor, twelve miles. Soil between this and Sultanpoor neither so fertile nor so well cultivated, as we found it on the other side of the Goomtee river, though it is of the same denomination – generally doomut, but here and there muteear. The term muteear embraces all good argillaceous earth, from the light brown to the black, humic or ulmic deposit, found in the beds of tanks and lakes in Oude. The natives of Oude call the black soil of Malwa and southern India, and Bundlekund, *muteear*. This black soil has, in its unexhausted state, abundance of silicates, sulphates, phosphates, and carbonates of alumina, potassa, lime, &c. &c., and of organic acids, combined with the same unorganic substances, to attract and fix ammonia, and collect and store up moisture, and is exceedingly fertile and strong.

Both salt-petre and common salt are made by lixiviation from some of the poor, oosur soils; but, from the most barren in Oude, carbonates of soda, used in making *glass* and *soap*, are taken.[a] The earth is collected from the surface of the most barren spots, and formed into small, shallow, round tanks, a yard in diameter. Water is then poured in, and the tank filled to the surface, with an additional supply of the earth, and smoothed over. This tank is then left exposed to the sun for two days, during the hottest and driest months of the year, March, April and May, and part of June, when the crust, formed on the surface,

[a] See Butter, *Southern Districts of Oud'h*, pp. 72–82, on manufacture of salt, soda, saltpetre and glass phials and bangles. Note that Butter claims specifically that no soap was produced at that time, p. 81.

is taken off. The process is repeated once; but in the second operation, the tank is formed around, and below by the debris, of the first tank, which is filled to the surface, after the water has been poured in, with the first *crust* obtained. The second crust is called the *reha*, which is carbonate or bicarbonate of soda. This is formed into small cakes, which are baked to redness in an oven, or crucible, to expel the moisture and carbonic acid, which it contains. They are then powdered to fine dust, which is placed in another crucible, and fused to liquid glass, the *reha* containing in itself sufficient silica to form the coarse glass used in making bracelets, &c. &c.

A superabundance of nitrates seem also to impair or destroy fertility in the soil, and they may arise from the decomposition of animal or vegetable matter, in a soil containing a superabundance of porous lime.[a] The atmospheric air and water, contained in the moist and porous soil, are decomposed. The hydrogen of the water combines with the nitrogen of the air, and water, contained in the moist and porous soil, are decomposed. The hydrogen of the water combines with the nitrogen of the air, and that given off by the decomposing organic bodies, and forms ammonia. The nitrogen of the ammonia then takes up the oxygen of the air and water, and becoming nitric acid, forms nitrates with the lime, potash, soda, &c., contained in the soil. Without any superabundance of lime in the soil, however, the same effects may be produced, when there is a deficiency of decaying vegetable and animal matter, as the oxygen of the decomposed air and water, having no organic substances to unite with, may combine with the nitrogen of the ammonia, and form nitric acid; which, uniting with the lime, potash, soda, &c. may form the superabounding nitrates destructive of fertility.

This superabundance of reha, or carbonate of soda, which renders so much of the surface barren, must, I conclude, arise from deposits of common salt, or chloride of sodium. The water, as it percolates through these deposits, towards the surface, becomes saturated with their alkaline salts; and, as it reaches the

[a] This dubious paragraph is retained mainly to avoid cutting unnecessarily into this generally interesting section on salt and glass-making. It is also perhaps interesting as an example of Sleeman's scientific turn of mind and interests.

surface, and becomes evaporated in the pure state, it leaves them behind at or near the surface. On its way to the surface, or at the surface, the chloride of sodium becomes decomposed by contact with *carbonates of ammonia and potassa – sulphuric and nitric acids.* In a soil, well supplied with decaying animal or vegetable matter, these carbonates or sulphates of soda, as they rise to the surface, might be formed into nutriment for plants, and taken up by their roots; or in one well flooded, occasionally, with fresh water, any superabundance of the salts, or their bases, might be taken up in solution and carried off. The people say, that the soil, in which these carbonates of soda (reha), abound, are more unmanageable than those in which nitrates abound – they tell me, that, with flooding, irrigating, manuring and well ploughing, they can manage to get crops from all but the soils in which this *reha* abounds.

The process, above described, by which the bracelet makers extract the carbonates of soda and potash from the earth of the small, shallow tanks, is precisely the same as that by which they are brought from the deep bed of earth below, and deposited on or near the surface. In both processes, the water, which brings them to the surface, goes off into the atmosphere, in a pure state, and leaves the salts behind. To make soap from the reha, they must first remove the silex which it contains.

There are no rocks in Oude, and the only form in which lime is found for building purposes and road pavements, is that of kunkur, which is a carbonate of lime, containing silica, and oxide of iron. In proportion, as it contains the last, the kunkur is more or less red. That which contains none, is of a dirty white. It is found in many parts of India in thin layers, or amorphous masses, formed by compression, upon a stiff clay substratum; but in Oude I have seen it only in nodules, usually formed on nuclei of flint or other hard substances. The kingdom of Oude must have once been the bed, or part of the bed, of a large lake,[a] formed by

[a] This theory is not now accepted; rather, as Spate and Learmonth put it, 'The great crescent of alluvium from the delta of the Indus to that of the Ganga represents the infilling of a foredeep warped down between the Gondwana block and the advancing Himalayas'; *India and Pakistan*, p. 41. Cf. M. H. Rahman, *L'Oudh. Etude de géographie économique sur les plaines de l'Oudh de Nord de l'Inde* (Paris, 1940), pp. 16–18, who expressly rejects the idea of a former lake or sea.

the diluvial detritus of the hills of the Himmalah[a] chain; and, as lime-stone abounds in that chain, the bed contains abundance of lime, which is taken up by the water, that percolates through it from the rivers, and from the rains and floods above. The lime thus taken up and held in solution with carbonic acid gas, is deposited around the small fragments of flint, or other hard substances, which the waters find in their way. Where the floods which cover the surface, during the rains, come in rivers, flowing from the Himmalah, or other hills, abounding in lime-stone rocks, they, of course, contain lime and carbonic acid gas, which add to the kunkur nodules, formed in the bed below; but in Oude, the rivers seldom overflow to any extent, and the kunkur is, I believe, formed chiefly from the lime, already existing in the bed.[1]

The sujjee is formed from the reha by filtration. A tank is formed on a terrace of cement. In a hole, at one corner, is a small tube. Rows of bricks are put down from one end to the other, with intervals between, for the liquor to flow through to the

[1] Doctor O'Shaughnessy, [Sir William Brooke O'Shaughnessey (1809–89) Edinburgh M.D. 1830; came to Bengal in 1833; Professor of Chemistry, Medical College Calcutta; F.R.S. 1843; Director-General of Telegraphs 1853; knighted 1856. Published works on medicine and chemistry.] the most eminent chemist now in India, tells me, that there are two marked varieties of kunkur in India, the red and the white, – that the red differs from the white, solely in containing a larger proportion of peroxide of iron – that the white consists of carbonate of lime, silica, alumina, and, sometimes, magnesia and protoxide of iron. He states, that he considers the kunkur to be deposited by calcareous waters, abounding in infusorial animalculae – that the waters of the annual inundation are rich in lime, and that all the facts that have come under his observation, appear to him, to indicate, that this is the source of the kunkur deposit, – which is seen in a different form in the Italian travertine, and the crescent nodules of the Isle of Sheppey, and, of Bologne.

Doctor O'Shaughnessy further states, that the *reha* earth, which I sent to him from Oude, is identical with the *sujjee muttee* of Bengal, and contains carbonate of soda, and sulphate of soda, as its essential characteristic ingredients, with silicious clay and oxide of iron. But in Oude, the term 'sujjee', is given to the carbonate and sulphate of soda, which remains after the silex has been removed from the reha. The reha is fused into glass, after the carbonic acid and moisture have been expelled by heat; and the sujjee is formed into soap, by the addition of lime, fat, and linseed oil, in the following proportions, I am told.

6 sujjee.   4 lime.   2½ fat.   1½ ulsee oil.

[a] Properly Himalaya, 'abode of snow'. Note that variations of the form used by Sleeman were common in the later eighteenth and early nineteenth centuries; see H. Yule and A. C. Burnell, *Hobson-Jobson. A glossary of colloquial Anglo-Indian words and phrases*...revised ed. W. Crooke (London, 1903), pp. 414–15.

tube. On these rows a layer of stout reeds is first placed; and, over them, another layer, composed of the leaves of these reeds. On this bed the coarse reha earth is placed, without being refined by the process, described in the text above. Some coarse common salt (kharee nimuck[a]), is mixed up with the reha. The tank is then filled with water, which filters slowly through the earth, and passes out through the tube into pans, whence it is taken to another tank, upon a wider terrace of cement, where it evaporates, and leaves the *sujjee* deposited. The second tank is commonly made close under the first, and the liquor flows into it through the tube, rendering pans unnecessary. It is only in the hot months of March, April, May, and part of June, till the rains begin to fall, that the reha and sujjee are formed. During the other nine months, the *Looneas*, who provide them, turn their hands to something else. The *reha*, deprived of its carbonic acid, and moisture by heat, is fused into glass. Deprived of silex, by this process of filtration, it is formed into sujjee, from which the soap is made.[1]

The country is well provided with mango and other fine trees, single and in clusters and groves; but the tillage is slovenly and scanty, strongly indicative of want of security to life, property and industry. No symptom of the residence of gardeners and other cultivators of the better classes, or irrigation, or the use of manure in tillage.

December 25, 1849. – Nawabgunge, eleven miles. The soil good, as indicated by the growth of fine trees on each side of the road, as far as we could see, over the level plain; and by the few fields of corn in sight; but the cultivation is deficient and slovenly. A great part of the road lay through the estate of Mundone, held

[1] On the process of filtration, above described, Doctor O'Shaughnessy observes: 'I do not clearly understand the use of the common salt, used in the extraction of soda, in the process you described. But many of the empirical practices of the natives prove, on investigation, to square with the most scientific precepts. For example, their proportions, in the manufacture of corrosive sublimate, are precisely identical with those which the *atomic theory* leads the European chemist to follow. The filtering apparatus, which you describe, is really admirable; and, I doubt much, whether the best practical chemist could devise any simpler or cheaper way of arriving at the object in view.'

[a] Khari-nimak, a factitious kind of salt; sulphate of soda used in medicine and for the adulteration of common salt. See glossary below.

by Davey Persaud, the tallookdar; and the few peasants, who stood by the side of the road, to watch their fields, as we passed, and see the cavalcade, told me, that the deficient tillage and population arose from his being in opposition to government, and diligently engaged in plundering the country generally, and his own estates in particular, to reduce the local authorities to his own terms. The government demand upon him is twenty thousand rupees. He paid little last year, and has paid still less during the present year, on the ground, that his estate yields nothing. This is a common and generally successful practice among Tallookdars, who take to fighting against the government, whether their cause be just or unjust. These peasants and cultivators told us, that they had taken to the jungles, for shelter, after the last harvest, till the season for sowing again commenced; remained in the fields, still houseless, during the night, worked in their fields in fear of their lives, during the day and apprehended, that they should have to take to the jungles again, as soon as their crops were gathered, if they were even permitted to gather them. They attributed as much blame to their landlord, as to the Nazim, Wajid Allee Khan. He, however, bears a very bad character; and is said to have, designedly, thrown a good deal of the districts, under his charge, out of tillage, in the hope, that no other person would venture to take the contract for it in that condition; and, that he should, in consequence, be invited to retain it on more favorable terms. He was twelve lakhs of rupees, in balance, when superseded, at the end of the year, in September last, by the present governor, Aga Allee, who manages the same districts, on a salary of two thousand rupees a month, without any contract for the revenues; but, with the understanding, that he is to collect, or at least, to pay, a certain sum.

The late contractor will, no doubt, relieve himself from the burthen of this balance, in the usual way. He will be imprisoned for a time, till he pays, or enters into engagements to pay, to the minister, and the influential men at Court, as much as they think he can be made to pay, in bribes, and some half of that sum into the Treasury, and have all the rest struck out of the accounts as irrecoverable – perhaps two lakhs in bribes, and one to the Treasury may secure him an acquittance, and a fair chance of employment hereafter. His real name is Wajid Allee; but as that is the name of the king, he is commonly called Ahmud Allee, that the royal ears may not take offence.

December 26, 1849. – Pertabghur, distance eight miles. In the course of fourteen years, almost all signs of one of the most healthful and most agreeable cantonments of the Bengal Army, have been effaced. Fine crops of corn now cover what were the parades for Cavalry, Infantry, and Artillery, and the gardens and compounds of officers' bungalows. The grounds, which were once occupied by the old cantonments, are now let out to cultivators, immediately under government, and they are well cultivated; but the tillage of the rest of the country, we have this-morning passed over, is scanty and slovenly. The Rajah of Pertabghur has, for sometime, been on bad terms with the contractors, greatly in arrears, and commonly in opposition to the government, having his band of armed followers in the jungles, and doing nothing but mischief. This is the case with most of the Tallookdars of the country, over which I have passed. Not one in five, or I may say, one in ten, attends the viceroys, because it would not be safe to do so; or pays the demands of government punctually, because there is no certainty in them.

I passed down the line of Captain Magness's corps, which is at present stationed at Pertabghur. It is as well dressed, and as fine a looking corps as any Infantry Regiment, in our own Native Army, and has always shown itself as good on service. It has eight guns attached to it, well provided and served. The artillery men, drivers, &c. &c., are as well dressed and as fit for their duties as our own. Stores and ammunition are abundant, but the powder is execrable. Captain Magness is a good officer. The guns are six-pounders, drawn by bullocks; and two gallopers of very small calibre, drawn by horses. They are not adapted for the duties they have to perform, which is chiefly against mud forts and strong holds; and four 9-pounders, two howitzers, and two mortars would be better. They are, however, well manned and provided with bullocks, ammunition and stores. The finest young men in Oude are glad to take service under Captain Magness; and the standard height of his men is, at present, five feet ten inches. He has some few men, good for nothing, called *sufarishies*, whom he is obliged to keep in on account of the persons by whom they are recommended, eunuchs, fiddlers, and Court favorites, of all kinds. In no country are there a body of finer looking recruits than Captain Magness now has at drill. All of the first families in the country, and of unquestionable courage and fidelity to their salt. He has four hundred Cavalry of what is called the *body guard*, men well dressed, and of fine appearance. These Cavalry are, however, likely soon to be taken from him and made over to some good for nothing Court favorite. He has about seven hundred men present with his Infantry corps. His adjutant, Yosuf Khan, speaks English well, and has travelled a good deal in England, Europe generally, and Palestine. He is a sensible unprejudiced man, and good soldier. Captain Magness attends the Nazim of the district; but, unfortunately, he, like all the other commandants of corps, and public servants of the State, is obliged to forage for fodder and fuel. A foraging party is sent out every day, be where they will, to take these things gratis, wherever they can find them most conveniently. Bhoosa, grass and wood, are the things which they are authorised to take, without payment, wherever they can find them; but they, of course, take a good many other things. The government allows nothing to any of its troops or establishments, for these things, except when they are in Lucknow. The consequence is, that there is hardly a good cover to any man's house, or sufficient fodder for the cattle of any village, during the hot season and rains.

December 27, 1849. – Halted at Pertabghur. I had a visit from many of the persons, who were in my service, when I was here, with my Regiment, thirty years ago, as watchmen, gardeners, &c. They continue to hold and till the lands, which they or their fathers then tilled; and the change in them is not so great, as that which has taken place within the same time, among my old native friends, who survive in the Saugor and Nerbudda districts,[a]

[a] Territories in central India which later formed part of the Central Provinces; the greater part came from cessions of territories by Maratha chiefs in 1817–18. Note that this was the area of Sleeman's initial civilian service in India.

where the air is less dry, and the climate less congenial to the human frame. The natives say, that the air and water of Malwa*ᵃ* may produce as good trees and crops as those of Oude, but can never produce such good soldiers. This, I believe, is quite true. The Sultanpoor district is included in the Banoda division of Oude; and the people speak of the *water* of this division for *tempering* soldiers, as we talk of the water of Damascus, for tempering sword blades. They certainly never seem so happy as when they are fighting in earnest with swords, spears and matchlocks. The *water* of the Byswara division is considered to be very little inferior to that of Banoda, and we get our sipahies from these two divisions almost exclusively.

Captain Magness's corps is, at present, attached to the Nazim of this district, with its guns, and squadron of horse, as an auxiliary force. Over and above this force, he has nine Regiments of Nujeebs, Detachments of other Corps, Artillery, Pioneers, &c., amounting, in all, according to the musters and pay drafts, to seven thousand seven hundred and seventy-eight men, for whom thirty-seven thousand seven hundred ninety-three rupees a month are drawn. Of these, fifteen hundred are dead or have deserted, or are absent on leave without pay. Their pay is all appropriated by the commandants of corps, or Court favorites. Fifteen hundred more are in attendance on the commandants of corps, who reside at the Capital, and their friends or other influential persons about the Court, or engaged in their own trades or affairs, having been put in to the corps by influential persons at Court, to draw pay, but do no duty. Of the remaining four thousand seven hundred and seventy-eight, one-third, or one thousand five hundred and ninety-two, are, what is called, *sufarishies*, or men who are unfit for duty, and have been put in by influential persons at Court, to appear at muster and draw pay. Of the remaining three thousand one hundred and eighty-six present, there would be no chance of getting more than two-thirds, or two thousand one hundred and twenty-four men, to fight on emergency – indeed, the Nazim would think himself exceedingly lucky, if he could get one-third to do so.

Of the forty-two guns, thirteen are utterly useless on the

ᵃ An area in central India over which the British gained supremacy in 1818.

117

ground; and out of the remaining twenty-nine, there are draft bullocks for only five. But there are no stores or ammunition for any of them; and the Nazim is obliged to purchase, what powder and ball he may require, in the bazars. None of the gun carriages have been repaired for the last twenty years, and the strongest of them would go to pieces after a few rounds. Very few of them would stand one round with good powder. Five hundred rupees are allowed for fitting up the carriage and tumbril of each gun, after certain intervals of from five to ten years; and this sum has, no doubt, been drawn over and over for these guns, during the twenty years, within which they have had no repairs whatever. If the local governor is permitted to draw this sum, he is sure never to expend one farthing of it on the gun. If the person, in charge of the ordnance at Lucknow, draws it, the guns and tumbrils are sent in to him, and returned with, at least, a coating of paint and putty, but seldom with any thing else. The two persons in charge of the two large parks at Lucknow, from which the guns are furnished, Anjum-od Dowlah, and Auces-od Dowlah, a fiddler, draw the money for the corn, allowed for the draft bullocks, at the rate of three pounds per diem for each, and distribute, or pretend to distribute, it through the agents of the grain dealers, with whom they contract for the supply; and the district officers, under whom these draft bullocks are employed, are never permitted to interfere. They have nothing to do but pay for the grain allowed; and the agents, employed to feed the bullocks, do nothing but appropriate the money for themselves and their employers. Not a grain of corn do the bullocks ever get.

The Nazim has charge of the districts of Sultanpoor, Haldeemow, Pertabghur, Jugdeespoor, and that part of Fyzabad, which is not included in the estate of Bukhtawar Sing, yielding, altogether, about ten and half lakhs of rupees to government. He exercises entire fiscal, judicial, magisterial and police authority, over all these districts. To aid him in all these duties, he has four deputies – one in each district – upon salaries of one hundred and fifty rupees each a month, with certain fees and perquisites. To inquire into particular cases, over all these districts, he employs a special deputy, paid out of his own salary.

All the accountants and other writers, employed under him, are appointed by the deputies and favorites of the minister; and, considering themselves as their creatures, they pay little regard to their immediate master, the Nazim. But over and above these men, from whom he does get some service, he has to pay a good many, from whom he can get none. He is, before he enters upon his charge, obliged to insert, in his list of civil functionaries, to be paid monthly, out of the revenues, a number of writers and officers, of all descriptions, *recommended* to him by these deputies and other influential persons at Court. Of these men he never sees or knows any thing. They are the children, servants, creatures, or dependants of the persons who recommend them and draw their pay. These are called *civil sufarishies*, and cost the State much more than the *military sufarishies*, already mentioned – perhaps not less than six thousand rupees a month in this division alone.

The Nazim is permitted to levy, for incidental expenses, only ten per cent over and above the government demand; and required to send one-half of this sum to Court, for distribution. He is ostensibly required to limit himself to this sum, and to abstain from taking the gratuities, usually exacted by the *revenue contractors*, for distribution among ministers and other influential persons at Court. Were he to do so, they would all be so strongly opposed to the *amanee*, or trust system of management, and have it in their power so much to thwart him, in all his measures and arrangements, that he could never, possibly, get on with his duties; and the disputes between them, generally, result in a compromise. He takes, in gratuities, something less than his contracting predecessors took, and shares, what he takes, liberally, with those whose assistance he requires at Court. These gratuities, or nuzuranas, never appeared in the public accounts; and were a governor, under the *amanee* system, to demand the full rates paid to *contractors*, the more powerful landholders would refer him to these public accounts, and refuse to pay till he could assure them of the same equivalents in *nanker* and other things, which they were in the habit of receiving from contractors. These, as a mere trust manager, he may not be able to give; and he consents to take something less. The

119

landholders know, that where the object is, to exact the means to gratify influential persons about Court, the Nazim would be likely to get good military support, if driven to extremity, and consent to pay the greater part of what is demanded. When the trust manager, by his liberal remittances to Court patrons, gets all the troops he requires, he exacts the full gratuities, and still higher and more numerous if strong enough.[1]

The system of government, under which Oude suffers during the reign of the best king, is a fearful one; and what must it be under a sovereign, so indifferent as the present is, to the sufferings of his people, to his own permanent interests, and to the duties and responsibilities of his high station. Seeing that our government attached much importance to the change, from the *contract* to the *trust* system of management, the present minister is putting a large portion of the country under that system, in the hope of blinding us. But there is, virtually, little or no change in the administration of such districts – the person who has the charge of a district under it, is obliged to pay the same gratuities to public officers and Court favorites, and he exacts the same, or nearly the same, from the landholders – he is under no more check than the contractor, and the officers and troops under him, abuse their authority in the same manner, and commit the same outrages upon the suffering people. Security to life and property is disregarded in the same manner; he confines himself as exclusively to the duties of collecting revenue; and is as regardless of security to life and property, and of fidelity to his engagements with the landholders in his jurisdiction. The trust management of a district differs from that of the contractors, only as the *wusoolee kubaz* differs from the *lakulamee* – though he does not enter into a formal contract to pay a certain sum, he is always

---

[1] The corps under Captains Magness, Bunbury, Barlow, and Subha Sing, are called *Komukee*, or auxiliary Regiments; and they are, every season, and sometimes, often in the same season, sold to the highest bidder, as a perquisite, by the minister. The services of Captain Magness and Captain Bunbury's corps were purchased, in this way, for 1850 and 1851, by Aga Allee, the Nazim of Sultanpoor, and he has made the most of them. No *contractor* ever exacted higher *nazuranas* or *gratuities* than he has, by their aid, this season, though he still holds the district as a trust manager. Ten, twenty, or thirty thousand rupees are paid for the use of one of these Regiments, according to the exigency of the occasion, or the time for which it may be required.

expected to pay such a sum, and if he does not, he is obliged to wipe off the balance in the same way, and is kept in jail till he does so, in the same way – indeed, I believe, the people would commonly rather be under a contractor, than a trust manager, under the Oude government, and this was the opinion of Colonel Low,[a] who, of all my predecessors, certainly knew most about the real state of Oude.

The Nazim of Sultanpoor has authority to entertain such Tehseeldars and *Jumogdars* as he may require, for the collection of the revenue. Of these he has, generally, from fifty to sixty employed, on salaries, varying from fifteen to thirty rupees a month each. The Tehseeldar is employed here, as elsewhere, in the collection of the land revenue, in the usual way; but the *Jumogdar* is an officer unknown in our territories. Some are appointed direct from Court, and some by the Nazims and Amils of districts. When a landholder has to pay his revenue direct to government (as all do, who are included in, what is called, the Hozoor Tehseel), and he neglects to do so punctually, a Jumogdar is appointed. The landholder assembles his tenants, and they enter into pledges to pay direct to the Jumogdar, the rents due by them to the landholder, under existing engagements, up to a certain time. This may be the whole, or less than the whole, amount due to government by the landholder. If any of them fail to pay, what they promise, to the Jumogdar, the landholder is bound to make good, the deficiency, at the end of the year. He also binds himself to pay to government, whatever may be due, over and above, what the tenants pledge themselves to pay to the Jumogdar. This transfer of responsibility, from the landholder to his tenants, is called '*Jumog Lagana*', or transfer of the jumma. The assembly of the tenants, for the purpose of such adjustment, is called *zunjeer bundee*, or linking together. The adjustment thus made, is called the *bilabundee*. The salary of the

[a] General Sir John Low (1788–1880): came to India in 1805; Resident with Baji Rao, the dispossessed Peshwa, at Bithur near Cawnpore from 1819 to 1825; Political Agent at Jaipur (1825) and then Gwalior (1830); Resident at Lucknow from 1831 to 1842; Agent to the Governor-General in Rajputana from 1848 to 1852; Resident at Hyderabad, 1852–3 and finally military member of the Governor-General's council from 1853 to 1858. See Low, *Fifty years with John Company*; also P. C. Gupta, *The last Peshwa and the English Commissioners 1818–1851* (Calcutta, 1944).

Jumogdar is paid by the landholder, who distributes the burthen of the payment upon his tenants, at a per centage rate. The Jumogdar takes written engagements from the tenants; and they are bound not to pay any thing to the landholder, till they have paid him (the Jumogdar), all that they are, by these engagements, bound to pay to him. He does all he can to make them pay punctually; but is not, properly, held responsible for any defalcation. Such responsibility rests with the landlords. Where much difficulty is expected from the refractory character of the landholder, the officer commanding the whole, or some part, of the troops, in the district, is often appointed the Jumogdar; and the amount, which the tenants pledge themselves to pay to him, is debited to him, in the pay of the troops, under his command. The Jumogdars, who are appointed by the Nazims and Amils, act in the same manner with regard to the landlords and tenants, to whom they are accredited, and are paid in the same manner. There may be one, or there may be one hundred, Jumogdars in a district, according to the necessity for their employment, in the collection of the revenue. They are generally men of character, influence, and resolution; and often useful to both, or all three parties; but when they are officers, commanding troops, they are often very burthensome to landlords and tenants. The Jumogdar has only to receive the sums, due, according to existing engagements, between the parties, and to see that no portion of them is paid to any other person. He has nothing to do with apportioning the demand, or making the engagements between tenants and landlords, or landlords and government officers.

The Canoongoes and Chowdheries in Oude, are commonly called Seghadars; and their duties are the same here as every where else in India.

December 28, 1849. – Twelve miles to Hundore, over a country more undulating, and better cultivated than any we have seen since we recrossed the Goomtee river at Sultanpoor. It all belongs to the Rajah of Pertabghur, Shumshere Bahadur, a Somebunsee, who resides at Dewlee, some six miles from Pertabghur. His family is one of the oldest and most respectable in Oude; but his capital of Pertabghur, where he used to reside till lately, is one of the most beggarly. He seems to have concentrated there all the beggars in the country; and there is not a house of any respectability to be seen. The soil, all the way, has been, what they call, the doomut, or doomuteea, which is well adapted to all kinds of tillage, but naturally less strong than muteear, or argillaceous earth, and yields scanty crops, where it is not well watered and manured.

The Rajah came to my camp in the afternoon, and attended me on his elephant in the evening, when I went round the town, and to his old mud fort, now in ruins, within which is the old residence of the family. He does not pay his revenue punctually, nor is he often prepared to attend the viceroy when required; and it was thought, that he would not come to me. Finding that the Korwar and other Rajahs, and large landholders, who had been long on similar terms with the local authorities, had come in, paid their respects, and been left free, he also ventured to my camp. For the last thirty years, the mutual confidence, which once subsisted between the government authorities and the great landholders of these districts, has been declining, and it ceased, altogether, under the last viceroy, Wajid Allee Khan, who appears to have been a man without any feeling of humanity or sense of honor. No man ever knew what he would be called upon to pay to government, in the districts under him; and almost all the respectable landholders prepared to defend, what they had, by force of arms; deserted their homes, and took to the jungles, with as many followers as they could collect and subsist as soon as he entered on his charge. The atrocities charged against him, and upon the best possible evidence, are numerous and great.

The country we have passed through to-day, is well studded with fine trees, among which the mhowa abounds more than usual. The parasite plant, called the bandha, or Indian mistletoe, ornaments the finest mhowa and mango trees. It is said to be a disease, which appears as the tree grows old, and destroys it if not cut away. The people who feel much regard for their trees, cut these parasite plants away; and there is no prejudice against removing them among Hindoos, though they dare not cut away a peepul tree, which is destroying their wells, houses, temples or tombs; nor do they, with some exceptions, dare to destroy a wolf, though he may have eaten their own children, or actually have one of them in his mouth. In all parts of India, Hindoos have a notion, that the family of a man, who kills a wolf, or even wounds it, goes soon to utter ruin; and so also the village, within the boundaries of which a wolf has been killed or wounded. They have no objection to their being killed, by other people, away from the villages; on the contrary, are very glad to have them so destroyed, as long as their blood does not drop on their premises. Some Rajpoot families in Oude, where so many children are devoured by wolves, are getting over this prejudice. The bandha is very ornamental to the fine mhowa and mango trees, to the branches of which it hangs suspended, in graceful festoons, with a great variety of colors and tints, from deep scarlet and green, to light red and yellow.

Wolves are numerous in the neighbourhood of Sultanpoor, and, indeed, all along the banks of the Goomtee river, among the ravines, that intersect them; and a great many children are carried off by them from towns, villages, and camps. It is exceedingly difficult to catch them, and hardly any of the Hindoo population, save those of the very lowest class, who live a vagrant life, and bivouac in the jungles, or in the suburbs of towns and villages, will attempt to catch or kill them. All other Hindoos have a superstitious dread of destroying or even injuring them; and a village community, within the boundary of whose lands a drop of wolf's blood has fallen, believes itself doomed to destruction. The class of little vagrant communities above mentioned, who have no superstitious dread of destroying any living thing, eat jackals and all kinds of reptiles, and catch all kinds of animals, either to feed upon them themselves, or to sell them to those who wish to keep or hunt them.

But it is remarkable, that they, very seldom, catch wolves, though they know all their dens, and could, easily, dig them out, as they dig out other animals. This is supposed to arise from the profit, which they make, by the gold and silver bracelets, necklaces and other ornaments, which are worn by the children, whom the wolves carry to their dens and devour, and are left at the entrance of their dens. A party of these men, lately brought to our camp, alive, a very large hyena, which was let loose and hunted down by the European officers, and the clerks of my office. One of the officers asked them, whether this was not the reason, why they did not bring wolves to camp, to be hunted down in the same way, since officers would give more for brutes that ate children, than for such as fed only on dogs or carrion. They dared not deny, though they were ashamed or afraid to acknowledge, that it was. I have myself, no doubt, that this is the reason, and that they do make a good deal, in this way, from the children's ornaments, which they find at the entrance of wolves' dens. In every part of India, a great number of children are, every day, murdered, for the sake of their ornaments, and the fearful examples that come daily to the knowledge of parents, and the injunctions of the civil authorities, are unavailing against this desire to see their young children decked out in gold and silver ornaments...[a]

[a] This subject interested Sleeman; see also the section on 'wolves nurturing children' (*JTKO*, vol. I, pp. 208–22) which is omitted here.

CHAPTER V

[Partabgarh and Baiswara 'districts', 29 December 1849– 7 January 1850]

[1852: I, 200] [1858: I, 223–4]

December 29, 1849. – Ten miles to Rampoor. Midway we passed over the border of the Sultanpoor district into that of Salone, whose Amil, Hoseyn Buksh, there met us with his *cortège*. Rampoor is the Residence of Rajah Hunmunt Sing, the Tallookdar of the two estates of Dharoopoor and Kalakunkur, which extend down to and for some miles along the left bank of the river Ganges. There is a fort in each of these estates, and he, formerly, resided in that of Dharoopoor, four miles from our present encampment. That of Kalakunkur is on the bank of the Ganges. The lands along, on both sides the road, over which we are come, are scantily cultivated, but well studded with good trees, where the soil is good for them. A good deal of it is, however, the poor oosur soil, the rest muteear, of various degrees of fertility...

[1852: I, 206–45] [1858: I, 230–71]

December 30, 1849. – Ten miles to Salone, over a pretty country, well studded with fine trees, and well tilled, except in large patches of oosur land, which occur on both sides of the road. The soil, doomateea, with a few short intervals of muteear. The Rajah of Pertabghur, and other great landholders of the Sultanpoor division, who had been, for some days, travelling with me; and the Nazim and his officers, took leave yesterday. The Nazim, Aga Allee, is a man of great experience in the convenances of Court and city life, and of some in revenue management, having long had charge of the estates, comprised in the 'Hozoor Tehseel', while he resided at Lucknow. He has good sense and an excellent temper, and his manners and deportment are courteous and gentlemanly. The Rajah of Pertabghur is a very stout and fat man, of average understanding. The rightful heir to the principality was Seorutun Sing, whom I have mentioned in my *'Rambles and Recollections'*, as a gallant young landholder, fighting, for his right, to the succession, while I was cantoned at Pertabghur in 1818.[a] He continued to fight, but in vain, as the revenue contractors were too strong for him. Gholam Hoseyn, the then Nazim, kept him down, while he lived, and Dursun Sing got him into his power by fraud, and confined him, for three years, in jail.

He died soon after his release, leaving one son, Rajah Dheer Sing, who still lives upon the portion of land which his father inherited. He has taken up the contest, for the right, bequeathed to him by his father; and his uncle, Golab Sing, the younger brother of Seoruttun, a brave, shrewd and energetic man, has been, for some days, importuning me for assistance. The nearest relations of the family told me, yesterday, that they were coerced, by the government authorities, into recognising the adoption of the present Rajah, though it was contrary to all Hindoo law and usage. Hindoos, they said, never marry into the same gote or family, and they never ought to adopt one of the relations of their wives, or a son of a sister, or any descendant in the female line, while there is one of the male line existing. Seoruttun Sing was the next heir in the male line; but the Rajah, having married a young girl in his old age, adopted, as his heir to the principality, her nearest relative, the present Rajah, who is of a different *gote*. The desire to keep the land, in the same family, has given rise to singular laws and usages, in all nations, in the early stages of civilization, when industry is confined, almost exclusively, to agriculture, and land is almost the only property valued. Among the people of the Himmaleh hills, as in all Sogdiana,[b] it gave rise to poly andry; and, among the Israelites and mahommedans, to the marriage of many brothers, in succession, to the same woman.

The Rajah of Dharoopoor, who resides at Rampoor, our last halting place, holds, as above stated, a tract of land, along the

[a] *R and R* (1915), p. 248.

[b] Part of the ancient Persian empire in central Asia between the Oxus and Jaxartes rivers, corresponding to the later emirate of Bukhara and the region of Samarkand.

left bank of the Ganges, called the Kalakunkur, in which he has lately built a mud fort, of reputed strength. He is a very sensible and active man, of pleasing manners. He has two grown up sons, who were introduced to me by him yesterday. The government authorities complain, of his want of punctuality, in the payment of his revenue; and he complains, with much more justice, of the uncertainty in the rate of the demand on the part of government, and its officers, or Court favorites, and in the character of the viceroys, sent to rule over them; but, above all, of the impossibility of getting a hearing at Court, when they are wronged and oppressed by bad viceroys. He went twice himself to Lucknow, to complain of grievous wrongs, suffered by him and his tenants, from an oppressive viceroy; but, though he had some good friends at Court, and among them Rajah Bukhtawar Sing, he was obliged to return without finding access to the sovereign, or his minister, or any one in authority over the viceroy. He told me:

that all large landholders, who had any regard for their character, or desire to retain their estates, and protect their tenants, were obliged to arm and take to their strongholds or jungles, as their only resource, when bad viceroys were sent – that if they could be assured, that fair demands only would be made, and that they would have access to authority, when they required to defend themselves from false charges, and to complain of the wrong doings of viceroys and their agents, none of them would be found in resistance against the government, since all were anxious to bequeath to their children a good name, as well as a good estate.

He promised punctual payment of his revenues to government, and strict obedience in all things, provided that the contractor did not enhance his demand upon him, as he now seemed disposed to do, in the shape of gratuities to himself and Court favorites. 'To be safe in Oude', he said, 'it is necessary to be strong; and prepared, always, to use your strength in resisting outrage and oppression, on the part of the king's officers.'

At Salone resides a holy mahommedan, Shah Puna Ata,[a] who is looked up to, with great reverence, by both mahommedans and Hindoos, for the sanctity of his character, and that of his ancestors, who sat upon the same religious *throne*, for throne his

[a] Cf. Butter, *Southern Districts of Oud'h*, p. 139.

simple mattress is considered to be. From the time that the heir is called to the *throne*, he never leaves his house, but stays at home, to receive homage, and distribute blessings and food to needy travellers of all religions. He gets from the king of Oude twelve villages, rent free, in perpetuity; and they are said to yield him twenty-five thousand rupees a year, with which he provides for his family, and for needy travellers and pilgrims. This eleemosynary endowment was granted, about sixty years ago, by the then sovereign, Asuf-od Dowlah. The lands had belonged to a family of Kumpureea Rajpoots, who were ousted for contumacy or rebellion, I believe. He was plundered of all he had, to the amount of some twenty thousand rupees, in 1834, during the reign of Nuseer-od Deen Hyder,[a] by Ehsan Hoseyn, the Nazim of Byswara and Salone, one of the sons of Sobhan Allee Khan, the then virtual minister; but some fifteen days after, he attacked the Tallookdar of Bhuderee, and lost his place in consequence. The popular belief is, that he became insane in consequence of the holy man's curses, and that his whole family became ruined from the same cause.

Bhuderee, which lies a few miles to the south of Salone, was then held by two gallant Rajpoot brothers, Jugmohun Sing and Bishonath Sing, the sons of Zalim Sing. In the month of October, A.D. 1832, Dhokul Sing got the contract of the district, and demanded, from Bhuderee, an increase of ten thousand rupees in its revenue. They refused to pay this increase. At the established rate they had always paid the government demand punctually, and been good subjects and excellent landlords. Dhokul Sing was superseded by Ehsan Hoseyn, in March, 1833; and he insisted upon having the increase of ten thousand. They refused to pay, and Ehsan Hoseyn besieged and attacked their fort in September. After defending themselves resolutely for five days, Bishonauth Sing consented to visit Ehsan Hoseyn, in his camp, on a solemn assurance of personal security; but he no sooner came to his tent than he was seized and taken to Rae Bareilly, the head-quarters, a prisoner, in the suite of the Nazim. He there remained confined, in irons, under charge of a wing of a Regiment, commanded by Mozim Khan, till February 1834, when

[a] Nasir-ud-din Haidar, reigned 1827–37.

he effected his escape, and went back to Bhuderee. In March, a large force was collected, with an immense train of artillery, to aid the Nazim, and he again laid siege to the fort. Having sent off their families before the siege began, and seeing, in the course of a few days, that they could not long hold out against so large a force, the two brothers buried eight out of their ten guns, left the fort at midnight with the other two, cut their way through the besiegers, and passed over a plain, six miles, to Ramchora, on the left bank of the Ganges, and within the British territory, followed by the whole of the Nazim's force.

A brisk cannonade was kept up, on both sides, the whole way, and a great many lives were lost. The two brothers thought they should be safe at Ramchora, under the protection of the British government; but the Nazim's force surrounded the place, and kept up a fire upon it. The brothers contrived, however, to send over the Ganges, the greater part of their followers, under the protection of their two guns, and the few men retained to defend and serve them. Jugmohun Sing at last consented to accept the pledge of personal security tendered by Rajah Seodeen Sing, the commander-in-chief of the attacking forces; but while he and his brother were on their way to the camp, with a few armed attendants, the soldiers of the Nazim, by whom they were escorted, attempted to seize and disarm them. They resisted and defended themselves. Others came to their rescue, and the firing recommenced. Jugmohun Sing, and his brother, Bishonath Sing, and all their remaining followers were killed. The two brothers lost about one hundred and fifty men, and the Nazim about sixty, in killed. The heads of the two brothers were taken off, forthwith, and sent to the king. Three villages, in the British territory, were plundered by the Oude troops on this occasion. This violation of our territory the king of Oude was called upon to punish; and Ehsan Hoseyn was deprived of his charge, and heavily fined, to pay compensation to our injured subjects.

Roshun-od Dowlah, the minister, was entirely in the hands of Sobhan Allee Khan; and, as long as he retained office, the family suffered no other punishment. When he, Roshun-od Dowlah, was, afterwards, deprived of office, he went to Cawnpore to reside, and Sobhan Allee and all his family were obliged to follow his fortunes. On his dismissal from office, Roshun-od Dowlah was put into jail, and not released till he paid twenty-two lakhs of rupees into the Treasury. He had given eight lakhs, in our Government promissory notes, to his wife, and three to his son, and he took some lakhs with him to Cawnpore, all made during the five years he held office. Sobhan Allee Khan, his deputy, was made to pay, into the Treasury, seven lakhs, and five in gratuities – all made during the same five years. Sobhan Allee died, last year, on a pilgrimage to Mecca, with the character of one of the ablest and least scrupulous of men; and his sons continue to reside at Cawnpore and Allahabad, with the character of having all the bad, without any of the good, qualities of their father. The widow of Jugmohun manages the estate, but she has adopted the nearest heir to her husband, the present Rajah of Bhuderee, a fine, handsome and amiable youth, of sixteen years of age, who is now learning Persian. He was one of the many chiefs, who took leave of me yesterday, and the most prepossessing of all. His adoptive mother, however, absorbs the estates of her weaker neighbours, by fraud, violence and collusion, like other landholders; and the dispossessed become leaders of gang robbers as in other parts.

The Shah receives something from the local authorities, and contributions from mahommedan Princes, in remote parts of India, such as Bhopal,[a] Seronge,[b] &c. &c. Altogether his income is said to amount to about fifty thousand rupees a year. He has letters from Governors General of India, Lieutenant Governors of the North Western Provinces and their Secretaries; and from Residents at the Court of Lucknow, all of a complimentary character. He has lately declared his eldest son to be his heir to the *throne*; and is said to have already put him upon it. I received from him the usual letter of compliments and welcome, with a present of a tame antelope, and some fruit and

---

[a] A state with an Indian ruler, in central India. Next to Hyderabad, Bhopal was the most important Muslim-ruled state in India; see *The Imperial Gazetteer of India*, [hereafter *IG*], 26 vols (London, 1908), vol. VIII, pp. 125–42.

[b] One of the three districts of the central Indian state of Tonk which was ruled by a Pathan prince. The first ruler, who acquired the state while a mercenary commander for the Maratha ruler, Jaswant Rao Holkar, had come from Moradabad district in Rohilkhand. *IG*, vol. XXII, pp. 408–9.

sugar; and I wrote him a reply in the usual terms. His name is Shah Puna Ata, and his character is held in high esteem by all classes of the people, of whatever creed, caste or grade.

The Bhuderee family give their daughters in marriage to the Bugheela Rajahs of Rewa,[a] and the Powar Rajahs of Ocheyra,[b] who are considered to be a shade higher in caste than they are among the Rajpoots. Not long ago they gave one hundred thousand rupees, with one daughter, to the only son of the Rewa Rajah, as the only condition on which he would take her. Golab Sing, the brother of Seoruttun Sing, of Pertabghur, by caste a Sombunsee, is said to have given, lately, fifty thousand rupees, with another daughter, to the same person. Rajah Hunmunt Sing, of Dharoopoor – who is, by caste, a Beseyn Rajpoot – the year before last went to Rewa, accompanied by some fifty brahmins, to propose an union between his daughter, and the same son of the Rewa Rajah. A large sum was demanded, but he pleaded poverty, and, at last, got the Rajah to consent to take fifty thousand rupees down, and seventy-five thousand at the last ceremony of the barat, or fetching home of the bride. When all had been prepared for this last ceremony, the Rajah of Rewa pleaded the heat of the weather, and his son would not come to complete it, and take away his bride. Hunmunt Sing collected one hundred *resolute brahmins*, and proceeded with them to Rewa, where they sat *dhurna* at the Rajah's door, without tasting food; and declared, that they would all die there unless the marriage were completed.

The Rajah did all he could, or could make his people do, to get rid of them; but, at last, afraid that some of the brahmins would really die, he consented that his son should go and fetch his bride, if Hunmunt Sing would pay down twenty-five thousand rupees more, to defray the cost of the procession, in addition to the seventy-five thousand. He did so, and his daughter was taken off in due form. He has another daughter to dispose of in the same way. The Rewa Rajah has thus taken five or six wives, for his son, from families a shade lower in caste; but the whole that

[a] A state in the Baghelkhand agency in central India; *IG*, vol. xxi, pp. 279–88.

[b] A state in the Sagar and Narbada territories (see above, p. 116, n. *a*) which was taken under direct British supervision in 1850 because of the incapacity of the ruler; Thornton, *Gazetteer*, vol. iii, pp. 786–7.

he has got with them, will not be enough to pay one of the Rajpoot families, a shade higher in caste than he is, in Rajpootana, to take one daughter from him. It costs him ten or twelve lakhs of rupees, to induce the Rajah of Oudeepoor, Joudhpoor, or Jypoor,[a] to take away, as his bride, a daughter of Rewa. All is a matter of bargain and sale. Those who have money must pay, in proportion, to their means, to marry their daughters, into families, a shade higher in caste or dignity; or to get daughters from them when such families are reduced to the necessity of selling their daughters to families of a lower grade.

Among brahmins it is the same. Take, for example, the Kunojee brahmins, among whom there are several shades of caste. The member of a family, a shade higher, will not give his son, in marriage, to a daughter of a family a shade lower, without receiving a sum, in proportion, to its means; nor will he give a *daughter* in marriage to such a family, till he is so exalted as to be able to disregard the feelings of his clan, or reduced to such a degree of poverty, as shall seem, to his clan, sufficient to justify it. This bargain and sale of sons and daughters prevails, more or less, throughout all Hindoo society, and is not, even now, altogether unknown among Christian nations. In Oude this has led to the stealing of young girls, from our own districts. Some men and women, from our districts, make a trade of it. They pretend to be of Rajpoot caste, and inveigle away girls from their parents, to be united, in marriage, to Rajpoots in Oude. They pretend to have brought them with the consent of their parents, of the same or higher caste, in our territories, and make large sums by the trade.

December 31, 1849. – Eight miles to Sotee, over a country well studded with trees, and generally well cultivated. The soil is, all the way, domuteea. The road, the greater part of the way, lies in the purgunnah of Nyne, held by Jugunnath Sing, a Kumpureea Rajpoot, and his nephew, and the collateral branches of their family. They have a belt of jungle, extending, for some

---

[a] Udaipur, Jodhpur and Jaipur: three of the most important of the Rajput states of Rajputana (now called Rajasthan). See *IG*, vol. xxiv, pp. 82–102; vol. xiv, pp. 179–98; and vol. xiii, pp. 382–99.

twelve miles, along the right bank of the Saee river, and on the right side of the road, and within from two to six miles from it, in some parts nearer, and in others more remote. Wild hogs, deer, neelgae, and wild cattle abound in this jungle, and do great injury to the crops in its vicinity. The peasantry can kill and eat the hogs and deer, but dare not kill or wound the wild cattle or neelgae. The wild cattle are said to be from a stock which strayed or were let loose in this jungle some centuries ago. They are described as fat, while the crops are on the ground, and well formed, some black, some red, some white, and some mixed, and to be as wild and active as the deer of the same jungle. They are sometimes caught by being driven into the Saee river, but the young ones are said to refuse all food, and die soon, if not released. Hindoos soon release them from the religious dread, that they may die in confinement. The old ones sometimes live, and are considered valuable. They are said to be finer in form than the tame cattle of the country; and, from July to March, when grass abounds, and the country around is covered, successively, with autumn and spring crops, more fat and sleek.

The soil is good and strong, and the jungle, which covers it very thick. It is preserved by a family of Kumpureea Rajpoots, whose whole possessions, in 1814, consisted of nine villages. By degrees they have driven out or murdered all the other proprietors, and they now hold no less than one hundred and fifty, for which they pay little or no revenue to government. The rents are employed in keeping up large bands of armed followers and building strong holds, from which they infest the surrounding country. The family has become divided into five branches, each branch having a fort or stronghold in the Nyn jungle, and becoming, by degrees, subdivided into smaller branches, who will thrive and become formidable, in proportion, as the government becomes weak. Each branch acts independantly in its depredations and usurpations from weaker neighbours; but all unite when attacked or threatened by the government.

Rajah Dursun Sing held the district of Salone, from 1827 to 1836; and, during this time, he made several successful attacks upon the Kumpureea Rajpoots of the Nyn jungle; and, during his occasional temporary residence, he had a great deal of the jungle, around his force, cut down; but he made no permanent arrangement for subduing them. In 1837, the government of this district was transferred to Kondon Lal Partak, who established a garrison in the centre of the jungle, had much of it cut down, and kept the Kumpureea barons effectively in check. He died in 1838, and Rajahs Dursun Sing and Bukhtawar Sing again got the government, and continued the *partaks* system, for the next five years, up to 1843. They lost the government for 1844 and 1845, but their successors followed the same system, to keep the Kumpureeas in order. Bukhtawar Sing got the government again for 1846 and 1847, and persevered in this system; but in 1848, the government was made over to Hamid Allee, a weak and inexperienced man. His deputy, Nourouz Allee, withdrew the garrison, and left the jungle to the Kumpureeas, who, in return, assigned to him three or four of their villages, rent free, in perpetuity, which, in Oude, means as long as the grantee may have the power or influence to be useful to the granters, or to retain the grants. Since that time the Kumpureeas have recovered all the lands they had lost, restored all the jungle that had been cut down, and they are now more powerful than ever. They have strengthened their old forts and built some new, and added greatly to the number of their armed followers, so that the governor of the district dares not do any thing to coerce them into the payment of the just demands of government, or to check their usurpations and outrages.

The present Nazim has with him two Nujeeb Regiments, one of nine hundred and fifty-five, and the other of eight hundred and thirty men; a squadron of horse and fourteen guns. The two corps are virtually commanded by fiddlers and eunuchs at Court. Of the men borne on the muster rolls and paid, not one half are present; of the number present, not one half are fit for the duties of soldiers; and of those fit for such duties, not one half would perform them. They get, nominally, four rupees a month, liable to numerous deductions – they are obliged to provide their own clothing, arms, accoutrements, and ammunition, except on occasions of actual fighting, when they are entitled to powder and ball from the government officer, under whom they are employed. He purchases powder in the bazars, or has it sent to him from

Lucknow; and, in either case, it is not more than one-third of the strength used by our troops. It is made in villages, and supplied to contractors, whose only object is to get the article at the cheapest possible rate; and that supplied to the most petted corps, is altogether unfit for service.

The arms, with which they are expected to provide themselves, are a matchlock and sword. They are often ten or twelve months in arrears, and obliged to borrow money for their own subsistence and that of their families, at twenty-four per cent interest. If they are disabled they have little chance of ever recovering the arrears of pay due to them; and if they are killed, their families have still less. Even the arms and accoutrements, which they have purchased with their own money, are commonly seized by the officers of government, and sold for the benefit of the State. Under all these disadvantages, the Nazim tells me, that he thinks it very doubtful whether any of the men of the two corps would fight at all on emergency. The cavalry are still worse off, for they have to subsist their horses, and if any man's horse should be disabled or killed, he would be at once dismissed with just as little chance of recovering the arrears of pay due to him. Of the fourteen guns, two only are in a state fit for service. Bullocks are provided for six, out of fourteen; but they are hardly able to stand from want of food, much less to draw heavy guns. I looked at them, and found that they had had no grain for many years, and very little grass or chaff, since none is allowed by government for their use, and little can be got by forage, or plunder, which is the same thing. One seer and half of grain, or three pounds, a day, for each bullock, is allowed and paid for by government; but the bullocks never get any of it. Of the six best guns, for which he has draft bullocks, the carriage of one went to pieces on the road yesterday, and that of another went to pieces, this-morning, in my camp, in firing the salute, and both guns now lie useless on the ground. He has one mortar, but only two shells for it; and he has neither powder nor ball for any of the guns. He was obliged to purchase, in the bazar, the powder required for the salute for the Resident.

The Nazim tells me, that he has entertained, at his own cost, two thousand Nujeebs or Seobundies, on the same conditions as those on which the others serve in the two Regiments, on duty under him – that is, they are to get four rupees a month each, and furnish themselves with food, clothing, a matchlock, sword, accoutrements and ammunition, except on occasions of actual fighting, when he is to provide them with powder and ball from the bazar. The minister, he tells me, promised to send him another Nujeeb corps – the Futteh Jung – from Khyrabad; but he has heard so bad an account of its discipline, that he might as well be without it. All the great landholders see the helpless state of the Nazim, and not only withhold from him the just dues of government, but seize upon and appropriate, with impunity, the estates of the small proprietors in their neighbourhood.

January 1, 1850. – Fourteen miles to Rae Bareilly, over a plain with more than usual undulation, and the same doomuteea light soil, tolerably cultivated, and well studded with trees of the finest kind. The festoons of the bandha hang gracefully from the branches, with their light green and yellow leaves, and scarlet flowers, in the dark green foliage of the mango and mhowa trees in great abundance. I saw them in no other, but they are, some-times, said to be found in the banyan, peepul and other trees, with large leaves, though not in the tamarind, babul and other trees, with small leaves. I examined those on the mango and mhowa trees, and they are the same in leaf and flower, and are said to be the same in whatever tree found. Rae Bareilly is in the estate of Shunkerpoor, belonging to Rana Benee Madho, a large landholder. He resides at Shunkurpoor, ten miles from this, and is strong, and not very scrupulous in the acquisition, by fraud, violence and collusion, of the lands of the small proprietors, in the neighbourhood. I asked Rajah Hunmunt Sing, of Dharoo-poor, as he was riding by my side, this-morning, whether he was not a man of bad character. He said – 'no, by no means, he is a man of great possessions, credit and influence, and of good repute.' But does he not rob smaller proprietors of their heredi-tary lands? 'If', replied the Rajah,

you estimate men's character, in Oude, on this principle, you will find hardly any landholder, of any rank, with a good one; for they have all been long doing the same thing – all have been augmenting their own estates by absorbing those of smaller proprietors, by what you will call fraud, violence, and collusion, but they are not thought the worse of for this by the government or its officers.

Nothing could be more true. Men who augment their estates in this way, purchase the acquiescence of temporary local officers, either by gratuities, or promises of aid in putting down other powerful and refractory landholders; or they purchase the patronage of Court favorites, who get their estates transferred to the 'Hozoor Tehseel', and their transgressions overlooked. Those who augment their resources in this way, employ them in maintaining armed bands, building forts, and purchasing cannon, to secure themselves in the possession; and to resist the government and its officers, who might, otherwise, make them pay in some proportion to their usurpations.

Benee Madho called upon me, after breakfast, and gave me the little of his history that I desired to hear. He is of the Byans Rajpoot clan, and his ancestors have been settled in Oude for about twenty-five generations, as landholders of different grades. The tallook, or estate, now belongs to him, and is considered to be a principality, to descend, entire, by the law of primogeniture, to the nearest male heir, unless the lands become divided during his life time, among his sons. Such a division has already taken place, as will be seen by the note below.[1]

The three and half shares held by his brothers and cousins, are liable to sub-division, by the Hindoo law of inheritance, or the custom of his family and clan; but his own share must descend, undivided, unless he divides it during his life time, or his heirs divide it during theirs; and consent to descend in the scale of landholders. He says, that during the five years, that Fakeer

[1] Abdool Sing, the Tallookdar of Shunkurpoor, had three sons; first, Doorga Buksh, to whom he gave three shares; second, Chundha Buksh, to whom he gave two shares; third, Bhowanee Buksh, to whom he gave one and half shares. The three shares of Doorga Buksh descended to his son, Sheopersaud, who died without issue. Chunda Buksh left two sons, Ramnaraen and Gor Buksh, Ramnaraen inherited the three shares of Sheopersaud, as well as the two shares of his father. He had three sons, Rana Benee Madho, Nirput Sing, and Jogray Sing, Benee Madho inherited the three shares, and one of the other two was given to Nirput Sing, and the other to Jogray Sing. Gorbuksh Sing left one son, Sheopersaud, who gets the one and half share of Bhowanee Buksh, whose son, Joorawun, died without issue. Benee Madho is now the head of the family; and he has more than quadrupled his three shares by absorptions, made in the way above mentioned.

Mahommed Khan was Nazim, a quarrel subsisted between him and the Tallookdar of Khujoor Gow, Rugonauth Sing, his neighbour – that Sahib Rae, the deputy of Fakeer Mahommed, who was himself no man of business, adopted the cause of his enemy, and persuaded his master to attack and rob him of all he had, turn him out of his estate, and make it over to Rugonath Sing. He went to Lucknow for redress, and remained there urging his claims for fourteen months, when he got an order from the minister, Ameen-od Dowlah, for the estate being restored to him, and transferred to the Hozoor Tehseel. He recovered his possessions, and the transfer was made; and he has, ever since, lived in peace. He might have added, that he has been, at the same time, diligently employed in usurping the possessions of his weaker neighbours.[1]

On our road, two miles from Rae Bareilly, we passed over a bridge, on the Saee river, built by *Reotee Ram*, the deputy of the celebrated eunuch, Almas Allee Khan, some sixty or seventy years ago. He, at the same time, planted an avenue of fine trees, from Salone to Rae Bareilly, twenty miles; and from Rae Bareilly to Dalamow, on the Ganges, south, a distance of fourteen miles more. Many of the trees are still standing and very fine; but the greater part have been cut down during the contests that have taken place between the government officers and the landholders, or between the landholders themselves. The troops in attendance upon local government authorities have, perhaps, been the greatest enemies to this avenue, for they spare nothing of value, either in exchange or esteem, that they have the power to take. The government and its officers feel no interest in such things, and the family of the planter has no longer the means to protect the trees, or repair the works.

Rae Bareilly is the head quarters of the local authorities in the Byswara district, and is considered to be one of the most healthy places in Oude. It is near the bank of the small river Saee, in a

[1] Benee Madho and Rugonath Sing have since quarrelled about the title of Rana. Benee Madho assumed the title, and Rugonath wished to do the same, but Benee Madho thought this would derogate from his dignity. They had some fighting, but Rugonath, at last, gave in, and Benee Madho purchased, from the Court, a recognition of his exclusive right to the title, which is a new one in Oude. They had each a force of five thousand brave men, besides numerous auxiliaries.

fine, open plain, of light soil; and must be dry at all seasons, as the drainage is good, and there are no jheels or jungles near. It would be an excellent cantonment for a large force; and position for large civil establishments. The town is a melancholy ruin, and the people tell me, that whatever landholder, in the district, quarrels with the local authorities, is sure as his first enterprise, to sack *Rae Bareilly*, as there is no danger in doing it. The inhabitants live so far from each other, and are separated by such heaps of ruins and deep water courses, that they can make no resistance. The high walls and buildings, all of burnt brick, erected in the time of Shahjehan,*a* are all gone to ruin. The plain, around the town, is open, level, well cultivated, and beautifully studded with trees. There is a fine tank, of puckah masonry, to the north-west of the town, built by the same Reotee Ram, and repaired by some member of his family, who holds and keeps in good order the pretty garden around it. The best place for a cantonment, courts, &c. is the plain which separates the town from the river Saee, to the south-east. They should extend along from the town to the bridge over the Saee river. The water of this river is said to be excellent, though not quite equal to that of the Ganges. There is good water in most of the wells, but in some it is said to be brackish. The bridge requires repair.

January 2, 1850. – We halted at Rae Bareilly, and I inspected the bullocks, belonging to the guns of Sobha Sing's Regiment, and some guns, belonging to the Nazim. The bullocks have been starved, are hardly able to walk, and quite unfit for any work. Some of the carriages of the guns are broken down, and those that are still entire, are so rotten, that they could not bear a march. This Regiment of Sobha Sing's was as good as any of those commanded by Captains Magness, Bunbury and Barlow, while commanded by the late Captain Buckley, and the native officers and sipahees, trained under him, are all still excellent; but they are not well provided. Like the others, this Regiment was to have had guns, permanently, attached to it, but the want of Court influence has prevented this. They now have them only when sent on service, from one or other of the batteries at

a Mughal emperor, reigned 1628–57.

Lucknow; and the consequence is, that they are good for nothing. Sobha Sing is at Court, in attendance on the minister, and his adjutant, Bhopull Sing, a near relative of the Rajah of Mynpooree,[a] commands. He seems to be a good soldier, and honest and respectable man.

The Nazim has with him this one *Komukee*, or auxiliary Regiment; and half of three Regiments of Nujeebs, amounting, according to the pay abstracts and muster rolls, to fifteen hundred men. He has one hundred Cavalry, and seven guns, of which one only is fit for use, and for that one he has neither stores, nor ammunition. He was obliged to purchase, in the bazar, the powder and cloth required to make up the cartridges, for a salute for the Resident. Of the fifteen hundred Nujeebs, not two-thirds are present, and of these hardly one-half are efficient. They are paid, armed, clothed and provided like the corps of Nujeebs, placed under the other local officers. The Tallookdars of the districts have not, as yet, presented themselves to the Nazim, but they have sent their agents, and, with few exceptions, shown a disposition to pay their revenues. The chief landholder, in the district, is Rambuksh, of Dondeea Kherah, a town, with a fort, on the bank of the river Ganges. He holds five of the purgunnahs as hereditary possessions; 1, Bhugwuntnuggur; 2, Dondeea Kherah; 3, Mugraen; 4, Punheen; 5, Ghutumpoor. The present Nazim has put all five under the management of government officers, as the only safe way to get the revenues, as Rambuksh is a bad paymaster. Had he not been so, as well to his *own retainers* as to the *king's officers*, the Nazim would not have been able to do this. It is remarked, as a singular fact, among Rajpoot landholders, that Rambuksh wants courage himself, and is too niggardly to induce others to fight for him with spirit. The last Nazim, Hamid Allee, a weak and inexperienced man, dared not venture upon such a measure, to enforce payment of balances.

He married the daughter of Fuzl Allee, the prime minister for fifteen months, during which time he made a fortune of some thirty or thirty-five lakhs of rupees, twelve of which Hamid

[a] Mainpuri district in the North-Western Provinces, the British–Indian province surrounding Oudh (later called Agra Province and linked with Oudh as the United Provinces of Agra and Oudh).

Allee's wife got. He was persuaded, by Gholam Allee, his deputy, and others, that he might aspire to be prime minister at Lucknow, if he took a few districts in farm, to establish his character and influence. In the farm of these districts, he has sunk his own fortune and that of his wife; and is still held to be a defaulter to the amount of some eighteen lakhs; and is now in jail. This balance he will wipe off in time, in the usual manner. He will beg and borrow to pay a small sum to the Treasury, and four times the amount in gratuities to the minister, and other persons, male and female, of influence at Court. The rest will be struck off as irrecoverable; and he will be released. He was a man respected at Delhi, as well on account of his good character as on that of his wealth; but he is here only pitied as an ambitious fool.

The wakeel, on the part of the king, with the Resident, has been uniting his efforts to those of Hoseyn Buksh, the present Nazim of Salone, to prevail upon Rajah Hunmunt Sing, the Tallookdar of Dharoopoor, to consent to pay an addition of ten or fifteen thousand rupees to the present demand of one hundred and sixteen thousand rupees a year, for his estate. He sturdily refused, under the assurance of the good offices of Rajah Bukhtawar Sing, who has, hitherto, supported him. Among other things, urged by him, to account for his inability to pay, is the obligation he is under to liquidate, by annual instalments, a balance due to Bukhtawar Sing himself, when he held the contract of the district many years ago. Bukhtawar Sing acknowledges the receipt of the instalments, and declares that they are justly due; but these payments are, in reality, nothing more than gratuities, paid for his continued good offices with the minister and Dewan. While Dursun Sing, and his brother, Bukhtawar, held the contract of Salone, the estate was put under management, and yielded one hundred and seventy-four thousand rupees a year, out of which they allowed a deduction, on account of nankar, or subsistence, of some twenty thousand. The Rajah and Bukhtawar Sing urge, that this was, for the most part, paid out of the property left by Byree Saul, to whom Himmut Sing succeeded; and that the estate can now be made to yield only one hundred and sixteen thousand, from which is to be deducted a nankar of forty thousand. They offer him a deduction of this forty thousand, out of a rent roll, rated at one hundred and thirty thousand; and threaten him with the vengeance of His Majesty if he refuses. He looks at their military force and smiles. The agents of all the Tallookdars, who are in attendance on the Nazim, do the same. They know, that they are strong, and see that the government is weak, and they cease to respect its rights and orders. They see, at the same time, that the government and its officers regard less the rights than the strength of the land-holders; and, from fear, favor the strong while they oppress and crush the weak.

January 3, 1850. – Gorbuksh Gunge, alias, Onae, fourteen miles. The soil of the country, over which we came, is chiefly a light doomuteea; but there is a good deal of what they call bhoor, or soil, in which sand superabounds. The greater part belongs to the estate of Benee Madho, and is admirably cultivated, and covered with a great variety of crops. The country is better peopled than any other part that we have seen since we recrossed the Goomtee. We passed through several villages, the people of which seemed very happy. But their habitations had the same wretched appearance – naked mud walls, with invisible mud coverings. The people told me, that they could not venture to use thatched or tiled roofs, for the king's troops, on duty with the local authorities, always took them away, when they had any. They were, they said, well secured from all other enemies; by their landlord. Bhopaul Sing, acting commandant of Sobha Sing's Regiment, riding with me, said,

Nothing can be more true than what the people tell you, sir; but the *Koomukee* Regiments, of which mine is one, have tents provided for them, which none of the Nujeeb and other corps have, and in consequence, these corps never take the choppers of the peasantry for their accommodations. The peasantry, however, always suffer, more or less, even from the Koomukee corps, sir, for they have to forage for straw, wood, fuel, bhoosa, &c., like the rest, and to take it wherever they can find it. When we have occasion to attack, or lay siege to a stronghold, all the roofs, doors and windows of the people are, of course, taken to form scaling ladders, batteries, &c.; and, it is lamentable, sir, to see the desolation created around, after even a very short siege.

Rajah Hunmunt Sing and Benee Madho were riding with me, and when we had passed through a large crowd of seemingly happy peasantry in one village, I asked Benee Madho (whose tenants they were), whether they would all have to follow his fortunes if he happened to take up arms against the government. 'Assuredly', said he, 'they would all be bound, in honor, to follow me, or to desert their lands at least.' And if they did not, I suppose you would deem it a *point of honor* to plunder them? 'That he assuredly would', said Rajah Hunmunt Sing; 'and make them the first victims'. And if any of them fell fighting on his side, would he think it a *point of honor* to provide for their families? 'That we all do', said he, 'they are always provided for, and taken the greatest possible care of.' And if any one is killed in fighting for the king? They did not reply to this question, but the adjutant, Bhopaul Sing, said, – 'his family would be left to shift for themselves – no one asks a question about them.' 'This', observed Rajah Bukhtawar Sing, 'is one of the great sources of the evil that exists in Oude. How can men be expected to expose their lives, when they know, that no care will be taken of their families, if they are killed or disabled.' It is the rule to give a disabled man one month's pay and dismiss him; and to give the family of any one killed in the service, two months' pay. But, though the king is charged for this, it is seldom that the wounded man, or the family of the killed, get any portion of it. On the contrary, the arrears of pay due, – which are, at all times, great, – are never paid to the disabled sipahee, or the family of the sipahee killed. If issued from the Treasury, they are appropriated by the commandants and their friends at Court; and the arms and accoutrements, which the deceased has purchased with his own money, are commonly sold for the benefit of the State, or its officers.

They mentioned that the family of the person who planted a mango tree, or grove, continued to hold it as their exclusive property in perpetuity; but, that the person who held the mhowa trees, was commonly expected to pay to the landlord, where there was one, and to the government officers, where there was not, a duty amounting to from four annas to two rupees a year, for each tree, according to its fruitfulness – that the proprietor often sold the fruit of one tree for twenty rupees the season. The fruit of one mango tree has, indeed, often been sold for a hundred rupees the season, where the mangoes are of a quality, much esteemed, and numerous. The groves and fine solitary trees, on the lands we have to-day passed through, are more numerous than usual; and the country being undulating and well cultivated, the scenery is beautiful; but, as every where else, it is devoid of all architectural beauty in works of ornament or utility – not even a comfortable habitation is any where to be seen. The great landholders live at a distance from the road, and in forts or strongholds.[a] These are generally surrounded by fences of living bamboos, which are carefully kept up as the best possible defence against attacks. The forts are all of mud, and when the walls are exposed to view they look ugly. The houses of the peasants, in the villages, are, for the most part, covered with mud, from which the water is carried off, by tubes of wood or baked clay, about two feet long. There are parapets around the roof, a foot or two high, so that it cannot be seen, and a village appears to be a mass of dead mud walls, which have been robbed of their thatched or tiled roofs. Most of the tubes, used for carrying off the water from the roofs, are the simple branches of the palm tree, without their leaves.

Among the peasantry, we saw a great many sipahees, from our Native Infantry Regiments, who have come home, on furlough, to their families. From the estate of Rajah Hunmunt Sing, in the Banoda district, there are one thousand sipahees in our service. From that of Benee Madho, in the Byswara district there are still more. They told us, that they and their families were very happy, and they seemed to be so; but Hunmunt Sing said, they were a privileged class, who gave much trouble and annoyance, and were often the terror of their non-privileged neighbours and co-sharers in the land. Benee Madho, as I have stated above, sometimes makes use of his wealth, power, and influence, to rob his weaker neighbours, of their estates. The lands, on which we are encamped, he got two years ago from their proprietor, Futteh Bahader, by foreclosing a mortgage, in which he and others had involved him. The gunge or

[a] See Appendix 1 below for some details of these forts and jungles.

bazar, close to our tents, was established by Gorbuksh, the uncle of Futteh Bahader, and became a thriving emporium, under his fostering care; but it has gone to utter ruin under his nephew, and heir, and the mortgagee. The lands around, however, could never have been better cultivated than they are; nor the cultivator better protected, or encouraged. It rained slightly, before sunset, yesterday, and heavily, between three and four this-morning; but not so as to prevent our marching.

This-morning, a male elephant, belonging to Benee Madho, killed one of his attendants near to our camp. He had three attendants, the driver and two subordinates. The driver remained in camp, while the two attendants took the elephant to a field of sugar cane, to bring home a supply of the cane, for his fodder for the day. A third subordinate had gone on to cut the cane and bind it into bundles. One of the two was on the neck of the elephant, and another walking, by the side, holding one of the elephant's teeth in his left hand, all the way to the field, and he seemed very quiet. The third attendant brought the bundles, and the second handed them up to the first on the back to be stowed away. When they had got up about a dozen, the elephant made a rush at the third attendant, who was bringing the bundles, threw him to the ground with his foot, knelt down upon him, and crushed him to death with his front. The second attendant ran off as soon as he saw the elephant make a rush at the third; and the first fell off under the bundles of sugar cane, as soon as the elephant knelt down to crush the third to death. When the elephant rose from the poor man, he did not molest, or manifest any wish to molest, either of the other two, but stood still, watching the dead body. The first, seeing this, ventured to walk up to him, to take him by the ear, and ask him what he meant. At first he seemed surly, and shoved the man off, and he became alarmed, and retired a few paces; but seeing the elephant show no further signs of anger, he again walked up, and took him by the ear familiarly. Had he ran or shown any signs of fear, the elephant would, he thought, have killed him also, for he had killed three men, in the service of his former proprietor, and was now in his annual fit of madness, or *must*. Holding the elephant by the ear, he led him to the first tree, and placed himself on the opposite side to see whether the animal had become quite sober. Seeing that he had, he again approached, and put upon his two fore legs the chain fetters, which they always have with them, suspended to some part of the body of elephants in this state. He could not venture to command the elephant to kneel down in the usual way, that he might get upon his neck; and, ascending the tree, he let himself down from one of the branches upon his back, where he sat. He then made the animal walk on, in fetters, towards camp; and, on the way, met the mahout, or driver, to whom the second attendant had reported the accident. The driver came up, and, after the usual volume of abuse on the elephant, his mother, father, and sundry female relations, he ordered the attendant to make him sit down that he might get on his neck. He did so in fear and trembling, and the driver got on his neck, while the attendant sat on his back, and the elephant took them to Benee Madho's village, close to my camp, where he was fastened, in chains, to a tree, to remain, for some months, on reduced allowances, till he should get over his madness. The body of the poor man was burnt with the usual ceremonies, and the first attendant told me, that his family would be provided for by Benee Madho, as a matter of course. I asked him how he or any other person could be found, to attend a beast of that kind. Pointing to his stomach, he said – 'We, poor people, are obliged to risk our lives, for this, in all manner of ways, – to attend elephants has been always my profession, and there is no other open to me; and we make up our minds to do whatever our duties require from us, and trust to Providence.' He told me that when the elephant shoved him off, he thought that in his anger, he might have forgotten him, and called out as loud as he could, – 'What, have you forgotten a service of six years, and do you intend to kill the man who has fed you so long.' That the beast seemed to recollect his voice and services, and became, at once, quiet and docile – 'that had he not so called out, and reminded the animal of his long services, he thought he should have been killed – that the driver came, armed with a spear, and showed himself more angry than afraid, as the safest plan in such cases.'

January 4, 1850. – Halted at the village of Onae, alias, Gorbuksh Gunge. It lost the name of Onae, after the proprietor, Gorbuksh who had built the Gunge, and made it a great emporium of trade in corn, cotton-cloth, &c. &c.; but is recovering it again, now that the Gunge has become a ruin, and the family of the builder has been dispossessed of the lands. I rode out in the morning to look at the neighbouring village of Doolarae-ka Gurhee, or the fort of Doolarae, and have some talk with the peasantry, who are Bys Rajpoots, of one of the most ancient Rajpoot families in Oude. They told me,

That their tribe was composed of two great families, Nyhussas and Synbunsies – that the acknowledged head of the Synbunsies was, at present Rugonath Sing, of Kojurgow, and that Hindpaul, Tallookdar of Korree Sudowlee, was the head of the Nyhussas; that Baboo Rambuksh, Tallookdar of Dhondeea Kheera, had the title of Row, and Dirg Bijee Sing, Tallookdar of Morarmow, that of Rajah – that is, he was the acknowledged Rajah of the clan, and Baboo Rambuksh, the Row, an inferior grade – that these families had been always fighting with each other, for the possession of each other's lands, from the time their ancestors came into Oude, a thousand years ago, except when they were united in resistance against the common enemy, the governor or ruler of the country – that one family got weak by the subdivision of the lands, among many sons or brothers, or by extravagance, or misfortune, while another became powerful, by keeping the lands undivided, and by parsimony and prudence; and the strong increased their possessions by seizing upon the lands of the weak, by violence fraud or collusion with the local authorities – that the same thing had been going on among them for a thousand years, with some brief intervals, during which the rulers of Oude managed, by oppression, to unite them all against themselves, or by prudence, to keep them all to their respective rights and duties – that Doolarae, who gave his name to the village, by building the fort, was of the Nyhussa family, and left two sons, and only two villages, Gurhee and Agoree, out of a very large estate, the rest having been lost, in the contests, with the other families of the tribe – that these two had become minutely subdivided among their descendants; and Bhugwan Das, Synbunsee, of Simree, four years ago, seized upon the Gurhee, in collusion with the local authorities; that Thakoor Buksh Nyhussa, Tallookdar of Rahwa, seized upon Agoree, in the same way – that the local authorities, designedly, assessed these villages, at a higher rate than they could be made to pay, and then, for a bribe, transferred them to the powerful Tallookdars, on account of default.

Gorbuksh Sing, Synbunsee, died some twenty years ago, leaving an estate, reduced from a greater number, to ninety

Diary of a Tour Through Oude

three villages. His nephew, Futteh Bahader, a child, was adopted by his widow, who continued to manage the whole till she died, four years after. The heir was still a boy; and Rugonath Sing, of Kajurgow, the head of the Synbunsee family, took advantage of his youth, seized upon the whole ninety three villages, and turned him out to beg subsistence among his relatives. In this he, Rugonath Sing, was, as usual, acting in collusion with the local authorities of the government. He continued to possess the estate for ten years, but to reside in his fort of Hajeepoor. Koelee Sing, a Guhlote, by caste, and a zumeendar of Bheeturgow, and its eight dependant villages, which formed part of the estate of Futteh Bahader, went to Court at Lucknow, and represented, that Rugonath Sing had no right whatever to the lands he held, and the Court had better make them over to him and the other zumindars, if they did not like to restore them to their rightful heir. Bheeturgow and its dependant eight villages, were made over to him; and ten sipahees, from Capt. Hyder Hearsey's Regiment, were sent to establish and support him in possession. Rugonath attacked them, killed two of the sipahees, and drove out Koelee Sing. He repaired to Court; and Mahomed Khan was sent out, as Special Commissioner, with orders to punish Rugonath Sing. He and Captain Hearsey attacked him in his fort of Hajeepoor, drove him out, and restored Futteh Bahader, to twenty-four villages; and reestablished Koelee Sing, in Bheeturgow, and the eight villages dependant upon it. Futteh Bahader was poor, and was obliged to tender the security of Benee Madho, the wealthy Tallookdar of this place, for the punctual payment of the revenue. The year before last, when a balance of revenue became due, he, the deputy, in collusion with Gholam Allee, seized upon all the twenty-four villages.

Futteh Bahader went to seek redress at Lucknow, but had no money to pay his way at Court, while Benee Madho had abundance, and used it freely, to secure the possession of so fine an addition to his estate. Futteh Bahader, as his last resource, got his uncle, Bustee Sing, of the 3d Cavalry, whom he called his father,[1] to present a petition, for redress, to the Resident, in

[1] He called Bustee Sing his *father*, as sipahees can seek redress through the Resident, for wrongs suffered by no others than their mothers, fathers, their children and themselves.

Diary of a Tour Through Oude

April, 1849. Gholam Allee was ordered to release Futteh Bahader, whom Benee Madho had confined, and send him to Lucknow. The order was not obeyed, and it was repeated in December, without effect; but his uncle's agent, Gorbuksh, was diligent at the Residency, and the case was made over, for investigation and decision, to the Ameen, Mahomed Hyat. Finding Futteh Bahadur still in confinement, with sundry members of his family, when I came here yesterday, I ordered him to be made over to the king's wakeel, in attendance upon me, to be sent to the Court, to prosecute his claim, and produce proofs of his right. Of his right there can be no question, and the property, of which he was robbed, in taking possession, and the rents, since received, if duly accounted for, would more than cover any balance, due by Futteh Bahader. When he gave the security of Benee Madho, for the payment of the revenue, he gave, at the same time, what is called, the Jumog of his villages to him; that is, bound his tenants to pay to him their rents, at the rate they were pledged to pay to him; and the quesion pending is, simply, what is fairly due to Benee Madho, over and above what he may have collected from them. Benee Madho had before, by the usual process of violence, fraud, and collusion, taken eighteen of the ninety-three villages, and got one for a servant; and all the rest had, by the same process, got into the possession of others; and Futteh Bahader had not an acre left when his uncle interposed his good offices with the Resident.[1] The dogs of the village of Doolarae-kee Gurhee followed us towards camp, and were troublesome to the horses and my elephant. I asked the principal zumeendar, why they were kept. He said they amused the children of the village, who took them out after the hares, and by their aid and that of the sticks, with which they armed themselves, they got a good many; that all they got for food, was the last mouthful of every man's dinner, which no man was sordid enough to grudge them – that when they wished to describe a very sordid man, they said – 'he would not even throw his last mouthful (koura) to a dog!'

[1] A punchaet was assembled at Lucknow, to decide the suit between Benee Madho and Futteh Bahader, at the instance of the Resident; and they awarded to Benee Madho, a balance due on account, of thirty thousand rupees which Futteh Bahader has to pay before he can recover possession of his estate.

Diary of a Tour Through Oude

January 5, 1850.[a] – Halted at Onae, in consequence of continued rain, which incommodes us, but delights the landholders and cultivators, whose crops will greatly benefit by it. The halting of so large a camp inconveniences them, however, much more than us; for they are called upon to supply us with wood, grass and straw, for which they receive little or no payment; for the king's people will not let us pay for these things, and pay too little themselves. Those who attend us, do not plunder along the road; but the followers of the local authorities, who attend us, through their respective jurisdictions, do so; and sundry fields of fine carrots, and other vegetables, disappear, as under a flight of locusts along the road. The camp followers assist them, and as our train extends from the ground we leave to that to which we are going, for twelve or fourteen miles, it is impossible, altogether, to prevent such injuries from so undisciplined a band. The people, however, say, they suffer much less than they would from one-fourth of the number under a contractor, marching without an European superior, and I give compensation in flagrant cases. Captain Weston acts as our provost marshall. He leaves the ground an hour or two after I do, and seizes and severely punishes any one found trespassing.

In my ride, this-morning, I found, that Nyhussa and Synbunsee are two villages, distant about ten miles from our camp, to the south-east – that all the Byses, who give the name of Byswara, to this large district, are called Tillokchundees, from Tilok-chund, the founder of the family in Oude. He had two sons, *Hurhur Deo* and *Prethee Chund*. Hurhur Deo had two sons, one of whom, Kurun Rae, established himself in Nyhussa, and the other, Khem Kurun, in Synbunsee. Their descendants have taken their titles from their respective villages. Prethee Chund's descendants established themselves in other parts, and the descendants of both bear the appellation of Tilokchundee Byses. The Rajahs and Rows are of the same family, and are so called from their ancestors having, at some time, had the title of Rajah and Row conferred upon them.

Rajah Seodursun Sing, of Simrotee, who resides in the village of Chundapoor upon his estate, four miles east of Bulla, has been

[a] The year is given incorrectly as 1851 in the original.

151

with me for the last five days. He is a strong man, and has been refractory occasionally; but, at present, he pays his revenue punctually, and keeps his estate in good order. He rendered good service yesterday in the way, in which all of his class might, by good management, be made to aid the government of Oude. A ruffian, by name, Mohiboollah, who had been a trooper in the king of Oude's service, contrived to get the lease of the estate of Bulla, which is about twenty miles, north-east, from our camp; and, turning out all the old landholders and cultivators, he there raised a gang of robbers, to plunder his neighbours and travellers. He had been only two months in possession, when he attacked the house of an old invalid subadar-major of the Honourable Company's service, (fifty-seventh Native Infantry,) on the 21st of December, 1849, robbed him of all he had, and confined him and all his family, till he promised, under good security, to pay, within twenty days, a ransom of one thousand two hundred rupees more. He had demanded a good deal more, but hearing that the Resident's camp was approaching he consented to take this sum four days ago, and released all his prisoners. The subadar presented a petition to me, and, after taking the depositions of the old zumeendars and other witnesses, I requested the king's wakeel, to send off a Company of Soubha Sing's Regiment, to arrest him and his gang.

They went off from Rae Bareilly, on the night of the 1st instant; but, finding that the subadar-major and his family had been released the day before, and that the village was full of armed men, ready to resist, they returned on the evening of the 2d. On the 3d, the whole Regiment, with its Artillery, and three hundred auxiliaries, under Rajah Seodursun Sing, left my camp, at Onae, at midnight, and before day light surrounded the village. There were about one hundred and fifty armed men in it; and after a little bravado, they all surrendered, and were brought to me. Mohiboollah had, however, gone off, on the pretence of collecting his rents, two days before; but his father and brother were among the prisoners. All who were recognized as having been engaged, in the robbery, were sent off prisoners to Lucknow, and the rest were disarmed and released.

Among those detained, were some notorious robbers, and the

gang would soon have become very formidable,. but for the accident of my passing near. He had got the lease of the estate through the influence of Akber-od Dowlah, one of the Court favorites, for the sole purpose of converting it into a den of robbers; and, the better to secure this object, he had got it transferred from the jurisdiction of the Nazim to the Hozoor Tehseel, over the manager of which the Court favorite had paramount influence. He was to share with his client the fruits of his depredations, and, in return, to secure him impunity for his crimes. Many of his retainers were among the prisoners, brought in to me, having been present at the distribution of the large booty acquired from the old subadar, some thirty or forty thousand rupees. The subadar had resided upon the estate of Seodursun Sing, but having, seven years ago, complained through the Resident, of over exactions, for the small patch of land he held, and got back the grain, which had been attacked for the rent, he was obliged to give it up, and reside in the hamlet he afterwards occupied near Bulla, whose zumeendars assured him of protection.[1] He had a large family, and a great deal of property in money and other valuables, concealed under ground. Mohiboollah first seized and sent off the subadar, and then had ramrods made red hot, and applied to the bodies of the children, till the females gave him all their ornaments, and pointed out to him all the hidden treasures. They were then all taken to Bulla and confined, till the subadar had pledged himself to pay the ransom demanded. I requested the king to take the estate from this ruffian, and restore it to its old proprietors, whose family had held it for several centuries, or bestow it, in lease, to some other strong and deserving person.

The Tilokchundee Byses take the daughters of other Rajpoots, who are a shade lower in caste, in marriage for their sons, but do not give their daughters, in marriage, to them in return. They have a singular notion, that no snake ever has destroyed

---

[1] The greater part of this property is understood to have been confided, in trust, to the old subadar, by some other minion of the Court, and the chief object of the gang was to get hold of it; as their patron, Akber-od Dowlah, had become aware, that his fellow minion had entrusted his wealth to the old subadar, after he had taken up his residence near Bulla. The estate was made over, in farm, to Benee Madho, as the best man to cope with Mohiboollah, should he return and form a new gang.

or ever can destroy one of the family, and seem to take no precautions against its bite. If bitten by a snake, they do not attempt any remedy, nor could Benee Madho recollect any instance of a Tilokchundee Bysee having died from a bite. He tells me, that some families, in every Rajpoot tribe in Oude, destroy their female infants, to avoid the cost of marrying them, though the king prohibited infanticide and suttee, in the year 1833. That infanticide does still prevail among almost all the Rajpoot tribes in Oude, is unquestionable.

January 6, 1850. – Yesterday evening we moved to Morowa, west, a distance of twelve miles, over a plain of bad oosur soil, scantily cultivated near the road. To the left and right of the road, at a little distance, there are some fine villages, thickly peopled, and situated in fine and well cultivated soil. The country is well wooded, except in the worst parts of the soil, where trees do not thrive. We saw a great deal of sugar cane in the distance, and a few pawn gardens. The population of the villages came to the high road to see us pass; and among them were a great many native officers and sipahees of our Regiments, who are at their homes, on furlough, Government having given a very large portion of the native army the indulgence of furlough, during the present cold season. They all seemed happy; but, to my discomfort, a vast number take advantage of this furlough, and my movements, to urge their claims against the government, its officers, and subjects. Nothing can be more wretched than the appearance of the buildings, in which the people of all grades live in these villages – mud walls without any appearance of coverings, and doors and windows worse than I have seen in any other part of India. Better would not be safe against the king's troops, and these would, certainly, not be safe against a slight storm – a good shower and a smart breeze, would level the whole of the villages with the ground, in a few hours. But, said the people, – 'the mud would remain, and we could soon raise up the houses again, without the aid of masons, carpenters, or blacksmiths'. It is enough that they are used to them.

Morowa is a large town, well situated and surrounded with groves of the finest trees, in great variety; and, to the surprise of the officers with me, they saw a respectable house, of burnt brick. It belongs to the most substantial banker and agricultural capitalist in these parts, *Chundun Lal*. These capitalists and their families are, generally, more safe than others, as their aid is necessary to the government and its officers, and no less so to the landholders, cultivators and people of all classes. Their wealth consists in their credit in different parts of India; and he who has most of it, may have little at his house to tempt the robber, while the government officers stand generally too much in daily need of his services and mediation to molest him. A pledge made by these officers to landholders and cultivators, or to these officers, by such persons, is seldom considered safe or binding, till the respectable banker or capitalist has ratified it by his mediation, to which all refer with confidence.

He understands the characters and means of all, and will not venture to ratify any pledge till he is assured of both the disposition and ability of the party to fulfil it. Chundun Lal is one of the most respectable of this class in Oude. He resides at this place, Morowa, but has a good landed estate in our territories, and banking establishments at Cawnpoor, and many other of our large stations. He is a very sensible, well informed man, but not altogether free from the failing of his class, a disposition to abuse the confidence of the government officers; and, in collusion with them, to augment his possessions in land, at the cost of his weaker neighbours. I am told here that the Tilokchund Byses, when bitten by a snake, do, sometimes, condescend to apply a remedy. They have a vessel full of water suspended above the head of the sufferer, with a small tube at the bottom, from which water is poured, gently, on the head, as long as he can bear it. The vent is then stopped till the patient is equal to bear more; and this is repeated four or five times, till the sufferer recovers. I have not yet heard of any one dying under the operation, or from the bite of a snake. I find no one that has ever heard of a member of this family dying of the bite of a snake. One of the Rajahs of this family, who called on me to-day, declared, that no member of this family had ever been known to die of such a bite; and he could account for it only 'from their being descended from Salbahun, the rival and conquerer of Bickermajeet, of

155

Ojein'.[a] This Salbahun[1] is said to have been a lineal descendant of the *snake-god*! He told me, that the females of this family could never wear cotton cloth of any colour but plain white – that when they could not afford to wear silk or satin, they never wore any thing but the piece of white cotton cloth, which formed, in one, the waist band, petticoat and mantle, or robe, (the dhootee and loongree,) without hemming or needle work of any kind whatever. Those who can afford to wear silk or satin, wear the petticoat and robe, or mantle, of that material, and of any colour. On their ankles, they can wear nothing but silver; and above the ankles, nothing but gold; and if not, nothing, not even silver, except on the feet and ankles. No Hindoo, of respectability, however high or wealthy, can wear any thing more valuable than silver, below the waist. The Tilokchundee Byses can never condescend to hold the plough; and, if obliged to serve, they enlist in the army or other public establishments of the Oude or other States...[2]

[1852: I, 247–50] [1858: I, 273–6]

January 7, 1850. – To Mirree, twelve miles, over a plain of light doomuteea soil, sufficiently cultivated, and well studded with trees. We passed Runjeet-ka Poorwa, half way – once a large and populous town, but now a small one. The fog was, however, too thick to admit of my seeing it. From this place to Lucknow, thirty miles, Seetlah Buksh, a deputy of Almas Allee Khan's, planted an avenue of the finest kind of trees. We had to pass through a mile of it, and the trees are in the highest perfection, and complete on both sides. I am told, that there are, however, many considerable intervals, in which they have been destroyed. The trees must have been planted about sixty years ago.

[1] Salbahan must have been one of the leaders of the Scithian armies, who conquered India, in the reign of Vickramadittea.

[2] The ground, on the north-west side of Morowa, would be good for a cantonment, as the soil is sandy, and the plain well drained. Water must lie during the rains on all the other sides, and the soil has more clay in it.

[a] The identification of Vikramaditya of Ujjain, who is reputed to have defeated the Sakas (or Scythians), remains obscure. See A. L. Basham, *The Wonder that was India* (London, 1954), p. 65.

Diary of a Tour Through Oude

I may here remark, that no native gentleman from Lucknow, save such as hold office in districts, and are surrounded by troops, can, with safety, reside in the country. He would be either suspected and destroyed by the great landholders around him, or suspected and ruined by the Court. Under a better system of government, a great many of these native gentlemen, who enjoy hereditary incomes, under the guarantee of the British Government, would build houses in distant districts, take lands and reside on them with their families, wholly or occasionally, and Oude soon be covered with handsome gentlemen's seats, at once ornamental and useful. They would tend to give useful employment to the people, and become bonds of union between the governing and the governed. Under such an improved system, our guarantees would be of immense advantage to the whole country of Oude, in diffusing wealth, protection, education, intelligence, good feeling, and useful and ornamental works. At present these guarantees are not so. They have concentrated at the Capital all who subsist upon them, and surrounded the sovereign and his Court, with an overgrown aristocracy, which tends to alienate him more and more from his people. The people derive no benefit from, and have no feeling or interest in common with, this city aristocracy, which tends more and more to hide their sovereign from their view, and to render him less and less sensible of his duties and high responsibilities; and what would be a blessing under a good, becomes an evil under a bad system, such as that which has prevailed since those guarantees began.

In this overgrown city, there is a perpetual turmoil of processions, illuminations, and festivities. The sovereign spends all that he can get in them, and has not the slightest wish to perpetuate his name by the construction of any useful or ornamental work beyond its suburbs. All the members of his family, and of the city aristocracy, follow his example, and spend their means in the same way. Indifferent to the feelings and opinions of the landed aristocracy, and people of the country, with whom they have no sympathy, they spend all that they can spare for the public, in gratifying the vitiated tastes of the overgrown metropolis. Hardly any work, calculated to benefit or gratify the people of the country, is formed or thought of by the members of the royal family or aristocracy or Lucknow; and the only one formed, by the sovereign, for many years is, I believe, the metalled road, leading from Lucknow to Cawnpoor on the Ganges.

One good these guarantees certainly have effected. They have tended greatly to inspire the people of the city with respect for the British Government, by whom the incomes of so large and influential a portion of the community and their dependants, are secured. That respect extends to its public officers and to Europeans generally; and in the most crowded streets of Lucknow, they are received with deference, courtesy and kindness, while in those of Hydrabad, their lives, I believe, are never safe without an escort from the Resident.

The people of the country respect the British Government, its officers, and Europeans generally, from other causes. Though the Resident has not been able to secure any very substantial or permanent reform in the administration, still he has often interposed with effect, in individual cases, to relieve suffering, and secure redress for grievous wrongs. The people of the country see, that he never interposes except for such purposes; and their only regret is, that he interposes so seldom; and that his efforts, when he does so, should be so often frustrated or disregarded. In the remotest village or jungle in Oude, as in the most crowded streets of the Capital, an European gentleman is sure to be treated with affectionate respect! and the humblest European is as sure to receive protection and kindness, unless he forfeits all claim to it by his misconduct.

The more sober-minded mahommedans of Lucknow and elsewhere are much scandalized at the habit which has grown up among them in the cities of India, of commemorating every event, whether of sadness or of joy, by brilliant illuminations and splendid processions, to amuse the idle populations of such cities. It is, they say, a reprehensible departure from the spirit of their creed, and from the simple tastes of the early mahommedans, who laid out their superfluities in the construction of great and durable works of ornament and utility. Certainly no event can be more sorrowful among mahommedans than that which is commemorated in the mohurrum, by illuminations and processions with the Tazeeas, and yet no illuminations are more brilliant, and no processions more noisy, costly and splendid. It is worthy of remark, that Hindoo Princes, in central and southern India, even of the brahmin caste, commemorate this event in the same way; and, in no part of India, are these illuminations and processions more brilliant and costly. Their object is solely to amuse the population of their Capitals, and to gratify the mahommedan women, whom they have under their protection, and their children, who must all be mahommedans.

CHAPTER VI

[Baiswara and Sundeela 'districts',
8–17 January 1850]

[1852: i, 251–9] [1858: i, 277–86]

January 8, 1850. – Nawabgunge, eleven miles, over a plain, the soil of which, near the road, is, generally, very poor oosur. No fruit or ornamental trees – few shrubs, and very little grass. Here and there, however, even near the road, may be seen a small patch of land, from which a crop of rice has been taken this season; and the country is well cultivated all along, up to within half a mile of the road, on both sides. Nawabgunge is situated on the new metalled road – fifty miles long – between Lucknow and Cawnpoor, and about mid-way between the two places.[1] It was built by the late minister, Nawab Ameen-od Dowlah, while in office, for the accommodation of travellers; and is named after him. It is kept up, at his expense, for the same purpose, now that he has descended to private life. There is a small house, for the accommodation of European gentlemen and ladies, as well as a double range of buildings – between which the road passes – for ordinary travellers, and for shop-keepers to supply them.

Some people told me, that even the worst of this oosur soil might be made to produce fair crops under good tillage; while others denied the possibility, though all were farmers or land-holders. All, however, agreed, that any but the *worst* might be made so by good tillage – that is, by flooding the land by means of artificial embankments, for two or three rainy seasons, and then cross-ploughing, manuring and irrigating it well. All say, that the soil, hereabouts, is liable to become oosur, if left fallow and neglected for a few years. The oosur, certainly, seems to

---

[1] The term Gunge, signifies a range of buildings, at a place of traffic, for the accommodation of merchants, and all persons engaged in the purchase and sale of goods, and for that of their goods and of the shop-keepers who supply them.

prevail most near the high roads, where the peasantry have been most exposed to the rapacity of the king's troops; and this tends to confirm the notion, that tillage is necessary in certain soils, to check the tendency of the carbonates or nitrates, or their alkaline bases, to superabundance. The abundance of the chloride of sodium in the soil, from which the superabounding carbonates of soda are formed, seems to indicate, unequivocally, that the bed, from which they are brought to the surface, by capillary attraction, must, at some time, have been covered by salt water. The soil of Scind, which was at one time covered by the sea, seems to suffer still more generally from the same super-abundance of the carbonates of soda, formed from the *chlorides of sodium*, and brought to the surface in the same manner. But in Scind the evil is greater and more general, from the smaller quantity of rain that falls. Egypt would, no doubt, suffer still more from the same cause, inasmuch as it has still less rain than Scind, but for the annual overflowing of the Nile. The greater part of the deserts, which now disfigure the face of the globe in hot climates, arise chiefly from the same causes; and they may become covered by tillage and population, as mankind becomes wiser, more social and more humane.

January 9, 1850. – Halted at Nawabgunge. A vast deal of grain of all sorts has, for the last two years, passed from Cawnpoor to Lucknow for sale. The usual current of grain is from the northern and eastern districts of Oude towards Cawnpoor;[a] but, for these two years, it has been from Cawnpoor to these districts. This is owing to two bad seasons in Oude generally, and much oppression in the northern and eastern districts in particular; and the advantage which the navigation of the Ganges affords to the towns, on its banks, on such occasions. The metalled road from Cawnpoor to Lucknow is covered almost with carts and vehicles of all kinds. Guards have been established upon it for the protection of travellers; and life and property are now secure upon it; which they had not been for many years, up to the latter end of 1849. This road has lately been completed

---

[a] Cf. Butter, *Southern Districts of Oud'h*, who claims that at that time (1839) there was no trade of grains from Oudh into the North-Western Provinces.

under the superintendance of Lieut. G. Sim, of the Engineers, and cost above two lakhs of rupees.[a]

The minister came out with a very large cortège yesterday, to see and talk with me, and is to stay here to-day. I met him, this morning, on his way out, to shoot in the lake; and it was amusing to see his enormous train contrasted with my small one. I told him, to the amusement of all around, that an English gentleman would rather get no air or shooting at all than seek them in such a crowd. The minister was, last night, to have received the Rajahs and other great landholders, who had come to my camp, but they told me, this-morning, that they had, some of them, waited all night, in vain, for an audience – that the money demanded by his followers, of various sorts and grades, for such a privilege, was much more than they could pay – that, to see and talk with a prime minister of Oude, was one of the most difficult and expensive of things. Rajah Hunmunt Sing, of Dharoopoor, told me, that he feared, his only alternative now was a very hard one, either to be utterly ruined by the contractor of Salone, or to take to his jungles and strongholds, and fight against his sovereign.[1]

Rajah Rambuksh, of Dondhea Kheera, is in the same predicament. He tells me, that a great part of his estate has been taken from him by Chundun Lal, of Morowa, the banker, already mentioned, in collusion with the Nazim, Kotab-od Deen, who depends so much on him, as the only capitalist in his district, – that he is obliged to conciliate him by acquiescing in the spoliation of others, – that he has already taken much of his lands, by fraud and collusion, and wishes to take the whole in the same way, – that this banker now holds lands, in the district, yielding above two laks of rupees a year, can do what he pleases, and is, every day, aggrandising himself and family by the ruin of others. There is some truth in what Rambuksh states, though he exaggerates a little the wrong which he himself suffers; and it is

---

[1] The Rajah was too formidable to be treated lightly, and the Amil was obliged to give in, and consent to take from him what he had paid to his predecessor; but, to effect this, the Rajah was, afterwards, obliged to go to Lucknow, and pay largely in gratuities.

[a] This was in fact the only regularly-made road in the kingdom; Thornton, *Gazetteer*, vol. IV, pp. 31, 37; and Butter, *Southern Districts of Oud'h*, p. 85.

lamentable, that all power and influence in Oude, of whatever kind, or however acquired, should be so sure to be abused, to the prejudice of both sovereign and people. When these great capitalists become landholders – as almost all do – they are apt to do much mischief in the districts, where their influence lies, for the government officers can do little in the collection of the revenue without their aid; and, as the collection of revenue is the only part of their duty, to which they attach much importance, they are ready to acquiesce in any wrong that they may commit, in order to conciliate them. The Nazim of Byswara, Kotab-od Deen, is an old and infirm man, and very much dependant upon Chundun Lal, who, in collusion with him, has certainly deprived many of their hereditary possessions, in the usual way in order to aggrandise his own family. He has, at the same time, purchased a great deal of land, at auction, in the Honourable Company's districts, where he has dealings, keeps the greater part of his wealth, and is prepared to locate his family, when the danger of retaining any of either in Oude becomes pressing. The risk is always great; but they bind the local authorities, civil and military, by solemn oaths and written pledges, for the security of their own persons and property, and those of their own persons and property, and those of their families and clients.

January 10, 1850. – At Nawabgunge, detained by rain, which fell heavily yesterday, with much thunder and lightning, and has continued to fall all night. It is painful and humiliating to pass through this part of Oude, where the families of so many thousands of our sipahees reside, particularly at this time when so large a portion of them are at their homes on furlough. The Punjab war[a] having closed, all the corps engaged in it, have, this year, been sent off to quiet stations, in our old provinces, and their places supplied by others, which have taken no share in that or any other war, of late. As a measure of economy, and with a view to indulge the native officers and sipahees of the corps, engaged in that war, Government has, this season, given a long furlough, to all the native army of Bengal. Some three hundred and fifty native officers and sipahees, from each Regiment, are,

[a] The Second Panjab War, 1848–9, the First having been 1845–6.

or are to be, absent on leave this season. This saves to Government a very large sum, in the extra allowance which is granted to native officers and sipahees, during their march from one station to another; and in the deductions which are made from the pay and allowances of those who go on furlough. During furlough, subadars receive 52 rupees a month, instead of 67; jemadars 17, instead of 24; havildars 9, instead of 14; naicks 7, instead of 12; and sipahees 5–8, instead of 7.

These native officers and sipahees, with all their gallantry on service, and fidelity to their salt, are the most importunate of suitors; and, certainly, among the most untruthful and unscrupulous in stating the circumstances of their claims, or the grounds of their complaints. They crowd around me, morning and evening, when I venture outside my tent, and keep me employed all day in reading their petitions. They cannot or will not understand, that the Resident is – or ought to be – only the channel through which their claims are sent for adjustment, through the Court to the Oude tribunals and local authorities; and that the investigation and decision must – or ought to – rest with them. They expect, that he will at once himself investigate and decide their claims, or have them investigated and decided, forthwith, by the local authorities of the district, through which he is passing; and, it is in vain to tell them, that the 'law's *delay*', is as often and as justly complained of in our own territory, as in Oude; whatever may be the state of its *uncertainty*.

The wrongs, of which they complain, are, of course, such as all men of their class, in Oude, are liable to suffer; but no other men, in Oude, are so prone to exaggerate the circumstances attending them, to bring forward, prominently, all that is favorable to their own side, and keep back all that is otherwise; and to conceal the difficulties which must attend the search after the truth, and those still greater which must attend the enforcement of an award when made. Their claims are often upon men who have well garrisoned forts, and large bands of armed followers, who laugh at the king's officers and troops, and could not be coerced into obedience, without the aid of a large and well appointed British force. For the immediate employment of such a force, they will not fail to urge the Resident, though they have,

Diary of a Tour Through Oude

to the commanding officer of their Company and Regiment, represented the debtor or offender, as a man of no mark, ready to do whatever the Resident, or the Oude authorities, may be pleased to order. On one occasion, no less than thirty lives were lost in attempting to enforce an award, in favor of a sipahee of our army.

I have had several visits from my old friend Sheikh Mahboob Allee, the subadar-major, who is mentioned in my essay on 'MILITARY DISCIPLINE'.[a] He is now an invalid pensioner in Oude; and, in addition to the lands, which his family held, before his transfer to the invalids, he has lately acquired possession of a nice village, which he claimed, in the usual way, through the Resident. He told me, that he had possession, but that he found it very difficult to keep cultivators upon it.

'And why is this, my old friend? Cultivators are abundant in Oude, and glad always to till lands, on which they are protected and encouraged by moderate rents, and a little occasional aid in seed, grain and stock; and you are now in circumstances to afford them both?' 'True, sir', said the old subadar, 'but the great refractory landholder – my neighbour – has a large force, and he threatens to bring it down upon me; and my cultivators are afraid, that they and their families will all be cut up some dark night, if they stay with me.' 'But what has your great neighbour to do with your village? Why do you not make friends with him?' 'Make friends with him, sir! – the thing is impossible.' 'And why, subadar sahib?' 'Sir, it was from him that the village was taken, by the orders of the Durbar, through the interposition of the Resident, to be made over to me; and he vows, that he will take it back, whatever number of lives it may cost him to do so.' 'And how long may he and his family have held it?' 'Only thirty or thirty-five years, sir.' 'And neither you nor your family have ever held possession of it for that time?' 'Never, sir, but we always hoped, that the favor of the British Government would, some day, get it for us.' 'And in urging your claim to the village, did you ever tell the Resident, that you had been so long out of possession?' 'No sir, we said nothing about *time*.' 'You know, subadar sahib, that in all countries a limit is prescribed in such cases, and, at the Residency, that limit is six years; and, had the Resident known, that your claim was of so old a date, he would never have interposed in your favor, more especially, when his doing so involved the risk of the loss of so many lives, first in obtaining possession for you, and then keeping you in it.'

Cases of this kind are very numerous.

[a] *On the Spirit of Military Discipline in our Native Indian Army* (Calcutta, 1841); cf. *R and R* (1915), p. xxxiii.

The estate of Rampoor, which we lately passed through, belonged to the grand father of Rajah Hunmunt Sing. His eldest son, Sungram Sing, died without issue, and the estate devolved on his second son, Bhow Sing, the father of Rajah Hunmunt Sing. The third brother separated from the family stock during the life of his father, and got, as his share, Sursae, Kuttra Bulleepoor, and other villages. He had five sons; first, Lokee Sing; second, Dirguj Sing; third, Hul Sing; fourth, Dul Sing; and fifth, Bul Sing, and the estate was, on his death, subdivided among them. Kuttra Bulleepoor, devolved on Lokee Sing, the eldest, who died without issue; and the village was subdivided among his four brothers, or their descendants. But Davey Buksh, the grand son, by adoption, of the second brother, Dirguj Sing, unknown to the others, assigned, in lieu of a debt, the whole village to a brahmin, named Bhyroo Tewaree, who, forthwith, got it transferred to the Hozoor Tehseel, through Matadeen, a havildar of the 5th Troop, 7th Regiment of Cavalry, who, in an application to the Resident, pretended, that the estate was his own. It is now beyond the jurisdiction of the local authorities, who could ascertain the truth; and all the rightful co-sharers have been, ever since, trying, in vain, to recover their rights. The brahmin and the havildar, with Sooklal, a trooper in the same Regiment, now divide the profits between them, and laugh at the impotent efforts of the old proprietors, to get redress. Gholam Jeelanee, a shop-keeper of Lucknow, seeing the profits derived by sipahees, from the abuse of this privilege, purchased a Cavalry uniform, jacket, cap, pantaloon, boots, shoes and sword, and on the pretence of being an invalid trooper of ours, got the signature of the Brigadier commanding the Troops in Oude, to his numerous petitions, which were sent for adjustment to the Durbar through the Resident. He followed this trade profitably for fifteen years. At last he got possession of a landed estate, to which he had no claim of right. Soon after he sent a petition to say, that the dispossessed proprietor had killed four of his relations and turned him out. This led to a more strict enquiry, when all came out. In quoting this case to the Resident, in a letter, dated the 16th of June, 1836, the king of Oude observes, – 'If a person, known to thousands in the city of Lucknow, is able, for fifteen years, to carry on such a trade successfully, how much more easy must it be for people in the country, not known to any in the city, to carry it on.' . . .

[1852: I, 274–6] [1858: I, 304–6]

January 11, 1850. – At Nawabgunge, detained by rain, which fell heavily all last night, to the great delight of the *landed interest*, and great discomfort of travellers. Nothing but mud around us – our tents wet through, but standing, and the ground inside of them dry. Fortunately there has been no strong wind with the heavy rain, and we console ourselves with the thought, that the small inconvenience which travellers suffer from such rain, at this season, is trifling, compared with the advantage, which millions of our fellow creatures derive from it. This is what I have heard all native travellers say, however humble or however great – all sympathise with the landed interests, in a country where industry is limited, almost exclusively, to the culture of the soil; and the revenue of the sovereign derived, almost exclusively, from the land. After such rains the cold increases – the spirit rise, – the breezes freshen, – the crops look strong, – the harvest is retarded, – the grain gets more sap and becomes perfect, – the cold season is prolonged, as the crops remain longer green, and continue to condense the moisture of the surrounding atmosphere. Without such late rain, the crops ripen prematurely, – the grain becomes shrivelled, and defective both in quantity and quality. While the rain lasts, however, a large camp is a wretched scene; for few of the men, women, and children, and still fewer of the animals it contains, can find any shelter at all!

January 12, 1850. – At Nawabgunge, still detained by rain. The minister had ordered out tents for himself and suite, on the 8th, but they had not come up, and I was obliged to lend him one of my best, and some others as they came up, or they would have been, altogether, without shelter. When he left them on the 10th, his attendants cut and took away almost all the ropes, some of the kanats – or outer walls – and some of the carpets. He knew nothing about it, nor will he ever learn any thing till told by me. His attendants were plundering in all the surrounding villages while he remained; and my people tried, in vain, to prevent them, lest they should themselves be taken for the plunderers. Of all this the minister knew nothing. The attendants on the contractors and other local officers are, if possible, still worse; and throughout the country the king's officers all plunder, or acquiesce in the plunder, utterly regardless of the sufferings of the people and the best interests of their sovereign. No precaution, whatever, is taken to prevent this indiscriminate plunder, by the followers of the local authorities; nor would any one of them think it worth his while to interpose, if he saw the roofs of the houses of a whole village moving off on the heads of his followers to his camp; or a fine crop of sugar cane, wheat or vegetables, cut down, for fodder, by them, before his face. It is the fashion of the country, and the government acquiesces in it.

Among the people no man feels mortified, or apprehends that he shall stand the worse in the estimation of the government or its officers, for being called and proved to be a robber. It is the trade of every considerable landholder in the country occasionally; and that of a great many of them perpetually; the murder of men, women and children, generally attends their depredations. A few days ago, when requested by the king, to apply to officers commanding stations, and magistrates of bordering districts, for aid in the arrest of some of the most atrocious of these rebels and robbers, I told His Majesty, that out of consideration for the poor people who suffered, I had made a requisition for that aid, for the arrest of three of the worst of them; but that I could make no further requisition until he did something to remove the impression now universal over Oude, that those who protected their peasantry, managed their estates well, obeyed the government in all things, and paid the revenue punctually, were sure to be oppressed, and, ultimately ruined, by the government and its officers, while those who did the reverse in all these things, were equally sure to be favored and courted...

[1852: I, 281–94] [1858: I, 311–25]

January 13, 1850. – Russoolabad, twelve miles, over a country better peopled and cultivated than usual, where the soil admits of tillage. There is a good deal that requires drainage, and still more that is too poor to be tilled without great labour and outlay in irrigation, manure, &c. The villages are, however, much nearer to each other, than in any other part of the country that we have passed over; and the lands, close around every village, are well cultivated. The landholders and cultivators told me, that the heavy rain we have had, has done a vast deal of good to the crops; and, as it has been followed by a clear sky and fine westerly wind, they have no fear of the blight, which might have followed, had the sky continued cloudy, and the winds easterly. Certainly nothing could look better than the crops of all kinds do now, and the people are busily engaged in ploughing the land for sugar cane, and for the autumn crops of next season.

I had some talk with the head zumeendar of Naraenpoor, about mid-way. He is of the Ditchit family of Rajpoots, who abound in the district we have now entered. We passed over the boundary of Byswara about three miles from our last encampment, and beyond that district there are but few Rajpoots of the Bys clan. These Ditchits give their daughters in marriage to the Bys Raj-poots, but cannot get any of theirs in return. Gunga Sing, the zumeendar, with whom I was talking, told me, that both the Ditchits and Byses put their infant daughters to death; and that the practice prevailed, more or less, in all families of these and, he believed, all other clans of Rajpoots in Oude, save the Sengers.[1] I asked him whether it prevailed in his own family, and he told me that it did, more or less, as in all others. I bid him leave me, as I could not hold converse with a person guilty of such atrocities; and told him, that they would be all punished for them in the next world, if not, in this.

Rajah Bukhtawar Sing, who was on his horse beside my elephant, said,

They are all punished in this world; and will, no doubt, be punished still more in the next – scarcely any of the heads of these landed aristocracy are the legitimate sons of their predecessors – they are all adopted, or born of women of inferior grade – the heads of families who commit or tolerate

---

[1] The Sengers are almost the only class of Rajpoots in Bundelkund, and Bog-hilcund, Rewa, and the Saugor territories, who used to put their female infants to death; and here, in Oude, they are almost the only class who do not.

such atrocities, become leprous, blind, deaf or dumb, or are carried off in early life, by some terrible disease – hardly any of them attain a good old age – nor can they boast of an untainted line of ancestors like other men – if they get sons they commonly die young. They unite themselves to women of inferior castes for want of daughters in families of their own ranks; and there is hardly a family among these proud Rajpoots, unstained by such connexions.[1] Even the reptile *Pausies* become *Rajpoots* by giving their daughters to Powars and other Rajpoot families, when, by robbery and murder, they have acquired wealth and landed property. The sister of Gunga Buksh, of Kasimgunge, was married to the Rajah of Etondeea, a Powar Rajpoot, in Mahona; and the present Rajah – Jode Sing – is her son. Gunga Buksh is a Pausee, but the family call themselves Rawats, and are considered to be Rajpoots, since they have acquired landed possessions, by the murder and ruin of the old proprietors – they all delight in murder and rapine – the curse of God is upon them, sir, for the murder of their own innocent children!

When I was sent out to inquire into the case of Brigadier Webber, who had been attacked and robbed, while travelling in his Palkee, with relays of bearers, from Lucknow to Seetapoor, I entered a house to make some enquiries, and found the mistress weeping. I asked the cause, and she told me, that she had had four children, and lost all – that three of them were girls, who had been put to death in infancy, and the last was a fine boy, who had just died! I told her, that this was a just punishment from God for the iniquities of her family, and that I would neither wash my hands nor drink water under her roof. I never do under the roof of any family in which such a cruel practice prevails. These Rajpoots are all a bad set sir. When men murder their own children, how can they scruple to murder other people. The curse of God is upon them, sir.

In the district of Byswara, (he continued) through which we have just passed, you will find, at least, fifty thousand men armed to fight against each other, or their government and its officers, – in such a space, under the Honourable Company's dominion, you would not find one thousand armed men of the same class. Why is this, but because you do not allow such crimes to be perpetrated. Why do you go on acquiring dominion over one country after another with your handful of European troops, and small force of native sipahees, but because God sees that your rule is just, and that you have an earnest desire to benefit the people, and improve the countries you take?

[1] A great number of girls are purchased and stolen from our territories, brought into Oude, and sold to Rajpoot families, as wives for their sons, on the assurance, that they are of the same or higher caste, and that their parents have been induced to part with them from poverty. A great many of our native officers and sipahees, who marry, while home on furlough, and are pressed for time, get such wives. Some of their neighbours are always bribed by the traders in such girls, to pledge themselves for the purity of their blood. If they ever find out the imposition, they say nothing about it.

He told me, that he had charge of the cattle under Saadut Allee Khan, when Lord Lake took the field at the first siege of Bhurtpoor.[a] That his master lent His Lordship five hundred elephants, eight thousand artillery bullocks, and five hundred horses – that two hundred and fifty of the elephants returned, but whether any of the bullocks and horses came back or not he could not say. The country, we came over to-day, is well studded with groves and fine single trees, but the soil is generally of the lighter doomuteea kind, which requires much labour and outlay in water and manure. The irrigation is all from wells and pools. In the villages we came through, we saw but few of the sipahees of our army, home on furlough – they are chiefly from the Byswara and Bunoda districts. We found our tents pitched upon a high and dry spot, with a tight soil of clay and sand. After the heavy rain we have had, it looked as if no shower had fallen upon it for an age. The mud walls of the houses we saw on the road were naked as usual. The rapacity of the king's troops, is, every where, directly or indirectly, the cause of this; and till they are better provided and disciplined, the houses in the towns and villages, can never improve.

The commandant, Imdad Hoseyn, of the Akberee or Telinga Regiment, on duty with the Amil of the Poorwa district, in which our camp was last pitched, followed me a few miles this morning, to beg, that I would try to prevail upon the Durbar to serve out clothing for his corps. He told me that the last clothing it got from the government was on the occasion of Lord Hasting's[b] visit to Lucknow, some thirty-three years ago, in 1817 – that many orders had been given, since that time, for new clothing, but there was always some one about Court, to counteract them from malice or selfishness – that his father, Zakir Allee, commanded the corps when it got the last clothing, and he succeeded him many years ago. The Telinga Regiments are provided with arms, accoutrements and clothing, by government. The sipahees formerly got five rupees a month, but for only ten months in the year – they now get four rupees and three

---

[a] The first siege of Bharatpur, 1805; see above p. 56, n. *a*.

[b] Francis Rawdon, first Marquis of Hastings and second Earl of Moira (1754–1826); succeeded as Irish Earl of Moira, 1793; general, 1803; Governor-General, October 1813–January 1823; created Marquis of Hastings, 1817.

and half annas a month, for all the twelve months. He is, he says, obliged to take a great many *sufarashies,* or men put in by persons of influence at Court, out of favor, or for the purpose of sharing in their pay; and under the deductions and other disadvantages, to which they are liable, he could get no good men to enlist. The corps, in consequence, has a wretched appearance; and, certainly, could not be made formidable to an enemy. The 'Akbery' is one of the Telinga corps of Infantry, and was intended to be, in all things, like those of Captains Barlow, Bunbury and Magness; but Imdad Hoseyn told me, that they had a certain weight at Court, which secured for their Regiments many advantages, necessary to make the corps efficient, while he had none – that they had occasional intercourse with the Resident, and were all at Court for some months in the year, to make friends, while he was always detached.

January 14, 1850. – Halted at Russoolabad, for our second set of tents, which did not come up till night, when it was too late to send them on to our next ground. We have two sets of sleeping and dining tents – one to go on and the other to remain during the night; but only one set of office tents. They are struck in the afternoon, when the office duties of the day are over, and are ready by the time we reach our ground the next morning. This is the way in which all public functionaries march in India. Almost all officers who have revenue charges, march through the districts under their jurisdiction, during the cold season, and so do many political officers, who have control over more than one native principality. I have had charges that require such moving, ever since the year 1822, or for some twenty-eight years; and with the exception of two intervals of absence, on medical certificate, in 1826 and 1836. I have been, every cold season, moving in the way I describe. No Resident, at the Court of Lucknow, ever before moved over the country as I am doing, to inquire into the condition of the people, the state of the country and character of the administration; nor would it be desirable for them to do so, unless trained to civil business, and able and disposed to commune freely with the people of all classes. The advantages would hardly counterbalance the disadvantages. When I apologise to the peasantry for the unavoidable trespasses of my camp, they always reply good humouredly, – 'the losses we suffer from them are small and temporary, while the good we hope from your visit is great and permanent'. Would that I could realise the hopes, to which my visit gives rise!!

January 15, 1850. – To Meeangunge, five miles, over a plain of good doomuteea soil, well studded with trees; but much of the land lies waste, and many of the villages and hamlets are unoccupied and in ruins. We passed the boundary of the Russoolabad district, about two miles from our last ground, and crossed into that of Meeangunge, or Safeepoor. The Russoolabad district was held in contract, for some years, by one of the greatest knaves in Oude, Buksh Allee, a dome by caste, whose rise to wealth and influence may be described as illustrative of the manners and customs of the Lucknow Court and government. This man and his deputy, Munsab Allee, reduced a good deal of the land of the district to waste, and depopulated many of its villages and hamlets by over exactions; and by an utter disregard of their engagements with the landholders and cultivators; and they were in league with many atrocious highway robbers, who plundered and murdered so many travellers along the high road, leading from Lucknow to Cawnpoor, which runs through the district, that it was deemed unsafe to pass it except in strong bodies. When I took charge of my office in January last, they used to seize every good looking girl, or young woman, passing the roads with parents and husbands, who were too poor to purchase redress at Court, and make slaves or concubines of them; and, feeling strong in the assurance of protection from the fiddlers in the palace, who are of the same caste, domes, Buksh Allee defied all authority, and kept those girls and women in his camp and house at Lucknow, while their parents and husbands, for months and years, in vain, besought all who were likely to have the least influence or authority, to interpose for their release. Some of them came to me, soon after I took charge; and, having collected sufficient proof of these atrocities, and of some robberies, which he had committed, or caused to be com-

mitted, along the high road, I insisted upon his being deprived
of his charges and punished. He remained, for many months,
concealed in the city, but was, at last, seized by some of the
Frontier Police, under the guidance of an excellent officer,
Lieutenant Weston, the Superintendent. I had prevailed on the
king to offer two thousand rupees for his apprehension, and the
two thousand rupees were distributed among the captors. The
girls and young women were released, their parents and husbands compensated for the sufferings they had endured, and
many of the persons who had been robbed by him and his
deputy, had the value of their lost property made good. Great
impediments were thrown in the way of all this by people of
influence about Court; but they were all surmounted by great
skill and energy on the part of Lieutenant Weston, and steady
perseverance on mine; and Buksh Allee remained in jail, treated
as a common felon, till all was effected. All had, in appearance,
been done by the king's officers, but in reality by ours, under his
Majesty's sanction; for it was clear, that nothing would be done,
unless we supervised and guided their proceedings. The district
is now held, in contract, by a very respectable man, Mahommed
Uskaree, who has taken it for four years.

The district of Safeepoor, in which we are now encamped, has
been held, in contract for five years, by Budreenath, a merchant
of Lucknow, who had given security for the former contractor.
He could not fulfill his engagements to government, and the
contract was made over to him as surety, on condition, that he
paid the balance. He has held it ever since, while his younger
brother, Kiddernath, has conducted their mercantile affairs at
Lucknow. Budreenath has always considered the affair as a mercantile speculation; and thought of nothing but the amount he
has to pay to government, and that which he can squeeze out of
the landholders and cultivators. He is a bad manager – the lands
are badly tilled, and the towns, villages and hamlets are scantily
peopled, and most wretched in appearance. Near the border we
passed one village, Mahommedpoor, entirely in ruins. After
some search we found a solitary man of the Pausee tribe, who
told us, that it had been held, for many generations, by the family
of Rugonath, a Gouree Rajpoot, who paid for it at an uniform

rate of six hundred rupees a year. About three years ago, the contractor demanded from him an increased rate, which he could not pay. Being sorely pressed, he fled to the jungles, with the few of his clan that he could collect, and ordered all the cultivators to follow his fortunes. They were of a different clan – mostly Bagheelas – and declined the honor. He urged, that if they followed him for a season or two, the village would be left untilled, and yield nothing to the contractor, who would be constrained to restore him to possession at the rate which his ancestors had paid – that his family had nothing else to depend upon, and if they did not desert the land, and take to the jungles and plunder with him, he must, of necessity, plunder them. They had never done so, and would not do so now. He attacked and plundered the village three times, killed three men, and drove all the rest to seek shelter and employment in other villages around. Not a soul but himself, our informant, was left, and the lands lay waste. Rogonath Sing rented a little land in the village of Gouree, many miles off, and in another district, still determined to allow no man but himself to hold the village or restore its tillage and population. This, said the Pausee, is the usage of the country, and the only way in which a landholder can honestly or effectually defend himself against the contractor, who would never regard his rights, unless he saw that he was prepared to defend them in this way, and determined to involve all under him in his own ruin – depopulate his estate, and lay waste his lands.

Meean Almas, after whom this place, Meeangunge, takes his name, was an eunuch. He had a brother, Rahmut, after whom the town of Rahmutgunge, which we passed some days ago, took its name. Meean Almas was the greatest and best man of any note that Oude has produced. He held for about forty years, this and other districts, yielding to the Oude government an annual revenue of about eighty lakhs of rupees a year. During all this time he kept the people secure in life and property, and as happy as people in such a state of society can be; and the whole country, under his charge, was, during his life time, a garden. He lived here in a style of great magnificence, and was often visited by his sovereign, who used, occasionally, to spend a month at a time with him at Meeangunge. A great portion of the lands, held by him, were among those made over to the British Government, on the division of the Oude territory, by the treaty of 1801, concluded between Saadut Allee Khan, and the then Governor General, Lord Wellesley.[a] The country was then divided into equal shares, according to the rent roll at the time. The half made over to the British Government has been, ever since, yielding more and more revenue to us, while that retained by the sovereign of Oude, has been yielding less and less to him; and ours now yields, in land revenue, stamp duty and the tax on spirits, two crore and twelve lakhs a year, while the reserved half now yields to Oude, only about one crore, or one crore and ten lakhs. When the cession took place, each half was estimated at one crore and thirty three lakhs. Under good management the Oude share might, in a few years, be made equal to ours, and, perhaps, better, for the greater part of the lands, in our share, have been a good deal impoverished by over-cropping, while those of the Oude share have been improved by long fallows. Lands of the same natural quality in Oude, under good tillage, now pay a much higher rate of rent than they do in our half of the estate.

Almas Allee Khan, at the close of his life, was supposed to have accumulated immense wealth; but when he died he was found to have nothing, to the great mortification of his sovereign who seized upon all. Large sums of money had been lent by him to the European merchants at Lucknow, as well as to native merchants all over the country. When he found his end approaching, he called for all their bonds and destroyed them. Mr. Ousely and Mr. Paul were said to have, at that time, owed to him more than three lakhs of rupees each. His immense income he had expended in useful works, liberal hospitality and charity. He systematically kept in check the Tallookdars, or great landholders; fostered the smaller, and encouraged and protected the better classes of cultivators, such as Lodhies, Koormies and Kachies, whom he called and considered his children. His reign over the large extent of country under his

[a] Richard Colley, Marquis Wellesley (1760–1842); eldest son of the first Earl of Mornington; succeeded, 1781; Governor-General, May 1798–July 1805; created Baron Wellesley, 1798; created Marquis, 1799.

jurisdiction, is considered to have been its golden age. Many of the districts, which he held, were among those transferred to the British Government, by the treaty of 1801; and they were estimated at the revenue which he had paid for them to the Oude government. This was much less than any other servant of the Oude government would have been made to pay for them, and this accounts, in some measure, for the new increased rate they yield to us. Others pledged themselves to pay rates which they never did or could pay, and the nominal rates, in the accounts, were always greater than the real rates. He never pledged himself to pay higher rates than he could and really did pay.

Now the Tallookdars keep the country in a perpetual state of disturbance, and render life, property and industry, every where insecure. Whenever they quarrel with each other, or with the local authorities of the government, from whatever cause, they take to indiscriminate plunder and murder – over all lands not held by men of the same class – no road, town, village, or hamlet, is secure from their merciless attacks – robbery and murder become their diversion – their sport – and they think no more of taking the lives of men, women and children, who never offended them, than those of deer or wild hogs. They not only rob and murder but seize, confine and torture all whom they seize, and suppose to have money or credit, till they ransom themselves with all they have or can beg or borrow. Hardly a day has passed since I left Lucknow, in which I have not had abundant proof of numerous atrocities of this kind committed by landholders, within the district through which I was passing, year by year, up to the present day. The same system is followed by landholders of smaller degrees and of this military class – some holders of single villages or co-sharers in a village. This class comprises Rajpoots of all denominations, Musulmans and Pausies. Where one co-sharer, in a village, quarrels with another, or with the government authorities, on whatever subject, he declares himself in a *state of war*, and adopts the same system of indiscriminate plunder and reckless murder. He first robs the house, and murders all he can of the family of the co-sharer, with whom he has quarrelled, or whose tenement he wishes to seize upon; and then gets together all he can of the loose characters around, employs them in indiscriminate plunder, and subsists them upon the booty, without the slightest apprehension that he shall thereby stand less high in the estimation of his neighbours, or that of the officers of government; on the contrary, he expects, when his *pastime* is over, to be, at least more feared and courted; and more secure in the possession of increased lands, held at lower rates. All this terrible state of disorder arises from the government not keeping faith with its subjects, and not making them keep faith with each other. I, one day, asked Rajah Hunmunt Sing, how it was, that men guilty of such crimes, were tolerated in society, and he answered by quoting the following Hindee couplet. 'Men reverence the man whose heart is wicked, as they adore and make offerings to the evil planet, while they let the good pass unnoticed, or with a simple salute of courtesy.'[1]

The contractor for this district, Budreenath, came to call in the afternoon, though he is suffering much from disease. He bears a good character with the government, because he contrives to pay its demand; but a very bad one among the people, from whom he extorts the means. He does not adhere to his engagements with the landholders and cultivators, but exacts, when the crops are ripe, a higher rate than they had engaged to pay at the commencement of tillage; and the people suffer not only from what he takes over and above what is due, but from the depredations of those whom such proceedings drive into rebellion. Against such persons he is too weak to protect them; and as soon as the rebels show, that they can reduce his income by plundering and murdering the peasantry, and all who have property in the towns and villages, he reestablishes them on their lands on their own terms. He had, lately, however, by great good luck, seized two very atrocious characters of this description, who had plundered and burnt down several villages, and murdered some of their inhabitants; and, as he knew that they would be released on the first occasion of thanksgiving at Lucknow – having the means to bribe Court favorites – he begged my permission to

---

[1] There is another Hindee verse to the same effect. 'Man dreads a crooked thing – the demon Rahoo[a] dares not seize the moon till he sees her full.' They consider the eclipse to be caused by the demon Rahoo seizing the moon in his mouth.

[a] Rahu, the king of the meteors and the guardian of the 'south-western' quarter, who is said to be the cause of the eclipse.

make them over to Lieutenant Weston, Superintendent of the Frontier Police, as robbers by profession. 'If they come back, sir, they will murder all who have aided in their capture, or given evidence against them, and no village or road will be safe.'

Some shop-keepers in the town complained, that the contractor was in the habit of forcing them to stand sureties, for the fulfilment, on the part of landholders, of any engagements they might make, to pay him certain sums, or to make over to him certain land produce at the harvets. This, they said, often involved them in heavy losses, as the landholders frequently could not, or would not, do either when the time came, and they were made to pay. This is a frequent practice throughout Oude. Shop-keepers and merchants who have property, are often *compelled*, by the contractors and other local officers, to give such security, for bad or doubtful paymasters, with whom they may happen to have had dealings or intercourse, and by this means robbed of all they have. All manner of means are resorted to to compel them – they and their families are seized and confined, and harshly or disgracefully treated, till they consent to sign the security bonds. The plea, that the bonds had been forced from them, would not avail in any tribunal to which they might appeal – it would be urged against them, that the money was for the *State*; and this would be considered as quite sufficient to justify the government officer who had robbed them...

[1852: I, 300–5] [1858: I, 332–7]

January 16, 1850. – We were to have gone, this morning, to Ouras, but were obliged to encamp at Burra, eight miles from Meeangunge, on the left bank of the Saee river, which had been too much increased by the late rains, to admit of our baggage and tents passing over immediately, on any thing but elephants. As we have but few of them, our tents were pitched on this side of the river, that our things might have the whole day before them, to pass over on carts and camels, as the river subsided. Ouras is three miles from our camp, and we are to pass through it and go on to Sundeela to-morrow. There is no bridge, and boats are not procurable on this small river, which we have to cross and recross several times.

Diary of a Tour Through Oude

The country from Meeangunge is scantily cultivated, but well studded with trees, and generally fertile under good tillage. The soil is the light doomuteea, but here and there very sandy and poor, running into what is called bhoor. The villages and hamlets which we could see are few and wretched. We have few native officers and sipahees, in our army, from the districts we are now in; and, I am, in consequence, less oppressed with complaints from this class of the Oude subjects. We met, near our tents, a party of soldiers, belonging to Rajah Ghalib Jung, a person already mentioned, and, at present, Superintendent of Police, along the Cawnpoor road, escorting a band of thieves, who robbed Major Scott, some ten months ago, on his way, by dawk, from Lucknow, and an European merchant, two months ago, on his way, by dawk, from Cawnpoor to Lucknow. They had been seized in the Sundeela districts, and the greater part of the stolen property found in their houses. They are of the Pausie tribe, and told me, that thieving was their hereditary trade; and that they had long followed it on the Cawnpoor road with success. The landholder, who kept them upon his estate and shared in their booty, was also seized; but made over to the revenue contractor, who released him after a few days' imprisonment, for a gratuity. Of these Pausies there are supposed to be about one hundred thousand families in Oude. They are employed as village watchmen; but, with few exceptions, are thieves and robbers by hereditary profession. Many of them adopt poisoning as a trade, and the numbers who did so were rapidly increasing, when Captain Hollings, the Superintendent of the Oude Frontier Police, arrested a great many of them, and proceeded against them as Thugs by profession, under Act III, of 1848.[a] His measures have been successfully followed up by Captain Weston, his successor; and this crime has been greatly diminished in Oude. It prevails still, however, more or less, in all parts of India.

[a] Act III of 1848, 'An Act for removing doubts as to the meaning of the words "Thug" and "Thuggee", and the expression "Murder by Thuggee", when used in the Acts of the Council of India', passed 26 February 1848; India Office, Records Dept, *India Acts 1846–51*. The basic legislation to deal with the thugs was Act XXX of 1836 and Act XVIII of 1837: see Kaye, *Administration of the East India Company*, p. 375. Kaye does not mention Act III of 1848.

These Pausies of Oude generally form the worst part of the gangs of refractory Tallookdars in their indiscriminate plunder. They use the bow and arrow expertly, and are said to be able to send an arrow through a man at the distance of one hundred yards. There is no species of theft or robbery in which they are not experienced and skillful; and they increase and prosper in proportion as the disorders in the country grow worse. They serve any refractory landholders, or enterprising gang robber, without wages, for the sake of the booty to be acquired.

Many of the sipahees of the Mobarick Pultun, on detached duty with the king's wakeel, in attendance upon me, were, this morning, arrested, while taking off the choppers from the houses of villages along the road, and around my camp, for fuel and fodder, in what they called the '*usual way*'. The best beams and rafters, and the whole of the straw were fast moving off to my camp; and when seized the sipahees seemed much surprised, and asked me what they were to do, as they had not received any pay for six months; and the government expected, that they would help themselves to straw and timber whereever they could most conveniently find it. All were fined; but the hope to put a stop to this intolerable evil, under the present system, is a vain one. The evil has the acquiescence and encouragement of the government and its functionaries, of all kinds and grades, throughout the country. It is distressing to witness, every day, such melancholy proofs of how much is done that ought not to be done, and how much that ought to be done is left undone, in so fine a country. A want of sympathy or fellow feeling between the governing and governed is common in all parts of India, but in no part that I have seen is it so marked as in Oude. The officers of the government delight in plundering the peasantry; and upon every local governor, who kills a landholder of any mark, rewards and honors are instantly bestowed, without the slightest inquiry as to the cause or mode. They know that no inquiry will be made; and, therefore, kill them when they can no matter how, or for what cause. The great landholders would kill the local governors with just as little scruple, did they not fear, that it might make the British Government interpose, and aid in the pursuit after them.

January 17, 1850. – Sundeela, about thirteen miles from our last camp, on the bank of the little river Saee, over a plain of good doomuteea soil, very fertile, and well cultivated in the neighbourhood of villages. The greater portion of the plain is, however, uncultivated, though capable of the best tillage; and shows more than the usual signs of maladministration. In this district there are only three Tallookdars, and they do not rob or resist the government at present. They distrust the government authorities, however, and never have any personal intercourse with them. The waste is entirely owing to the bad character of the contractors, and the license given to the troops and establishments under them. The district is now held in *amanee* tenure, and under the management of Hoseyn Buksh, who entered into his charge only six weeks ago. He is without any experience in, or knowledge of, his duties. He has three Regiment of Nujeebs, on duty, under him, and all who are present came out to meet me. Any thing more unlike soldiers it would be difficult to conceive. They are feared only by the honest and industrious. Wherever the Amil goes they go with him, and are a terrible scourge to the country – by far the worst that the country suffers under.

The first thing necessary to effect a reform is, to form out of these disorderly and useless bodies a few efficient Regiments, – do away with the purveyance system, on which they are now provided with fuel, fodder, carriage, &c. – pay them liberally and punctually – supply them with good clothing, arms, accoutrements and ammunition; and concentrate them at five or six points, in good cantonments, whence they can move quickly to any part, where their services may be required. No more than are indispensably required, should attend the local authorities, in their circuits. All the rest should remain in cantonments till called for on emergency; and when so called for, they should have all the conveyance they require, and the supplies provided for them. The conveyance at fixed rates, and the supplies at the market price, in good bazaars. For police duties and revenue collections there should be a sufficient body of men kept up, and at the disposal of the revenue and police authorities. The military establishments should be under the control of a different authority. But all this would be of no avail, unless the corps were under able commanders, relieved from the fear of Court favorites; and under a commander-in-chief who understood his duty, and had influence enough to secure all that the troops required to render them efficient, and not a child of seven years of age.

Several of the villages of Sundeela are held by Syud zumeendars, who are peaceable and industrious subjects, and were generally better protected than others, under the influence of Chowdhere, Sheik Hushmut Allee, of Sundeela, an agricultural capitalist and landholder, whom no local authority could offend with impunity. His proper trade was to aid landholders of high and low degree, by becoming surety for their punctual payment of the government demand, and advancing the instalments of that demand himself when they had not the means, and thereby saving them from the visits of the local authorities, and their rapacious and disorderly troops; but in an evil hour he ventured to extend his protection a little further, and to save them from the oppressions of an unscrupulous contractor, he undertook to manage the district himself, and make good all the government demand upon it. He was unable to pay all that he had bound himself to pay. His brother was first seized by the troops and taken to Lucknow. He languished under the discipline to which he was there subjected; and when, on the point of death, from what his friends call a *broken heart*, and the government authorities *cholera morbus*,[a] he was released. He died immediately after his return home; and Hushmut Allee was then seized and taken to Lucknow, where he is now confined. The people here lament his absence as a great misfortune to the district, as he was the only one among them who ever had authority and influence, united with a fellow feeling for the people, and a disposition to promote their welfare and happiness.

[a] The term, first recorded from 1819, for 'Asiatic', 'Epidemic' or 'Malignant' cholera which is endemic in India.

END OF FIRST VOLUME

DIARY

OF A

TOUR THROUGH OUDE,

IN

DECEMBER 1849, & JANUARY & FEBRUARY, 1850.

BY

THE RESIDENT

Lieutenant-Colonel W. H. Sleeman.

VOLUME II.

PRINTED AT LUCKNOW IN A PARLOUR PRESS.

1852.

The title page of the 1858 edition reads:

A / Journey / through the / Kingdom of Oude, / in 1849–1850; /

By direction of the Right Hon. the Earl of Dalhousie, / Governor-General. /

With Private Correspondence relative / to the Annexation of Oude to British India, &c. /

By Major-General Sir W. H. Sleeman, K.C.B. / Resident at the Court of Lucknow. /

In Two Volumes. / Vol. II. /

London: / Richard Bentley, / Publisher in Ordinary to Her Majesty. / 1858. /

[Title page reproduced by courtesy of the Curators of the Bodleian Library, Oxford.]

DIARY OF A
TOUR THROUGH OUDE

VOLUME II

CHAPTER VII

[Sundeela, Bangur and Sandee 'districts',
18–28 January 1850]

[1852: ɪɪ, 1–3] [1858: ɪɪ, 1–4]
The baronial proprietors in the Sundeela district are Murdun
Sing, of Dhurawun, with a rent roll of 38,000; Gunga Buksh, of
Atwa, with one of 25,000; Chundeeka Buksh, of Birwa, with
one of 25,000; and Somere Sing, of Rodamow, with one of
34,000. This is the rent roll declared and entered in the accounts; but it is much below the real one. The government
officers are afraid to measure their lands, or to make any enquiries on the estates into their value, lest they should turn
robbers and plunder the country, as they are always prepared to
do. They have always a number of armed and brave retainers
ready to support them in any enterprise, and can always add to
their number on emergency. There is never any want of loose
characters ready to fight for the sake of plunder alone. A Tallookdar, however, when opposed to his government, does not
venture to attack another Tallookdar or his tenants. He stands
too much in need of his aid, or at least of his neutrality and
forbearance.

January 18, 1850. – Halted at Sundeela. To the north of the
town there is a large uncultivated plain of *oosur* land, that would
answer for cantonments; but the water lies, for some time after

rain, in many places. The drainage is defective, but might be made good towards a rivulet to the north and west. There is another open plain to the west of the town, between the suburbs and the small village of Ausoo Serae, where the Trigonometrical Survey[a] has one of its towers. It is about a mile from east to west, and more from north to south, and well adapted for the location of troops and civil establishments. The climate is said to be very good. The town is large and still populous, but the best families seem to be going to decay, or leaving the place. There are a good many educated persons from Sundeela in our civil establishments who used to leave their families here; but life and property have become so very insecure, that they now always take them with them to the districts in which they are employed, or send them to others. There are many good houses of burnt brick and cement, but they are going fast to decay, and are all surrounded by numerous mud-houses without coverings, or with coverings of the same material, which are hidden from view by low parapets. These houses have a wretched appearance.

The Amil has twelve guns with him; but the bullocks are all so much out of condition from want of food, that they can scarcely walk; and the Amil was obliged to hire a few plough bullocks, from the cultivators, to draw out two guns to my camp to fire the salute. They get no grain, and there is little or no grass anywhere on the fallow and waste lands, from the want of rain during June, July and August. The Amil told me, that he had no stores or ammunition for the guns; and that their carriages were all gone, or going, to pieces, and had received no repairs whatever for the last twelve years. I had, in the evening, a visit from Rajah Murdun Sing, of *Dharawun*; a stout and fat man, who bears a fair character. He is of the Tilokchundee Bys clan, who cannot intermarry with each other, as they are all of the same gote or family. It would, according to their notions, be incestuous.

[a] The 'Great Trigonometrical Survey' of India which was begun in 1801 from a baseline in Madras Presidency. See G. F. Heaney, 'The story of the Survey of India', *The Geographical Magazine*, vol. xxx, no. 4 (Aug. 1957), pp. 182–90; R. H. Phillimore, *Historical Records of the Survey of India*, 4 vols (Dehra Dun: Survey of India, 1945–); and C. B. Markham, *A Memoir on the Indian Surveys* (London, 2nd ed. 1878, reprint Amsterdam, 1968).

Diary of a Tour Through Oude

January 19, 1850.– Hutteeah Hurrun, thirteen miles. The plain level as usual, and of the loose doomuteea soil, fertile in natural powers every where, and well tilled around the villages, which are more numerous than in any other part that we have passed over. The water is every where near the surface, and wells are made at little cost. A well is dug at a cost of from five to ten rupees; and in the muteear, or argillaceous soil, will last for irrigation for forty years. To line it with burnt bricks without cement will cost from one to two hundred rupees; and to add cement will cost a hundred more. Such lining is necessary in light soil, and still more so in sandy or *bhoor*. They frequently line their wells at little cost with long thick cables, made of straw and twigs, and twisted round the surface inside. The fields are every where irrigated from wells or pools, and near villages well manured; and the wheat and other spring crops are excellent. They have been greatly benefitted by the late rains, and in no case injured. The ground all the way covered with white hoar frost, and the dews heavy in a cloudless sky. Finer weather I have never known in any quarter of the world...

[1852: ii, 5–13] [1858: ii, 6–15]

A good deal of the land, distant from villages, lies waste, though capable of good tillage; and from the all-pervading cause, the want of confidence in the government and its officers, and of any feeling of security to life, property and industry. Should this cause be removed, the whole surface of the country would become the beautiful garden, which the parts well cultivated and peopled now are. It is all well studded with fine trees – single and in clusters and grove. The soil is good – the water near the surface, and to be obtained in any abundance at little outlay – and the peasantry are industrious, brave and robust. Nothing is wanted but good and efficient government, which might be easily secured. I found many Kunojee Brahmins in the villages along the road, who tilled their own fields without the aid of ploughmen; and they told me, that when they had no longer the means to hire ploughmen, they were permitted to hold their own ploughs – that is, they were not excommunicated for doing so.

In passing along with wheat fields close by on our left, while the sun is a little above the horizon on the right, we see a *glory* round the shadows of our heads as they extend into the fields. All see these *glories* around their own heads, but cannot see them around those of their neighbours. They stretch out from the head and shoulders, with gradually diminished splendour to some short distance. This beautiful and interesting appearance arises from the leaves and stalks of the wheat being thickly bespangled with dew. The observer's head being in the direct rays of the sun, as they pass over him to that of his shadow in the field, he carries the glory with him. Those before and behind him see the same glory around the shadows of their own heads, but cannot see it round that of the head of any other person before or behind; because he is on one or other side of the direct rays which pass over them. It is best seen when the sky is most clear, and the dew most heavy. It is not seen over bushy crops such as the arahur, nor on the grass plains.

January 20, 1850. – Beneegunge, eight miles, over a slightly undulating plain of light, sandy soil, scantily cultivated, but well studded with fine trees of the best kind. Near villages, where the land is well watered and manured, the crops are fine and well varied. All the pools are full from the late rain, and they are numerous and sufficient to water the whole surface of the country, with a moderate fall of rain in December or January. If they are not available, the water is always very near the surface, and wells can be made for irrigation at a small cost. The many rivers and rivulets, which enter Oude from the Himmaleh chain and Tarae forest, and flow gently through the country towards the Ganges, without cutting very deeply into the soil, always keep the water near the surface, and available in all quarters and in any quantity for purposes of irrigation. Never was country more favored by nature, or more susceptible of improvement under judicious management. There is really hardly an acre of land that is not capable of good culture, or that need be left waste, except for the sites of towns and villages, and ponds for irrigation, or that would be left waste under good government. The people understand tillage well, and are

190

industrious and robust – capable of any exertion under protection and due encouragement.

The government has all the revenues to itself, having no public debt, and paying no tribute to any one, while the country receives from the British Government alone fifty lakhs, or half a million a year; first, in the incomes of guaranteed pensioners, whose stipends are the interest of loans received by our Government at different times from the sovereigns of Oude, as a provision for their relatives and dependants in perpetuity, and as endowments for their mausoleums and mosques, and other religious and eleemosynary establishments; second, in the interest paid for Government securities held by people residing in Oude; third, in the payment of pensions to the families of men who have been killed in our service; and to invalid native officers and sipahees of our army residing there; fourth, in the savings of others who still serve in our army, while their families reside in Oude; and those of the native officers of our civil establishments, whose families remain at their homes in Oude; fifth, in the interest on a large amount of our Government securities held by people at Lucknow, who draw the interest not from the Resident's Treasury, but from the General Treasury in Calcutta, or the Treasuries of our bordering districts, in order to conceal their wealth from the king and his officers. Over and above all this our Government has to send into Oude, to be expended there, the pay of five regiments of infantry, and a company of artillery, which amounts to some six or seven lakhs more. Oude has so many places of pilgrimage, that it receives more in the purchase of the food and other necessaries required by the pilgrims, during their transit and residence, than it sends out with pilgrims who visit shrines and holy places in other countries. It requires little from other countries, but a few luxuries for the rich in shawls from Kashmere and the Punjab, silks, satins, broad cloth, muslins, guns, watches, &c. &c. from England.

A great portion of the salt and saltpetre required is raised within Oude; and so is all the agricultural produce, except in seasons of drought; and the arms required for the troops are manufactured in Oude, with the exception of some few cannon and shells, and the musquets and bayonets for the few disciplined regiments. The royal family and some of the Mahommedan gentlemen at Lucknow send money occasionally to the shrines of Mecca, Medina, Kurbala and Nujuf Ashruf,[a] in Turkish Arabia; and some Hindoos send some to Benares and other places of worship, to be distributed in charity, or laid out in useful works in their name. Some few Hindoo and Mahommedan gentlemen, when they have lost their places and favor at the Oude Court, go and reside at Cawnpoor, and some few other places in the British territory for greater security; but, generally, it may be said, that, in spite of all disadvantages, mahommedan gentlemen from Oude, in whatever country they may serve, like to leave their families in Oude, and to return and spend what they acquire among them. They find better society there than in our own territories, or societies more to their tastes – better means for educating their sons – more splendid processions, festivals and other inviting sights, in which they and their families can participate without cost – more consideration for rank and learning, and more attractive places for worship and religious observances. The little town of Kakoree, about ten or twelve miles from Lucknow, has, I believe, more educated men, filling high and lucrative offices in our civil establishments, than any other town in India, except Calcutta. They owe the greater security, which they there enjoy, compared with other small towns in Oude, chiefly to the respect in which they are known to be held by the British Government and its officers; and to the influence of their friends and relatives, who hold office about the Court of Lucknow.

January 21, 1850.[b] – Sakin, ten miles north west. The country well studded with fine trees, and pretty well cultivated; but the soil is light from a superabundance of sand; and the crops are chiefly autumn, except in the immediate vicinity of villages, and

---

[a] Mecca and Medina, which are associated with Muhammad, are in Arabia; see *The Encyclopaedia of Islam* [*EI*], vol. iii (London, 1936), pp. 83–92 and 436–48. Kerbela (Meshhed Husain), the burial place of Husain, and al-Nadjaf (Meshhed Ali), the site of the tomb of Ali, are now in Iraq; see *EI*, vol. iii, pp. 477–9 and 815–16.

[b] Date given incorrectly as 1849 in original.

cut in December. The surface, on which they stood this season, appears to be waste, except where the stalks of the jowar and bajara are left standing for sale and use, as fodder for cattle. These stalks are called kurbee, and form good fodder for elephants, bullocks, &c. &c. during the cold, hot and rainy season. They are said to keep better when left on the ground – after the heads have been gathered – than when stacked. The sandy soil, in the vicinity of villages, produces fine spring crops of all kinds, wheat, gram, sugar-cane, arahur, tobacco, &c. &c., being well manured by drainage from the villages, and by the dung stored and spread over it; and that more distant would produce the same, if manured and irrigated in the same way. The head men, or proprietors, of some villages along the road mentioned

that the fine state in which we saw them was owing to their being strong and able to resist the government authorities when disposed – as they generally were – to oppress or rackrent them – that the landholders owed their strength to their union, for all were bound to turn out and afford aid to their neighbour on hearing the concerted signal of distress – that this league, *'offensive and defensive'*, extended all over the Bangur district, into which we entered about midway between this and our last stage; and that we should see how much better it was peopled and cultivated, in consequence, than the district of Mahomdee, to which we were going – that the strong only could keep any thing under the Oude government; and as they could not be strong without union, all landholders were solemnly pledged to aid each other, *to the death,* when oppressed or attacked by the local officers.

They asked Captain Weston, who was some miles behind me, what was the Resident's object in this tour – whether the Honourable Company's Government was to be introduced into Oude? He told them, that the object was solely to see the state of the country and condition of the people, with a view to suggest to the king's government any measures that might seem calculated to improve both; and asked them whether they wished to come under the British rule. They told him – 'that they should like much to have the British rule introduced, if it could be done, without worrying them with its complicated laws, and formal and distant courts of justice, of which they had heard terrible accounts.'

Diary of a Tour Through Oude

The Nazim of the Tundeeawun, or Bangur district, met me on his border, and told me

that he was too weak to enforce the king's orders, or to collect his revenues – that he had with him one efficient company of Captain Bunbury's corps, with one gun in good repair, and provided with draft bullocks, in good condition; and that this was the only force he could rely upon; while the landholders were strong, and so leagued together for mutual defence, that, at the sound of a matchlock, or any other concerted signal, all the men of a dozen large villages would, in an hour, concentrate upon and defeat the largest force the king's officers could assemble – that they did so almost every year, and often frequently within the same year – that he had, nominally, eight guns on duty with him; but the carriage of one had already gone to pieces; and those of the rest had been so long without repair, that they would go to pieces with very little firing – that the draft bullocks had not had any grain for many years, and were hardly able to walk; and he was, in consequence, obliged to hire plough bullocks, to draw the gun required to salute the Resident; but he had only ten days ago received an order to give them grain himself, charge for it in his accounts, and hold himself responsible for their condition – that they had been so starved, that he was obliged to restrict them to a few ounces a day at first, or they would have all died from over eating.

This order has arisen from my earnest intercession in favour of the artillery draft bullocks; but so many are interested in the abuse, that the order will not be long enforced. Though the grain will, as heretofore, be paid for from the Treasury, it will, I hear, be given to the bullocks only while I am out on this tour.

In the evening some cultivators came to complain, that they had been robbed of all their bhoosa (chaff) by a sipahee from my camp. I found, on enquiry, that the sipahee belonged to Captain Hearsey's five companies of Frontier Police – that these companies had sixteen four-bullock hackeries attached to them for the carriage of their tents and luggage; and that these hackeries had gone to the village, and taken all that the complainants had laid up for their own cattle for the season – that such hackeries formerly received twenty-seven rupees eight annas a month each, and their owners were expected to purchase their own fodder; but that this allowance had, for some years, been cut down to fourteen rupees a month, and they told *to help themselves to fodder wherever they could find it* – that all the hackeries hired by the king and his local officers, for the use of troops, establishments,

&c. &c. had been reduced, at the same rate, from twenty-seven eight annas a month to fourteen, and their owners received the same order. All villages, near the roads, along which the troops and establishments move, are plundered of their bhoosa, and all those within ten miles of the place, where they may be detained for a week or fortnight, are plundered in the same way.

The Telinga corps and Frontier Police are alone provided with tents and hackeries by government. The Nujeeb corps are provided with neither. The Oude government formerly allowed, for each four-bullock hackery, thirty rupees a month, from which *two rupees and half* were deducted for the perquisites of office. The owners of the hackeries were expected to purchase bhoosa and other fodder for their bullocks at the market price; but they took, what they required, without payment, in *collusion with* the officers under whom they were employed, or in *spite* of them; and the Oude government, in 1845, cut the allowance down to seventeen rupees and half, out of which *three rupees and half* are cut for perquisites, leaving fourteen rupees for the hackeries; and their owners and drivers have the free privilege of helping themselves to bhoosa and other fodder wherever they can find them. Some fifty or sixty of these hackeries were formerly allowed for each Telinga corps with guns – now only twenty-two are allowed; and when they move they must, like Nujeeb corps, seize what more they require. They are allowed to charge nothing for their extra carriage, and, therefore, pay nothing!

January 22, 1850.[a] – Tundeeawun, eight miles west. The country level, and something between doomuteea and muteear, very good, and in parts well cultivated, particularly in the vicinity of villages; but a large portion of the surface is covered with jungle, useful only to robbers and refractory landholders, who abound in the pergunnah of Bangur. In this respect it is reputed one of the worst districts in Oude. Within the last few years, the king's troops have been frequently beaten and driven out with loss, even when commanded by an European officer. The landholders and armed peasantry of the different villages unite their *quotas*

[a] Date given incorrectly as 1849 in original.

of auxiliaries, and concentrate upon them on a concerted signal, when they are in pursuit of robbers and rebels. Almost every able bodied man of every village in Bangur is trained to the use of arms of one kind or another, and none of the king's troops, save those who are disciplined and commanded by European officers, will venture to move against a landholder of this district; and when the local authorities cannot obtain the aid of such troops, they are obliged to conciliate the most powerful and unscrupulous by reductions in the assessment of the lands, or additions to their *nankar*...

[1852: II, 19–38] [1858: II, 21–42]

It would be of advantage to remove the regiment of Oude local infantry from Seetapoor to Tundeeawun, where its presence and services are much more required. The climate is as good, and all that native soldiers require for food and clothing are cheaper. The drainage is good; and to the east of the town there is one of the finest plains for a cantonment that I have ever seen. There are but few wells, but new ones can be made at a trifling cost; and the Oude government would willingly incur the outlay required for these and for all the public buildings required for the new cantonments, to secure the advantage of such a change. The cost of the public buildings would be only 12,000 rupees; and the same sum would have to be given in compensation for private buildings – total 24,000. The refractory landholders would soon be reduced to order, and prevented from any longer making their villages dens of robbers as they now do; and the jungles around would all soon disappear. These jungles are not thick, or unhealthy, consisting of the small dhak or palas tree, with little or no under wood; and the surface they now occupy would soon be covered with fine spring crops, and studded with happy village communities, were people encouraged, by an assurance of protection, to settle upon it, and apply their capital and labour to its cultivation. The soil is every where of the finest quality, the drainage is good, and there are no jheels. There are a few ponds, yielding the water required for the irrigation of the spring crops, during their progress to maturity, from November to March. They are said all to become dry in the hot season. It is,

I think, capable of being made the finest part of this fine country of Oude.

It was in contemplation to make the road from Lucknow to Shajehanpoor and Bareilly pass through this place, Tundeeawun, by which some thirty miles of distance would be saved, and a good many small rivers and watercourses avoided. Why this design was given up I know not; but I believe the only objection was the greater insecurity of this line from the bad character of the great landholders of the Bangur and Sandee Palee districts; and the greater number of thieves and robbers who, in consequence, reside in them. There has been but little outlay in works of any kind in the old line through Seetapoor; and when measures have been taken to render this line more secure, a good road will, I hope, be made through Tundeeawun. It was once a populous place, but has been falling off for many years, as the disorders in the district have increased. The Nazim resides here. The last Nazim, Hoseyn Allee, who was removed to Khyrabad, at the end of last year, is said to have given an increase of *nankar* to the refractory landholders of this district during that year, to the extent of forty thousand rupees a year. to induce them to pay the government demand, and desist from plunder. By this means he secured a good reputation at Court, and the charge of a more profitable and less troublesome district; and left the difficult task of resuming this lavish increase of the *nankar* to his successor, Seonath, the son of Dilla Ram, who held the contract of the district for some twenty years up to the time of his death, which took place last year. Seonath is a highly respectable and amiable man; but he is very delicate in health, and, in consequence, deficient in the vigour and energy required to manage so turbulent a district. He has, however, a deputy in Kidder Nath, a relative, who has all the ability, vigour and energy required, if well supported and encouraged by the Oude Durbar. He was deputy under Dilla Ram, for many years, and the same under Hoseyn Allee, last year. He is a man of great intelligence and experience; and one of the best officers of the Oude government that I have yet seen.

There are two kinds of recognised perquisites, which landholders enjoy in Oude, and in most other parts of India. The *nankar* and the *seer* land. The *nankar* is a portion of the recognised rent roll acknowledged by the ruler to be due to the landholder for the risk, cost and trouble of management; and for his perquisite as hereditary proprietor of the soil, when the management is confided to another. It may be ten, twenty, or one hundred per cent upon the rent roll of the estate, which is recognised in the public accounts, as the holder happens to be an object of fear or of favor, or otherwise; and the real rent roll may be more or less than that which is recognised in the public accounts. The actual rent, which the landholder receives, may increase with improvements, and he may conceal the improvement from the local authorities, or bribe them to conceal it from government; or it may diminish from lands falling out of tillage, or becoming improverished by over-cropping, or from a diminution of demand for land produce; and the landholder may be unable to satisfy the local authorities of the fact, or to prevail upon them to represent the circumstance to government. The amount of the *nankar* once recognised, remains the same till a new rate is recognised by government. But when the government becomes weak, the local authorities assume the right to recognise new rates, to suit their own interest; and pretend that they do so to promote that of their sovereign.

I may instance the Amil of this district last year. He was weak, while the landholders were strong. They refused to pay, on the plea of bad seasons. He could send no money to the Treasury, and was in danger of losing his place. The man who had to pay a revenue of ten thousand, could not be induced to pay five. He enjoyed an acknowledged *nankar* of two thousand upon a recognized rent roll of twelve thousand; and, to induce him to pay, he gives him an increase to this *nankar* of one thousand, making the *nankar* three thousand, and reducing the revenue to nine thousand. Being determined to render the increase to his *nankar* permanent, whether the government consents or not, the landholder agrees to pay the ten thousand for the present year. The collector sends the whole, or a part of the one thousand, as gratuities to influential men at Court, and enters it in the public accounts as irrecoverable balance. The present Amil, finding that the increase to the *nankar* has not been acknowledged by government, demands the full ten thousand rupees for the present year. The landholder refuses to pay any thing, takes to the jungles, and declares, that he will resist till his permanent right to the increase be acknowledged.

The Amil has taken the contract at the rate of last year, as the government had sanctioned no increase to the *nankar*, and he pleads in vain for a remission in the rate, which he pledged himself to pay, or an increase of means to enforce payment among so turbulent and refractory a body of landholders. As I have before mentioned, the Oude government has, this season, issued an order to all revenue collectors to refuse to recognise any increase to the *nankar*, that has been made since the year A.D. 1814, or Fusilee 1222, when Saadut Allee died; as none has, since that year, received the sanction of government, though the *nankar* has been more than doubled within that period in the manner above described by local authorities. The increase to the *nankar*, and the alienation, in rent free tenure, of lands liable to assessment in 1814, by local authorities, and influential persons at Court, are supposed to amount, in all Oude, to forty lakhs of rupees a year. None of them have been formally recognised by the Court, but a great part of them has been tacitly acquiesced in by the minister and Dewan for the time being. They cannot enforce the order for reverting to the *nankar* of 1814; and if they attempt to do so, the whole country will be in disorder. Indeed, the minister knows his own weakness too well, to think seriously of ever making such an attempt. The *seer* lands are those which the landholders and their families till themselves, or by means of their servants, or hired cultivators. Generally they are not entered at all in the rent rolls; and when they are entered, it is at less rates than are paid for the other lands. The difference between the no rent, or less rates, and the full rates, is part of their perquisites. These lands are, generally, shared out among the members of the family as hereditary possessions.

January 23, 1850. – Behta, ten miles, over a plain of fine muteear soil. The greater part of the surface is, however, covered by a low palas jungle. The jungle remains, because no one will venture to lay out his capital in rooting up the trees and shrubs, and bringing the land under culture where the fruits of his industry, and his own life, and those of his family, would be so very insecure; and because the powerful landholders around require the jungles to run to when in arms against the government officers, as they commonly are. The land, under this jungle, is as rich in natural powers, as that in tillage; and nothing can be finer than the crops are in the cultivated parts, particularly in those immediately around villages. There are numerous large trees in the jungles; but the fine peepul and banyan trees are torn to pieces for the use of the elephants and camels of the establishments of the local officers, and for the cows, bullocks and buffaloes of the peasantry. The cows and buffaloes are said to give greater quantities of milk when fed on the leaves of these trees, than when fed on any thing else, available in the dry season; but the milk is said to be of inferior quality. All the cultivated and peopled parts are beautifully studded with single trees and groves.

No respectable dwelling house is any where to be seen; and the most substantial landholders live in wretched mud hovels, with invisible covers. I asked the people why, and was told, that they were always too insecure to lay out any thing in improving their dwelling houses; and, besides, did not like to have such local ties, where they were so liable to be driven away by the government officers, or by the landholders in arms against them, and their reckless followers. The local officers of government, of the highest grade, occupy houses of the same wretched description, for none of them can be sure of occupying them a year, or of ever returning to them again when once removed from their present offices; and they know, that neither their successors, nor any one else, will ever purchase or pay rent for them. No mosques, mausoleums, temples, seraees, colleges, courts of justice, or prisons, to be seen in any of the towns or villages. There are a few Hindoo shrines at the half dozen places that popular legends have rendered places of pilgrimage; and a few small tanks and bridges made in olden times by public officers, when they were more secure in their tenure of office than they now are. All the fine buildings, raised by former rulers and their officers, at the old capital of Fyzabad, are going fast to ruin. The old city of Ajoodheea is a ruin, with the exception of a few buildings along the bank of the river raised by wealthy Hindoos in honour of Ram, who once lived and reigned there, and is believed, by all Hindoos, to have been an incarnation of Vishnoo.[a]

I have often mentioned, that the artillery draft bullocks receive no grain, and are every where so poor, that they can hardly walk, much less draw heavy guns and tumbrils. The reason is this; the most influential men at Court obtain the charge of feeding the cattle in all the different establishments, and charge for a certain quantity of grain, or other food, at the market price, for each animal. They contract for the supply of the cattle with some grain merchant of the city, who undertakes to distribute it through his own agents. The contractor, for the supply of the artillery draft bullocks, sends an agent with those in attendance upon every collector of the land revenue, and he gives them as little as possible. The contractor, afraid of making an enemy of the influential man at Court, who could, if he chose, deprive him of his contract or place, never presumes to interfere; and the agent gives the poor bullocks no grain at all. The collector, or officer in charge of the district, is, however, obliged, every month, to pay the agent of the contractor the full market price of the grain supposed to be consumed, that is one sere and half a day by every bullock. The same, or some other influential person at Court, obtains and transfers, in the same way, the contract for the feeding of the elephants, horses, camels, bullocks and other animals kept at Lucknow for use, or amusement; and none of them are in much better condition than the draft bullocks of the artillery in the remote districts – all are starved or nearly starved, and objects of pity. Those who are responsible for their being fed, are too strong in Court favour, to apprehend any punishment for not feeding them at all.

In my ride this morning I asked the people of the villages, through and near which we passed, whether infanticide prevailed. They told me, that it prevailed amongst almost all the Rajpoot families of any rank in Oude – that very poor families of those

[a] For the 'incarnations' (avataras) of Vishnu, see Dowson, *Dictionary of Hindu Mythology*, pp. 33–8.

classes retained their daughters, because they could get something for them from the families of lower grade into which they married them; but that those who were too well off in the world, to condescend to take money for their daughters from lower grades, and were obliged to incur heavy costs in marrying them into families of the same or higher grade, seldom allowed their infant daughters to live. 'It is strange', I observed, 'that men, who have to undergo such heavy penance for killing a cow, even by accident, should have to undergo none for the murder of their own children; nor to incur any odium among the circle of society in which they live – not even among Brahmins and the ministers of their religion.' 'They do incur odium and undergo penance', said Rajah Bukhtawur Sing – 'do they not?' said he to some Brahmins standing near – they smiled, but hesitated to reply. 'They know they do', said the Rajah, 'but are afraid to tell the truth, for they and their families live in villages belonging to these proud Rajpoot landholders, and would be liable to be turned out of house and home were they to tell what they know.' One of the Brahmins then said,

all this is true, sir, but after the murder of every infant, the family considers itself to be an object of displeasure to the deity; and after the twelfth day they send for the family priest, (Prohut) and, by suitable gratuities, obtain absolution – this is necessary, whether the family be rich or poor; but when the absolution is given, nothing more is thought or said about the matter – the Gour and other Rajpoots, who can afford to unite their daughters in marriage to the sons of Chouhans, Byses and other families of higher grade, though they cannot obtain theirs in return for their sons, commit less murders of this kind than others; but all the Rajpoot clans commit more or less of them; habit has reconciled them to it; but it appears very shocking to us Brahmins, and all other classes – they commonly bury the infants alive as soon as possible after their birth. We, sir, are helpless, living, as we do, among such turbulent and pitiless landholders, and cannot presume to admonish or remonstrate – our lives would not be safe for a moment, were we to say any thing, or seem to notice such crimes.

I do not think that any landholder of this class, in the Bangur district, would feel much compunction for the commission of any crime that did not involve their expulsion from caste, or degradation in rank. Great crimes do not involve these penalties – they incur them only by small peccadillos, or offences deemed

Diary of a Tour Through Oude

venal among other societies. The government of Oude, as it is
at present constituted, will never be able to put down, effectually,
the great crimes which now stain almost every acre of land in its
dominions. It is painful to pass over a country abounding so
much in what the evil propensities of our nature incite men to
do, when not duly restrained; and so little in what the good
prompt us to perform and create, when duly protected and encouraged, under good government.

January 24, 1850. – Sandee, fourteen miles, over a plain of light
domuteea soil, which becomes very sandy for the last four or
five miles. The crops are scanty upon the more sandy parts,
except in the vicinity of villages; but there is little jungle, and
no undue portion of fallow for so light a soil. About five miles
from our last ground, we came through the large and populous
village of Bawun; about three miles further, through another of
nearly the same size, Sungeechamow; and about three miles
further on, through one still larger, Admapoor, which is
three miles from Sandee. Sandee and Nawabgunge join each
other, and are on the bank of the Gurra river, a small stream,
whose waters are said to be very wholesome. We passed the
boundary of the Bangur district just before we entered the village
of Sungeechamow, which lies in that of Sandee.

There is a Hindoo shrine on the right of the road between
Sandee and Adamapoor, which is said to be considered very
sacred, and called Burmawust. It is a mere grove, with a few
priests, on the bank of a large lake, which extends close up to
Sandee on the south. The river Gurra flows under the town
to the north. The place is said to be healthy, but could hardly
be so, were this lake to the west or east, instead of the south,
whence the wind seldom blows. This lake must give out more
or less of malaria that would be taken over the village, for
the greater portion of the year, by the prevailing easterly
and westerly winds. I do not think the place so eligible for
a cantonment as Tundeeawun, in point either of salubrity,
position, or soil.[a]

[a] Sleeman added a manuscript note to the 1852 edition: 'and I am now satisfied
that Tundeeawun is not so healthy a place as I supposed'. This was not printed in
1858, cf. vol. II, p. 31.

January 25, 1850. – Halted at Sandee. The lake on the south side, mentioned yesterday, abounds in fish, and is covered with wild fowl; but the fish we got from it yesterday was not good of its kind. There are very fine groves of mango trees close to Sandee, planted by merchants and shop-keepers of the place. The oldest are still held by the descendants of those by whom they were first planted more than a century ago; and no tax whatever is imposed upon the trees of any kind, or upon the lands on which they stand. Many young groves are growing up around, to replace the old ones as they decay; and the greatest possible security is felt in the tenure by which they are held by the planter, or his descendants, though they hold no written lease, or deed of gift; and have neither written law nor court of justice to secure it to them. Groves and solitary mango, semul, tamarind, mhowa and other trees, whose leaves and branches are not required for the food of elephants and camels, are more secure in Oude than in our own territories; and the country is, in consequence, much better provided with them. While they give beauty to the landscape, they alleviate the effects of droughts to the poorer classes from the fruit they supply; and droughts are less frequently and less severely felt in a country, so intersected by fine streams, flowing from the Tarae forest, or down from the perpetual snows of neighbouring hills, and keeping the water always near the surface. These trees tend also to render the air healthy, by giving out oxygen in large quantities during the day, and absorbing carbonic acid gas. The river Gurra enters the Ganges about twelve miles below Sandee. Boats take timber on this stream from the Phillibeet[a] district to Cawnpoor. It passes near the town of Shajehanpoor; and the village of Palee, twenty miles north-west from Sandee, where we shall have to recross it.

January 26, 1850. – Busora, twelve miles north-west from Sandee, over a plain of light sandy soil, or bhoor, with some intervals of oosur. The tillage extends over as much of the surface as it ought in so light a soil; and the district of Sandee Palee generally is said to be well cultivated. It had been under the

---

[a] Now written as Pilibhit.

charge of Hafiz Abdoollah, a very honest and worthy man, for seven years up to his death, which took place in November last. He is said never to have broken faith with a landholder; but he was too weak in means to keep the bad portion under control; and too much occupied in reading or repeating the *koran*, which he knew all by heart, as his name imports. His son, Ameer Gholam Allee, a lad of only thirteen years of age, has been appointed his successor. He promises to be like his father in honesty and love of the holy book.

About half way we passed the village of Bhanapoor, held by zumeendars of the *Dhaukuree* Rajpoot clan, who told me, that they give their daughters in marriage to the Rykwars, but more to the Sombunsie Rajpoots, who abound in the district, and hold the greater part of the lands – that these Sombunsies have absorbed almost all the lands of the other classes by degrees, and are now seizing upon theirs – that the Sombunsies give their daughters in marriage only to the Rathore and Chouhan Rajpoots, few of whom are to be found on the Oude side of the Ganges; and, in consequence, that they take, such as they preserve, to our districts on the other side of that river, but murder the greater part rather than condescend to marry them to men of the other Rajpoot clans whom they deem to be of inferior grade, or go to the expense of uniting them in marriage to clans of higher or equal grade in Oude. Some Sombunsies, who came out to pay their respects from the next village we passed, told us, that they did not give their daughters even to the Tilokchundee Bys Rajpoots; but in this they did not tell the truth.

At the next village, the largest in the parish, Barone, the chief landholder, Kewul Sing, came out and presented his offering of a fine fighting ram. He was armed with his bow, and 'quiver full of arrows'; but told me, that he thought a good gun, with pouch and flask, much better, and he carried the bow and quiver merely because they were lighter. He was surrounded by almost all the people of the town, and told me, that the family held in copartnership fifty-two small villages, immediately around *Barone* – that this village had been attacked and burnt down by Captain Bunbury and his regiment the year before last, without any other cause, that they could understand, save that he had recommended him not to encamp in the grove close by. The fact was, that none of the family would pay the government demand, or obey the old Amil, Hafiz Abdoollah; and it was necessary to make an example. On being asked whether his family and clan, the Sombunsies, preserved or destroyed their daughters, he told me, in the midst of his village community, that he would not deceive me – that they, one and all, destroyed their infant daughters; but that one was, occasionally, allowed to live (*ek-adh*) – that the family was under a taint for twelve days after the murder of an infant, when the family priest (Prohut) was invited and fed in due form; that he then declared the absolution complete, and the taint removed.

The family priest was present, and I asked him what he got on such occasions. He said, that to remove the taint, or grant absolution after the murder of a daughter, he got little or no money; he merely partook of the food prepared for him in due form; but that, on the birth of a son, he got ten rupees from the parents. All the assembled villagers bore testimony to the truth of what the patriarch and the priest told me. They said, that no one would enter a house in which an infant daughter had been destroyed, or eat or drink with any member of the family, till the Prohut had granted the absolution, which he did after the expiration of twelve days, as a matter of course, depending, as he did, upon the good will of the landholders, who were all of the same clan, Sombunsies. Few other Brahmins will condescend to eat, drink or associate with these family and village priests, who take the sins of such murders upon their own heads. The old patriarch rode on with me upon his pony, five miles to my tents, as if I should not think the worse of him for having murdered his own daughters, and permitted others to murder theirs. I told him, that I could hold no converse with men who were guilty of such crimes; and that the vengeance of God would crush them all, sooner or later. For his only excuse he told me, that it was a practice, derived from a long line of ancestors, wiser and better than they were; and that it prevailed in almost every Rajpoot family in the country – that they had, in consequence, become reconciled to it, and knew not how to do without it. Family pride is the cause of this terrible evil.

Diary of a Tour Through Oude

The estate of Kateearee, on the left hand-side of the road to-wards the Ramgunga and Ganges is held by Runjeet Sing, of the Kuteear Rajpoot clan. His estate yields to him about one hundred and twenty thousand rupees a year, while he is assessed at only sixteen thousand. While Hakeem Mehndee was in banishment at Futtehgurh, about fifteen years ago, he became intimate with Runjeet Sing, of Kuteearee; and when he afterwards became minister, in 1837, he is said to have obtained for him the king's seal and signature to a perpetual lease at this rate, from which is deducted a *nankar* of four thousand, leaving an actual demand of only twelve thousand. Were such grants, in perpetuity, respected in Oude, the ministers and their minions would soon sell the whole of His Majesty's dominions, and leave him a beggar. He has not yet been made to pay a higher rate; not, however, out of regard for the king's pledge, but solely out of that for Runjeet's fort of Dhunmutpoor, on the bank of the Ganges, his armed bands, and his seven pieces of cannon. He has been diligently employing all his surplus rents in improving his defensive means; and, besides his fort and guns, is said to have a large body of armed and disciplined men. He has seized upon a great many villages around, belonging to weaker proprietors: and is every year adding to his estate in this way. In this the old Amil, Hafiz Abdoollah, acquiesced, solely because he had not the means, nor the energy to prevent it. He got his estate excluded from the jurisdiction of the local authorities, and placed in the Huzoor Tuhseel. Like others of his class, who reside on the border, he has a village in the British territory to reside in, unmolested, when charged by the Oude authorities with heavy crimes and balances. He had been attacked and driven across the Ganges, in 1837, for contumacy and rebellion; deprived of his estate, and obliged to reside at Futtehgurh, where he first became acquain-ted with Hakeem Mehndee. The Oude government has often remonstrated against the protection which this contumacious and atrocious landholder receives from our subjects and autho-rities.[1] Crimes in this district are not quite so numerous as in

[1] See Resident's letter to Government North-Western Provinces, 3rd August, 1837. King's letter to the Resident, 7th April, 1837. The same to the same, 19th May, 1837. Depositions and urzies.

Bangur; but they are of no less atrocious a character. The thieves and robbers of Bangur, when taken and taxed with being so, say, 'of course we are robbers – if we were not how should we have been permitted to reside in Bangur?' All are obliged to fight and plunder with the landholders, or to rob for them on distant roads, and in distant villages. My camp has been robbed several times within the time I have been out, and the property has been traced to villages in the Sundeela and Bangur districts. In the Sundeela district it can be recovered, when traced, with a small force, and the thieves taken; but in the Bangur district it would require a large military force, well commanded, and a large train of artillery to recover the one or seize the other.

A respectable landholder of this place, a Sombunsie, tells me

that the custom of destroying their female infants has prevailed from the time of the first founder of their race – that a rich man has to give food to many Brahmins, to get rid of the stain, on the twelfth or thirteenth day; but, that a poor man can get rid of it by presenting a little food, in due form, to the village priest – that they cannot give their daughters in marriage to any Rajpoot families, save the Rhathores and Chouhans – that the family of their clan who gave a daughter to any other class of Rajpoots, would be excluded from caste immediately and for ever – that those who have property have to give all they have with their daughters to these Chouhans and Rhathores, and reduce themselves to nothing; and can take nothing from them in return, as it is a great stain to take 'kuneea dan', or virgin price, from any one – that a Sombunsie may, however, when reduced to great poverty, take the 'kuneea dan' from the Chouhans and Rhathores, for a virgin daughter, without being excommunicated from the clan; but even he could not give a daughter to any other clan of Rajpoots without being excluded for ever from caste – that it was a misfortune, no doubt; but it was one that had descended among them from the remotest antiquity, and could not be got rid of – that mothers wept and screamed a good deal when their first female infants were torn from them; but after two or three times giving birth to female infants, they become quiet and reconciled to the usage; and said, 'do as you like' – that some poor parents of their clan did certainly give their daughters for large sums to wealthy people of lower clans, but lost their caste for ever by so doing – that it was the dread of sinking, in substance, from the loss of property, and in grade, from the loss of caste, that alone led to the murder of female infants – that the dread prevailed more or less in every Rajpoot clan, and led to the same thing; but most in the clan that restricted the giving of daughters in marriage to the smallest number of clans.

The infant is destroyed in the room where it is born, and there buried. The floor is then plastered over with cow dung; and, on the thirteenth day, the village or family priest must cook and eat his food in that room. He is provided with wood, ghee, barley, rice and tillee (sesamum). He boils the rice, barley and sesamum in a brass vessel, throws the ghee over them when they are dressed, and eats the whole. This is considered as a *hom*, or burnt offering; and, by eating it in that place, the priest is supposed to take the whole *hutteea*, or sin, upon himself, and to cleanse the family from it. I am told, that they put the milk of the mudar shrub – 'asclepias gigantea' – into the mouth of the infant to destroy it, and cover the mouth with the faeces that first pass from the infant's bowels. It soon dies; and, after the expiation, the parents again occupy the room, and there receive the visits of their family and friends, and gossip as usual! Rajah Bukhta-war Sing tells me, that he has heard the whole process frequently described in this way by the midwives who have attended the birth. These midwives are, however, generally sent out of the room, with the mother, when the infant is found to be a girl. In any law for the effectual prevention of this crime, it would be necessary to prescribe a severe punishment for the priest, as an accessory after the fact. The only objection to this is, I think, that it might deprive the Court of the advantage of an important witness, when required, at the trial of the parents; but, when necessary, he might be admitted as king's evidence. All the people here that I talk to on the subject, say, that the crime has been put down in the greater part of the British territories; and that judicious measures, honestly and firmly carried out, would put it down in Oude, and do away with the scruples which one clan of Rajpoots have, to give their daughters in marriage to another. Unable to murder their daughters, they would be glad to dispose of them in marriage to all clans of Rajpoots. It might be put down in Oude, as it was put down by Mr. Willoughby,[a] of Bombay, in the districts under his charge, by making the abolition one of the conditions on which all persons of the

---

[a] J. P. Willoughby, of the Bombay Civil Service, who was responsible for the campaign against infanticide in Kathiawar in the 1830s; see Kaye, *Administration of the East India Company*, pp. 567–71.

Rajpoot clans hold their lands, and strictly enforcing the observance of that condition. The government of Oude, as now constituted, could do nothing whatever towards putting it down in
this or any other way.

January 27, 1850. – Palee, eight miles, north-west. The road half
way from Sandee to Busora, and half way from Busora to Palee,
passes over a very light, sandy soil – bhoor. I have already stated
that kutcha wells, or wells without burnt brick and cement,
will not last in this sandy soil, while it stands more in need
of irrigation. The road, for the last half way of this morning's
stage, passes over a good doomuteea soil. The whole country is,
however, well cultivated, and well studded with fine trees; and
the approach to Palee is, at this season, very picturesque. The
groves of mango and other fine trees, amidst which the town
stands, on the right bank of the Gurra river, appear very beautiful, as one approaches, particularly now that the surrounding
country is covered by so fine a carpet of rich spring crops. The
sun's rays falling upon such rich masses of foliage, produce an
infinite variety of form, color and tint, on which the eye delights
to repose. We intended to have our camp on the other side of
the river, but no good ground could be found for it without
injury to the crops, within three miles from Palee, and we must
cross it on our way to Shahabad to-morrow.

This small river flows along a little to the right of our march
this morning. About half way we passed a very pretty village,
held and cultivated by families of Kunojee Brahmins, who *condescend* to hold and drive their own ploughs. Other families of
this class pride themselves upon never condescending to drive
their own ploughs; and consider themselves, in consequence, a
shade higher in caste. Other Brahmin families have different
shades, or degrees, of caste, like the Kunojeeas; but I am not
aware that any family of any other class of Brahmins condescend
to hold their own ploughs. I told them, that 'God seemed to
favour their exertions, and bless them with prosperity, for I had
not seen a nicer village or village community.' They seemed to
be all well pleased with my compliment. At Palee resides Bulb-
huder Sing, a notorious robber, who was lately seized and sent

as a felon to Lucknow. After six months' confinement, he bribed himself out, got possession of the estate, which he now holds, and to which he had no right whatever, and had it excluded from the jurisdiction of the local authorities, and transferred to the 'Hozoor Tuhseel'. He has been ever since diligently employed in converting it into a den of robbers; and, in the usual way, seizing upon other people's lands, stock and property, of all kinds.

Hundreds in Oude are doing the same thing in the same way. Scores of those, who suffer from the depredations of this class of offenders, complain to me every day; but I can neither afford them redress, nor hold out any hope of it from any of the Oude authorities. It is a proverb, 'that those who are sentenced to six years imprisonment in Oude, are released in six months, and those who are sentenced to six months, are released in six years'. Great numbers are released every year at Lucknow for *thanksgivings*, or *propitiation*; if the king or any member of his family becomes sick, prisoners are released, that they may recover; and when they recover, others are released as a grateful, and, at the same time, profitable acknowledgment, since the government relieves itself from the cost of keeping them; and its servants appropriate the money paid for their ransom. Those who are in for long periods are, for the most part, great offenders, who are the most able and most willing to pay high for their release – those who are in for short ones are, commonly, the small ones, who are the least able and least disposed to give any thing. The great offenders again are those who are most disposed, and most able, to revenge themselves on such persons as have aided the government in their arrest or conviction; and they do all they can to murder and rob them and their families and relatives, as soon as they are set at large, in order to deter others from doing the same. This would be a great evil in any country, but is terrible in Oude, where no police is maintained for the protection of life and property. The cases of atrocious murders and robberies, which come before me every day and are acknowledged by the local authorities, and neighbours of the sufferers, to have taken place, are frightful. Such sufferings, for which no redress is to be found, would soon desolate any part of India less favoured by nature...

Diary of a Tour Through Oude

[1852: II, 41–3] [1858: II, 45–7]

January 28, 1850. – Shahabad, ten miles. We crossed, close under Palee, the little river Gurra, which continued, for some miles, to flow along, in its winding course, close by on our left. It is here some five or six miles to the south-west of the town. The soil we have come over is chiefly muteear, or the doomuteea tightened by a mixture of clay, or argillaceous earth. Rich crops of rice are grown on this muteear, which retains its moisture so much better than the looser doomuteea soil.

Half way we came through a nice village, the lands of which are subdivided between the members of a large family of Kunojee Brahmins, who came out to see us pass, and pay their respects. The cultivation was so fine, that I *hoped* they were of the class who condescended to hold their own ploughs. I asked them, and they, with seeming pride, told me, that they did not – that they employed servants to hold their ploughs for them When I told them, that this was their *misfortune*, they seemed much amused; but were all well behaved and respectful, though they must have thought my notion a very odd one.

The little Gurra flows from the Oude Tarae forest by the town of Phillibheet, where boats are built, to be taken down to Cawnpoor, on the Ganges, for sale. About four hundred, great and small, are supposed to be taken down the Gurra every year, in the season of the rains. They take down the timber of the Tarae forest, rice and other things; and all are sold with their cargoes at Cawnpoor, or other places on the Ganges. The timbers are floated along on both sides of the boats. Palee is a nice place for a cantonment, or seat of public civil establishments; and Shahabad is no less so. The approach to both, from the south east, is equally beautiful, from the rich crops which cover the ground up to the houses; and the fine groves and majestic single trees which surround them.

Shahabad is a very ancient and large town, occupied chiefly by Pathan musulmans, who are a very turbulent and fanatical set of fellows. Subsookh Rae, a Hindoo, and the most respectable merchant in the district, resided here; and, for some time, consented to officiate as the deputy of poor old Hafiz Abdoollah, for the management of the town, where his influence was great. He had lent a good deal of money to the heads of some of the Pathan families of the town; but, finding few of them disposed to repay, he was, last year, obliged to refuse further loans. They determined to take advantage of the coming mohurrum festival, to revenge the *affront*, as men commonly do, who live among such a fanatical community. The tazeeas are commonly taken up, and carried in procession, ten days after the new moon is first seen, at any place where they are made; but in Oude all go by the day in which the moon is seen from the capital of Lucknow. As soon as she is seen at Lucknow, the king issues an order, throughout his dominions, for the tazeeas to be taken in procession ten days after. She was this year, in November, first seen on the 30th of the month at Lucknow; but at Shahabad, where the sky is generally clearer, she had been seen on the 29th. The men, to whom Subsookh Rae had refused further loans, determined to take advantage of this incident, to wreak their vengeance; and when the deputy promulgated the king's order for the tazeeas to be taken in procession ten days after the 30th, they instigated all the mahomedans of the town, to insist upon taking them out ten days after the 29th; and persuaded them, that the order had been fabricated, or altered, by the malice of their Hindoo deputy, *to insult their religious feelings*. They were taken out accordingly, and having to pass the house of Subsookh Rae, when their excitement, or spirit of religious fervor, had reached the highest pitch, they there put them down, broke open the doors, entered in a crowd, and plundered it of all the property they could find, amounting to above seventy thousand rupees. Subsookh Rae was obliged to get out, with his family, at a back door, and run for his life. He went to Shajehanpoor, in our territory, and put himself under the protection of the magistrate. Not content with all this they built a small miniature mosque at the door with some loose bricks, so that no one could go either out or in, without the risk of knocking it down, or so injuring this *mock mosque*, as to rouse, or enable the evil-minded to rouse, the whole mahomedan population against the offender. Poor

Subsookh Rae has been utterly ruined, and ever since seeking in vain for redress. The government is neither disposed, nor able, to afford it; and the poor boy, who has now succeeded his *learned* father in the contract, is helpless. The little mock mosque, of un-cemented bricks, still stands as a monument of the insolence of the mahomedan population, and the weakness and apathy of the Oude government.

CHAPTER VIII

[Mahomdee 'district', 29 January–4 February 1850]

[1852: II, 44–62] [1858: II, 48–68]

[*January 29, 1850*. There is no entry under this date.]

Lalta Sing, of the Nikomee Rajpoot tribe, whom I had lately an opportunity of assisting, for his good services, in arresting outlaws from our territories, has just been to pay his respects. Our next encamping ground is to be on his estate of Kurheya and Para. He tells me – that very few families of his tribe now destroy their female infants – that tradition ascribes the origin of this evil to the practice of the mahomedan emperors of Delhi, to demand daughters in marriage from the Rajpoot princes of the country – that some of them were too proud to comply with the demand, and too weak to resist it in any other way than that of putting all their female infants to death. This is not impossible. He says, that he believes the *Dhankuries*, whom I have described above, to be really the only tribe of Rajpoots among whom no family destroys its infant daughters in Oude – that all tribes of Rajpoots get money with the daughters they take from tribes, a shade lower in caste, to whom they cannot give theirs in return; and pay money with the daughters they give in marriage to tribes a shade higher, who will not give their daughters to them in return. The native collector of Shahabad, a gentlemanly mahomedan, came out two miles to pay his respects on my approach, and we met on a large space of land, lying waste, while all around was covered with rich crops – 'Pray why is this land left waste?' 'It is, sir, altogether unproductive.' 'Why is this – it seems to me to be just as good as the rest around, which produces such fine crops?' 'It is called *khubtee*, slimy, and is said to be altogether barren'. 'I assure you, sir', said Rajah Bukhtawar Singh, 'that it is good land, and capable of yielding good crops, under good tillage, or it would not produce the fine grass you see upon it. You must not ask men like this about the kinds and qualities of soils, for they really know nothing whatever about them – they are *city gentlemen's sons*, who get into high places, and pass their lives in them without learning any thing, but how to screw money out of such as we are, who are born upon the soil, and depend upon its produce, all our lives, for subsistence. Ask him, sir, where either he, or any of his ancestors, ever knew any thing of the difference between one soil and another.'

The collector acknowledged the truth of what the old man said; and told me, that he really knew nothing about the matter; and had merely repeated what the people told him. This is true with regard to the greater part of the local revenue officers employed in Oude. 'One of these city gentlemen, sir', said Bukhtawar Sing, 'when sent out as a revenue collector, in Saadut Allee's time, was asked by his assistants what they were to do with a crop of sugar-cane, which had been attached for balances, and was becoming too ripe, replied, *'cut it down to be sure and have it stacked!'* He did not know that sugar-cane must, as soon as cut, be taken to the mill, or it spoils.' 'I have heard of another', said the old Rusaldar Nubbee Buksh, 'who, after he entered upon his charge, asked the people about him, to show him the tree on which grew the fine *istamalee*[1] rice, which they used at Lucknow.' 'There is no question, sir', said Bukhtawar Sing, 'that is too absurd for these cockney[a] gentlemen to ask when they enter upon such revenue charges as these – they are the aristocracy of towns and cities, who are learned enough in books and court ceremonies and intrigues, but utterly ignorant of country life, rural economy, and agricultural industry.'

For a cantonment, or civil station, the ground to the north of Shahabad, on the left hand side of the road leading to Mahomdee, seems the best. It is a level plain of a stiff soil formed of clay and sand, and not very productive.

The country, from Sandee and Shahabad to the rivers Ganges

---

[1] The *istamalee* rice is rice of fine quality, which has been kept for some years before used. To be good, rice must be kept for some years before used, and that only which has been so kept is called *istamalee* or *useable*.

[a] Used contemptuously from c. 1826 of 'townsmen'. Note its use also in this way in the Table of Contents, p. 45.

and Ramgunga, is one rich sheet of spring cultivation; and the estate of Kuteearee, above described, is among the richest portions of this sheet. The portions on which the richest crops now stand, became waste during the disorders, which followed the expulsion of Runjeet Sing in the usual way in 1837, and derived the usual benefit from the salutary fallow. A stranger passing through such a sheet of rich cultivation, without communing with the people, would little suspect the fearful crimes that are every year committed upon it, from the weakness and apathy of the government, and the bad faith and bad character of its officers and chief landholders. The land is tilled in spite of all obstacles, because all depend upon its produce for subsistence; but there is no indication of the beneficial interference of the government, for the protection of life, property and character, and for the encouragement of industry, and the display of its fruits. The land is ploughed, and the seed sown often by stealth at night, in the immediate vicinity of a sanguinary contest between the government officers and the landholders; it is only when the latter are defeated, and take to the jungles, or the Honorable Company's districts, and commence their indiscriminate plunder, that the cultivator ceases from his labours, and the lands are left waste.

Runjeet Sing, two or three years ago, seized upon the village of Mulatoo, in his vicinity, to which he had no claim whatever, and he has forcibly retained it. It had long paid government ten thousand a year; but he has consented to pay only one thousand. Lands yielding above nine thousand he has cut off from its rent roll, and added to those of his hereditary villages, on the borders. Last year he seized upon the village of Nudua, with a rent roll of fourteen hundred rupees; and he holds it with a party of soldiers and two guns. The Amil lately sent out a person, with a small force to demand the government dues; but they were driven back, as he pretends, that he got it in mortgage from Dumber Sing, who had taken a short lease of that and other khalsa villages, and absconded as a defaulter; and that he has purchased the lands from the cultivating proprietors; and is, therefore, bound to pay no revenue, whatever, for them to the king. All defaulters and offenders, who take refuge on his estate, he instigates to plunder, and provides with gangs, on condition of getting the greater part of the booty. He thinks that he is sure of shelter in the British territory, should he be driven from Oude. He feels also sure of aid from other large land-holders of the same class in the neighbourhood.

January 30, 1850. – Kurheya Para, twelve miles, over a plain of excellent muteear soil, a good deal of which is covered with jungle. Para is a short distance from Kurheya, and our camp is midway between the two villages. The boundary of the Sandee Palee and Mahomdee districts we crossed about four miles from our present encampment. This district of Mahomdee was taken in contract by Hakeem Mehndee, at three lakhs and eleven thousand rupees a year, in 1804 A.D.; and, in a few years, he brought it into full tillage, and made it yield above seven lakhs. It has been falling off ever since it was taken from him, and now yields only between three and four lakhs. The jungle is studded with large peepul trees, which are all shorn of their small branches and leaves. The landholders and cultivators told me, that they were taken off by the cowherds who grazed their buffaloes, bullocks and cows, in these jungles – that they formed their chief, and, in the cold season, their best food, as the leaves of the peepul tree were supposed to give warmth to the stomach, and to increase the quantity of the milk – that the cowherds were required to pay nothing for the privilege of grazing their cattle in these jungles, by the person to whom the lands belonged, because they enriched the soil with their manure, and all held small portions of land under tillage, for which they paid rent – that they had the free use of the peepul trees in the jungles, but were not permitted to touch those on the cultivated lands and in villages.

White ants are so numerous in the argillaceous muteear soil, in which their feed abounds, that it is really dangerous to travel on an elephant, or *swiftly* on horseback, over a new road cut or enlarged through any portion of it that has remained long untilled. The two fore legs of my elephant went down, yesterday morning, into a deep pit made by them, but concealed by the new road, that has been made over it, for the occasion of my visit, near Shahabad; and it was with some difficulty that he extricated them. We have had several accidents of the same kind since we came out. In cutting a new road they cut through large ant hills, and leave no trace of the edifices, or the gulf below them, which the little insects have made in gathering their food, and raising their lofty habitation. They are not found in the bhoor, or oosur soils; and in comparatively small numbers in the doomuteea, or lighter soil; but they abound in the muteear soil in proportion to its richness. Cultivation, where the crops are irrigated, destroys them; and the only danger is in passing over new roads cut through jungle, or lands that have remained long untilled; or along the sides of old pathways, from which these land marks have been removed in hastily widening them for wheeled carriages.

A brahmin cultivator, whose cart we had been obliged to press into our own service for this stage, came along with me almost all the way. He said

the spring crops of this season, sir, are, no doubt, very fine; but in days of yore, before the curse of *Bhurt Jee* (the brother of Ram)[a] came upon the landholders and cultivators of Oude, they were much finer – when he set out from his capital of Ajoodheea, for the conquest of Ceylon, he left the administration to his brother, Bhurt Jee, who made a liberal settlement of the land tax. He put a ghurra, or pitcher, with a round bottom, turned upside down, into every half acre (beegha) of the cultivated land, and required the landholder, or cultivator, to leave upon it, as much of the grain produced, as the rounded bottom would retain, which could not be one ten thousandth part of the produce; he lived economically, and collected, at this rate, during the many years that his brother was absent. But when his brother returned and approached the boundary of his dominions, he met hosts of landholders and cultivators, clamouring against the *rapacity and oppression* of his brother's administration! The humanity of Ram's disposition was shocked, sir, at all this; and he became angry with his brother, before he heard what he had to say. When Bhurt had satisfied his brother, that he had not taken from them the thousandth part of what he had a right to take, and Ram had, indeed, taken from them himself, he *sighed* at the wickedness and ingratitude of the agricultural classes of Oude; and the baneful effects of this sad *sigh* has been upon us

[a] Bharata, son of Dasaratha, the king of Ayodhya, and the half-brother of Rama-chandra. Bharata's mother brought about Rama's exile from the kingdom and tried to seat Bharata on the throne, but he refused to supplant his elder brother and, instead, ruled for him during his exile; Dowson, *Dictionary of Hindu Mythology*, p. 47.

ever since, sir, in spite of all we can do to avert them. In order to have the blessing of God upon our labours, it is necessary for us to fulfil, strictly, all the responsibilities under which we hold and till the land; first, to pay punctually the just demands of government, second, all the wages of the labour employed; third, all the charities to the poor; fourth, all the offerings to our respective tutelary gods; fifth, a special offering to Mahabeer, alias Hunooman.[a] These payments and offerings, sir, must all be made before the cultivator can safety take the surplus produce to his store room for sale and consumption.

Old Bukhtawar Sing, who was riding by my side, said – 'a conscientious farmer or cultivator, sir, when he finds that his field yields a great deal more than the usual returns – that is when it yields twenty, instead of the usual return of ten, gives the whole in charity, lest evil overtake him from his unusual good luck and inordinate exultation.'

I asked the brahmin cultivator, why all these offerings were required to be made by cultivators in particular. He replied – 'There is, sir, no species of tillage in which the lives of numerous *insects* are not sacrificed; and it is to atone for these numerous murders, and the ingratitude to Bhurt, that cultivators, in particular, are required to make so many offerings'; and, he added

much sin, sir, is no doubt brought upon the land by the murder of so many female infants. I believe, sir, that all the tribes of Rajpoots murder them; and I do not think that one in ten is suffered to live. If the family, or village, priest did not consent to eat with the parents, after the murder, no such murders could take place, sir; for none, even of their nearest relatives, will ever eat with them, till the brahmin has done so.

The bearers of the tonjohn, in which I sat, said

we do not believe, sir, that one girl in twenty, among the Rajpoots, is preserved. Davey Buksh, the Gonda Rajah, is, we believe, the only one of the Biseyn Rajpoot tribe who preserves his daughters;[1] his father did the same, and his sister, who was married to the Bhudoreea Rajah of Mynpooree, came to see him lately, on the occasion of a pilgrimage to Ajoodheea, on the death of her husband – of the six Kulhuns families of Chehdwara, two only preserve their daughters, Surnam Sing, of Arta, and Jeskurn, of Kumeear; but whether their sons, or successors, in the estates, will do the same, is uncertain.

[1] There are a great many families of the Biseyn Rajpoots, who never destroy their infant daughters.

[a] Hanuman, the king of the monkeys, whose exploits are celebrated in the story of Rama-chandra (the *Ramayana*); Dowson, *Dictionary of Hindu Mythology*, pp. 116–17.

These bearers are resident of that district. I may here remark, that oak trees, in the hills of the Himmaleh chain, are disfigured in the same manner, and for the same purpose, as the peepul and banyan trees are here; their small branches and leaves are torn off to supply fodder for bullocks and other animals. The ilex[a] of the hills has not, however, in its nakedness, the majesty of the peepul and banyan of the plains, though neither of them can be said to be 'when unadorn'd, adorn'd the most'.

January 31, 1850. – Puchgowa, north-east, twelve miles, over a plain of doomuteea soil, a good deal of which is out of tillage at present. On the road we came through several nice villages, the best of which was occupied, exclusively, by the families of the Kunojeea brahmin proprietors, and the few persons of inferior caste, who ploughed their lands for them, as they are a shade too high in caste, to admit of their holding their own ploughs. They are, however, very nice people, and seemed very much pleased at being put so much at their ease, in a talk with the great man, about their own domestic and rural economy. They told me, that they did not permit Rajpoots to reside in, or have any thing to do with, their village. Why? – 'Because, sir, if they once get a footing among us, they are, sooner or later, sure to turn us all out.' How?

They get lands by little and little at lease, soon refuse to pay rent, declare the lands to be their own, collect bad characters for plunder, join the Rajpoots of their own clan, in all the villages around, in their enterprises, take to the jungles on the first occasion of a dispute, attack, plunder and burn the village, murder us and our families, and soon get the estate for themselves, on their own terms, from the local authorities, who are wearied out by the loss of revenue arising from their depredations; our safety, sir, depends upon our keeping entirely aloof from them.

Under a government so weak, the only men who prosper, seem to be these landholders of the military classes, who are strong in their union, clan feeling, courage and ferocity. The villages here are numerous, though not large; and by far the greater part are occupied by Rajpoots of the Nikomee tribe.

The Amil of the Mahomdee district, Krishun Sahae, had come out so far as Para, to meet me, and have my camp supplied. He

[a] The holm-oak, or evergreen-oak.

had earned a good reputation, as a native collector, of long standing, in the Shajehanpore district, under Mr. Buller; but being ambitious, to rise more rapidly than he could hope to do under our settled government, he came to Lucknow with a letter of introduction from Mr. Buller to the Resident, Colonel Richmond[a] – paid his court to the Durbar – got appointed Amil of the Mahomdee district, under the *amanee* system, paid his nazuranas on his investiture, in October last, and entered upon his charge. A few days ago it pleased the minister to appoint, to his place, Aboo Toorab Khan, the nephew and son-in-law of Moonowur-ood Dowla; and orders were sent out immediately, by a camel messenger, to the commandants of the corps on duty with Krishun Sahae, to seize and send him, his family, and all his relations and dependants, with all the property to be found upon them, to Lucknow. The wakeel, whom he kept at Court for such occasions, heard of the order for the supercession and arrest, and, forthwith, sent off a note to his master, by the fastest foot messenger he could get. The camel messenger found, that the Amil had left Mahomdee, and gone out two stages to Para, to meet the Resident. He waited to deliver his message to the commandants and subordinate civil officers of the district, and see that they secured all the relatives, dependants and property of the Amil, that could be found. The foot messenger, more wise, went on, and delivered his letter to Krishun Sahae, at Para, on the evening of Tuesday the 29th. He ordered his elephant very quietly, and, mounting, told the driver to take him to a village on the road to Shajehanpoor.

On reaching the village about midnight, the driver asked him whither he was going – 'I am flying from my enemies', said Krishun Sahae; 'and we must make all haste, or we shall be overtaken before we reach the boundary.' 'But', said the driver, 'my house and family are at Lucknow, and the one will be pulled to the ground, and the other put into jail, if I fly with you.' Krishun Sahae drew out a pistol, and threatened to shoot him if he did not drive on as told. They were near a field of sugar-cane, and the driver hedged away towards it, without the Amil's perceiving his intention. When they got near the field, the

---

[a] Colonel A. F. Richmond, C.B., Resident at Lucknow, 1845–9.

elephant dashed in among the cane, to have a feast; and the driver, in his *seeming* effort to bring him out, fell off and disappeared under the high cane. The Amil did all he could to get out his elephant; but the animal felt, that he was no longer in danger of severe treatment from above, and had a very comfortable meal before him, in the fine ripe cane, and would not move. The poor Amil was obliged to descend, and make all possible haste on foot across the border, attended by one servant, who had accompanied him in his flight. The driver ran to the village, and got the people to join him in the pursuit of his master, saying, that he was making off with a good deal of the king's money. With an elephant load of the king's money in prospect, they made all the haste they could; but the poor Amil got safely over the border into British territory. They found the elephant dining, very comfortably, on the sugar cane. After abusing the driver and all his female relations for deluding them with the hope of a rich booty, they permitted him to take the empty elephant to the new Amil at Mahomdee. News of all this reached my camp last night.

I omitted to mention, that at Busora, on the 27th, a Rajpoot landholder, of the Sombunsie tribe, came to my camp, with a petition, regarding a mortgage; and mentioned, that he had a daughter, now two years of age; that when she was born he was out in his fields, and the females of the family put her into an earthen pot, buried her in the floor of the apartment, where the mother lay, and lit a fire over the grave – that he made all haste home, as soon as he heard of the birth of a daughter, removed the fire and earth from the pot, and took out his child. She was still living, but two of her fingers, which had not been sufficiently covered, were a good deal burnt. He had all possible care taken of her, and she still lives; and both he and his wife are very fond of her. Finding that his tale interested me, he went home for the child; but his village was far off, and he has not been able to overtake me. He had given no orders to have her preserved, as his wife was confined sooner than he expected; but the family took it for granted, that she was to be destroyed; and, in running home to preserve her, he acted on the impulse of the moment. The practice, of destroying female infants, is so general among this tribe, that a family commonly destroys the daughter, as soon as born, when the father is from home, and has given no special orders about it, taking it to be his wish, as a matter of course. Several respectable landholders of the Chouhan, Nikomee, and other tribe of Rajpoots, were talking to me yesterday evening; and as they were connected, by marriage, with Rajpoot families of the same and higher clans, in the British territories, I asked them, whether some plan could not be devised, to suppress the evil in Oude, as it had been suppressed there; for the disorders, which prevailed, seemed to me to be only a visitation from above, for such an all-pervading sin. They told me, that there would be little difficulty in putting down this system, under an honest and strong government, that would secure rights, enforce duties, and protect life and property, as in the British territories. Atrocious and cruel as this crime is in Oude, it is hardly more so than that which, not long ago, prevailed in France and other nations of Europe, of burying their daughters, alive, in nunneries, in order to gratify the same family pride.

It is painful to me to walk out of my tent of an evening; for I have, every day, large crowds seeking redress for grievous wrongs, for which I see no hope of redress – men and women, who have had their dearest relatives murdered, their houses burnt down – their whole property taken away – their lands seized upon – their crops destroyed by ruffians residing in the same or neighbouring villages, and actually in the camp of the Amil, without the slightest fear of being punished or made to surrender any portion of what they have taken. The government authorities are too weak, even to enforce the payment of the government demand, and have not the means to seize or punish offenders of any kind, if they have the inclination. In some districts they not only acquiesce in the depredations of these gangs of robbers, but act in collusion with their leaders, in order to get their aid in punishing defaulters, or pretended defaulters, among the landholders. They murder the landholders, and as many as possible of their families; and, as a reward for their services, the local authorities make over their lands to them at reduced rates.

The Nazim of Sandee Palee told me, on taking leave, that he had only two wings of Nujeeb Regiments with him, one of which was fit for some service, and, in consequence, spread over the district on detached duties. The other was with him; but out of the five hundred, for which he had to issue monthly pay, he should not be able to get ten men to follow him on any emergency. They are obliged to court and conciliate the strong and reckless, who prey upon the weak and industrious; and, in consequence, become despised and detested by the people. I feel like one moving among a people afflicted with incurable diseases, who crowd around him in hope, and are sent away in despair. I try to make the local authorities exert themselves in behalf of the sufferers; but am told, that they have already done their utmost in vain – that if they seize robbers and murderers, and send them to Lucknow, they are sure to purchase their enlargement, and return to wreak their vengeance on them, and on all who have aided them in their arrest and conviction – that if they attempt to seize one of the larger landholders, who refuses to pay the government demand, seizes upon the lands of his weaker neighbours, and murders and robs them indiscriminately, he removes across the Ganges, into one of the Hon'ble Company's districts, and thence sends his myrmidons, to plunder and lay waste the whole country, till he is invited back by a weak and helpless government, upon his own terms – that formerly British troops were employed, in support of the local authorities, against offenders of this class; but that, of late years, all such aid and support have been withdrawn from the Oude government, while the offenders find all they require from the subjects and police authorities of the bordering British districts.

The country we passed over to-day, between Para and Puchgowa, is a plain, beautifully studded with groves and fine solitary trees, in great perfection. The bandha, or mistle toe, upon the mhowa and mango trees, are in full blossom, and add much to their beauty – the soil is good, and the surface, every where, capable of tillage, with little labor or outlay; for the jungle, where it prevails the most, is of grass and the small palas trees – butea frondosa – which may be easily uprooted. The whole surface of Oude is, indeed, like a gentleman's park of the most beautiful description, as far as the surface of the ground and the foliage go. Five years of good government would make it one of the most beautiful parterres in nature. To plant a large grove, as it ought to be, a Hindoo thinks it necessary to have the following trees: –

(1) The banyan, or burgut.	(11) Kytha, feronia elephantum.
(2) Peepul, ficus religiosa.	(12) Kuthal, or jack.
(3) Mango.	(13) Moulsaree, mimusops elengi.
(4) Tamarind.	(14) Kuchnar, bauhinea variegata.
(5) Jamun, eugenia jambolana.	(15) Neem, melia azadirachta.
(6) Bele, cratoeva marmelos.	(16) Bere, fizyphus jujuba.
(7) Pakur, ficus venosa.	(17) Horse radish, sahjuna.
(8) Mhowa, bassia latifolia.	(18) Sheeshum, dalbergia sisa.
(9) Oula, phyllanthus emblica.	(19) Toon, adrela toona.
(10) Goolur, ficus glomerata.	(20) Chundun, or sandal.

Where he can get, or afford to plant, only a small space, he must confine himself to the more sacred, and generally useful, of these trees; and they are the handsomest in appearance. Nothing can be more beautiful than one of those groves surrounded by fields teeming with rich spring crops, as they are at present; and studded here and there with fine single banyan, peepul, tamarind, mhowa and cotton trees, which, in such positions, attain their highest perfection, as if anxious to display their greatest beauties, where they can be seen to the most advantage. Each tree has there free space for its roots, which have the advantage of the water supplied to the fields around in irrigation, and free current of air, whose moisture is condensed upon its leaves and stems by their cooler temperature, while its carbonic acid and ammonia are absorbed and appropriated to their exclusive use. Its branches, uncommoded by the proximity of other trees, spread out freely, and attain their utmost size and beauty.

I may here mention what are the spring crops, which now, in a luxuriance, not known for many years from fine falls of rain in due season, embellish the surface, over which we are passing.

SPRING CROPS

(1) Wheat.	(8) Moong, (pulse.)
(2) Barley.	(9) Peas, of three kinds.
(3) Gram.	(10) Mustard.
(4) Arahur, of two kinds, (pulse.)	(11) Sugar-cane, of six kinds.
(5) Musoor, (pulse.)	(12) Koosum, (safflower.)
(5) Alsee, (linseed.)	(13) Opium.
(7) Surson, (a species of fine mustard.)	(14) Palma christi.

Diary of a Tour Through Oude

February 1, 1850. – Mahomdee, eleven miles, over a level plain of muteear soil, of the best quality, well supplied with groves and single trees of the finest kind; but a good deal of the land is out of tillage, and covered with the rank grass, called garur, the roots of which form the fragrant khus, for tatties, in the hot winds; and dhak (butea frondosa) jungle. Several villages, through and near which we passed, belong to brahmin zumeendars, who were driven away, last year, by the rapacity of the contractor, Mahomed Hoseyn, a senseless oppressor, who was, this year, superseded by a very good officer and worthy man, who was driven out with disgrace, as described yesterday, while engaged in inviting back the absconded cultivators to these deserted villages, and providing them with the means of bringing their lands again into tillage. Hoseyn Allee had seized and sold all their plough bullocks, and other agricultural stock, between the autumn and spring harvests, together with all the spring crops, as they became ripe, to make good the increased rate of revenue demanded; and they were all turned out beggars, to seek subsistence, among their relatives and friends, in our bordering district of Shajehanpoor. The rank grass and jungle are full of neelgae and deer of all kinds; and the cowherds, who remain to graze their cattle on the wide plains, left waste, find it very difficult to preserve their small fields of corn from their trespass. They are said to come in herds of hundreds around these fields during the night, and to be frequently followed by tigers, several of which were killed last year, by Captain Hearsey of the Frontier Police. Waste lands, more distant from the great Tarae forest, are free from tigers.

I had a long talk with the brahmin communities of two of these villages, who had been lately invited back from the Shajehanpoor district, by Krishun Sahae, and resettled on their lands. They are a mild, sensible, and most respectable body, whom a sensible ruler would do all, in his power, to protect and encourage; but these are the class of landholders and cultivators whom the reckless governors of districts, under the Oude government, most grievously oppress. They told me –

'that nothing could be better than the administration of the Shajehanpoor district by the present collector and magistrate, Mr. Buller, whom all classes loved and respected; that the whole surface of the country was under tillage, and the poorest had as much protection as the highest in the land; that the whole district was, indeed, a garden.' 'But the returns, are they equal to those from your lands in Oude?' 'Nothing like it, sir, they are not half as good; nor can the cultivator afford to pay half the rate that we pay when left to till our lands in peace.' 'And why is this?' 'Because, sir, ours is sometimes left waste to recover its powers, as you now see all the land around you, while theirs has no rest.' 'But do they not alternate their crops, to relieve the soil?' 'Yes, sir, but this is not enough – ours receive manure from the herds of cattle and deer that graze upon it while fallow; and we have greater stores of manure than they have, to throw over it when we return and resume our labors. We alternate our crops, at the same time, as much as they do; and plough and cross plough our lands more.' 'And where would you rather live – there, protected as the people are from all violence, or here, exposed, as you are, to all manner of outrage and extortion?' 'We would rather live here, sir, if we could; and we were glad to come back.' 'And why? There the landholders and cultivators are sure that no man will be permitted to exact a higher rate of rent or revenue than that which they voluntarily bind themselves to pay during the period of a long lease; while here you are never sure that the terms of your lease will be respected for a single season?' 'That is all true, sir, but we cannot understand the "*aen* and *kanoon*" (the rules and regulations), nor should we ever do so; for we found that our relations, who had been settled there for many generations, were just as ignorant of them as ourselves. Your courts of justice (adawluts), are the things we most dread, sir; and we are glad to escape from them as soon as we can, in spite of all the evils we are exposed to on our return to the place of our birth. It is not the fault of the European gentlemen, who preside over them, for they are anxious to do, and have justice done, to all; but, in spite of all their efforts, the wrong doer often escapes, and the sufferer is as often punished.

The truth, sir, is seldom told in these courts. There they think of nothing but the number of witnesses, as if all were alike; here, sir, we look to the quality. When a man suffers wrong, the wrong doer is summoned before the elders, or most respectable men of his village or clan; and if he denies the charge, and refuses redress, he is told to bathe, put his hand upon the peepul tree, and declare aloud his innocence. If he refuses, he is commanded to restore what he has taken, or make suitable reparation for the injury he has done; and if he refuses to do this, he is punished by the odium of all, and his life becomes miserable. A man dares not, sir, put his hand upon that sacred tree and deny the truth – the gods sit in it and know all things; and the offender dreads their vengeance. In your adawluts, sir, men do not tell the truth so often as they do among their own tribes, or village communities – they perjure themselves in all manner of ways, without shame or dread; and there are so many men about these courts, who understand the "Rules and Regulations", and are so much interested

Diary of a Tour Through Oude

in making truth appear to be falsehood, and falsehood truth, that no man feels sure that right will prevail in them in any case. The guilty think they have just as good a chance of escape as the innocent. Our relations and friends told us, that all this confusion of right and wrong, which bewildered them, arose from the multiplicity of the "Rules and Regulations", which threw all the power into the hands of bad men, and left the European gentlemen helpless!'

'But you know that the crime of murdering female infants, which pervades the whole territory of Oude, and brings the curse of God upon it, has been suppressed in the British territory, in spite of these "*aens* and *kanoons*"?' 'True, sir, it has been put down in your bordering districts; but the Rajpoot families, who reside in them, manage to escape your vigilance, and keep up the evil practice. They intermarry with Rajpoot families in Oude, and the female infants, born of the daughters they give in marriage to Oude families, are destroyed in Oude, without fear or concealment; while the daughters they receive in marriage, from Oude families, are sent over the border into Oude, when near their confinement, on the pretence of visiting their relations. If they give birth to boys, they bring them back with them into your districts; but if they give birth to girls, they are destroyed in the same manner, and no questions are ever asked about them.' 'Do you ever eat or drink with Rajpoot parents who destroy their female infants?' 'Never, sir! we are brahmins, but we can take water in a brass vessel from the hands of a Rajpoot, and we do so when his family is unstained with this crime; but nothing would ever tempt us to drink water, from the hands of one, who permitted his daughters to be murdered.' 'Do you ever eat with the village or family priest, who has given absolution to parents, who have permitted their daughters to be murdered, by eating in the room where the murder has been perpetrated?' 'Never, sir; we abhor him as a participator in the crime; and nothing would ever induce one of us to eat or associate with him – he takes all the sin upon his own head, by doing so, and is considered by us as an outcast from the tribe, and accursed! It is they who keep up this fearful usage. Tigers and wolves cherish their offspring, and are better than these Rajpoots, who, out of family or clan pride, destroy theirs. As soon as their wives give birth to sons, they fire off guns, give largely in charity, make offerings to shrines, and rejoice in all manner of ways; but when they give birth to poor girls, they bury them alive, without pity, and a dead silence prevails in the house; it is no wonder, sir, that you say, that the curse of God is upon the land in which such sins prevail!'...

[1852: II, 74–81] [1858: II, 81–8]

February 2, 1850. – Halted at Mahomdee. The spring crops around the town are very fine, and the place is considered to be very healthy. There is, however, some peculiarity in the soil,

229

opposed to the growth of the poppy. The cultivators tell me, that they have often tried it; that it is stinted in growth, whatever care be taken of it, and yields but little juice, and that of bad quality; though it attains perfection in the Shahabad and other districts around. The doomuteea soil is here esteemed better than the muteear, though it requires more labour in the tillage. It is said that *mote* and *mash*, two pulses, do not thrive in the muteear soil so well as in the doomuteea.

February 3, 1850. – Poknapoor, eight miles. We crossed the Goomtee about midway, over a bridge of boats that had been prepared for us. The boats come up the river thus far for timber, and were detained for the occasion. The stream is here narrow, and said to flow from a basin (the phoola talao), in the Tarae forest, some fifty miles to the north, at Madhoo Tanda. There is some tillage on the verge of the stream on the other side; but from the river to our tents, four miles, there is none. The country is level and well studded with groves and fine single trees, bur, peepul, mhowa, mango, &c., but covered with rank grass. Near the river is a belt of the sakhoo and other forest trees, with underwood, in which tigers lodge and prey upon the deer, which cover the grass plain; and frequently upon the bullocks, which are grazed upon it in great numbers. Several bullocks have been killed and eaten by them within the last few days; and an old fakeer, who has, for some months, taken up his lodging on this side the river, under a peepul tree, in a straw hut, just big enough to hold him, told us, that he frequently saw them come down to drink, in the stream, near his lodging. We saw a great many deer in passing, but no tigers. The soil, near the river, is sandy, and the ground uneven, but still cultivable; and on this side of the sandy belt, it is all level and of the best kind of doomuteea. Our tents are in a fine grove of mango trees, in the midst of a waste, but level and extensive, plain of this soil, not a rood of which is unfit for the plough, or incapable of yielding crops of the finest quality. It is capable of being made, in two or three years, a beautiful garden.

The single trees, which are scattered all over it, have been shorn of their leaves and small branches, by the cowherds, for their cattle; but they would all soon clothe themselves again under protection. The groves are sufficiently numerous, to furnish sites for the villages and hamlets required. All the large sakhoo trees have been cut down and taken away on the ground we have come over, which is too near the river for them to be permitted to attain full size. Not an acre or a foot of the land is oosur, or unfit for tillage. Poknapoor is in the estate of Etowa, which forms part of the pergunnah of Peepareea, to which Bahadur Sing, the person above described, lays claim. He holds a few villages round his residence at Pursur; but the pergunnah is under the management of a government officer, under the Amil of Mahomdee. The Rajah, Syud Ashruf Allee Khan, of Mahomdee, claims a kind of suzerainty over all the district, and over this pergunnah of Peepareea among the rest. From all the villages, tilled and peopled, he is permitted to levy, an income for himself, at the rate of two rupees a village. This the people pay with some reluctance, though they recognize his right.

The zumeendars of Poknapoor are Kunojee brahmins, who tell me, that they can do almost every thing in husbandry, save holding their own ploughs – they can drive their own harrows and carts, reap their own crops, and winnow and tread out their own corn; but if they once condescend to *hold their own ploughs*, they sink in grade, and have to pay twice as much, as they now pay, for wives for their sons, from the same families, and take half of what they now take for their daughters from the same families, into which they now marry them. They have, they say, been settled in these pergunnahs, north-east of the Goomtee river, for fifty-two generations, as farmers and cultivators; and their relatives, who still remain at Aslamabad, a village one koss south-east of Mahomdee, which was the first abode of the tribe in Oude, have been settled there for no less than eighty-four generations. They form village communities, dividing the lands among the several members, and paying, over and above the government demand, a liberal allowance to the head of the village and of the family settled in it, to maintain his respectability, and to cover the risk and cost of management, either in kind, in money, or in an extra share of the land.

The lands of Poknapoor are all divided into two equal shares, one held by *Dewan*, and the other by *Ramnath*, who were both among the people with whom I conversed. Teekaram, who has a share in Dewan's half, mentioned, that about thirteen years ago, the Amil, Khwaja Mahmood, wanted to increase the rate of the government demand on the village, from the four hundred, which they had long paid, to four hundred and fifty – that they refused to pay, and Hindoo Sing, the Rajpoot tallookdar of Rehreea, one koss east of Poknapoor, offered to take the lease at four hundred and fifty, and got it. They refused to pay, and he, at the head of his gang of armed followers, attacked, plundered and burnt down the village, and killed his, Teekaram's, brother, Girdharee, with his two sons; and inflicted three severe cuts, of a sabre, on the right arm of the wife, who is now a widow among them. Hindoo Sing's object was, to make this village a permanent addition to his estate; but, to his surprise, the Durbar took serious notice of the outrage, and he fled into the Shajehanpoor district, where he was seized by the magistrate, Mr. Buller, and made over to the Oude authorities for trial. He purchased his escape from them in the usual way; but soon after offered to surrender, to the collector, Aboo Torab Khan, on condition of pardon for all past offences.

The collector begged the brahmins to consent to pardon him for the murders, on condition of getting, from Hindoo Sing, some fifty beeghas of land, out of his share in Rehreea. They said they would not consent to take five times the quantity of the land among such a turbulent set; but should be glad to get a smaller quantity, rent free, in their own village, for the widow of Girdharee. The collector gave them twenty-five beeghas, or ten acres, in Poknapoor; and this land Teekaram still holds, and out of the produce, supports the poor widow. A razeenamah, or pardon, was given by the family; and Hindoo Sing has, ever since, lived in peace upon his estate. The lease of the village was restored to the brahmin family, at the reduced rate of two hundred and fifty; but soon after raised to four hundred, and again reduced to two hundred and fifty, after the devastation of Bahadur Sing and Bhoder Sing.

These industrious and unoffending brahmins say, that since these Rajpoot landholders came among them, many generations ago, there has never been any peace in the district, except during the time that Hakeem Mehndee held the contract, when the whole plain, that now lies waste, became a beautiful *chummun* (parterre) – that since his removal, as before his appointment, all has been confusion – that the Rajpoot landholders are always quarrelling, either among themselves, or with the local government authorities; and, whatever be the nature or the cause of quarrel, they always plunder and murder, indiscriminately, the unoffending communities of the villages around, in order to reduce these authorities to their terms – that when these Rajpoot landholders leave them in peace, the contractors seize the opportunity to increase the government demand, and bring among them the king's troops, who plunder them just as much as the rebel landholders, though they do not often murder them in the same reckless manner. They told me, that the hundreds of their relatives, who had gone off during the disorders, and taken lands, or found employment in our bordering districts, would be glad to return to their old lands, groves and trees, in Oude, if they saw the slightest chance of protection; and the country would soon become again the beautiful parterre, which Hakeem Mehndee left it thirty years ago, instead of the wilderness, in which they were now so wretched – that they ventured to cultivate small patches, here and there, not far from each other, but were obliged to raise platforms, upon high poles, in every field, and sit upon them all night, calling out to each other, in a loud voice, to keep up their spirits, and frighten off the deer which swarmed upon the grass plain, and would destroy the whole of the crops, in one night, if left unprotected – that they were obliged to collect large piles of wood around each platform, and keep them burning all night, to prevent the tigers from carrying off the men who sat upon them – that their lives were wretched amidst this continual dread of man and beast; but the soil and climate were good, and the trees and groves, planted by their forefathers, were still standing and dear to them; and they hoped, now that the Resident had come among them, to receive, at no distant day, the protection they required. This alone is required, to render this the most beautiful portion of Oude, and Oude the most beautiful portion of India.

February 4, 1850. – Gokurnath, thirteen miles, north-east, over
a level plain of the same fine muteear soil, here and there running
into doomuteea and bhoor, but in no case into oosur. The first
two miles, over the grass plain, and the next four, through a belt
of forest trees, with rank grass and underwood, abounding in
game of all kinds, and infested by tigers. Bullocks are often taken
by them, but men seldom. The sal, alias sakhoo, trees are here
stinted, gnarled and ugly, while, in the Tarae forest, they are
straight, lofty and beautiful. The reason is, that beyond the
forest their leaves are stripped off and sold for *plates*. They are
carried to distant towns, and stored up, for long periods, to form
breakfast and dinner plates; and the people, in the country, use
hardly any thing else. Plates are formed of them, by sewing
several together, when required; and they become as pliable as
leather, even after being kept for a year or more, by having a
little water sprinkled over them. They are long, wide and tough,
and well suited to the purpose. All kinds of food are put upon
them, and served up to the family and guests. The cattle do not
eat them, as they do leaves of the peepul, bur, neem, &c. &c.
The sakhoo, when not preserved, is cut down, when young, for
beams, rafters, &c. &c. required in building. In the Tarae forest,
the proprietors of the lands, on which they stand, preserve them
till they attain maturity, for sale to the people of the plains; and
they are taken down the Ghagra and other rivers, that flow
through the forest, to the Ganges; and vast numbers are sold in
the Calcutta market. The fine tall sakhoos, in the Tarae forest,
are called 'sayer'; the knotted, stinted and crooked sakhoos,
beyond the forest, are called 'khohurs'.

There are but few teak (or sagwun) trees in this part of the
Tarae forest. The country is, every where, studded with the same
fine groves and single trees, and requires only tillage to become
a garden. From the belt of jungle to our camp at Gokurnath,
seven miles, the road runs over an open grass plain, with here
and there a field of corn. The sites of villages are numerous, but
few of them are occupied at present. All are said to have been in
a flourishing state, and filled by a happy peasantry, when Hakeem Mehndee lost the government. Since that time these villages
and hamlets have diminished, by degrees, in proportion as the

rapacity of the contractors, and the turbulence of the Rajpoot landholders, have increased.

The first village we passed through, after emerging from the belt of jungle, was Pureylee, which is held and occupied by a large family of cultivating proprietors, of the Koormee caste. Up to the year 1847, it had, for many years, been in a good condition, and paid a revenue of two thousand rupees a year to government. In that year Ahmud Allee, the collector, demanded a thousand more. They could not pay this: and he sold all their bullocks and other stock to make up the demand. The lands became waste as usual; and Lonee Sing, of Mitholee, offered the next contractor one thousand rupees a year for the lease, and got it. The village has now been permanently absorbed in his estate in the usual way; and, as the Koormees are a peaceful body, they have quietly acquiesced in the arrangement, and get all the aid they require from their new landlord. Before this time they had held their lands, as proprietors, directly under government. From allodial[1] proprietors they are become feudal tenants, under a powerful Rajpoot chief.

[1] By allodial, I mean, lands held in proprietary right, immediately under the crown, but liable to the land tax.[a]

[a] Cf. the definition of the Oxford dictionary: 'of or pertaining to an allodium', that is, 'an estate held, not of a superior, but in absolute ownership'.

CHAPTER IX

[Khyrabad 'district', 5–13 February 1850]

[1852: II, 82–6] [1858: II, 89–94]

Lonee Sing, who visited me yesterday afternoon, with a respectable train, has, in this and other ways, less creditable, increased his estate of *Mitholee*, from a rent roll of forty, to one of one hundred and fifty thousand rupees a year, out of which he pays fifty thousand to government; and he is considered one of its best subjects. He is, as above stated, of the Ahbun Rajpoot clan, and a shrewd and energetic man. The estate was divided into six shares. It had formed one under Rajah Davey Sing, whose only brother, Bhujun Sing, lived united with him, and took what he chose to give him for his own subsistence and that of his family. Davey Sing died without issue, leaving the whole estate to his brother, Bhujun Sing, who had two sons, Dul Sing and Maun Sing, among whom he divided the estate.[1] Dul Sing had six sons, but Maun Sing had none. He, however, adopted Bhowanee Sing, to whom he left his portion of the estate. Dul Sing's share became subdivided among his six sons, but Khunjun Sing, the son of his eldest son, when he became head of the family, got together a large force, with some guns, and made use of it, in the usual way, by seizing upon the lands of his weaker neighbours. He attacked his nephew, Bhowanee Sing, and took all his lands; and got, on one pretence or another, the greater part of those of his other relatives.

He died without issue, leaving his possessions, and military force, to Lonee Sing, his brother, who continued to pursue the same course. In 1847 he, with one thousand armed men, and five guns, attacked his cousin, Monnoo Sing, of Mohlee, the head of the family of the fourth son of Dul Sing, killed four and wounded two persons; and, in collusion with the local governor,

---

[1] *Mitholee* contains the sites of one thousand four hundred and eighty-six villages, only one-third of which are now occupied.

Diary of a Tour Through Oude

seized upon all his estate. Redress was sought for in vain; and, as I was passing near, Monnoo Sing, and his brother Chotee Sing, came to me at Mahomdee to complain. Monnoo Sing remained behind sick, at Mahomdee, but Chotee Sing followed me on. He rode on horseback behind my elephant, and I made him give me the history of his family as I went along, and told him to prepare for me a genealogical table, and an account of the mode in which Lonee Sing had usurped the different estates of the other members of the family. This he gave to me on the road between Poknapoor and Gokurnath, by one of his belted attendants[a], who, after handing it up to me on the elephant, ran along under the nose of Rajah Bukhtawur Sing's fine chestnut horse, without saying a word.

I asked the Rajah whether he knew Lonee Sing –

'Yes', said he, 'every body knows him – he is one of the ablest, best, and most substantial men in Oude; and he keeps his estate in excellent order, and is respected by all people.' 'Except his own relations', said the belted attendant – 'these he robs of all they have, and no body interposes to protect them, because he has become wealthy, and they have become poor!' 'My good fellow,' said the Rajah, 'he has only taken what they knew not how to hold, and with the sanction of the king's servants.' 'Yes', replied the man, 'he has got the sanction of the king's servants, no doubt, and any one, who can pay for it, may get that now-a-days, to rob others of the king's subjects. Has not Lonee Sing robbed all his cousins of their estates, and added them to his own, and thereby got the means of bribing the king's servants, to let him do what he likes.' 'What,' said the Rajah, with some asperity, 'should you, a mere soldier, know about State affairs? Do you suppose, that all the members of any family can be equal? Must there not be a head to all families, to keep the rest in order? Nothing goes on well in families or governments where all are equal, and there is no head to guide; and the head must have the means to guide the rest.' 'True,' said the belted attendant, 'all can't be equal in the rule of States; but in questions of private right, between individuals and subjects, the case is different; and the ruler should give to every one his due, and prevent the strong from robbing the weak. I have five fingers in my hand – they serve me, and I treat them all alike. I do not let one destroy or molest the other.' 'I tell you,' said the Rajah, with increasing asperity, 'that there must be heads of families, as well as heads of States, or all would be confusion; and

[a] A 'chaprasi' or the bearer of a 'chapras' or badge-plate inscribed with the name of the office to which the bearer is attached; usually an office messenger wearing such a badge on a cloth or leather belt. In Bombay, according to *Hobson-Jobson* (p. 220), this man was called a 'puttywalla' or 'man of the belt'.

237

Lonee Sing is right in all that he has done – don't you see what a state his district is in, now that he has taken the management of the whole upon himself? I dare say, all the waste that we see around us, has arisen from the want of such heads of families.' 'You know,' said the man, 'that this waste has been caused by the oppression of the king's officers, and their disorderly and useless troops; and the strong striving to deprive the weak of their rights.'

'You know nothing about these matters,' said the Rajah, still more angrily – 'the wise and strong are every where striving to subdue the weak and ignorant, in order, that they may manage, what they hold, better than they can – don't you see how the British Government are going on, taking country after country, year after year, in order to manage them better than they were managed under others; and don't you see how these countries thrive under their strong and just government? Do you think that God would permit them to go on, as they do, unless He thought, that it was for the good of the people who come under their rule?' Turning to me, the Rajah continued – 'When I was one day riding over the country with Colonel Low, the then Resident, as I now ride with you, sir, he said, with a sigh – "in this country of Oude what darkness prevails! No one seems to respect the right of another; and every one appears to be grasping at the possessions of his neighbour, without any fear of God or the king!" "True, sir," said I, "but do you not see, that it is the necessary order of things, and must be ordained by Providence. Is not your Government going on, taking country after country, and benefitting all it takes? And will not Providence prosper their undertakings as long as they do so? – the moment they come to a stand, all will be confusion – sovereigns cannot stand still, sir; the moment *their bellies are full* (their ambition ceases), they and the countries they govern retrograde – no sovereign in India, sir, that has any regard for himself, or his country, can, with safety, sit down and say, that *his belly is full* – (that he has no further ambition of conquest) – he must go on to the last." '[1]

The poor belted attendant of Chotee Sing was confounded with the logic and eloquence of the old Rajah, and said nothing more; and Chotee Sing himself kept quietly behind on his horse, with his ears well wrapped up in warm cloth, as the morning was a very cold one, and he was not well. He looked very grave; and evidently thought the Rajah had outlived his understanding. But the fact is, that the Rajah has, by his influence at Court, taken all

[1] The Rajah's reasoning was drawn from the practice in Oude, of seizing upon the possessions of weaker neighbours, by means of gangs of robbers. The man who does this, becomes the slave of his gangs, as the imperial robber, who seizes upon smaller States by means of his victorious armies, becomes their slaves, and, ultimately, their victim. The history of India is nothing more than the biography of such men, and the Rajah has read no other.

the lands held by his two elder nephews, Rughbur Sing and Ramadeen, and made them over to their youngest brother, Maun Sing, whom he has adopted, made his heir, and the head of the family. He has, in consequence, for the present, a strong fellow-feeling with Lonee Sing; and, in all this oration at least, 'his wishes were father to his thoughts'. . .

[1852: II, 88–94] [1858: II, 96–102]

The portion of the estate of Mitholee, held by Lonee Sing, now contains the sites of six hundred and four villages, about one half of which are occupied – four hundred and eighty-four of these lie in the Mahomdee district, and one hundred and twenty in that of Khyrabad. The number and names of the villages are still kept up in the accounts.

February 5, 1850. – Kurrunpoor Mirtaha, ten miles, over a plain of fine muteear soil, scantily cultivated, but bearing excellent spring crops, where it is so. Not far from our last camp, at Gokurnath, we entered a belt of jungle, three miles wide, consisting chiefly of stinted, knotty and crooked sakhoo trees, with underwood and rank chopper grass. This belt of jungle is the same we passed through, as above described, between Pokna-poor and Gokurnath. It runs from the great forest to the north, a long way down, south-east, into the Khyrabad district. From this belt to our present ground, six miles, the road passes over a fine plain, nine-tenths of which is covered with this grass, but studded with mango groves and fine single trees. The forest runs along to the north of our road, which lay east, from one to three miles distant, and looked very like a continued mango grove. The level plain of rich soil extends up through the forest to the foot of the hills: and is all the way capable of the finest cultivation. Here and there the soil runs into light doomuteea; and, in some few parts, even into bhoor, in proportion as the sand abounds; but, generally, the soil is the fine muteear, and very fertile. The whole plain is said to have been in cultivation thirty years ago, when Hakeem Mehndee held the contract; but the tillage has been falling off ever since, under the bad or oppressive management of successive contractors.

The estate, through which we have been passing, is called Bharwara, and contains the sites of nine hundred and eighty-nine villages, about one tenth of which are now occupied. The land-holders are all of the Ahbun Rajpoot tribe; but a great part of them have become musulmans. They live together, however, though of different creeds, in tolerable harmony; and eat together on occasions of ceremony, though not from the same dishes. No member of the tribe ever forfeited his inheritance by changing his creed. Nor did any one of them, I believe, ever change his creed, except to retain his inheritance, liberty, or life, threatened by despotic and unscrupulous rulers. They dine on the same floor, but there is a line marked off to separate those of the party who are Hindoos, from those who are musulmans. The musulmans have mahomedan names, and the Hindoos Hindoo names; but both still go by the common patronymic name of Ahbuns. The musulmans marry into musulman families, and the Hindoos into Hindoo families of the highest castes, Chouhans, Rathores, Rykwars, Janwars, &c. &c. Of course all the children are of the same religion and caste as their parents. They tell me, that the conversion of their ancestors was effected by force, under a prince, or chief, called 'Kala Pahar'. This must have been Mahomed Firmally, alias, Kala Pahar, to whom his uncle Bheilole,[a] king of Delhi, left the district of Bahraetch, as a separate inheritance, a short time before his death, which took place A.D. 1488. This conversion seems to have had the effect of doing away with the murder of female infants in the Ahbun families, who are still Hindoos; for they could not get the musulman portion of the tribe to associate with them if they continued it.

The estate of Bharwara is divided into four parts. Hydrabad, Hurunpoor, Aleegunge and Sekunderabad. Each division is sub-divided into parts, each held by a separate branch of the family; and the sub-division of these parts is still going on, as the heads of the several branches of the family die, and leave more than one son. The present head of the Ahbun family is Mahommed Hussan Khan, a musulman, who resides in his fort, in the village of Julalpoor, near the road over which we passed. The small fort

---

[a] Bahlul Lodi, the first Lodi Sultan of Delhi, reigned 1451–89.

240

is concealed within, and protected by a nice bamboo fence, that grows round it. He holds twelve villages, rent free, as *nankar*, and pays revenue for all the rest that compose his share of the great estate. The heads of families, who hold the other shares, enjoy, in the same manner, one or more villages, rent free, as *nankar*. These are all well cultivated, and contain a great many cultivators of the best classes, such as Koormees, Lodhies and Kachies.

We passed through one of them, Kamole, and I had a good deal of talk with the people, who were engaged in pressing out the juice of sugar-cane. They told me, that the juice was excellent; and that the syrup, made from it, was carried to the district of Shajehanpoor, in the British territory, to be made into sugar. Mahommed Hussan Khan came up, as I was talking with the people, and joined in the conversation. All seemed to be delighted with the opportunity of entering, so freely, into conversation with a British Resident, who understood farming, and seemed to take so much interest in their pursuits. I congratulated the people on being able to keep so many of their houses well covered with grass choppers; but they told me

that it was with infinite difficulty they could keep them, or any thing else they had, from the grasp of the local authorities, and the troops and camp followers, who attended them, and desolated the country like a flock of locusts – that they are not only plundered but taxed by them – first, the sipahees take their choppers, beams and rafters off their houses – then the people, in charge of artillery bullocks and other cattle, take all their stores of bhoosa, straw, &c. &c., and threaten to turn the cattle loose, on their fields, if not paid a gratuity – the people, who have to collect fuel for the camp (bildars), take all their stores of wood, and doors and windows also, if not paid for their redemption – then the people, in charge of elephants and camels, threaten to denude of their leaves and small branches, all the peepul, burgut and other trees, most sacred, and dear to them, near their homes, unless paid for their forbearance. And, though last not least, men, women and children are seized, not only to carry the plunder and other burthens gratis for sipahees and servants of all kinds and grades, and camp-followers, but to be robbed of their clothes, and made to pay ransoms to get back, while all the plough bullocks are put in requisition to draw the guns, which the king's bullocks are unable to draw themselves. In short, that the approach of king's servants is dreaded as one of the greatest calamities that can befall them.

I should here mention, that all the Telinga Regiments, fourteen in number, are allowed tents and hackeries to carry them. The way in which the bullocks of such carts are provided with fodder, has been already mentioned. But no tents, or conveyance of any kind, are allowed for the Nujeeb corps, thirty-two in number. Whenever they move – and they are almost always moving – they seize whatever conveyance and shelter they require from the people of the country around. Each battalion, even in its ordinary incomplete state, requires four or five hundred porters, besides carts, bullocks, horses, ponies, &c. &c. Men, women and children, of all classes, are seized, and made to carry the baggage, arms, accoutrements, and *cages of pet birds*, belonging to the officers and sipahees of these corps. They are stripped of their clothes, confined and starved from the time they are seized; and, as it is difficult to catch people to relieve them, along the road, they are commonly taken on two or three stages. If they run away they forfeit all their clothes, which remain in the hands of the sipahees; and a great many die along the road of fatigue, hunger and exposure to the sun. Numerous cruel instances of this have been urged by me on the notice of the king, but without any good effect. The line of march of one of these corps is like the road to the temple of Juggurnath![a] When the corps is about to move, detachments are sent out to seize conveyance of all kinds; and for one cart required and taken, fifty are seized, and released for a donation, in proportion to their value, the respectability of the proprietors, and the necessity for their employment at home at the time. The sums thus extorted by detachments, they share with their officers, or they would never be again sent on such lucrative service.

It appears, that in this part of Oude, the people have not, for many years, suffered so much from the depredations of the refractory landholders as in other parts; and that the desolate state of the district arises, chiefly, from the other three great evils that afflict Oude, the rack-renting of the contractors – the divisions

[a] Jagannatha or 'Lord of the Universe', a representation of Krishna at Puri in Orissa which is visited by large numbers of pilgrims for festivals when the figure is bathed or taken in procession in a large car; Dowson, *Dictionary of Hindu Mythology*, p. 129.

they create and foster among landholders; and the depredations of the troops and camp-followers who attend them. But the estate has become much subdivided, and the shareholders, from this cause, and the oppression of the contractors, have become poor and weak; and the neighbouring landholders of the Janwar and other Rajpoot tribes, have taken advantage of their weakness, to seize upon a great many of their best villages. Out of Kurumpoor, within the last nine years, Anorud Sing, of Oel, a Janwar Rajpoot, in collusion with local authorities, has taken twelve; and Umrao Sing, of Mahewa, of the same tribe, has taken eighteen, making twenty villages from the Kurumpoor division. These landholders reside in the Khyrabad district, which adjoins that of Mahomdee, near our present camp.

The people, everywhere, praise the climate – they appear robust and energetic, and no sickness prevails, though many of the villages are very near the forest. The land, on which the forest stands, contains, in the ruins of well built towns and fortresses, unquestionable signs of having once been well cultivated, and thickly peopled; and it would soon become so again under good government. There is nothing in the soil to produce sickness; and, I believe, the same soil prevails up through the forest to the hills. Sickness would, no doubt, prevail for some years, till the underwood, and all the putrid leaves, should be removed. The water that stagnates over them, and percolates through the soil, into the wells, from which the people drink, and the exhalations which arise from them, and taint the air, confined by the dense mass of forest trees, underwood and high grass, are, I believe, the chief cause of the diseases which prevail in this belt of jungle.

It is, however, remarkable, that there are two unhealthy seasons in the year in this forest, one at the latter end of the rains, in August, September and October; and the other before the rains begin to fall, in the latter part of April, the whole of May and part of June. The diseases in the latter are, I believe, more commonly fatal than they are in the former; and are considered, by the people, to arise solely from the poisonous quality of the water, which is often found in wells, to be covered with a thin crust of petrolium [*sic*]...

Diary of a Tour Through Oude

[1852: ii, 98–122] [1858: ii, 107–33]

The state of the Bharwara district may be illustrated by that of one of its four divisions, or mahals, Alleegunge. In the last year of Hakeem Mehndee's rule (1818), this division was assessed at one hundred and thirty-eight thousand rupees, with the full consent of the people, who were all thriving and happy. The assessment was, indeed, made by the heads of the principal Ahbun families of the district, with Mahommed Hussan Khan, as chief assessor. One hundred and thirty-two thousand were collected, and six thousand were remitted in consequence of a partial failure of the crops. Last year, by force and violence, the landholders of this division were made to agree to an assessment upon the lands, in tillage, of ten thousand and five hundred rupees, of which not six thousand can be collected. The other three divisions are in the same state. Not one-tenth of the land is in tillage, nor are one-tenth of the villages peopled. The soil is really the finest that I have seen in India; and I have seen no part of India in which so small a portion of the surface is unfit for tillage. The moisture rises to the surface just as it is required; and a tolerable crop is got by a poor man, who can't afford to keep a plough, and merely burns down the grass and digs the surface with his spade, or pickaxe, before he sows the seed. Generally, however, the tillage, in the portion cultivated, is very good. The surface is ploughed and cross-ploughed from six to twenty, or even thirty, times in the season; and the harrow and roller are often applied till every clod is pulverized to dust.

The test of first-rate preparation for the seed is, that a ghurra, or earthen pitcher, full of water, let fall upon the field, from a man's head, shall not break. The clods, in the muteear soil, are so pulverized only in the fields that are to be irrigated; or to the surface of which moisture rises from below as the weather becomes warm. The people say, that it does so rise, when required, in land, even a good way from the forest; and that the clods are, in consequence, not necessary to retain it. This is the only part of India in which I have known the people take ratoon, or second crops of sugar-cane from the same roots; and the

244

Diary of a Tour Through Oude

farmers and cultivators tell me, that the second crop is almost as good as the first. The fields, in tillage, are well supplied with manure, which is very abundant where so large a portion of the surface is waste, and affords such fine pasture. They are also well watered, for the water is near the surface; and in the tight muteear soil, a kutcha well, or well without masonry, will stand good for twenty seasons. To make pucka wells, or wells lined with burnt bricks and cement, would be costly. Each well of this kind costs about one hundred rupees. The kutcha wells, which are lined with nothing, or with thick ropes of twigs and straw, cost only from five to ten rupees. The people tell me, that oppression and poverty have made them less fastidious than they were formerly – that formerly it was considered disgraceful to plough with buffaloes, or to use them in carts; but they are now in common use for both purposes – that vast numbers of the Kunojee brahmins and others, who could not formerly drive their own ploughs, drive them now; and that all will, in time, condescend to do so, as the penalties of higher payments, with and for daughters in marriage, cease to be exacted from men whose necessities have become so pressing.

February[a] 6, 1850. – Halted at Kurunpoor, where the gentlemen of my camp shot some floricans,[b] hares, partridges and a porcupine along the bank of the small river Oel, which flows along from north-west to south-east, within three miles of Kurunpoor.

February[c] 7, 1850. – Teekur, twelve miles. The road, for three miles, lay through grass jungle to the border of the Khyrabad district, whence the plain is covered with cultivation, well studded with trees, clusters of bamboos, and well peopled with villages, all indicating better management. A great many fields are reduced to the fine dust, above described, to receive the sugarcane, which is planted in February. The soil is muteear; but has, in many parts, become impaired by over-cropping. The people

[a] Date given incorrectly as March in original.
[b] Bengal floriken (Hindustani, *likh*), a small bustard (*Sypheotides bengalensis*) found in the Ganges plain, especially in the tarai; H. Whistler, *Popular Handbook of Indian Birds* (London, 1949), pp. 447–9.
[c] Date given incorrectly as March in original.

told me, that the crops were not so rich as they ought to be from the want of manure, which is much felt here, where there is so little pasture for cattle. The wheat has almost everywhere received an orange tint from the geerwa, or blight, which covers the leaves; but, happily, has not as yet settled upon the stalks to feed on the sap. This blight, the cultivators say, arises from the late and heavy rain they have had, and the easterly wind that prevailed for a few days. The geerwa is a red fungus, which, when it adheres to the stems, thrusts its roots through the pores of the epidermis, and robs the grain of the sap as it ascends. When easterly winds and sultry weather prevail, the pores of the epidermis appear to be more opened and exposed to the in-roads of these fungi, than at other times. If the wind continue westerly for a fortnight more, little injury may be sustained; but should easterly winds and sultry weather prevail, the greater part may be lost – 'We cultivators and landholders', said Bukhtawur Sing, 'are always in dread of something, and can never feel quite easy – if little rain falls, we complain of the want of more – if a good deal comes down, we are in dread of this blight, and never dare to congratulate ourselves on the prospect of good returns.' To the justice and wisdom of this observation all assented.[1]

The landholders of this purgunnah are chiefly Janwar Rajpoots. Kymara, a fine village, through which we passed, about five miles from Kurunpoor, is the residence of the present head of this family, Rajah Ajeet Sing. He has a small fort close by, in which he is now preparing to defend himself against the king's forces. The poor old man came out with all his village community, to meet and talk with me, in the hope that I might interpose to protect him. He is weak in mind and body, has no son, and, having lately lost his only brother, and declared heir to the estate, his cousins, and more distant relations, are scrambling for the inheritance. The usual means of violence, collusion and intrigue have been had recourse to. The estate is in the Huzoor Tuhseel, and not under the jurisdiction of the

[1] Westerly winds and cold weather prevailed, and the blight did little apparent injury to the crops; but the wheat crops, generally, over Oude and the adjoining districts, was shrivelled and deficient in substance. It had 'run to stalk' from the excess of rain.

contractor of Khyrabad. The old man seemed care-worn and very wretched; and told me, that the contractor, whom I should meet at Teekur, had only yesterday received orders from Court, to use all his means to oust him from possession, and make over the estate to his cousin, Jodha Sing, who had lately left him, in consequence of a dispute, after having, since the death of his brother, aided him in the management of the estate – that he had always paid his revenues to the king punctually; and, last year, he owed a balance of only one hundred and sixty rupees, when *Anrod Sing*, his distant relative, wanted him to declare his younger brother, Dirj Bijee Sing, his heir, to the estate, in lieu of Jodha Sing.

This he refused to do, and Anrod Sing came, with a force of two thousand armed men, supported by a detachment from Captain Barlow's regiment, and laid siege to his fort, on the pretence, that he was required to give security for the more punctual payment of the revenue. To defend himself, he was obliged to call in the aid of his clan and neighbours, and expend all that he had or could borrow; and, at last, constrained to accept Anrod Sing's security, for no merchants would lend money to a poor man in a state of siege. Anrod Sing had now gone off to Lucknow, and bribed the person in charge of the Huzoor Tuhseel, Gholam Ruza Khan, one of the most corrupt men in the corrupt Court of Lucknow, to get an order issued by the minister to have him turned out, and the estate made over to Jodha Sing, from whom he would soon get it on pretence of accumulated balances; and make it over, in perpetuity, to his brother, Dirj Bijee Sing. In this attempt, the old man said, a good many lives must be lost and crops destroyed, for his friends would not let him fall without a struggle.

As soon as we left the poor old man, Bukhtawur Sing said

This, sir, is the way in which government officers manage to control and subdue these sturdy Rajpoot landholders. While they remain united, as in the Bangur district, they can do nothing with them, and let them keep their estates on their own terms; but the moment a quarrel takes place between them, they take advantage of it – they adopt the cause of the strongest, and support him in his aggressions upon the other members of his family or clan, till all become weak by division and disorder, and submit. Forty or fifty years ago, sir, when I used to move about the country, on circuit, with Saadut Allee Khan – the then sovereign – as I now move with you, there were many Rajpoot landholders in Oude, stronger than any that defy the government now; but they dared not then hold their heads so high as they do now. The local officers, employed by him, were men of ability, experience and character, totally unlike those now employed. Each had a wing of one of the Honorable Company's regiments, and some good guns with him; and was ready and able to enforce his master's orders, and the payment of his just demands; but since his death, the local officers have been falling off in character and strength, while the Rajpoot landholders have risen in pride and power. The aid of the British troops has, by degrees, been altogether withdrawn; and the landholders of this class despise the Oude government, and many of them resist its troops whenever they attempt to enforce the payment of even its most moderate demands. The revenues of the State fall off as the armed bands of these landholders increase; and families, who, in his time, kept up only fifty armed men, have now five hundred, or even a thousand or two two thousand, and spend, what they owe to government, in maintaining them. To pay such bands they withhold the just demands of the State – rob their weaker neighbours of their possessions, and plunder travellers on the high way, and men of substance, wherever they can find them.

When Saadut Allee made over one-half of his dominions to the British Government, in 1801, he was bound to reduce his military force, and rely altogether upon the support of your government. He did so; but the force he retained, though small, was good; and while that support was afforded, things went on well – he was a wise man, and made the most of the means he had. Since that time, sir, the Oude force has been increased four-fold, as your aid has been withdrawn; but the whole is not equal to the fourth part, which served under Saadut Allee. You see how insignificant it everywhere is, and how much it is despised even by the third class Rajpoot landholders. You see, also, how they everywhere prey upon the people, and are dreaded and detested by them – the only estates free from their inroads, are those under the 'Huzoor Tuhseel', into which the Amils, and their disorderly hosts, dare not enter. If the landholders could be made to feel, that they would not be permitted to seize other men's possessions, nor other men to seize theirs, as long as they obeyed the government and paid its just dues, they would disband these armed followers, and the king might soon reduce his. He will never make them worth any thing – there are too many worthless, but influential, persons about the Court, interested in keeping up all kinds of abuses, to permit this. These abuses are the chief source of their incomes – they rob the officers and sipahees, and even the draft bullocks; and you, everywhere, see how the poor animals are starved by them.

Within a mile of the camp I met the Nazim, Hoseyn Allee Khan, who told me, that Rajah Goorbuksh Sing, of Ramnuggur

Dhumeree, had fulfilled all the engagements entered into before me at Byramghat, on the Ghagra, on the 6th of December, and was no longer opposed to the government; and that the only large landholder in his district, who remained so at present, was Seobuksh Sing, of Kateysura, a strong fort, mounted with seven guns, near the road, over which I am to pass the day after to-morrow, between Oel and Lahurpoor. As he came up on his little elephant, along the road, I saw half a dozen of his men, mounted on camels, trotting along through a fine field of wheat, now in ear, with as much unconcern as if they had been upon a fine sward, to which they could do no harm. I saw one of my people, in advance, make a sign to them, on which they made for the road as fast as they could. I asked the Nazim how he could permit such trespass. He told me – 'that he did not see them; and, unless his eye was always upon them, he could not prevent their doing mischief, for they were the king's servants, who never seemed happy, unless they were trespassing upon some of his majesty's subjects.' Nothing, certainly, seems to delight them so much as the trespasses of all kinds, which they do commit upon them.

February[a] *8, 1850.* – Oel, five miles, over a plain of the same fine muteear soil, beautifully cultivated, and studded with trees, intermixed with numerous clusters of the graceful bamboo. A great grand-son of the monster, Nadir Shah,[b] of Persia, Ruza Kolee Khan, who commands a battalion in the king of Oude's service, rode by me, and I asked him whether he ever saw such a cultivated country in Persia.

'Never,' said he: 'Persia is a hilly country, and there is no tillage, like this, in any part of it. I left Persia, with my father, twenty-two years ago, when I was twenty-two years of age, and I have still a very distinct recollection of what it was then'. 'There is no country in the world, sir', said the Nazim, 'like Hindoostan, when it enjoys the blessings of a good government. The purgunnah of Kheree, in which we now are, is all held by the heads of three families of Janwar Rajpoots, Rajah Ajub Sing, of Kymara,

[a] Date given incorrectly as March in original.
[b] Nadir Shah, King of Persia, 1736–47; defeated the Indian imperial armies near Panipat in 1739 and, after a peaceful entry into Delhi, he caused thousands to be massacred in retaliation for the killing of several hundred of his troops; *Oxford History of India*, 3rd ed. by P. Spear (1958), pp. 436–7.

Anrod Sing, of Oel, and Umrao Sing, of Mahewa. There are only sixty-six villages of khalsa, or crown lands left, yielding twenty-one thousand rupees a year. The rest have been all absorbed by the heads of these Rajpoot families.

	Villages.		Jumma.
Kymara,	82		13,486 0 0
Oel,	170		54,790 0 0
Mahewa,	70		20,835 0 0
	322		89,111 0 0
Khalsa,	66		21,881 0 0
	388		1,10,992 0 0

These heads of families have each a fort, surrounded by a strong fence of bamboos, and mounted with good guns; and the king cannot get so large a revenue from them, as he did thirty years ago, in the time of Hakeem Mehndee, though their lands are as well tilled now as they were then, and yield more rent to their holders. They spend it all, in keeping up large armed bands, to resist the government; but they certainly take care of their cultivators, and tenants of all kinds, and no man dares molest them.'

'But,' said Bukhtawur Sing, 'this beautiful scene would all be changed were they encouraged, or permitted, to contend with each other for the possession of the lands. I, yesterday, saw a great number of the merchants of Kymara following the Resident's camp; and, on asking them why, they told me, that the order from Court, obtained by Gholam Ruza, for you (the Nazim) to assist the Oel chief, Anrod Sing, in despoiling Rajah Ajub Sing of his estate, had driven out all who had no fields of corn, or other local ties to detain them, and had any thing to lose by remaining. The chief and his retainers were repairing their fort, and preparing to fight for their possessions to the last; and if you take your disorderly force against them, according to orders, the crops, now in the ground, will be all destroyed; and the numerous fields, now prepared to receive sugar-cane and the autumn seed, will be left waste – they will make reprisals upon Oel – others of their clan will join in the strife, and this district will be what that of Bharwara, which we have just left, now is. The merchants are in the right, sir, to make off – no property, in such a scene, is ever safe – there is no property, sir, like that in the Hon'ble Company's paper[a] – it is the only property that we can enjoy in peace – you feel no anxiety about it! It doubles itself in fifteen or sixteen years; and you go on from generation to generation enjoying your five per cent, and neither fearing nor annoying any body.'

The two villages of Oel and Dhukwa adjoin each other, and form a large town; but the dwelling houses have a wretched

[a] East India Company bonds, bearing 5 per cent interest; see above, Introduction, p. 20.

appearance, consisting of naked mud walls, with but a few more grass choppers, than are usually found upon them in Oude towns. There is a good looking temple, dedicated to Mahadeo,[a] in the centre of the town, and the houses are close upon the ditch of the fort, which has its bamboo fence inside its ditch and outer mud walls. I have written to the Durbar to recommend, that the order, for the attack upon Rajah Ajub Sing, be countermanded, and more pacific measures adopted for the settlement of the claims of the Exchequer and Anrod Sing, upon poor old Ajub Sing. The Kanoongoes of this place tell me, that the dispute has arisen from a desire, on the part of the old man's wife, to set aside the just claim of Jodha Sing, the old man's nephew, to the inheritance, in favor of a lad whom she has adopted and brought up, by name Teeka Sing, in whose name the estate is now managed by a servant – that Jodha Sing is the rightful heir, and managed the estate well for his uncle, after the death of his brother, till lately, when his aunt persuaded his uncle to break with him, which he did with reluctance – that Jodha Sing now lives in retirement at his village of Barkerwa – that Anrod Sing's design upon the inheritance for his younger brother, Dirj Bijee Sing, is unjust; and that he is, in consequence, obliged to prosecute it on the pretence of recovering money due, and supporting the claim of Jodha Sing; and in collusion with the officers of government – that Gholam Ruza, who has charge of the Huzoor Tuhseel, is ready to adopt the cause of any one who will pay him; and that Anrod Sing is now at Lucknow paying his Court to him, and getting these iniquitous orders issued.

Oel was transferred to the Huzoor Tuhseel in 1834, Kymara in 1836, and Mahewa in 1839. These Rajpoot landholders do not often seize upon the lands of a relative at once, but get them, by degrees, by fraud and collusion with government officers, so that they may share the odium with them. They instigate these officers to demand more than the lands can pay; offer the enhanced rate, and get the lands at once; or get a mortgage, run up the account, and foreclose by their aid. They no sooner get the estate than they reduce the government demand, by collusion or violence, to less than what the former proprietor had paid.

[a] Shiva, 'the great god'; Dowson, *Dictionary of Hindu Mythology*, p. 193.

February[a] *9, 1850.* – Lahurpoor, twelve miles, over a plain of doomuteea soil, well studded with groves and single trees, but not so fully cultivated the last half way as the first. For the first half way the road lies through the estate of Anrod Sing, of Oel; but for the last it runs through that of Seobuksh Sing, a Gour Rajpoot, who has a fort near the town of Kuteysura, five miles from Lahurpoor, and seven from Oel. It is of mud, and has a ditch all round, and a bamboo fence inside the outer walls. It is of great extent, but not formidable against well provided troops. The greater part of the houses, in the town, are in ruins, and Seobuksh has the reputation of being a reckless and improvident landholder. He is said not only to take from his tenants higher rates of rent than he ought; but to extort from them, very often, *a property tax*, highly and capriciously rated. This is what the people call the *bhalmansae*, of which they have a very great abhorrence. 'You are a *bhala manus* (a gentleman, or man of substance)', he says to his tenant, 'and must have property worth at least a thousand rupees – I want money sadly, and must have one-fifth – give me two hundred rupees.' This is what the people call '*bhalmansae*', or rating a man according to his substance; and to say that a landlord, or governor, does this, is to say that he is a reckless oppressor, who has no regard to obligations or to consequences. There are manifest signs of the present landholder, Seobuksh Sing, being of this character; but others, not less manifest of his grand-father having been a better man, in the fine groves which surround Lahurpoor, and the villages between this place and Kuteysura, all of which are included in his estate. These groves were, for the most part, planted during the life of his grand-father by men of substance, who were left free to dispose of their property as they thought best.

All the native gentlemen, who rode with me, remarked on the beauty of the approach to Lahurpoor, in which a rich carpet of spring crops covers the surface up to the groves, and extends along under the trees, which have been recently planted. There are many young groves about the place, planted by men who have acquired property by trade, and by the savings out of the salaries and perquisites of office at Lahurpoor, which is the

[a] Date given incorrectly as March in original.

residence of the Nazim, or local governor, during several months in the year; and the landlord, Seobuksh, cannot venture to exact his *property tax* from them. The air and water are much praised, and the general good health of the troops, civil establishments, and residents of all classes, show that the climate must be good. The position, too, is well chosen with reference to the districts, and the character of the people under the control of the governor of the Khyrabad district. The estate of Seobuksh is very extensive. The soil is all good, and the plain level, so that every part of it is capable of tillage. Rutun Sing, the father of Seobuksh, is said to have been a greater rack-renter, rebel and robber than his son is, and together they have injured the estate a good deal, and reduced it from a rent roll of one hundred thousand to one of forty. Its rent roll is now estimated, in the public accounts, at 54,640, out of which is deducted a *nankar* of 17,587, leaving a government demand of only 37,053. This he can't pay; and he has shut himself up sullenly in his mud fort, where the Nazim dares not attack him. He is levying contributions from the surrounding villages, but has not yet plundered or burnt down any. He was lately in prison for two years, but released on the security of Rajah Lonee Sing, of Mitholee, whose wife is his wife's sister. He, however, says, that he was pledged to produce him when required, not before the *present Nazim*, but his *predecessor*; and that he is no longer bound by this pledge. This reasoning would, of course, have no weight with the government authorities, nor would it be had recourse to were Lonee Sing less strong. Each has a strong fort, and a band of steady men. The Nazim has not the means to attack Seobuksh, and dares not attack Lonee Sing, as his estate of Pyla is in the 'Huzoor Tuhseel', and under the protection of Court favorites, who are well paid by him.

Lonee Sing's estate of Mitholee is in the Mahomdee district, and under the jurisdiction of the Amil; and it is only the portion, consisting of one hundred and four recently acquired villages, which he holds in the Pyla estate, in the Khyrabad district, that has been made over to the Huzoor Tuhseel.[1] He offered an

---

[1] Anrod Sing holds twenty-eight villages in the Pyla estate, acquired in the same way as those held by Lonee Sing.

increased rate for these villages to the then Amil, Bhowood Dowlah, in the year A.D. 1840. It was accepted, and he attacked, plundered and murdered a good many of the old proprietors, and established such a dread among them, that he now manages them with little difficulty. Basdeo held fourteen of these villages under mortgage, and sixteen more under lease. He had his brother, maternal uncle, and a servant, killed by Lonee Sing, and is now reduced to beggary. Lonee Sing took the lease in March 1840, and commenced this attack in May.

The Nazim had with him the force noted below; but, being unable to get any duty from the three regiments first named, he offered to dispense with the two first, on condition, that the command of the third should be placed at his disposal for his son or nephew.

Infantry. (1) Futteh Aesh Nujeebs. (2) Wuzeeree ditto. (3) Zuffer Mobaruk Telinga. (4) Futteh Jung ditto. Ruza Kolee Khan. (5) Captain Barlow's ditto. Eleven Guns.

This request was complied with; and, on paying a fee of five thousand rupees, he got the dress of investiture,[a] and offered it to Lieutenant Orr, a very gallant officer, the second in command of Captain Barlow's corps, as the only way to render the corps so efficient as he required it to be. The Durbar took away the two regiments; but, as soon as they heard that Lieutenant Orr was to command the third, they appointed Fidda Hoseyn, brother of the ruffian Mahommed Hoseyn, who had held the district of Mahomdee, and done so much mischief to it. Fidda Hoseyn, of course, paid a high sum for the command to be exacted from his subordinates, or the people of the district, in which it might be employed; and the regiment has remained worse than useless. Of the eleven guns, five are useless on the ground, and without bullocks. The bullocks for the other six are present, but too weak to draw any thing. They had had no grain for many years; but within the last month they have had one half seer each per day, out of the one seer and half paid for by government. There

[a] A dress of honour or khilat: some article of costume presented by a superior authority to an inferior as a mark of distinction; H. H. Wilson, *A Glossary of Judicial and Revenue Terms*, ed. A. C. Ganguli and N. D. Basu (Calcutta, 1940), p. 448.

is no ammunition, stores, or any thing else for the guns, and the best of the carriages are liable to fall to pieces with the first discharge. They are not allowed to repair them, but must send them in, to get them changed for others when useless. The Durbar knows, that if they allow the local officers to charge for the repair of guns, heavy charges will be made, and no gun ever repaired; and the local officers know, that if they send in a gun to be repaired at Lucknow, they will get in exchange one *painted* to look well, but so flimsily done up that it will go to pieces the first or second time it is fired.

Captain Barlow's corps is a good one, and the men are finer than any that I have seen in our own infantry regiments, though they get only five rupees a month each, while ours get seven. They prefer this rate under European officers in the Oude service, to the seven rupees a month, which sipahees get in ours, though they have no pension establishment, or extra allowance while marching. They feel sure, that their European commandants will secure them their pay sooner or later – they escape many of the harrassing duties to which our sipahees are liable – they have leave to visit their homes one month in twelve – they never have to march out of Oude, to distant stations, situated in bad climates – they get fuel and fodder, and often food, for nothing – their baggage is always carried for them at the public cost. But, to secure them their pay, arms, accoutrements, clothing, &c. &c. the commandant must be always about the Court himself, or have an *ambassador* of some influence there at great cost. Captain Barlow is almost all his time at Court, as much from choice as expedience, drawing all his allowances and emoluments of all kinds, while his second in command performs his regimental duties for him. The other officers like this, because they know, that the corps could not possibly be kept in the state it is without it. Captain Barlow has lately obtained three thousand rupees for the repair of his six gun carriages, tumbrils, &c. &c., that is five hundred for each. They had not been repaired for ten years – hardly any of the others have been repaired for the last twenty or thirty years.

The Nazim of this district of Khyrabad has taken the farm of it for one year at nine lakhs of rupees, that is one lakh and half less than the rate at which it was taken by his predecessor last year. He tells me, that he was obliged to enter into engagements to pay in gratuities fifty thousand to the minister, of which he has as yet paid only five thousand; twenty-five thousand to the Dewan, Balkishun, and seven thousand to Gholam Ruza, who has charge of the Huzoor Tuhseel – that he was obliged to engage to pay four hundred rupees a month, in salaries, to men named by the Dewan, who do no duty, and never shew their faces to him; and similar sums to the creatures of the minister and others – that he was obliged to pay gratuities to a vast number of understrappers[a] at Court – that he was not made aware of the amount of these gratuities, &c. &c. till he had received his dress of investitute, and had merely promised to pay what his predecessor had paid – that when about to set out, the memorandum of what his predecessor had paid, was put into his hand, and it was then too late to remonstrate or draw back. There may be some exaggeration in the rate of the gratuities demanded; but that he has to pay them to the persons named I have no doubt whatever, because all men in charge of districts have to pay them to those persons, whether they hold the districts in contract or in trust.

The Zuffer Mobaruk regiment, with its commandant, Fidda Hoseyn, is now across the Ghagra in charge of Dhorehra, an estate in the forest belonging to Rajah Arjun Sing, who has absconded in consequence of having been ruined by the rapacity of a native collector last year; and they are diligently employed in plundering all the people who remain. The estate paid 2,75,000 a year till these outrages began; and it cannot now pay fifty thousand. Arjun Sing and Seobuksh Sing, of Kuteysura, are the only refractory landholders in the Khyrabad district at present.

February[b] *10, 1850.* –Halted at Lahurpoor. There is good ground for large civil and military establishments to the south of the town, about a mile out, on the left of the road leading to Khyrabad. It is a fine open plain of light soil. New pucka wells would

---

[a] Subordinates or underlings.
[b] Date given incorrectly as March in original.

be required; and some low ground, near the south and north, would require to be drained, as water lies in it during the rains. There is excellent ground nearer the town on the same side, but the mango groves are thick and numerous, and would impede the circulation of air. The owners would, moreover, be soon robbed of them were a cantonment, or civil station, established among, or very near to, them. The town and site of any cantonment, or civil station, should be taken from the Kuteysura estate, and due compensation made to the holder, Seobuksh. The town is a poor one; and the people are keeping their houses uncovered, and removing their property under the apprehension, that Seobuksh will attack and plunder the place. All the merchants and respectable landholders, over the districts bordering on the Tarae forest, through which we have passed, declare, that all the colonies of Budukh dacoits, who had, for many generations, up to 1842, been located in this forest, have entirely disappeared. Not a family of them can now be found any where in Oude. Six or eight hundred of their brave and active men used to sally forth every year, and carry their depredations into Bengal, Behar, and all the districts of the north-west provinces. Their suppression has been a great benefit conferred upon the people of India by the British Government.

February[a] *11, 1850.* – Kusreyla, ten miles, over a plain of excellent muteear soil scantily cultivated, but studded with fine trees, single and in groves. Kusreyla is among the three hundred villages which have been lately taken in mortgage from the proprietors, and in lease from government, by Monowur-od Dowlah, the nephew and heir of the late Hakeem Mehndee. He is inviting and locating in these villages many cultivators of the best classes; and they will all soon be in a fine state of tillage. No soil can be finer, and no acre of it is incapable of bearing fine crops. The old proprietors and lessees, to whom he had lent money on mortgage, have persuaded him to foreclose, that they may come under so substantial and kind a landholder. They prefer holding the sub-lease under such a man, to holding the lease directly under government, subject to the jurisdiction of

[a] Date given incorrectly as March in original.

the Nazim. Monowur-od Dowlah pays forty thousand rupees a year for the whole to government, and has had the whole transferred to the 'Huzoor Tuhseel'.

The Nazim of Khyrabad rode by my side during this morning's march, and at my request he described the mutiny which took place in two of the regiments that attended him in the siege of Bhitolee, just before I crossed the Ghagra at Byramghat. These were the Futteh Aesh, and the Wuzeeree. Their commandants are Allee Hoseyn, a creature of one of the singers, Kootab Allee; and Mahommed Akhbur, a creature of the minister's. They were earnestly urged by the minister and Nazim to join their regiments for the short time they would be on this important service, but in vain; nothing could induce them to quit the Court. All the corps mentioned above, as attending the Nazim, were present, and the siege had begun when, on the 17th of November, some shopkeepers in camp, having been robbed during the night by some thieves, shut up their shops, and prepared to leave the camp in a body. The siege could not go on if the traders all left the place; and he sent a messenger to call the principal men that he might talk to them. They refused to move, and the messenger, finding that they were ready to set out, seized one of them by the waist band, and when he resisted, struck him on the head with a stick, and said, he would make him go to his master. The man called out to some sipahees of the Wuzeeree regiment, who were near, to rescue him – they did so – the messenger struggled to hold his grasp, but was dragged off and beaten – he returned the blows – the sipahees drew their swords – he seized one of the swords and ran off towards his master's tent, waving it over his head, to defend himself, followed by some of the sipahees. The others ran back to the grove in which their regiment and the Futteh Aesh were bivouaced – both regiments seized their arms and ran towards the Nazim's tents; and when they got within two hundred yards commenced firing upon them. The Nazim had with him only a few of his own armed servants. They seized their arms, and begged permission to return the fire, but were restrained till the regiment came near, and two tomandars, or officers, who stood by the Nazim, were shot down, one dead, and the other disabled.

His men could be restrained no longer, and they shot down two of the foremost of the assailants. The Nazim then sent off to Lieutenant Orr, who was exercising his corps with blank cartridge on the parade; and, supposing that one of these regiments was doing the same thing near the Nazim's tents, he paid no attention to them. He and his brother, the Adjutant, ran forward, and entreated the two regiments to cease firing; and the Nazim sent out Syud Seoraj-od Deen (the commandant of the Bhurmar regiment, stationed in the adjoining district of Ramnugger Dhumeree, who had just come to him on a visit), with the koran in his hand, to do the same. The remonstrances of both were in vain. They continued to fire upon the Nazim, and Lieutenant Orr went off to bring up his regiment, which stood ready to move on the parade. Alarmed at this the two regiments ran off to their grove, and the firing ceased.

During all this time the other two regiments, the Zuffer Mobaruk and Futteh Jung, stood looking on as indifferent spectators; and afterwards took great credit to themselves for not joining in this attempt to blow up the viceroy, who was obliged, the next day, to go to their camp and apologise humbly for his men having presumed to return their fire, which he declared that they had done without his orders! On his doing this, they consented to forego their claim to have the unhappy messenger sent to their camp to be *executed*; and to remain with him during the siege. As to taking any part in the siege and assault on the fort, that was altogether out of their line. Ruza Kolee Khan, the commandant of the Futteh Jung, was at Lucknow during this mutiny, but he joined a few days after. Lieutenant Orr gave me the same narrative of the affair at the dinner table last night; and said, that he and his brother had a very narrow escape – that his regiment would have destroyed all the mutineers had they been present; and he left them on the parade lest he might not be able to restrain them in such a scene. Even this mutiny of the two regiments could not tempt their commandants to leave Court, where they are still enjoying the favour of their patrons, the minister and the singers, and a large share of the pay and perquisites of their officers and sipahees, though the regiments have been sent off to the two disturbed districts of Sundeela and Salone.

They dare not face the most contemptible enemy, but they spare not the weak and inoffensive of any class, age or sex. A respectable landholder, in presenting a petition, complaining of the outrages committed upon his village and peasantry, said a few days ago

The oppression of these revenue collectors, and their disorderly troops, is intolerable, sir – they plunder all who cannot resist them, but cannot lift their arms, or draw their breath freely in the presence of armed robbers and rebels – it is a proverb, sir, that *insects* prey upon soft *wood*; and these men prey only upon the peaceful and industrious, who are unable to defend themselves.

The Nazim tells me, that the lamentations of the poor people, plundered and maltreated, were incessant and distressing during the whole time these two corps were with him; and that he could exercise no control whatever over them, protected as they were, in all their iniquities, by the Court favour their two commandants enjoyed at Lucknow.

I asked Bukhtawur Sing, before the Nazim overtook us this morning, why it was, that these governors always took so many troops with them when they moved, from place to place, merely to settle accounts and inspect the crops. 'Some of them', said he,

take all the troops they can muster, to show that they are great men – but, for the most part, they are afraid to move without them. They, and the greater part of the landholders, consider each other as natural and irreconcileable enemies; and a good many of those, who hold the largest estates, are at all times in open resistance against the government. They have their Vakeels with the contractors when they are not so, and spies when they are. They know all his movements, and would waylay and carry him off if not surrounded with a strong body of soldiers, for he is always moving over the country, with every part of which they are well acquainted. Besides, under the present system of allowing them to forage or plunder for themselves, it is ruinous to any place to leave them in it for even a few days – no man, within several miles, would preserve shelter for his family, or food for his cattle, during the hot and rainy months – he is obliged to take them about with him to distribute, as equally as he can, the terrible burthen of maintaining them. Now that the sugar-cane is ripe, not one cane would be preserved in any field within five miles of any place where the Nazim kept his troops for ten days.

February[a] *12, 1850.* – Seetapoor, nine miles, over a plain of muteear soil, the greater part of which is light, and yields but

[a] Date given incorrectly as March in original.

Diary of a Tour Through Oude

scanty crops without manure, which is very scarce. Immediately about the station and villages, where manure is available, the crops are good. The wind continues westerly, the sky is clear, and the blight does not seem to increase.

The 2nd regiment of Oude local infantry is stationed at Seetapoor, but it has no guns, or cavalry of any kind. Formerly there was a corps of the Hon'ble Company's native infantry here, with two guns and a detail of artillery. The sipahees of this corps, and of the 1st Oude local infantry, at Sultanpoor, are somewhat inferior in appearance to those of our own native infantry regiments; and still more so to the Oude corps under Captains Barlow, Magness and Bunbury. They receive five rupees eight annas a month pay, and batta, or extra allowance, when marching; and the same pay as our own sipahees of the line (seven rupees a month), when serving with them. But the commandants cannot get recruits equal to those that enlist in our regiments of the line, or those that enlist in the corps of the officers above named. They have not the rest and the license of the one, while they have the same drill and discipline, without the same rate of pay as the other. They have now the privilege of petitioning through the Resident like our sipahees of the line, and that of the pension establishment, while Barlow's, Bunbury's and Magness' corps have neither. They have none but internal duties – they are hardly ever sent out to aid the king's local authorities, and do not escort treasure even for their own pay. It is sent to them by drafts from Lucknow on the local collectors of the district in which they are cantoned; and the money required for the Resident's Treasury, a great portion of which passes through the Seetapoor cantonments, is escorted by our infantry regiments of the line, stationed at Lucknow, merely because a General Order exists, that no irregular corps shall be employed on such duties, while any regular corps, near, has a relief of guards present. The corps of regular infantry, at Shajehanpoor, escorts the treasure six marches to Seetapoor, where it is relieved by a detachment from one of the regular corps at Lucknow, six marches distant.

The native officers and sipahees of these two corps have leave of absence to visit their families just as often, and for just as

261

long periods, as those of the corps under the three above named officers, that is, for one month out of twelve. The native officers and sipahees of these three corps are not, however, so much drilled, or restrained, as those of the two Oude local corps, in which no man dares to help himself, occasionally, to the roofs of houses, and the produce of fields or gardens; nor to take presents from local authorities, as they are hardly ever sent out to assist them. The native officers and sipahees, of the very best of the king of Oude's corps, do all this more or less; and they become, in consequence, more attached to their officers and the service. Moreover, the commandants of the two corps of Oude local infantry never become *mediators* between large landholders and local governors, as those of the king of Oude's corps so often do; nor are any landed estates ever assigned to them for the liquidation of their arrears of pay, and confided to their management. So highly do the native officers of these three Oude *Komukee* corps appreciate all the privileges and perquisites they enjoy, when out on duty under district officers, that they consider short periods of guard duty in the city, where they have none of them, as serious punishments.

The drainage about Seetapoor is into the small river Surain, which flows along on the west boundary, and is excellent; and the lands in and about the station are, at all times, dry. The soil, too, is good; and the place, on the whole, is well adapted for the cantonment of a much larger force.

February[a] *13, 1850.* – Khyrabad, east, nine miles, over a plain of doomuteea soil with much oosur. A little outlay and labour seem, however, to make this oosur produce good crops. On entering the town on the west side, we passed over a good stone bridge over this little stream, the Surain; and to the east of the town is another over the still smaller stream of the Gond. Khyrabad is not so well drained as Seetapoor, nor would it be so well adapted for a large cantonment. It is considered to be less healthy. There is an avenue of good trees all the way from Seetapoor to Khyrabad, a distance of six miles, planted by

[a] Date given incorrectly as March in original.

Diary of a Tour Through Oude

Hakeem Mehndee. Our camp being to the eastern extremity of the town, renders the distance nine miles.

Yesterday, at Seetapoor, I had a visit from Monowur-od Dowla, late prime minister, and Moomtaz-od Dowla, grand son to the late king, Mahommed Allee Shah, on their way out to the Tarae forest to join Hindoo Rao, the brother of the Byza Bae, of Gwalior,[a] in pursuit of tigers. . .

[1852: II, 123–4] [1858: II, 135–6]

At Khyrabad there is a handsome set of buildings, consisting of a mausoleum over his father, a mosque, an *imambara*, and a *kudum rusool*, or shrine with the print of the prophet's foot – erected by Mucka Durzee, a tailor in the service of the king, who made a large fortune out of his master's favors, and who still lives, and provides for their repair and suitable endowment. These buildings are, like all others of the same kind, infested by a host of professional religious mendicants, of both sexes and all ages, who make the air resound with their clamours for alms. Not only are such buildings so infested, but all the towns around them. I could not help observing to the native gentlemen, who attended me – 'that when men planted groves and avenues, and built reservoirs, bridges, caravan seraes, and wells, they did not give rise to any such sources of annoyance to travellers – that they enjoyed the water, shade, and accommodation, without cost or vexation, and went on their way blessing the donor'. 'That', said an old Rusaldar, 'is certainly taking a new and just view of the case – but still it is a surprising thing to see a man, in this humble sphere of life, raising and maintaining so splendid a pile of buildings.'

The town of Khyrabad has still a good many inhabitants; but the number is fast decreasing. It was the residence of the families of a good many public officers in our Service, and that of Oude; and the local authorities of the district used to reside here. They do so no longer; and the families of public officers have

---

[a] Baiza Bai, the wife of Daulat Rao Sindhia of Gwalior who, after her husband's death in 1827, tried to run the state but was eventually forced to leave. She returned later and died in Gwalior in 1862: *R and R* (1915), p. 303, fn. 1 by V. A. Smith. See the note of Sleeman's biography of Baiza Bai, *ibid*, p. xxxvii.

almost all gone to reside at other places. Life and property have become exceedingly insecure; and attacks by gang robbers so frequent, that no man thinks his house and family safe for a single night. Government officers are entirely occupied in the collection of revenue; and they disregard altogether the sufferings and risks to which the people of towns are exposed. The ground around the place is low, and the climate is inferior to that of Seetapoor. Salt and saltpetre are made from the soil immediately round the town. . .

CHAPTER X

[Baree Biswa, Ramnuggur Dhumeree and Dureeabad Rudowlee 'districts', 14–24 February 1850]

[1852: ii, 196–204] [1858: ii, 214–23]

February 14th, 1850. – Peernuggur, ten miles, south-east, over a plain of the same soil, but with more than the usual proportion of oosur. Trees and groves as usual, but not quite so fine or numerous. The Nazim of Khyrabad took leave of me on his boundary as we crossed it about midway, and entered the district of 'Baree Biswa', which is held in farm by Lal Bahader, a Hindoo, who there met us. This fiscal officer has under him the 'Jafiree', and 'Tagfore' Regiments of nujeebs, and eight pieces of cannon. The commandants of both corps are in attendance at court, and one of them, Imdad Hoseyn, never leaves it. The other does condescend some times to come out to look at his regiment when *not on service.* The draft bullocks for the guns have, the Nazim tells me, had a little grain within the last month, but still, not more than a quarter of the amount for which the king is charged. Peernuggur is now a place of little note upon the banks of the little river Sae, which here flows under a bridge built by Asuf-od Dowlah some sixty years ago. Gang robberies are here as frequent as in Khyrabad, and the respectable inhabitants are going off in the same manner. One which took place in July last year is characteristic of the state of society in Oude, and may be mentioned here. Twelve sipahees of the 59th Regiment Native Infantry, then stationed at Bareilly, lodged here for the night, in a surae, on their way home on furlough. Dal Partuk, a Brahman by caste, and a man of strength and resolution, resided here, and cultivated a small patch of land. He had two pair of bullocks, which used to be continually trespassing upon other men's fields and gardens, and embroiling him with the people, till one night they disappeared. Dal Partuk called upon his neighbours, who had suffered from their trespasses, to restore them or pay the volume; and threatened to rob, plunder, and burn down the town if they did not.

A great number of pausees reside in and around the town; and he knew, that he could collect a gang of them, for any enterprise of this sort at the shortest notice. The people were not disposed to pay the value of his lost bullocks; and they could not be found. While he was meditating his revenge, his relation, Dhokul Partuk, was, by a trifling incident, driven to take the field as a robber. An oil vender – a female – from a neighbouring village had presumed to come to Peernuggur, and offer oil for sale. The oil venders of the town, dreading the consequences of such competition, went forthwith to the little garrison, and prayed for *protection*. One of the sipahees went off to the silversmith to whom the oil vender had sold two pence worth of oil; and, finding the oil vender still with him, proceeded at once to seize both, and take them off to the garrison as criminals. Dhokul Partuk, who lived close by, and had his sword by his side, went up and remonstrated with the sipahee, who, taking him to be another silversmith, struck him across the face with his stick. Dhokul drew his sword, and made a cut at the sipahee, which would have severed his head from his body had he not fallen backwards. As it was, he got a severe cut in the chest, and ran off to his companions. Dhokul went out of the town with his drawn sword, and no one dared to pursue him. At night he returned, took off his family to a distant village, became a leader of a band of pausee bowmen, and invited his kinsman, Dal Partuk, to follow his example.

Together they made an attack at night upon the town, and burnt down one quarter of the houses. Dal Partuk offered to come to terms, and live in the town again if the people would pay the value of his lost bullocks, and give him a small income of five rupees a month. This they refused to do; and the plunder and burning went on. At last they made this attack upon the party in the surae, which happened to be so full, that several of the sipahees and others were cooking outside the walls. None of the travellers had arms to defend themselves, and those inside closed the doors as soon as they heard the alarm. The pausees with their bows and arrows killed two of the sipahees who were outside; and while the gang was trying to force open the doors of the surae, the people of the town, headed by a party of eight pausee bowmen of their own, attacked and drove them back. These bowmen followed the gang for some distance, and killed several of them with their arrows. The sipahees who escaped proceeded in all haste to the Resident, and the frontier police has since succeeded in arresting several of the gang; but the two leaders have hitherto been screened by Goorbuksh Sing and other great landholders in their interest. The eight pausees, who exerted themselves so successfully in defence of the town and surae, were expecting an attack from the pausees of a neighbouring village, and ready for action when the alarm was given.

These parties of pausee bowmen have each under their charge a certain number of villages, whose crops and other property they are pledged to defend for the payment of a certain sum, or a certain portion of land rent-free. In one of these under the Peernuggur party, three bullocks had been stolen by the pausees of a neighbouring town. They were traced to them; and as they would neither restore them nor pay their value, the Peernuggur party attacked them one night in their sleep, and killed the leader and four of his followers, to deter others of the tribe from trespassing on property under their charge. They expect, they told us, to be attacked in return some night, and are obliged to be always prepared; but have not the slightest apprehension of ever being called to account for such things by the officers of government. Nor would Dal and Dhokul Partuk have any such apprehension, had not the Resident taken up the question of the murder of the Honourable Company's sipahees as an international one. After plundering and burning down a dozen villages, and murdering a score or two of people, they would have come back, and reoccupied their houses in the town without any fear of being molested or *questioned* by government officers. Nor would the people of the town object to their residing among them again, provided they pledged themselves to abstain, in future, from molesting them. Goorbuksh Sing, only a few days ago, offered the contractor, Hoseyn Allee, the sum of five

thousand rupees, if he would satisfy the Resident, that Dal Partuk had nothing whatever to do with the Peernuggur dacoitee;
and thereby induce him to discontinue the pursuit.

The people of towns and villages, having no protection whatever from the government, are obliged to keep up, at their own
cost, this police of pausee bowmen, who are bound only to protect those who pay them. As their families increase beyond the
means derived from this, their only legitimate employment, their
members thieve in the neighbouring or distant villages, rob on
the highroads, or join the gangs of those who are robbers by
profession; or take the trade in consequence of disputes and
misunderstandings with government authorities or their neighbours. In Oude – and indeed in all other parts of India, under a
government so weak and indifferent to the sufferings of its subjects – all men who consider arms to be their proper profession,
think themselves justified in using them, to extort the means of
subsistence from those who have property when they have none,
and can no longer find what they consider to be suitable employment. All Rajpoots are of this class; and the greater part of the
landholders in Oude are Rajpoots. But a great part of the
Mahommedan rural population are of the same class; and no
small portion of the Brahman inhabitants, like the two Partuks
above named, consider arms to be their proper profession; and
all find the ready means of forming gangs of robbers out of these
pausee bowmen, and the many loose characters to whom the
disorders of the country give rise. A great many of the officers
and sipahees of the king's nujeeb and other regiments, are every
month discharged for mutiny, insubordination, abuse of
authority, or neglect of duty, or merely to make room for men
more subservient to court favourites; or, because they cannot, or
will not, pay the demanded gratuity to a new and useless commandant appointed by court favour. The plunder of villages has
been the daily occupation of these men during the whole period
of their service; and they become the worst of this class of loose
characters, ready to join any band of freebooters. Such bands are
always sure to find a patron among the landholders ready to
receive and protect them, for a due share of their booty, against
any force that the king's officers may send after them; and, if

they prefer it as less costly, they can always find a manager of a district ready to do the same, on condition, that they abstain from plundering within his jurisdiction. The greater part of the land is, however, cultivated, and well cultivated under all this confusion and consequent insecurity. Tillage is the one thing needful to all; and the persons from whom trespasses on the crops are most apprehended are the reckless and disorderly trains of government officials.

[*February 15th, 1850.* There is no entry under this date.]

February 16th, 1850. – Biswa, eighteen miles, east, over a plain of excellent soil, partly doomut but chiefly mutteear, well studded with trees and groves, scantily cultivated for the half of the way, but fully and beautifully for the second half. The wheat beginning to change colour as it approaches maturity, and waving in the gentle morning breeze – intervening fields covered with mixed crops of peas, gram, ulsee, teora, surson, mustard, all in flower, and glittering like so many rich parterres – patches here and there of the dark-green *arahur* and yellow sugar-cane rising in bold relief – mangoe groves, majestic single trees, and clusters of the graceful bamboo studding the whole surface, and closing the distant horizon in one seemingly continued line of fence – the eye never tires of such a scene, but would like, now and then, to rest upon some architectural work of ornament or utility, to aid the imagination in peopling it.

The road for the last six miles passes through the estate of Nawab Allee, a Mahommedan landholder, who is a strong man, and a good manager and pay master. His rent roll is about four hundred thousand rupees a year, and he pays government about one hundred and fifty thousand. His hereditary possession was a small one; and his estate has grown to the present size in the usual way. He has lent money in mortgage, and foreclosed – he has given security for revenue due to government, by other landholders, who have failed to pay, and had their estates made over to him. He has given security for the appearance, when called for, of others; and on their failing to appear – perchance at his own instigation – had their lands made over to him by the government demand upon them. He has offered a higher rate of revenue for lands than present holders could make them yield; and, after getting possession, brought the demand down to a low rate in collusion with government officers. Some three-fourths of the magnificent estate which he now holds, he has obtained in these and other ways by fraud, violence, or collusion within the last few years. He is too powerful and wealthy to admit of any one's getting his lands out of his hands, after they have once passed into them, no matter how.

The Chowka river flows from the forest towards the Ghagra, about ten miles to the east from Biswa; and I am told, that the richest sheet of cultivation in Oude is within the delta formed by these two rivers.[1] At the apex of this delta stands the fort of Bhitolee, which I have often mentioned as belonging to Rajah Goorbuksh Sing, and being under siege by the contractor of the Khyrabad district when we passed the Ghagra in December. Biswa is a large town well situated on a good soil, and open plain; and its vicinity would be well suited for a cantonment, or seat for civil establishments. Much of the cloth called sullum[a] used to be made here for export to Europe; but the demand has ceased, and with it the manufacture.

February 17th and 18th, 1850. – Detained at Biswa by rain.

February 19th, 1850. – Yesterday evening came to Kaharpore, ten miles, over a plain of the same fine soil, mutteear of the best quality, running here and there into doomuttea and even bhoor. Cultivation good, and the plain covered with rich spring crops, except where the ground is being prepared to receive the autumn seed in June next. It is considered good husbandry to

[1] This delta contains the following noble estates, 1 Dhorehra, 2 Eesanuggur, 3 Chehlary, 4 Rampore, 5 Bhitolee, 6 Mullahpore, 7 Seonta, 8 Nigaseen, 9 Bhera Jugdeopore. The Turae forest forms the base of this delta, and the estates of Dhorehra, Eesanuggur, and Bhera Jugdeopore lie along its border. They have been much injured by the king's troops within the last three years. Bhitolee is at the apex.

[a] I have been unable to obtain any information about sullum cloth, but *IG*, vol. viii, p. 250, notes that Biswan (=Biswa) was celebrated formerly for cotton prints.

plough, cross plough, and prepare the lands thus early. The spring crops are considered to be more promising than they have been at any other season for the last twenty years. The farmers and cultivators calculate upon an average return of ten and twelve fold; and say, that in other parts of Oude, where the lands are richer, there will be one of fifteen or twenty of wheat, gram, &c. The pucka beega, two thousand seven hundred and fifty-six square yards, requires one maund of seed of forty seers, of eighty rupees of the king's and Company's coinage the seer.[1] The country as usual studded with trees, single, and in clusters and groves, intermingled with bamboos, which are, however, for the most part of the smaller, or hill kind.

On reaching camp, I met, for the first time, the great land-holder, Nawab Allee, of Mahmoodabad. In appearance, he is a quiet gentlemanly man of middle age and stature. He keeps his lands in the finest possible state of tillage, however objectionable the means by which he acquires them. His family have held the estates of Mahmoodabad and Belehree for many generations as zumeendars, or proprietors; but they have augmented them greatly, absorbing into them the estates of their weaker neighbours...

[1852: II, 208–12] [1858: II, 227–32]

Nawab Allee has always money at command to purchase influence at Court when required; and he has also a brave and well

---

[1] The pucka beega in Oude is about the same as that which prevails over our North-Western Provinces, two thousand seven hundred and fifty-six and a quarter square yards, or something more than one-half of our English statute acre, which is four thousand eight hundred and forty square yards. This pucka beega takes, of seed wheat, one maund, or eighty lbs.; and yields, on an average, under good tillage, eight returns of the seed, or eight maunds, or six hundred and forty pounds, which at one rupee the maund yields eight rupees, or sixteen shillings. The stock required in Oude in irrigated lands is about twenty rupees the pucka beega. The rent on an average two rupees.

In England an acre, on an average, requires two and three quarter bushels of seed wheat, or one hundred and seventy-six pounds, or two maunds and sixteen seers, and yields twenty-four bushels, or one thousand five hundred and thirty-six pounds. This at forty shillings the quarter (512 lbs.) would yield six pounds sterling. The stock required in England is estimated at ten pounds sterling per acre, or ten times the annual rent.

It is difficult to estimate the rate of rent on land in England, since the reputed owner is said to be 'only the ninth and last recipient of rent'.

armed force, with which to aid the governor of the district, when he makes it worth his while to do so, in crushing a refractory landholder. These are the sources of his power, and he is not at all scrupulous in the use of it – it is not the fashion to be so in Oude.

February 20th, 1850. – Came on sixteen miles to Futtehpore, in the estate of Nawab Allee, passing Mahmoodabad half way. Near that place we passed through a grove of mangoe and other trees called the 'Lak Peree', or the grove of a hundred thousand trees, planted by his ancestors forty years ago. The soil is the same, the country level, studded with the same rich foliage, and covered with the same fine crops. As we were passing through his estate, and were to encamp in it again to-day, Nawab Allee attended me on horseback; and I endeavoured to impress upon him and the Nazim the necessity of respecting the rights of others, and more particularly those of the old Chowdheree Pertab Sing.

'Why is it,' I asked, 'that this beautiful scene is not embellished by any architectural beauties – Sheikh Sadee,[a] the poet, so deservedly beloved by you all – old and young – Hindoos and Mahommedans – says, "the man who leaves behind him, in any place, a bridge, a well, a church, or a caravansurae never dies." – Here not even a respectable dwelling house is to be seen, much less a bridge, a church, or a caravansurae?' 'Here, sir,' said old Bukhtawur, 'men must always be ready for a run to the jungles – unless they are so they can preserve nothing from the grasp of the contractors of the present day, who have no respect for property or person – for their own character or for that of their sovereign – the moment that a man runs, to save himself, family and property, they rob and pull down his house, and those of all connected with him. When a man has nothing but mud walls with invisible mud covers, they give him no anxiety – he knows that he can build them up again in a few days, or even a few hours when he comes back from the jungles; and he cares little about what is done to them during his absence. Had he an expensive house of burnt brick and mortar he could never feel quite free – he might be tempted to defend it, and lose some valuable lives; or he might be obliged to submit to unjust terms. Were he to lay out his money in expensive mosques, temples, and tombs they would restrain him in the same way; and he is content to live without them, and have his loins always girded for fight or flight.' 'True,'

a Sadi (1184–1291), famous Persian poet; born in Shiraz; among his best-known works is *Gulistan* (1258).

said Nawab Allee, 'very true – we can plant groves and make wells, but we cannot venture to erect costly buildings of any kind. You saw the Nazim of Khyrabad only a few days ago bringing all his troops down upon Rampore, because the landlord, Goman Sing, would not consent to the increase, he demanded, of ten thousand, upon seventeen thousand rupees a year, which he had hitherto paid. Goman Sing took to the jungles; and in ten days his fine crops would all have been destroyed, and his houses levelled with the ground, had you not interposed, and admonished both. The one at last consented to take, and the other to pay an increase of five thousand. – Only three years ago, Goman Sing's father was killed by the Nazim in a similar struggle; and landholders must always be prepared for them.'

February 21st, 1850. – Bureearpore, ten miles, south-east, over a plain of the same fine soil, well cultivated, and carpetted with the same fine crops and rich foliage. Midway we entered the district of Ramnuggur Dhumeree, held by Rajah Gorbuksh Sing under the security of Seoraj-od Deen, the person who attempted in vain to arrest the charge of the two Regiments upon the Khyrabad Nazim, by holding up the *sacred Koran* over his head. He met me on his boundary, and Nawab Allee and the Nazim of Baree Biswa took their leave. Nawab Allee's brother, Abud Allee, came to pay his respects to me yesterday evening. He is a respectable person in appearance, and a man of good sense. The landscape was, I think, on the whole richer than any other that I have seen in Oude; but I am told that it is still richer at a distance from the road where the poppy is grown in abundance, and opium of the best quality made.[1]

Still lamenting the want of all architectural ornament to the scene, and signs of manufacturing and commercial industry, to show that people had property, and were able to display and enjoy it, and gradations of rank, I asked whether people invested their wealth in the loans of our Government.

'Sir', said Bukhtawur Sing, 'the people who reside in the country know nothing about your Government paper – it is only the people of the capital

---

[1] Opium sells in Oude at from three to eight rupees the seer according to its quality. In our neighbouring districts it sells at fourteen rupees the seer, in the shops licensed by Government. Government, in our districts, get opium from the cultivators and manufacturers at three rupees and half the seer. The temptation to smuggle is great, but the risk is great also, for the police in our districts is vigilant in this matter.

that hold it, or understand its value – the landholders and peasantry would never be able to keep it in safety, or understand when and how to draw the interest.' 'Do they spend more in marriage and other ceremonies than the people of other parts of India, or do they make greater displays on such occasions?' 'Quite the reverse, Sir', said Seoraj-od Deen – 'they dare not make any display at all – only the other day Gunga Buksh, the refractory landholder of Kasimgunge, attacked a marriage procession in the village of —— carried off the bridegroom, and imprisoned him till he paid the large ransom demanded from him. In February last year Imam Buksh Behraleen, of Oseyree, having quarrelled with the Amil, attacked and carried off a whole marriage party to the jungles. They gave up all the property they had, and offered to sign bonds for more, to be paid by their friends for their ransom, but he told them, that *money* would not do – that their families were people of influence, and must make the king's officers restore him to his estate upon his own terms, or he would keep them till they all died. They exerted themselves, and Imam Buksh got back his estate upon his own terms; but he still continues to rob and plunder – these crimes are to them diversions from which there is no making them desist. There are a dozen gang leaders of this class at present in the belt of jungle which extends westward from our right up to within fourteen miles of the Lucknow cantonments; and the plunder of villages, murder of travellers, and carrying off of brides and bridegrooms from marriage processions, are things of every day occurrence. There are also in these parts a number of pausee bowmen, who not only join in the enterprises of such gangs as in other districts, but form gangs of their own, under leaders of their own caste, to rob travellers and plunder villages.

Gunga Buksh of Kasimgunge, has his fort in this belt of jungle, and he and his friends and relations take good care, that no man cuts any of it down, or cultivates the lands. With the gangs which he and his relatives keep up in this jungle, he has driven out the greater part of the Syud proprietors of the surrounding villages, and taken possession of their lands. After driving out the king's troops from the town of Dewa, and exacting ransoms from many of the inhabitants, whom he seized and carried off in several attacks, he, in October last, brought down upon it all the ruffians he could collect – killed no less than twenty-nine persons – chiefly Syuds and land proprietors – and took possession of the town and estate. The chief proprietor, Bakur Allee, was killed among the rest; and Gunga Buksh burnt his body, and suspended his head to a post in his own village of Luseya. He dug down his house, and those of all his relations who had been killed with him; and now holds quiet possession of his estate.'

This was all true. The Resident, on the application of Haffiz-od Deen, a native judicial officer of Moradabad district – one of the family which had lost so many members in this atrocious attack – urged strongly on the Durbar the necessity of punishing

Gunga Buksh and his gang. The Ghunghor Regiment of Infantry, with a squadron of cavalry, and six guns, was sent out in October, 1849, for the purpose, under a native officer. On the force moving out, the friends of Gunga Buksh at Court caused the commandant to be sent for on some pretext or other; and he has been detained at the capital ever since. The force has, in consequence, remained idle, and Gunga Buksh has been left quietly to enjoy the fruits of his enterprise. The Amil, having no troops to support his authority, or even to defend his person in such a position, has also remained at Court. No revenue has been collected, and the people are left altogether exposed to the depredations of these merciless robbers. The belt of jungle is nine miles long and four miles wide; and the west end of it is within only fourteen miles of the Lucknow cantonments, where we have three Regiments of Infantry, and a company of Artillery.

[1852: II, 221–33] [1858: II, 244–56]

February 22nd, 1850. – This part of Oude, comprising the districts of Dureeabad Rudowlee, Ramnuggur Dhumeree, Dewa Jehangeerabad, Jugdispoor and Hydergur, has more mud forts than any other though they abound in all parts; and the greater part of them are garrisoned in the same way by gangs of robbers. It is worth remarking, that the children in the villages hereabout play at fortification as a favorite amusement, each striving to excell the others in the ingenuity of his defences. They all seem to feel, that they must some day have to take a part in defending such places against the king's troops; and their parents seem to encourage the feeling. The real mud forts are concealed from sight in beautiful clusters of bamboos or other ever-green jungle, so that the passer by can see nothing of them. Some of them are exceedingly strong, against troops unprovided with mortars and shells. The garrison is easily shelled out, by a small force, or starved out by a large one; but one should never attempt to breach them with round shot, or take them by an escalade or a rush.

It is still more worthy of remark, that these great landholders, who have recently acquired their possessions by the plunder and murder of their weaker neighbours, and who continue their system of pillage, in order to aquire the means to maintain their gangs, and add to these possessions, are those who are most favored at Court, and most conciliated by the local rulers; because they are more able and more willing than others to pay for the favors of the one, and set at defiance the authority of the other. They often get their estate transferred from the jurisdiction of the local governors to that of the person in charge of the Hozoor Tuhseel at Lucknow. Almost all the estates of this family of Rawuts have been so transferred. Local governors cannot help seeing or hearing of the atrocities they commit, and feeling some *sympathy* with the sufferers; or at least some apprehension, that they may lose revenue by their murder, and the absorption of their estate; but the officer in charge of the Hozoor Tuhseel sees or hears little of what they do, and cares nothing about the sufferers as long as their despoilers pay him liberally. If the local governor reports their atrocities to government, this person represents it as arising solely from enmity; and describes the sufferers as lawless characters, whom it is meritorious to punish. If the Court attempts to punish or coerce such characters, he gives them information, and does all he can to frustrate the attempt. If they are taken and imprisoned he soon gets them released; and if their forts and strongholds have been taken and pulled down, he sells them the privilege of rebuilding or repairing them. It is exceedingly difficult at all times, and often altogether impossible, to get one of these robber landholders punished, or effectually put down, so many and so formidable are the obstacles thrown in the way by the Court favorite, who has charge of the Hozoor Tuhseel, and their other friends at the capital. Those who suffer from their crimes have seldom any chance of redress. Having lost their all, they are no longer in a condition to pay for it; and without payment nothing can be got from the Court of Lucknow.

February 23rd, 1850. – Badoosura, ten miles, south-east, over a plain covered with rich crops and fine foliage – soil muteear generally, but in some parts doomut – tillage excellent. Passed over some more sites of Bhur towns. The Oude territory abounds with these sites, but nothing seems to be known of the history of the people to whom they belonged. They seem to have been systematically extirpated by the Mahommedan conquerors in the early part of the fourteenth century. All their towns seem to have been built of burnt brick, while none of the towns of the present day are so. There are numerous wells still in use which were formed by them of the finest burnt brick and cement; and the people tell me, that others of the same kind are frequently discovered in ploughing over fields. I have heard of no arms, coins or utensils peculiar to them having been discovered, though copper sunuds, or deeds of grant from the Rajahs of Kunoje,[a] to other people in Oude, six hundred years ago, have been found. The Bhurs must have formed town and village communities in this country at a very remote period, and have been a civilized people, though they have not left a name, date, or legend inscribed upon any monument. Brick ruins of forts, houses and wells, are the only relicts to be found of these people. Some few of the caste are still found in the humblest grade of society as cultivators, police officers, &c. in Oude and other districts north of the Ganges. Up to the end of the thirteenth century, their sovereignty certainly extended over what are now called the Byswara and Banoda districts; and Sultanpore, under some other name, appears to have been their capital. It was taken and destroyed early in the fourteenth century by Allah-od Deen, Sultan of Delhi, or by one of his generals, and named Sultanpore.[b] Chandour was another great town of these Bhurs. I am not aware of any temples having been found to indicate their creed.[1]

[1] The Bhur Goojurs must, I conclude, have been of the same race.

[a] The greatest of the rajas of Kanauj was Harshavardhana (reigned 606–47). The Pratihara kings (c. 750–1018) made Kanauj their capital but their power was broken by Mahmud of Ghazni in 1018. In the twelfth century, Kanauj passed into the control of a line of Rajput kings, the Rathors, the last of whom, Jai Chand, was defeated by Muhammad Ghuri in 1194. The city was finally destroyed by Sher Shah in 1540.

[b] Ala-ud-din Sikandar Sani Muhummad Shah, the third Khalji Sultan of Delhi, reigned from 1296–1316. There is some uncertainty as to which king of Delhi caused the destruction of Sultanpur. Butter (*Southern Districts of Oud'h*, p. 141) and Thornton (*Gazetteer*, vol. iv, p. 610), both claim that Kai Kubad (= Mu'izz ud-din Kaiqubad), the last of the 'Slave' Kings of Delhi (reigned 1287–90) was responsible. *IG*, vol. xxiii, p. 137, leaves the question unsettled but claims that the name of the destroyer was Ala-ud-din.

The landholders, who have become leaders of gang robbers, are more numerous here than in any other part of Oude that I have seen, save Bangur, but they are not here as there, so strongly federated. The Amil is so weak, that, in despair, he connives at their atrocities and usurpations as the only means of collecting the government revenue, and filling his own pockets. The pausee bowmen are here much more formidable than they are even in Bangur. There they thieve, and join the gangs of the refractory landholders; but here they have powerful leaders of their own tribe, and form formidable independent gangs. They sometimes attack and plunder villages, and spare neither age nor sex. They have some small strongholds in which they assemble from different villages over pitchers of spirits, made from the fruit of the mhowa tree, and purchased for them by their leaders; and, having determined upon what villages to attack, proceed at once to work before they get sober. Every town and village, through which we pass, has suffered more or less from their atrocities; and the people are in a continual state of dread. In 1842, the pausees, who resided in the village of Chindwara, in the Dewa district, ran off to avoid being held responsible for the robbery of a merchant, in the neighbourhood. They were pacified and brought back; but the landholder was sorely pressed by the government collector to pay up his balance of revenue, and he, in turn, pressed the pausees to pay up the balances due by them for rents. They ran off again, but their families were retained by the landholder. The pausees gathered together all of their clan that they could muster from the surrounding villages, attacked the landholder's house, killed his mother, wife, four of his nephews, the wife of one of his nephews, two of the king's sipahees who attempted to defend them, and several of the landholder, Yakoob Husuns' servants, and plundered him of every thing he had. The landlord himself happened to be absent on business, and was the only one of the family who escaped. In all, twenty-nine persons were murdered by the pausees on that occasion. They were all permitted to come back and settle in the village, as if nothing had happened; the village was made over to another, and Yakoob Husun has ever since been supplicating in vain for redress at the king's gate.

About three miles from Badoosura, we passed from the Ramnuggur district into that of Dureeabad Rodowlee; but the above description is applicable to both, though in a somewhat less degree to Ramnuggur than to Dureeabad. It is equally applicable to the Dewa district, which we left on our right yesterday, mid-way between our road and Lucknow. There Gunga Buksh Chowdheree and his relatives have large gangs engaged in plundering towns, and seizing upon the lands of their weaker and more scrupulous neighbours. In the Dureeabad district, the leaders of gangs are chiefly of the Behraleea tribe of Rajpoots, so called after the district of Behralee, in which they reside.

I, this morning, asked Nowsing, a landholder of the Rykwar Rajpoot clan, who came to me, in sorrow, to demand redress for grievous wrongs, whether he did not think, that all the evils they suffered, arose from murdering their female infants?

'No, Sir, I do not.' – 'But the greater part of the Rajpoot families do still murder them, do they not?' 'Yes, Sir, they still destroy them; and we believe, that the father who preserves a daughter will never live to see her suitably married, or, that the family into which she does marry, will perish or be ruined.' 'Do you recollect any instances of this?' 'Yes, Sir, my uncle, Dureeao, preserved a daughter, but died before he could see her married; and my father was obliged to go to the cost of getting her married into a Chouhan family, at Mynpooree, in the British territory. My grandfather, Nathoo, and his brother, Rughonath, preserved each a daughter, and married them into the same Chouhan families of Mynpooree. These families all became ruined, and their lands were sold by auction; and the three women returned upon us, one having two sons and a daughter; and another two sons – we maintained them for some years with difficulty; but this year, seeing the disorder that prevailed around us, they all went back to the families of their husbands. – It is the general belief among us, Sir, that those who preserve their daughters never prosper; and, that the families into which we marry them are equally unfortunate.' 'Then you think that it is a duty imposed upon you from above, to destroy your infant daughters; and that the neglect and disregard of that duty brings misfortunes upon you?' 'We think it must be so, Sir, with regard to our own families or clan!'

I am satisfied, that these notions were honestly expressed, however strange they may appear to others – habit has brutalized them, or rendered them worse than brutes in regard to their female offspring. They derive profit, or save expense and some mortification by destroying them; and readily believe anything that can tend to excuse the atrocity to themselves or to others. The facility with which men and women persuade themselves of a religious sanction for what they wish to do, however cruel and iniquitous, is not, unhappily, peculiar to any class or to any creed. These Rajpoots know that the crime is detestable not only to the few christians they meet, but to all Mahommedans, and to every other class of hindoos among whom they live and move. But the Rajpoots, among whom alone this crime prevails, are the dominant class in Oude; and they can disregard the feelings and opinions of the people around them with impunity. The greater part of the land is held by them, and in the greater part of the towns and villages their authority is paramount. Industry is confined almost exclusively to agriculture. They have neither merchants nor manufacturers to form, or aid in forming, a respectable and influential middle class; and the public officers of the state they look upon as their natural and irreconcileable enemies. When the aristocracy of Europe buried their daughters alive in nunneries, the state of society was much the same as it now is in Oude. The king has prohibited both infanticide and suttee. The latter, being essentially a public exhibition, the local authorities have continued, in great measure, to put down; but the former was certainly never more common than it is at present, for the Rajpoot landholders were never before more strong and numerous. That suttees were formerly very numerous in Oude, is manifest from the numerous suttee tombs we see in the vicinity of every town, and almost every village; but the Rajpoots never felt much interested in them – they were not necessary either to their pride or purse.[1]

February, 24th, 1850. – Dureeabad, ten miles, south-east, over a plain of good soil – doomut and mutteear – covered with the same rich crops and fine foliage. There is at present no other district in Oude, abounding so much in gang robbery and other crime, as this of Dureeabad Rodoulee, in which the Amil,

---

[1] Suttee, infanticide, suicide, the maiming of any one, or making any one an eunuch, were all prohibited by the king of Oude, on the 15th of May, 1833, as reported to Government by the Resident on the 6th November, 1834. These prohibitions were reported to the Resident, by the king, on the 14th of June, 1833.

Girdhara Sing, is notoriously conniving at these crimes from a consciousness of utter inability to contend with the landholders who commit them, or employ men to commit them. Yet he has, at his disposal, a force that ought to be sufficient to keep in order a district five times as large. He has the Jannissar battalion of nujeebs, under Seetla Buksh at present; the Zoolfukar Sufderee battalion of nujeebs, under Bhow-od Dowlah, who never leaves Court; and the Judeed, or new Regiment, consisting of a thousand men. He has nine guns, and a squadron of horse. Of the guns, five are on the ground, utterly useless; four will bear firing a few rounds. For these four he has bullocks, but they are not yet in condition. Of the seer and half of corn, drawn for each bullock per diem, only half a seer is given. Of the corps more than one-half of the men are at Lucknow, in attendance upon Court favourites; and of the half present not one-third are fit for the work of soldiers.

The Amil rode by my side, and I asked him about the case of the marriage procession.

'Sir', said he, 'what you heard from Seoraj-od Deen, is all true. Imam Buksh had a strong fort in his estate of Ouseyree, five miles to our right, where he had a formidable gang, that committed numerous dacoitees and highway robberies in the country around. I was ordered to attack him with all my force – he got intimation, and assembled his friends to the number of five thousand – I had not half the number – we fought till he lost seventy men, and I had thirty killed and fifteen wounded – he then fled to the jungles, and I levelled his fort with the ground. He, however, continued to plunder; and at last seized the bridegroom, and all the marriage party, and took them to his bivouac in the jungles. The family was very respectable and made application to me, and I was obliged to restore him to his estate, where he has lived ever since in peace. I attacked him in November, 1848, and he took off the marriage party in February following.' 'But', said a poor hackery driver, who was running along by my side, and had yesterday presented me a petition, 'you forgot to get back my two carts and bullocks which he still keeps, and uses for his own purpose, though I have been importuning you ever since.' 'And what did he do to you when he got you into the jungles?' 'He tied up and flogged all who seemed respectable, and worth something, such as merchants and shopkeepers; and poked them with red hot ramrods till they paid all they could get, and promised to use all the influence and wealth of their families, to force the Amil to restore him to his estate on his own terms.' 'And, were the parties married after their release?' 'Yes, Sir, we were released in April, after the Amil had been made to consent to his terms; and they were married in May; but I could not get back my two carts.' 'And on what term did you restore this Imam Buksh to his estate?' 'I granted him a lease, Sir,' said the Amil, 'at the same rate, of five thousand rupees a year, which he had paid before.'

Stopping to talk with the peasantry of a village who had come out to the road side to pay their respects and see the procession, I asked them how, amidst such crimes and disorders, they could preserve their crops so well.

'Sir', said they, 'we find it very difficult, and expensive to do so; and shall find it still more so when the crops are cut and stacked, or have been threshed and stored – then these gangs of robbers have it all their own way, and burn and plunder all over the country – we are obliged to spend all we have in maintaining watchmen for our fields.' 'But the pausee bowmen have an allowance for this duty, have they not?' 'Yes, Sir, they have all an allowance. Every cultivator, when he cuts his crop, leaves a certain portion standing for the pausee who has guarded it, and this we call his *Bisar*. Over and above this he has a portion of land from the proprietor, or holder of the village, which he tills himself or gets tilled by others.' 'And they are strong and faithful watchmen, are they not?' 'Yes, Sir, they are; and though they will thieve and join gangs of robbers in any enterprise, they will never betray their trust. They consider it a *point of honour* not to trespass on fields or property under the guardianship of members of their own class, with whom they are on good terms; or to suffer any persons whatever to trespass on what is under their own care. The money which we send to the treasuries is commonly entrusted to pausees; and their fidelity and courage may be relied upon. The gang robbers do little injury to our fields while the crops are green, for they take animals of hardly any kind with them in their enterprises; and, having to move to and from their points of attack as quickly as possible, they could carry little of our crops with them – they are, too, afraid of the arrows of the pausee bowmen at night, if they venture to trespass upon our fields.' – 'And, are these pausee bowmen paid at the rate you mention all over the country?' 'No, Sir, they are, in some parts, paid in what is called the beega arhaeya, or two seers and half of grain from every beega. From a pucka beega, they get pucka two and half seers; and from a kutcha beega, a kutcha two and half seers.'[1] 'Your crops, my friends, are finer than I have ever before seen them in Oude.' 'Yes, Sir, they are very fine, but how we shall gather them God only knows, with such gangs of desperate robbers all around us. – The alarm is sounded every night, and we have no rest – the government authorities are too weak to protect us, or too indifferent to our sufferings; and we cannot afford to provide the means to protect ourselves.'

[1] The kutcha measure bears the same relation to the pucka in weight, as in land measurement.

Diary of a Tour Through Oude

As we went on, I asked the Amil what had become of Ahburun Sing, of Kyampore, the landholder who murdered his father to get possession of his estate.

'Ahburun Sing, Sir, is still in possession of his estate of Kyampore, and manages it exceedingly well.' 'I thought he had taken to the jungles with his gang, like the rest of his class, after such a crime, in order to reduce you to terms?' 'It was, his father, Sir, Aman Sing, that was doing this – he was the terror of the country – neither road nor village was safe from him – he murdered many people, and plundered and burnt down many villages; and all my efforts to put him down were vain. At last I came to an understanding with his eldest son, who remained at home in the management of the estate, and was on bad terms with his father. He had confidential persons always about his father for his own safety; and when he was one night off his guard, he went at the head of a small band of resolute men, and seized him. He kept him in prison for six months, and told me, that while so much plunder was going on around, he did not feel secure of keeping his father a single night – that many of his old followers wanted him back as their leader, and would certainly rescue him if he was not disposed of – that he could not put him to death, lest he should be detested by his clan as a parricide; but, if I would make a feigned attack on the fort, he would kill him, and make it appear that he had lost his life in the defence of it. I moved with all the force I had against the fort, discharged many guns against the walls, made a feint attempt at escalade; and, in the midst of the confusion *Aman Sing was killed*. As soon as this was done, I returned with my force, the son remained in possession of the estate, and all the surrounding country was delighted to hear, that so atrocious a character had been got rid of.'

This was all true, and the Amil did not seem to think, that any one who listened to him could suppose that he had done any thing dishonourable in all this – he seemed to think, that all must feel as he did, seeing his utter inability to cope with these baronial robbers in any other way, and the evils they every day inflicted upon the people. This Aman Sing was the most formidable of these robbers in this district, and the highroad from Lucknow to Fyzabad was, for some time, closed by his gang. Of those whom he robbed, he used to murder all who appeared likely to be able to get a hearing at Court, or at the Residency...

CHAPTER XI

[Dureeabad Rudowlee 'district' and the return to Lucknow, 25–8 February 1850]

[1852: ii, 287–92] [1858: ii, 315–20]

February 25, 1850. – Halted at Dureeabad. I here saw the draft bullocks attached to the guns, with Captain Orr's companies of Frontier Police. They are of the best kind, and in excellent condition. They have the same allowance of a seer and a half of grain a day, which is drawn for every bullock attached to His Majesty's artillery. The difference is that they get all that is paid for in their name, while the others get one-third; and really got none when on detached duty till lately. On Fridays, Captain Orr's bullocks get only half; and this is, I believe, the rule with all the others that get any at all. His bullocks are bred in the Nanpara, Nigasun, Dhorehra and other district in the Oude Tarae, and are of an excellent quality for work. They cost from 40 to 75 rupees a pair. In these districts of the Tarae forest, the cows are allowed to go almost wild in large grass preserves, where they are defended from Tigers; and the calves are taken from them, when a year old, to be taken care of at home, till sold for the dairy or for work. Captain Orr's bullocks have no grazing ground, nor are they sent out at all to graze – they get nothing but bhoosa (chaff) and corn. Of bhoosa they get as much as they can eat, when on detached duty, as they take it from the peasantry without payment; but when at Lucknow, they are limited to a very small quantity, as government has to pay for it. On the 15th of May, 1833, the king prohibited any one from taking bhoosa, without paying for it, either for private or public cattle; and directed, that bhoosa, for all the artillery bullocks, should be purchased at the harvests, and charged for in the public accounts; but the orders was disregarded like that against the murder of female children.

Diary of a Tour Through Oude

February 26, 1850. – Sidhore, sixteen miles, W.S.W. The country, a plain, covered, as usual, with spring crops and fine foliage; but intersected midway by the little river Kuleeanee, which causes undulations on each side. The soil chiefly doomut and light, but fertile. It abounds more in white ants than such light soil generally does. We passed through the estate of Soorujpoor Behreylee, in which so many of the baronial robbers, above described, reside, and through many villages beyond it, which they had lately robbed and burnt down, as far as such villages can be burnt. The mud walls and coverings are as good as bomb-proofs against the fire, to which they are always exposed from these robbers. Only twenty days ago, Chundee Behraleea and his party attacked the village of Siswae, through which we passed a few miles from this – plundered it and killed three persons, and six others perished in the flames. They served several others, in the neighbourhood, in the same manner; and have, within the same time, attacked and plundered the town of Sidhore itself several times. The boundary, which separates the Dureeabad from the Sidhore district, we passed some four miles back; and the greater part of the villages, lately attacked, are situated in the latter, which is under a separate Amil, Aga Ahmud, who is, in consequence, unable to collect his revenue. The Amil of Dureeabad, Girdhara Sing, on the contrary, acquiesces in all the atrocities committed by these robbers, and is, in consequence, able to collect his revenue, and secure the favor of the Court. Some of the villages of the estate, held by the widow of Singjoo, late Rajah of Soorujpoor, are under the jurisdiction of the Sidhore Amil; and, as she would pay no revenue, the Amil took a force, a few days ago, to her twelve villages of Sonowlee, within the Dureeabad district, and seized and carried off some three hundred of her tenants, men, women and children, as hostages for the payment of the balance due, and confined them, pell mell, in a fort. The clamour of the rest of the population, as I past, was terrible, all declaring that they had paid their rents to the *Ranee,* and that she alone ought to be held responsible. She, however, resided at Soorujpoor, within the jurisdiction, and under the protection, of the Amil of Dureeabad.

The Behraleea gangs have lately plundered the five villages of

Sadutpoor, Luloopoor, Bilkhundee, and Subahpoor, belonging to Soorujbulee, the head Canoongo, or Chowdheree of Dureeabad, who had never offended them. Both the Amils were with me for the latter part of the road; and the dispute beteeen them ran very high. It was clear, however, that Girdhara Sing was strong in his league with the robbers, and conscious of being able to maintain his ground at Court; and Aga Ahmud was weak in his efforts to put them down, and conscious of his being unable much longer, to pay what was required, and keep his post. He has with him two Companies of Nujeebs and two of Telingas, and eight guns. The guns are useless and without ammunition, or stores of any kind; and the Nujeebs and Telingas cannot be depended upon. The best pay master has, certainly, the best chance. It is humiliating and distressing to see a whole people suffering such wrongs as are, every day, inflicted upon the village communities and town's people of Dureeabad, Rodowlee, Sidhore and Dewa, by these merciless freebooters; and impossible not to feel indignant at a government that regards them with so much indifference.

A respectable young agricultural capitalist from Biswa, Seetaram, rode along, by my side, this-morning, and I asked him, over whom these suttee tombs, near Biswa and other towns, were, for the most part, raised.

'Sir', said he, 'they are chiefly over the widows of brahmins, bankers, merchants, Hindoo public officers, tradesmen and shop-keepers.' 'Are there many such tombs, in Oude, over the widows of Rajpoot landholders?' 'I have not seen any, sir, and have rarely heard of the widow of a Rajpoot landholder burning herself.' 'No sir', said Bukhtawar Sing, 'how should such women be worthy to become suttees? they dare not become suttees, sir, with the murder of so many innocent children on their heads. Sir, we brahmins and other respectable Hindoos feel honored in having daughters; and never feel secure of a happy life hereafter, till we see them respectably married – this, sir, is a duty the deity demands from us, and the neglect of which we do not believe he can ever excuse. When the bridegroom comes sir, to fetch our daughter, the priest reads over the marriage service, and the parents of the girl wash her feet and those of her bridegroom; and, as they sit together after the ceremonies, put into her arms a tray of gold and silver jewels, and rich clothes, such as their condition in life enables them to provide; and then invoke the blessing of God upon their union – and then, and not till then, do they feel, that they have done their duty to their child. What can men and women, who murder their daughters, as soon as they are born, ever hope for in this life or in a future state? What can widows, conscious of such crimes, expect from ascending the funeral pile, with the bodies of their deceased husbands, who have caused them to commit such crimes?' 'And you think that there really is merit in such sacrifices on the part of widows, who have done their duties in this life?' 'Assuredly I do, sir, – if there were none, why should God render them so insensible to the pain of burning? I have seen many widows burn themselves in my time, and watched them from the time they first declared their intention to their death; and they all seemed to me to feel nothing whatever from the flames – nothing, sir, but support from above could sustain them through such trials. Depend upon it, sir, that no widow of a Rajpoot murderer of his own offspring would ever be so supported; they knew very well that they would not be so; and, therefore, very wisely never ventured to expose themselves to the trial – faithful wives and good mothers only could so venture. The Rajpoots, sir, and their wives were pleased at the prohibition, because others could no longer do what they dared not do!' 'What do you think, Seetaram?' 'I think, sir, that this crime of infanticide had its origin solely in family pride, which will make people do almost any thing. These proud Rajpoots did not like to put it in any man's power to call them *salahs* or *sussoors* (brothers-in-law or fathers-in-law).'[1]

[1852: II, 295–8] [1858: II, 323–6]

February 27, 1850. – Sutrick, sixteen miles west, over a plain of muteear soil, tolerably well cultivated, and very well studded with trees of the finest kinds, single, in clusters and in groves. The mango trees are in blossom and promise well. The trees are said to bear only one season out of three, but some bear in one season, and others in another, so that the market is always supplied, though in some seasons more abundantly than in others. A cloudy sky and easterly wind, while the trees are in blossom, are said to be very injurious. A large landholder told me, that they never took a tax upon any of the trees, nor even the mhowa trees, but the owner could not, except upon particular occasions, dispose of one to be cut down, without the permission of the zumeendar, upon whose lands it stood. He might cut down one without his permission, for building or repairing his house, or for fuel, on any occasion of marriage in his family, but not

---

[1] These are terms too often made use of as abuse all over India. To call a man sussoor or salah, in abuse, is to say to him, I have dishonored your daughter or your sister!

287

otherwise. A good many fine trees were, he said, destroyed by the local officers of government. Having no tents, they collected the roofs of houses from a neighbouring village, in hot or bad weather, cut away the branches to make rafters, and left the trunks as pillars, to support the roofs, and under this treatment, they soon died. He told me that cow dung was cheaper, for fuel, than wood, in this district; and, consequently, more commonly used in cooking; but that they gathered cow dung for fuel only during four months in the year, November, December, January and February; all that fell during the other eight months, was religiously left, or stored for manure. In the pits in which they stored it, they often threw some of the inferior green crops of autumn, such as kodo and kotkee; but the manure most esteemed among them was *pig's dung* – this, he said, was commonly stored and sold by those who kept pigs. The best muteear and doomut soils, which prevail in this district, are rented at two rupees a kutcha beegah, without reference to the crop, which the cultivator might take from them; and they yielded, under good tillage, from ten to fifteen returns of the seed, in wheat, barley, gram, &c. There are two and half or three kutcha beegahs in a pucka beegah; and a pucka beegah is from 2,750 to 2,760 square yards.

Sutrick is celebrated for the shrine of Shouk[a] Salar, alias *Borda Baba*, the father of Syud Salar,[b] whose shrine is at Bahraetch. This person, it is said, was the husband of the sister of Mahmood, of Ghuznee. He is supposed to have died a natural death at this place, while leading the armies of his sovereign against the Hindoos. His son had royal blood in his veins, and his shrine is held to be the most sacred of the two. A large fair is held here in March, on the same days that this fair takes place at Bahraetch. All our Hindoo camp followers paid as much reverence to the shrine as they passed as the mahommedans. It is a place without trade or manufactures; but a good many respectable mahommedan families reside in it, and have built several small but neat mosques of burnt bricks. There is little thoroughfare in the wretched road that passes through it.

[a] In the Table of Contents, this is given as 'Shaikh', which is probably more correct.
[b] See above, p. 69, n. *a*.

Diary of a Tour Through Oude

The Hindoos worship any sign of manifested might or power, though exerted against themselves, as they consider all might and power to be conferred by the deity for some useful purpose, however much that purpose may be concealed from us. 'These invaders, however merciless and destructive to the Hindoo race', say they, 'must have been sent on their mission by God for some great and useful purpose, or they could not possibly have succeeded as they did – had their proceedings not been sanctioned by Him, he could, at any moment, have destroyed them all, or have interposed to arrest their progress.' These, however, are the speculations of only the thinking portion – at the bottom of the respect shown to such mahommedan shrines, by the mass of Hindoos, there is always a strong ground-work of *hope* or *fear* – the soul or spirit of the savage old man, who had been so well supported on earth, must still, they think, have some influence at the Court of Heaven, to secure them good or work them evil; and they invoke or propitiate him accordingly. They would do the same to the tomb of Alexander, Jungez Khan, Tymour, or Nadir Shah,[a] without any perplexing inquiries as to their creed or liturgy.

February 28, 1850. – Chinahut, eleven miles, west, over a plain intersected by several small streams, the largest of which is the Rete, near Sutrick. There is a good deal of kunkur lime in the ground, over which we have passed to-day, but the tillage is good, where the land is at all level, and the crops are fine. The plain is cut up, here and there, by some ravines, but they are small and shallow, and render but a small portion of the surface unfit for tillage. The banks of the small streams are, for the most part, cultivated up to the water's edge.

We passed the Rete, over a nice bridge, built by Rajah Bukhtawar Sing, twenty-five years ago, at a cost of twenty-five thousand rupees, out of his own purse. He told me, that one morning, in the rains, he came to the bank of this river, on his way to Lucknow from Jeytpoor, a town which we passed yester-

[a] Alexander invaded India in 326–5 B.C.; Chingis Khan's conquests in Central Asia in the 1220s brought disturbance to north India; Timur the Lame sacked Delhi in 1398; and Nadir Shah sacked Delhi in 1739.

day, and found it so swollen, that he was obliged to purchase some large earthen jars, and form a raft upon them to take over himself and followers. While preparing his raft, which took a whole day, he heard that from five to ten persons were drowned, in attempting to cross this little river, every year, and that people were often detained upon the bank for four or five days together. He resolved to save people from all this evil; and, as soon as he got home, set about building this bridge, and got it ready before the next rains. It is a substantial work, with three good arches...

[1852: ii, 301–2] [1858: ii, 329–31]

Passing a mahommedan village, I asked some of the landholders, who walked along by the side of my elephant, to talk of their grievances, whether they ever used *pig's dung* for manure. They seemed very much surprised and shocked, and asked how I could suppose that mahommedans could use such a thing.

'Come', said Bukhtawar Sing, 'do not attempt to deceive the Resident – he has been all over India, and knows very well that mahommedans do not keep or eat pigs; but he knows also, that there is no good cultivator in Oude, who does not use the dung of pigs for manure; and you know that there is no other manure save pigeons' dung that is so good.' 'We often purchase *manure* from those who prepare it', said the landholders, 'and do not ask questions about what it may be composed of; but the greater part of the manure we use is the cow dung, which falls in the season of the rains, and is stored exclusively for that purpose. In the dry months, sir, the dung of cows, bullocks, buffalows, &c. is gathered, formed into cakes, and stacked for fuel; but in the rains it is all thrown into pits and stored for manure.'

Chinahut is the point from which we set out on the 2d of December, and here I was met by the prime minister, Nawab Allee Nakee Khan, and the chancellor of the exchequer, Maharajah Balkrishun, to whom I explained my views as to the measures which ought to be adopted to save the peaceful and industrious portion of His Majesty's subjects, from the evils which now so grievously oppress them. Here closes my pilgrimage of three months in Oude; and I can safely say, that I have learnt more of the state of the country, and the condition and requirements of the people, than I could possibly have learnt in a long life, passed exclusively at the Capital of Lucknow. Any general remarks that I may have to make, on what I have seen and heard, during the pilgrimage, I must defer to a future period.

At four in the afternoon, I left Chinahut and returned to Lucknow. At the old Race Stand, about three miles from the Residency, I was met by the heir apparent,[a] and drove with him, in his carriage, to the Furra Buksh Palace,[b] where we alighted for a few minutes, to go through the usual tedious ceremonies of an oriental court. On the way we were met by Mr. Hamilton, the Chaplain, and his lady, Doctor and Mrs. Bell, and Captain Bird, the first assistant, and his brother and guest. After the ceremony, I took leave of the Prince, and reached the Residency at six o'clock. My wife and children had left me at Peernuggur, to return, for medical advice, to the Residency, where I had the happiness to find them well, and glad to see me. Having broken my left thigh bone, near the hip joint, in a fall from my horse, in April, 1849, I was unable to mount a horse during the tour, and went in a tonjohn, the first half of the stage, and on an elephant the last half, that I might see as much as possible of the country, over which we were passing. The pace of a good elephant is about that of a good walker, and I had, generally, some of the landholders and cultivators riding or walking by my side to talk with.

W. H. SLEEMAN[c]

[a] Mirza Muhammad Hamid Ali.

[b] Farhat Bakhsh Palace was built by Claud Martin, a French adventurer who built a number of important buildings in Lucknow; he sold it to Nawab Saadat Ali who reigned from 1798 to 1814.

[c] The 1858 edition is not signed; but it has a final line after the text: 'End of the Tour'.

APPENDIX I

The forts and jungles of the taluqdars

In the abridgement of the text of the Diary, obvious digressions into family or general history have been omitted wherever possible because they tend to interrupt the description of the state of Oudh in mid-century which, it seems to me, is the main value of Sleeman's work and which is certainly the aspect of his Diary which I have tried to bring to the fore in this edition. The following pages from the latter part of volume II are also, in their original context, a digression, but they do contain material on the forts and other defences of the taluqdars which is highly relevant to an understanding of the institutions of local power which were so important in mid-nineteenth-century Oudh. It seems useful, therefore, to preserve this material, but in some way that does not break the general flow of the Diary itself; hence this appendix reprints these ten or so pages in their entirety. In addition to the material on the forts and jungles, these pages contain some comments and speculations by Sleeman arising from a consideration of this local scene which relate quite directly to the consideration of his attitudes towards India which I have outlined in the Introduction to this volume and these also seem to be worth preserving here.

It should be noted that the term 'jungle' is derived from the Hindustani word *jangal* which refers, as H. H. Wilson puts it in his *Glossary of Judicial and Revenue Terms*, to 'a forest, a thicket; any tract overrun with bushes or trees, or suffered to be overspread with vegetation'.[a] Dr Fayrer's description of the Umeriah jungle near Lucknow in which he and his Lucknow companions used to hunt in the mid-1850s, is perhaps useful here: 'an extensive tract of country covered with low brushwood of the dak and corunda trees and long grass in which were nylgye, hog-deer, antelope, hares, peafowl, black and grey partridges'.[b]

[1852: ii, 254–64] [1858: ii, 279–90]

After reading such narratives,[c] an English man will naturally ask, what are the means by which such atrocious gangs are enabled to escape the hands of justice. He will recollect the history of the MIDDLE AGES and think,

---

[a] Wilson, *Glossary*, ed. Ganguli and Basu, p. 361.
[b] *Recollections of My Life*, p. 89. 'Nylgye' are Sleeman's neelgae; see Glossary, below.
[c] This extract is preceded by a long catalogue of the crimes committed, and the tortures etc. practised, by various gangs of robbers in Daryabad Rudauli district, which I have not felt it necessary to reproduce here; see 1858, vol. ii, pp. 257–78.

of strong baronial castles, rugged hills, deep ravines, and endless black forests. They have no such things in Oude.[1] The whole country is a level plain, intersected by rivers, which, with one exception, flow near the surface, and have either no ravines at all, or very small ones. The little river Gomtee winds exceedingly, and cuts into the soil, in some places, to the depth of fifty feet. In such places there are deep ravines, and the landholders along the border improve these natural difficulties by planting and preserving trees and underwood in which to hide themselves and their followers, when in arms against their government. Any man who cuts a stick in these jungles, or takes his camels or cattle into them, to browze or graze without the previous sanction of the landholder, does so at the peril of his life. But landholders in the open plains and on the banks of rivers, without any ravines at all, have the same jungles.

In the midst of this jungle, the landholders have generally one or more mud forts, surrounded by a ditch and a dense fence of living bamboos, through which cannon shot cannot penetrate, and man can enter only by narrow and intricate pathways. They are always too green to be set fire to; and, being within range of the matchlocks from the parapet, they cannot be cut down by a besieging force. Out of such places the garrison can be easily driven by shells thrown over such fences, but an Oude force has seldom either the means or the skill for such purposes. When driven out by shells, or any other means, the garrison retires at night, with little risk, through the bamboo fence, and surrounding jungle and brushwood, by paths known only to themselves. They are never provided with the means of subsistence for a long siege; and when the Oude forces sent against them are not prepared with the means to shell them out, they sit down quietly, and starve or weary them out. This is commonly a very long process, for the force is seldom large enough to surround the place at a safe distance from the walls and bamboo fence, so as to prevent all access to provisions of all kinds, which the garrison is sure to get from their friends and allies in the neighbourhood; the garrison generally having the sympathy of all the large landholders around, and the besieging force being generally considered the common and irreconcilable enemy of all.

As soon as the garrison escapes, it goes systematically and diligently to work in plundering indiscriminately all the village communities, over the most fertile parts of the surrounding country, which do not belong to baronial proprietors like themselves, till it has made the government authorities agree to its terms, or reduced the country to a waste. The leaders of the gang may sometimes condescend, to quicken the process, by appropriating a portion of their plunder to bribing some influential person at Court, who gets an injunction issued to the local authorities, to make some arrangement for terminating the pillage; and consequent loss of

[1] The Terae forest, which borders Oude to the north, is too unhealthy to be occupied by any but those who have been born and bred in it. The gangs I am treating of are composed of men born and bred in the plains; and they cannot live in the Terae forest.

revenue, or he will be superseded or forfeit his contract. The rebel then returns with his followers, repairs all the mischief done to his fort, improves its defences, and stipulates for a remission of his revenue for a year or more, on account of the injury sustained by his crops or granaries. The unlucky Amil, whose zeal and energy have caused the necessity for this reduction, is probably thrown into jail till 'he pays the uttermost farthing', or bribes influential persons at Court to get him released on the ground of his poverty.

I may here mention the jungles in Oude which have been created, and are still preserved, by landholders, almost solely for the above purposes. They are all upon the finest soil, and in the finest climate; and the lands they occupy might almost all be immediately brought into tillage, and studded by numerous happy village communities.

I may however, before I begin to describe them, mention the fact, that many influential persons at Court, as well as the landholders themselves, are opposed to such a salutary measure. If brought under tillage, and occupied by happy village communities, all the revenue would or might flow in legitimate channels into the king's treasury; whereas, in their present state, they manage to fill their own purses, by gratuities, from the refractory landholders who occupy them, or from the local authorities, who require permission from Court to coerce them into obedience. Of these gratuities such a salutary measure would deprive them; and it is, in consequence, exceedingly difficult, to get a jungle cut down, however near it may be to the city where wood is so dear, and has to be brought from jungles, five or ten times the distance.

IN THE SULTANPORE DISTRICT

1st. The Jungle of Paperghat, about one hundred miles south-east from Lucknow, on the bank of the Gomtee river, ten miles long and three wide, or thirty square miles. In this jungle, Dirgpaul Sing, Taullookdar of Nanneemow, has a fort; and Rostum Sing, Taullookdar of Dera, has another.

2nd. The Dostpore Jungle, one hundred and twenty miles south-east from Lucknow, on the bank of the Mujhoee river, twelve miles long, and three broad, or thirty-six square miles.

3rd. The Khapra Dehee Jungle, one hundred miles south-east from Lucknow, on the plain. About ten miles long, and six miles broad; or sixty square miles.

4th. The Jugdeespore Jungle, on the bank of the Gomtee river, fifty miles south-east from Lucknow, sixteen miles long and three miles broad forty-eight square miles. Allee Buksh Khan, Taullukdar, has the fort of Tanda, in this jungle, on the bank of the Kandoo rivulet, which flows through it into the Gomtee. The fort of Bechoogur, in this jungle, is held by another Taullukdar.

5th. Gurh Ameytee, seventy miles from Lucknow, south-east, on the bank of the Sae river – nine miles long and three broad, or twenty-seven square miles. Rajah Madhoe Sing has a fort in this jungle; and is one of the very worst but most plausible men in Oude.

6th. Daoodpore Jungle, seventy miles south-east from Lucknow, on the plain, four miles long and three broad, or twelve square miles. The Beebee or lady Sagura has her fort and residence in this jungle.

7th. Duleeppore Jungle, one hundred and ten miles east from Lucknow, on the bank of the Sae river, – ten miles long, and three miles wide – thirty square miles. Seetla Buksh, who is always in rebellion, has a fort in this jungle.

8th. The Matona Jungle, fifty miles south-east from Lucknow, on the bank of the Gomtee river, twelve miles long and three wide – square miles thirty-six. Allee Buksh Khan, a notoriously refractory Taullukdar, has a fort in this jungle.

IN THE ULDEEMOW DISTRICT

9th. Mugurdhee Jungle, one hundred and forty miles east from Lucknow, on the bank of Ghogra river, eight miles long and three broad – square miles twenty-four.

10th. Putona Jungle, one hundred and twenty miles east from Lucknow, on the bank of the Tonus river, eight miles long and four miles broad – square miles thirty-two.

11th. Mudungur Jungle, one hundred and twenty miles east from Lucknow on the bank of the Tonus river, six miles long and three miles broad – square miles eighteen. Amreys Sing and Odreys Sing, sons of Surubdowun Sing (who was killed by the king's troops thirty years ago), hold the fort of Mudungur in this jungle.

12th. Bundeepore Jungle, east from Lucknow one hundred and forty miles, on the plain, seven miles long and one broad – seven square miles.

13th. Chunderdeeh, south-east from Lucknow, one hundred and ten miles, on the bank of the Gomtee river – seven miles long and three miles wide – square miles twenty-one.

IN THE DUREEABAD DISTRICT

14th. Soorujpore Behreyla Jungle, east from Lucknow forty miles, on the bank of the Kuleeanee river, sixteen miles long and four miles broad – square miles sixty-four. Chundee Sing has a fort in this jungle, and the family have been robbers for several generations. The widow of the late notorious robber, Rajah Singjoo, the head of the family, has a still stronger one.

15th. Guneshpore Jungle, sixty miles south-east from Lucknow, on the bank of the Gomtee river, six miles long and two broad – twelve square miles. Maheput Sing, an atrocious robber, holds his fort of Bhowaneegur, in this jungle.

The forts and jungles of the taluqdars

IN THE DEWA JEHANGEERABAD DISTRICT

16th. The Kasimgunge and Bhetae Jungle, eighteen miles north-east from Lucknow, sixteen miles long and four miles wide – square miles sixty-four, on the bank of the little river Reyt. Gunga Buksh holds the forts of Kasimgunge and Atursae, in this jungle, Thakur Purshad, those of Bhetae and Buldeogur; and Bhugwunt Sing that of Munmutpore. Other members of the same family hold those of Ramgura Paharpore. The whole family are hereditary and inveterate robbers.

IN THE BANGUR DISTRICT

17th. Tundeeawun Jungle, on the plain, west from Lucknow, seventy-two miles, twelve miles long and six broad – square miles seventy-two.

IN THE SALONE DISTRICT

18th. The Naen Jungle, eighty miles south from Lucknow, on the bank of the Sae river, six-teen miles long and three wide – square miles forty-eight. Jugurnath Buksh, the Taullookdar, holds the fort of Jankeebund, in this jungle; and others are held in the same jungle by members of his family.

19th. The Kutaree Jungle, on the bank of the Kandoo river, south-east from Lucknow sixty miles, eight miles long and three broad – square miles twenty-four. Surnam Sing, the Taullukdar, has a fort in this jungle.

IN THE BYSWARA DISTRICT

20th. The Sunkurpore Jungle, south from Lucknow, seventy miles, on the plain. Ten miles long and three wide – square miles thirty.

Benee Madhoe, the Taullukdar, has three forts in this jungle.

IN THE HYDERGUR DISTRICT

21st. The Kohlee Jungle, fifty miles south-east from Lucknow, on the bank of the Gomtee river, three miles long and one and half wide – square miles four and half. The rebels and robbers in this jungle trust to the natural defences of the ravines and jungles.

22nd. Kurseea Kuraea Jungle, south-east from Lucknow fifty miles, on the bank of the Gomtee river, three miles long and one wide – square miles three – the landholders trust in the same way to natural defences.

IN THE KHYRABAD AND MAHOMDEE DISTRICTS

23rd. Gokurnath Jungle, north-west from Lucknow, one hundred miles, extending out from the Terae forest, and running south-east, in a belt thirty miles long and five wide – square miles one hundred and fifty.

The forts and jungles of the taluqdars

Husun Rajah, the Taullookdar of Julalpore, has a fort in this jungle. Sheobuksh Sing, the Taullookdar of Lahurpore, holds here the fort of Katesura; and Omrow Sing, the Taullookdar of Oel, holds two forts in this jungle.

IN THE BAREE AND MUCHREYTA DISTRICTS

24th. The Suraen Jungle, north-west from Lucknow, thirty-four miles, along the banks of the Suraen river, twelve miles long and three miles wide – square miles thirty-six. In this jungle Jowahir Sing holds the fort of Basae Deeh; Khorrum Sing, that of Seogur; Thakur Rutun Sing, that of Jyrampore. They are all landholders of the Baree district, and their forts are on the *north* bank of the Saraen river. Juswunt Sing holds the fort of Dhorhara; Dul Sing, that of Gundhoreea; Rutun Sing holds two forts, Alogee and Pupnamow. – They are all landholders of the Muchreyta district, and their four forts are on the *south* bank of the Suraen river.

This gives twenty-four belts of jungle beyond the Terae forest, and in the fine climate of Oude, covering a space of eight hundred and eighty-six square miles, at a rough computation.[1] In these jungles the landholders find shooting, fishing, and security for themselves and families, grazing ground for their horses and cattle, and fuel and grass for their followers; and they can hardly understand how landholders of the same rank, in other countries, can contrive to live happily without them. The man who, by violence, fraud, and collusion, absorbs the estates of his weaker neighbours, and creates a large one for himself, in any part of Oude, however richly cultivated and thickly peopled, provides himself with one or two mud forts, and turns the country around them into a jungle, which he considers to be indispensable as well to his comfort as to his security.

The atrocities described in the above narrative, were committed by Bhooree Khan,[a] in the process of converting his estate of Dewa into a jungle, and building strongholds for his gang, as it increased and became more and more formidable. Having converted Deogow into a jungle, and built his strongholds, he would, by the usual process of violence, fraud and collusion with local authorities, have absorbed the small surrounding estates of his weaker neighbours, and formed a very large one for himself. The same process, no doubt, went on in England successively under the Saxons, Danes, and Normans; and in every country, in Europe under successive invaders and conquerors, or as long as the baronial proprietors of the soil were too strong to be coerced by their sovereign as they are in Oude.

An Englishman may further ask how it is, that a wretch guilty of such cruelties to men who never wronged him, to innocent and unoffending

---

[1] The surface of the Oude territory, including the Turae forest, is supposed to contain twenty-three thousand seven hundred and thirty-nine square miles. The Turae forest includes, perhaps, from four to five thousand square miles; but within the space there is a great deal of land well tilled and peopled.

[a] 1858, vol. II, pp. 262–79.

females and children, can find, in a society, where slavery is unknown, men to assist him in inflicting them, and landholders of high rank and large possessions, to screen and shelter him when pursued by his government. He must, for the solution of this question, also go back to the MIDDLE AGES, in England and the other nations of Europe, when the baronial proprietors of the soil, too strong for their sovereigns, committed the same cruelties, found the same willing instruments in their retainers, and members of the same class of landed proprietors, to screen, shelter and encourage them in their iniquities.

They acquiesce in the atrocities committed, by one who is in armed resistance to the government to day, and aid him in his enterprises openly or secretly, because they know, that they may be in the same condition, and require the same aid from him tomorrow – that the more sturdy the resistance made by one, the less likely will the government officers be to rouse the resistance of others. They do not sympathise with those who suffer from his depredations, or aid the government officers in protecting them, because they know, that they could not support the means required to enable them to contend successfully with their sovereign, and reduce him to terms, without plundering and occasionally murdering the innocent of all ages and both sexes, and that they may have to raise the same means in a similar contest tomorrow. They are satisfied, therefore, if they can save their own tenants from pillage and slaughter. They find, moreover that the sufferings of others enable them to get cultivators and useful tenants of all kinds, upon their own estates, on more easy terms, and to induce the smaller allodial or khalsa proprietors around, to yield up their lands to them, and become their tenants with less difficulty. It was in the same manner, that the great feudal barons aggrandised themselves in England, and all the other countries of Europe in the MIDDLE AGES.

In Oude all these great landholders look upon the sovereign and his officers – except when they happen to be in collusion with them for the purpose of robbing or coercing others – as their natural enemies, and will never trust themselves in their power without undoubted pledges of personal security. The great feudal tenants of the crown in England, and the other nations of Europe, did the same, except when they were in collusion with them for the purpose of robbing others of their rights; or fought under their banners for the purpose of robbing or destroying the subjects and servants of some other sovereign whom he chose to call his enemy.

Only one of these sources of union between the sovereign and his great landholders is in operation in Oude. Some of them are every year in collusion with the governors of districts for the purpose of coercing and robbing others; but the sovereign can never unite them under his banners for the purpose of invading and plundering any other country, and thereby securing for himself and them, present *glory*, wealth, and high sounding titles, and the admiration and applause of future generations. The strong

The forts and jungles of the taluqdars

arm of the British Government is interposed between them and all sur-rounding countries; and there is no safety valve for their unquiet spirits in foreign conquests – they can no longer do as Ram[a] did two thousand seven hundred years ago, lead an army from Ajodheea to Ceylon – they must either give up fighting or fight among themselves, as they appear to have been doing ever since Ram's time; and there are at present no signs of a disposition to send out another 'Sakya Guntama'[b] from Lucknow or Kapila vastee, to preach peace and good will to 'all the nations of the earth' – they would much rather send out fifty thousand more brave soldiers to fight 'all the nations of the east', under the banners of the Hon'ble East India Company.

An English statesman may further ask how it is, that so much disorder can prevail in a small territory like Oude without the gangs, to which it must give rise, passing over the border, to deprecate upon the bordering districts of its neighbours. The conterminous districts on three sides belong to the British Government, and that on the fourth or north belongs to Nepaul. The leaders of these gangs know, that if the British Government chose to interpose and aid the Oude government with its troops, it could crush them in a few days; and that it would do so if they ventured to rob and murder within its territory. They know also, that it would do the same if they ventured to cross the northern border, and rob and murder within the Nepaul territory. They, therefore, confine their depredations to the Oude territory, seeing that, as long as they do so, the British Govern-ment remains quiet.

[a] The story of the expedition of Ram, or Rama-chandra, the eldest son of Dasaratha, King of Ayodhya, to Ceylon (or Lanka) to rescue his wife, Sita, from the 'demon' king, Ravana, is told in the epic poem *Ramayana*.

[b] Gautama, the Buddha, was born in c. 560 B.C. near Kapilavastu (now in the Nepal tarai, north of Basti district). His father was the chief of the Sakya clan and as such ruled a small kingdom of which Kapilavastu was the capital. Gautama is also called Sakyamuni, 'the sage of the Sakyas'.

APPENDIX 2

A note on the administrative divisions of Oudh, c. 1850

One of the difficulties that has faced users of Sleeman's Diary in the past has been the problem of establishing clearly the administrative units which he mentions during his journey. He refers to 'districts' by name and he indicates when he is moving from one to another; but he neither shows the boundaries of these 'districts' on his map nor does he provide a complete list of them at any point. What is more confusing still, he uses the term 'district' in referring to three different administrative units: parganas, chaklas and the areas controlled by nazims. It is in an attempt to clarify this usage and to establish Sleeman's route more clearly that I have prepared this brief note and the sketch map which accompanies it. The map gives an *indication* only (it can hardly do more given our present knowledge) of the chakla boundaries; and it traces Sleeman's route through them.

The basic administrative units for the purpose of revenue collection in Oudh in the 1840s were parganas and chaklas. The parganas (of which there were 70) were tracts of land comprising a considerable number of villages, which were controlled by kanungos; the chaklas (of which there were 12) were larger units comprising several parganas, which were controlled by chakladars. Nazims, who were appointed at times to control *ad hoc* groupings of chaklas (or parts thereof), had powers similar to chakladars over these larger areas.[a] This practice of giving nazims rights over varying groups of chaklas from time to time seems to be the basis for the idea that the administrative divisions of the Kingdom were wholly arbitrary.[b] It does not seem in fact to have been the case that the basic units were arbitrary, and the following list, given by Butter in 1839, seems to be accurate[c]; Sleeman's spelling, where different, is given in brackets.

[a] See C. W. McMinn, *Introduction to the Oudh Gazetteer* (a proof copy in the India Office Library), p. 280. Sleeman, p. 118 gives the example of the Nazim of Partabgarh who, he says, has control of Partabgarh, Sultanpur, Haldeemow, Jugdeespoor (pargana) and part of Faizabad 'districts'. The Nazims' position can be compared with that of the British–Indian divisional Commissioner who supervised the work of the collectors in a group of 5 or 6 districts.

[b] Henry Lawrence, *Essays on the Indian Army and Oude* (Serampore, 1858), p. 293.

[c] Butter, *Southern Districts of Oud'h*, pp. 97–8. This list is reproduced by Thornton, *Gazetteer*, vol. IV, pp. 38–9. Irwin, *The Garden of India; or Chapters in Oudh History and Affairs*, p. 123, gives a similar list of chaklas and quotes the number of parganas as 70.

The administrative divisions of Oudh, c. 1850

I. Chakla Sultanpur:
    (1) Sultanpur   (4) Isauli
    (2) Jagdispur   (5) Tappa Asl
    (3) Chanda   (6) Bilahri

II. Chakla Aldemau (Haldeemow or Uldeemow):
    (1) Aldemau   (4) Berhar
    (2) Akbarpur   (5) Tanda
    (3) Dostpur

III. Chakla Partabgarh (Pertabghur):
    (1) Partabgarh   (3) Dalipur Patti
    (2) Amethi

IV. Chakla Pachhamrat (Pachhimrath):
    (1) Manglasi   (3) Rampur
    (2) Rat-Haveli (Faizabad)

V. Chakla Bainswara (Baiswara or Byswara):
    (1) Ranjitpurua   (8) Majranw
    (2) Harha   (9) Haidargarh
    (3) Ateha   (10) Rae Bareli
    (4) Mauhranwa   (11) Dalamau
    (5) Kumranwa   (12) Sarendi
    (6) Daundiakhera   (13) Bardar
    (7) Hasnganj

VI. Chakla Salon (Salone):
    (1) Salon Khass   (3) Jayis
    (2) Parsadipur   (4) Ateha

VII. Chakla Ahladganj:
    (1) Ahladganj   (3) Manikpur
    (2) Bihar   (4) Rampur

VIII. Chakla Gonda-Bahraich (Bahraetch):
    (1) Bahraich   (4) Bari
    (2) Gonda Khass   (5) Atraula
    (3) Muhammadabad

IX. Chakla Sarkar-Khairabad (Khyrabad):
    (1) Khairabad   (8) Sandila
    (2) Nimkharmisrik   (9) Malihabad
    (3) Khirilahrpur   (10) Kakori
    (4) Bangur   (11) Bijnaur
    (5) Muhemdi   (12) Kasmandi
    (6) Bilgiram   (13) Malanwa
    (7) Fattehpur-Biswa

The administrative divisions of Oudh, c. 1850

X. Chakla Sandi (Sandee):

    (1) Sandi   (3) Saromannagar

    (2) Pali   (4) Shahabad

XI. Chakla Rasulabad (Russolabad):

    (1) Rasulabad or Miyanganj   (4) Unnam or Unnaw

    (2) Safipur   (5) Muhan

    (3) Asiman

XII. Chakla Lakhnau (Lucknow):

    (1) Rudauli Daryabad   (4) Kursi

    (2) Goshaenganj   (5) Sidhaur

    (3) Dewe-Jahangirabad

The sketch map included here shows the chakla boundaries on the basis of (a) Butter's map of the southern districts[a] and (b) the indications in Sleeman and the known location of parganas in the northern districts.[b] It is not possible at this stage to draw the pargana boundaries with any measure of accuracy, but further research should make this possible. For the moment this map, rough as it necessarily is, may suffice to give some definition to the map of mid-nineteenth-century Oudh and some clearer indication than hitherto of Sleeman's passage through it.[c]

  [a] Butter, *Southern Districts of Oud'h*, plate II facing p. 2.

  [b] See map of Oudh in 1870 in India Office Library. I have also used a map of Oudh in 1848, drawn by the Survey of India, to locate some places on Sleeman's route.

  [c] For the tour in terms of the British Indian districts see Irwin, *Garden of India*, p. 141.

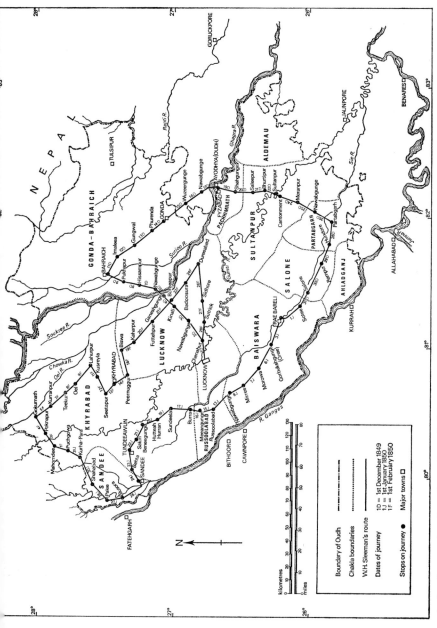

A sketch map showing the major administrative divisions of Oudh, *circa* 1850, and the daily stages of Sleeman's tour

List of the Nawabs and Kings of Oudh

1	Saadat Khan, son of Mir Muhammad Nasir	1724
2	Safdar Jang, nephew of (1)	1739
3	Shuja-ud-daula, son of (2)	1754
4	Asaf-ud-daula, son of (3)	1775
5	Wazir Ali, son of (4)	1797
6	Saadat Ali	1798
7	Ghazi-ud-din Haidar, son of (6)	1814
8	Nasir-ud-din Haidar, son of (7)	1827
9	Ali Shah, son of (6)	1837
10	Amjad Ali Shah, son of (9)	1842
11	Wajid Ali Shah, son of (10)	1847

Ghazi-ud-din Haidar was the first King of Oudh and the title passed to his successors.

Source: C. H. Philips (ed.), *Handbook of Oriental History* (London, reprint 1963), p. 92.

Glossary

This glossary is based on several established handbooks of Indian terminology and Anglo–Indian usage; the sources for each entry are indicated by means of the abbreviations listed below. Where, as in a few cases, I have been unable to trace a word, I have nevertheless included it here, along with Sleeman's explanation, both because it may be useful in cases where he uses the word in another place without explanation and because it seems to me to be important to have as complete a checklist as possible of the terms that he uses. The glossary lists words under the spelling used by Sleeman; but the transcriptions given by the authorities are also recorded where necessary.

AID   G. C. Whitworth, *An Anglo-Indian Dictionary. A glossary of Indian terms used in English, and of such English or other Non-Indian terms as have obtained special meanings in India* (London, 1885)

BCS   E. A. H. Blunt, *The Caste System of Northern India with special reference to the United Provinces of Agra and Oudh* (London, 1931)

CRAG   W. Crooke, *A Rural and Agricultural Glossary for the N-W Provinces and Oudh* (Calcutta, 1888)

EM   H. M. Elliot, *Memoirs on the History, Folklore, and Distribution of the Races of the North-Western Provinces of India; being an amplified edition of the original Supplemental Glossary of Indian Terms.* Revised by J. Beames, 2 vols (London, 1869)

HJ   H. Yule and A. C. Burnell, *Hobson-Jobson. A glossary of colloquial Anglo-Indian words and phrases, and of kindred terms, etymological, historical, geographical and discursive.* New ed. by W. Crooke (London, 1903)

HOH   C. H. Philips (ed.), *Handbook of Oriental History* (London, reprint 1963)

SDO   D. Butter, *Outlines of the Topography and Statistics of the Southern Districts of Oud'h and of the Cantonment of Sultanpur-Oud'h* (Calcutta, 1839)

WG   H. H. Wilson, *A Glossary of Judicial and Revenue Terms, and of Useful Words occurring in official documents relating to the administration of the government of British India.* Edited by A. C. Ganguli and N. D. Basu (Calcutta, 1940). First published 1855

Glossary

adawlut: adalat: court of justice. WG, pp. 12–13; HJ, pp. 4–6.

aen: ain, aeen: secular laws, statutes, rules, regulations. WG, p. 21.

amanee: amani: held in trust or deposit; applied especially to the collection of revenue directly from cultivators by officers of government upon the removal or suspension of intermediate claimants. WG, p. 32.

amanut: amanat: deposit, charge; anything held in trust. WG, p. 32.

Ameen: amin: a confidential agent, a trustee, a commissioner; used of a revenue officer or judicial officer. WG, p. 35.

amil: a collector of revenue for the government or for a revenue farmer; also himself a farmer of, or contractor for, the revenue; invested with supreme authority in the districts which he farms – 'as is still [i.e. 1855] the case in several native states, especially Oudh and Hyderabad'. WG, p. 34.

arahur: arhar: *Cytisus cajan,* a kind of pulse. WG, p. 48.

bajara: bajra: *Panicum spicatum,* a species of millet. WG, p. 77.

bandha: Sleeman says this is a form of mistletoe; above p. 123.

banyan tree: Indian fig tree, *Ficus indica* or *F. Bengalensis;* also called bar or bargat. HJ, pp. 65–7; EM, vol. II, p. 254.

barat: a bridal procession. WH, p. 98.

batta: bhata: additional allowance for public servants or soldiers, especially when in the field or on other special grounds. Often confused with batta which is the amount allowed for rates of exchange. WG, p. 122; HJ, pp. 72–4.

bazar: bazar: a market or market place. The markets known as hat or gunge (ganj) (qq.v.) are sometimes included in a bazar. WG, p. 106.

Beebee: bibi: Muslim term for a lady, a wife. CRAG, p. 46; HJ, p. 78.

beega arheya: Sleeman defines as payment of 2½ seers (q.v.) of grain from each beegha (q.v.) cultivated; see above p. 282.

beegha: bigha: land measure which varied in different areas and at different times. The standard bigha used in the North-Western Provinces' revenue surveys was 3,025 square yards (i.e., 5/8 of an acre); in Bengal it was 1,600 square yards. WG, p. 132.

bhala manus, bhalamansae: Sleeman says that this is a property tax levied by zamindars and rated according to a man's substance. bhala manus = 'gentleman'. Above p. 252.

bhoor: bhur: a very sandy soil with little fertility. WG, p. 129; CRAG, p.44.

bhoosa: bhusa: chaff and husks of cereals used as fodder; straw. WG, p. 130; CRAG, p. 45; HJ, pp. 92–3.

Bhuduk: badhak, budhuk: a killer or murderer. Badhak dacoits were associated with Thugs and murdered those whom they robbed. They resided chiefly on the borders of Oudh. WG, pp. 67–8.

Bhur Goojurs: caste name compounded of Bhur and Goojur (qq.v).

Bhurs: Bhar, Bhur: name of an 'aboriginal tribe'. WG, p. 118; EM, vol. I, pp. 33–4.

Glossary

bilabundee: bilabandi, bilahbandi: an account of the revenue settlement specifying the name of each unit on which revenue is paid (i.e., each 'mahal') and the amount due from each. WG, p. 133; EM, vol. ii, p. 242.

bildars: beldar, bildar: one who uses a mattock or spade (bel); a pioneer or sapper. WG, p. 109; HJ, p. 94; EM, vol. i, p. 16.

Brahmin: Brahman: caste category; see WG, p. 143, for a list of the major divisions distinguished in northern India.

bur tree: bar: s.v. banyan tree.

burgut tree: bargat: s.v. banyan tree.

bynamahs: bai-nama: a deed of sale. WG, pp. 73–4.

canoongoes: kanungo: lit. the expounder of the regulation or statute (kanun); a village or district revenue officer who kept the land records. Later used of this officer at the tahsil level. WG, p. 405; HJ, p. 157.

cantonment: pronounced cantoonment: a military station. HJ, p. 158.

choppers: chhappar: a thatched roof. HJ, p. 160; CRAG, p. 64.

chowderies: chaudhari, chaudhri: headman or leading man of a village, profession or trade. WG, p. 163; CRAG, p. 60.

chuckladar: chakledar: the superintendent, proprietor or renter of a chakla, an area comprising a number of parganas (s.v. purgunna). WG, p. 152.

chummun: chaman: As Sleeman says this is a garden with flower beds; above p. 233.

coss: s.v. koss.

crores: kror, but commonly crore: ten million units or 100 lakhs (q.v.); written 1,00,00,000. WG, p. 467.

dacoits: dakait: an armed robber, one of a gang of armed robbers. WG, p. 184; HJ, p. 290.

dawk: dak: transport by relays of men and horses, hence the mail. HJ pp. 299–300.

dewan: diwan: a royal court or council; a chief officer of state. Under Muslim governments he was the financial minister charged with the task of collecting the revenue and remitting it to the treasury, and he was invested with extensive judicial powers in civil and financial causes. WG, p. 225; HOH, p. 63.

dhak tree: a common tree, *Butea frondosa*, with brilliant red flowers; also called palas. The flowers produce a yellow dye and the wood is used for the hom (q.v.). EM, vol. i, pp. 243–4; HJ, p. 312.

dhootee: dhoti: loin cloth worn tucked under the legs and fastened at the waist. CRAG, p. 85; HJ, p. 314.

dhurna: dharna: a method of compelling payment by sitting at the door and fasting; while the suitor remains, the debtor must also fast. If the suitor dies, the consequences fall on the debtor. Originally Brahmans

Glossary

were employed by creditors using this method. WG, p. 215; HJ, pp. 315–17.

Dome: dom: a caste group engaged in menial and scavenging tasks but also musicians and the wives were often actresses. Elliot says that in Oudh, the term was used for sweepers. WG, pp. 228–9; EM, vol. I, pp. 84–5; BCS, p. 346.

doomut, doomuteea: domat, domatiya: a type of soil, comprising clay (matiar) and sand (bhur). WG, p. 229; CRAG, p. 90.

durbar: darbar: a royal court, a levee; also the executive government. WG, p. 193; HJ, p. 331.

dustuk: dastak: a pass or permit; a summons or writ served on a revenue defaulter to compel him to pay the balance due. WG, p. 198; HJ, p. 334.

ek-adh: 'one or more, one or so, some, few'; J. T. Platts, *A dictionary of Urdu, Classical Hindi and English* (London, 2nd ed. 1895), p. 113. Cf. *Bhargava's Standard Illustrated Dictionary of the Hindi Language,* comp. and ed. R. C. Pathak (Banaras, 5th ed. [1946]).

fakeer: fakir: any poor or indigent person but usually applied to a Muslim (and sometimes a Hindu) religious mendicant who subsists on alms. WG, pp. 241–2; HJ, p. 347.

Fusilee: fasli: the harvest year; introduced by the emperor Akbar as from A.D. 1555 (= 963 Hijra); that initial year was to be called Fasli 963. WG, p. 246.

garur: rank grass used for making khus (q.v.).

geerwa: girva: red rust in cereals. CRAG, p. 111.

ghaut: ghat: a quay or wharf; steps on the bank of a river. WG, p. 273; HJ, pp. 369–70.

ghee: ghi: clarified or oiled butter used for cooking; it is also drunk. WG, p. 276.

ghurra: ghara: earthern water pot or jar. WG, p. 271; HJ, p. 372.

gohars: Sleeman defines as 'auxiliaries'; above p. 60.

Goojurs: gujar: a caste group, cultivators and pastoralists but known in the past for their martial and predatory character. WG, p. 293; EM, vol. I, pp. 99–102.

Gosaen: gosain: a religious mendicant. Some gosains followed secular occupations and there were others who were vagrants and who robbed or extorted forced contributions. WG, pp. 285–6.

gote: gotra: an exogamous group, descended from a common ancestor, within the endogamous caste group. EM, vol. II, p. 331; WG, p. 287; J. Hutton, *Caste in India* (OUP, 4th ed. 1963), p. 281.

gram: a pulse, *Cicer arietinum*; called chana. HJ, p. 392; CRAG, p. 56.

gunge: ganj: a market place where grain and other provisions are sold generally wholesale. WG, p. 258.

Glossary

hackeries: hakeri, but commonly hackery: a cart drawn by bullocks; HJ says that originally it was applied to light carriages drawn by bullocks for personal transport but that it subsequently came to be used only of ordinary bullock carts. HJ, pp. 407–8; WG, p. 315.

hat: a market held only on certain days; a fair. WG, p. 315.

havildars: havildar: an Indian non-commissioned officer with a rank equivalent to sergeant. HJ, p. 412; AID, p. 119.

hom: homa: burnt offering, oblations of ghi and other articles put into fire as part of domestic religious observances. WG, p. 327.

Hozoor Tehseel: huzur: 'the presence, the royal presence' and hence the state or government; tahsil: the collection of public revenues, especially from land. Thus huzur tahsil is the collection of land revenue by the chief fiscal officer of government without the intervention of any third party. Note Sleeman's point that estates pay directly to the government and that the local authorities in the district have nothing to do with them. WG, pp. 320, 801.

hutheea: hatya: killing, murder; personal injury or violence. WG, p. 316.

ijara: ijara: a farm or lease of the revenue of a village or district. WG, p. 333.

imambara: a building in which the Muslim festival of Mohurrum (q.v.) is celebrated and the service in commemoration of the martyrs is performed. Tazeeas (tazias) (q.v.) are stored there at other times. Also sometimes used as a mausoleum for the family of the founder. WG, p. 337.

istamalee: Sleeman says that it is rice which has been kept for several years before being used; see above p. 216.

Jannissar: Janissary or Janizary: originally a body of Turkish infantry, founded in 1330 and constituting the Sultan's bodyguard and the main part of the standing army. Abolished in 1826 after an attempted mutiny in which a large number of the force were massacred. By extension the term denoted any body of Turkish infantry and hence any Turkish soldier, especially an escort for a traveller in Asia.

jemadars: jamadar: second-ranking Indian officer; in infantry next below subadar (q.v.) and in cavalry next to rusaldar (risaldar) (q.v.). HJ, p. 458; AID, p. 133.

jowar: jawar: a species of millet, *Holcus sorghum.* WG., p 368; CRAG, p. 139 which gives juar.

jumogdars: jamog: a conditional mortgage; a jamogdar is a person who lends a proprietor a sum of money and then recovers the loan from the cultivators. CRAG, p. 129; EM, vol. II, p. 189, which gives usage as eastern Oudh, Benares and lower Doab districts.

Glossary

Kachies: kachhi: a cultivator caste, noted as market gardeners. WG, p. 384; EM, vol. i, pp. 145–6.

kanats: kanat: walls of a tent or an external screen of canvas surrounding a tent. WG, p. 400.

kanoon: kanun: rule, regulation or statute. WG, p. 405.

khalsa: khalisa but sometimes spelt and pronounced khalsa: the exchequer; as applied to lands it meant those of which the revenue went directly to the government; hence lands or villages held immediately from government and of which the state is the manager or holder. WG, p. 431.

kharee nimuck: khari-nimak: a factitious kind of salt; sulphate of soda which is used for adulteration of common salt. WG, p. 436; CRAG, p. 157.

khohurs: Sleeman explains this as the opposite of sayer (q.v.), i.e., not producing income? See above p. 234. Literally means 'uneven'.

khubtee: Sleeman explains as 'slimy'; above p. 215.

khus: khaskhas: a sweet-scented grass root (*Andropogon muricatum*) used for making screens (called tatti) for doors and windows in the season of hot winds; the screens are kept wet and so reduce the temperature as the winds pass through them. WG, p. 440; CRAG, p. 158; HJ, pp. 283, 903.

kodo: a small millet, *Paspalum frumentaceum*, one form of which has the property of intoxicating when made into bread. WG, p. 458; EM, vol. ii, pp. 373–4; CRAG, p. 165.

koloo: kolhu: the country sugarcane mill. CRAG, p. 165.

komukee: kumaki, from Persian kumak, 'aid'; hence various uses with the idea of auxiliary; Mughal usage in sense of auxiliary troops. HJ, p. 251.

Koormies: kurmi: caste of agriculturists. WG, p. 478.

koss: sometimes coss; measure of distance varying from one to two miles in different localities but usually taken as about two miles. WG, p. 462; HJ, pp. 261–2; EM, vol. ii, pp. 194–6.

kotkee: kutki: a small millet, *Panicum miliare*. CRAG, p. 173.

kubz: kabz: receipt or acknowledgement; in village accounts it is the patwari's (s.v. putwaries) receipt for the instalment of rent. WG, pp. 382–3.

kudum rusool: kadam-i-rasul: as Sleeman says, a shrine containing an imprint of the foot of the Prophet Muhammad (= rasul = the messenger of God). WG, pp. 385, 704.

kuneea dan: kanyadan: the giving of a girl in marriage; a gift to a girl upon her marriage, a dowry. WG, p. 406; CRAG, p. 147.

kunkur: kankar: various sorts of coarse limestone found in the soil; also gravel, hard sand; used for road-making. WG, p. 403; CRAG, p. 146.

Kunojee: Kanauji: that is, coming from the city of Kanauj; the term is used to denote a number of north Indian social groups. Cf. Kanyakubja. WG, p. 406.

Glossary

kurbee: karbi: stems of millet cut up for fodder. CRAG, p. 147.

kutcha: kachcha: 'raw, crude, unripe, uncooked'; used with a wide range of examples; it is the opposite of pukka (pakka) (q.v.). HJ, pp. 287, 734; WG, pp. 383, 622.

lakhs: lakh: one hundred thousand units, written 1,00,000. HJ, pp. 500–1; HOH, p. 68.

lakulame kubz: lakalam-baki: undisputed balance of an account, rent or revenue; see also kubz, 'receipt'. WG, p. 483.

Lodhees: lodhi, lodha: a cultivating caste. WG, p. 491.

Looneas: lonia: a caste of salt-makers. WG, p. 492.

loongree: lungi: cloth worn by Muslims as a waist cloth; wrapped around body and ends tucked in but not carried through legs as with dhoti (dhootee, q.v.). CRAG, p. 179; HJ, p. 525, which gives 'lungooty'.

mango: the fruit of the tree *Mangifera Indica*; called am or amba in north India; HJ suggests that mango is from a Portuguese adaptation of the Tamil name. CRAG, pp. 7–8; HJ, pp. 553–5.

mash: a kind of pulse; usually applied to urad (*Phaseolus radiatus*) but sometimes to mung (*P. mungo*) which are in fact very similar. CRAG, pp. 189, 195, 282–3.

mhowa: mahua: the tree *Bassia latifolia*; the fruit or nut is eaten. CRAG, p. 182.

Mohtamin: Sleeman gives 'Quartermaster-General'; above, p. 74.

Mohurrum: muharram: the first month of the Muslim year; the tenth day of that month is the anniversary of the assassination of Hasan and Husain at Kerbala and it is therefore the great day of mourning for the Shia. A festival, lasting over the first ten days, is muharram. *The Encyclopedia of Islam*, vol. III (London, 1936), pp. 689–90; WG, p. 555.

mohurs: muhar: a gold coin of the value of Rs 16. WG, p. 555.

moonshee: munshi: a writer or secretary. WG, p. 567.

Moraes: murao, morao: a caste of cultivators; cf. Kachie (kachhi). EM, vol. I, pp. 145–6; BCS, p. 352.

mote: moth: a kind of pulse (*Phaseolus acontitifolius*). CRAG, p. 194.

mudar: madar: a shrub (*Asclepias gigantea*). HJ records that the acrid milky juice of the plant (= ak) was supposed to be used for infanticide. HJ, p. 593; CRAG, p. 180; SDO, p. 41.

must: mast: 'drunk'; applied to male animals in state of periodical excitement. HJ, p. 604.

muteear: matiar, matiyar: a bluish or blackish clay soil. WG, p. 229; CRAG, pp. 189–90.

naib: a deputy, a lieutenant. WG, p. 578.

naicks: naik, nayak: an Indian non-commissioned officer, a corporal. HJ, p. 614; AID, p. 219; WG, pp. 593–4.

Glossary

nanker: nankar: an allowance on the revenue demand given to the occupant or landlord as maintenance. WG, pp. 585–6; CRAG, p. 202.

Nawab: the plural of naib (q.v.) but used honorifically in the singular; originally denoted a viceroy or governor of a province but later became a title of a man of high rank upon whom it was conferred without office being attached to it. WG, p. 578; HOH, p. 70

Nawab Wuzeer: The first two Nawabs of 'independent' Oudh, Saadat Khan and Safdar Jang (who reigned 1720–54), were also the wazirs ('Finance Ministers'; s.v. wuzeer) of the Mughal emperor, and under Safdar Jang the office became hereditary to the family.

nazim: the superior officer or governor of a province charged with the administration of criminal law and justice. WG, p. 594.

neelgae: nilgai, nilgau: 'blue cow', the popular name for a large antelope of slaty-blue colour. HJ, pp. 621–2.

neem: nim: the tree, *Azadarichta Indica*. CRAG, p. 207.

nujeebs: najib (Arabic): 'a kind of half-disciplined infantry'; a militia of 'gentlemen volunteers'. HJ, p. 631.

nuzuranas, nazuranas: nazrana: a gift, or present, especially from an inferior to a superior; particularly applied to sums received as gratuities. WG, p. 596.

oosur: usar: land infested with salts and unfit for cultivation. WG, p. 856; CRAG, p. 283.

owl: aul: any great calamity such as plague, cholera, etc. HJ, pp. 649–50.

paemalee: paimali: trampling underfoot, laying waste; compensation for damage to standing crops by the passage of troops. WG, p. 619.

palankeens: palanquin: a box litter for travelling; it had a pole projecting before and behind which was borne on the shoulders of 4 or 6 men. HJ, pp. 659–61.

palas: another name for the dhak tree, q.v.

Passies, Pausies: pasi: a watchman; a caste of watchmen, labourers and (formerly) toddy tappers; also used as retainers. WG, p. 644; BCS, p. 353.

Pathans: the usual name for people of Afghan descent settled in India and especially Rohilkhand. WG, p. 647.

pawn: pan: a combination of betel leaves, areca nut, lime and spices, which is chewed. WG, p. 627; HJ, p. 689.

peepul: pipal: the tree, *Ficus religiosa*, which is one of the most important of Indian trees. Often associated with the temple or a prominent place in a village. The Bo tree of Ceylon. HJ, pp. 108, 691–2.

prohut: purohita: a family priest, one who conducts domestic ceremonies for a household or family. WG, pp. 683–4.

Glossary

pukka: pakka: 'ripe, finished, cooked' etc.; the opposite of kutcha (q.v.). HJ, p. 734; WG, p. 622.

Pultun: paltan: corruption of battalion, with some confusion with platoon; it is the usual Indian word for a regiment of Indian infantry and is not used of a European regiment. SDO says that it consisted of 12 companies (tuman) of 100 men each. HJ, p. 737; SDO, p. 102.

purgunna: pargana: a tract of land comprising many villages; several parganas go to make a chakla or zila. WG, p. 640.

putwaries: patwari: village accountant whose job is to record accounts relating to land, produce, cultivation, changes in ownership and past assessment. WG, p. 646.

Rajpoots: rajput, literally 'son of a king'. The name of a caste category. See WG for description of clan structure. WG, pp. 695–6.

ratoon: Sleeman says that this is a second crop of sugar cane; above p. 244.

Rawut: rawat: name of a caste. WG, p. 706.

razeenamas: razi nama: a written assent, a deed of agreement or concurrence, usually implying an amicable settlement; also, a testimonial signed by the plaintiff indicating that he is satisfied with a decision. WG, p. 707.

reeasuts: riasut: 'government rule', a term affected by zamindars when speaking of their own authority. WG, pp. 691, 709.

reha: reh: impure carbonate of soda; impregnates some soils and makes them barren (rehar) land. WG, p. 708; CRAG, p. 243.

rupee: rupiya; commonly rupee: standard silver coin. On the range of variations in value see the articles in WG, pp. 714–15 and HJ, pp. 774–6. The 1850 Oudh rupee, the 'Shamshere-shahi' was valued at par with the Company rupee: S. N. Prasad, *Paramountcy under Dalhousie* (Delhi, 1964), Appendix V, 'Some Indian coins in 1850', p. 210.

rusaldar: risaldar: Indian officer commanding a troop of irregular cavalry (a risala). WG, p. 710; HJ, p. 762; AID, p. 268.

sagwun: sagwan, sagun: the teak tree, *Tectona grandis.* HJ, p. 910.

sakhoo: the sal tree, *Shorea robusta.* O. Spate and A. Learmonth, *India and Pakistan* (London, 3rd ed. 1967), p. 80.

salah: sala: a wife's brother; 'to call a stranger by such an appellation is one of the most aggravated terms of abuse in Bengal'. WG, p. 738; CRAG, p. 248.

saraees: sarai: a large building, a rest house for travellers. AID, p. 281; HJ, pp. 811–12.

sayer: sair: 'remainder', the other sources of revenue accruing to government in addition to land revenue (customs, transit dues etc.). Also for individual landlords, 'manorial dues', that is, items of income not included in the produce of cultivation such as rent from fisheries, timber, etc. WG, p. 725; HJ, pp. 798–801; CRAG, p. 247.

Glossary

seer: ser: measure of weight which varied but was about 2 lb. WG, p. 759.

seer (land): sir: lands in a village cultivated by zamindars themselves (with labourers or tenants at will) as their own special share of the lands. WG, p. 778.

seghadars: Sleeman says that kanungos and chaudharis were called seghadars in Oudh; above p. 122.

semul: semal, sembhal: the 'cotton tree', *Bombax Malabaricum*. HJ, p. 807.

seobundies: sebundy from Persian sihbandhi: irregular troops used for revenue or police duties. HJ, p. 805.

sipahees: sipahi, commonly sepoy: an Indian soldier, disciplined and dressed in European style. HJ, pp. 809–11.

subadars: subadar: the chief Indian officer of a company of sipahis. HJ, pp. 856–7; AID, p. 301.

sufarishies: Sleeman says 'men who are unfit for duty, and have been put in by influential persons at Court, to appear at muster and draw pay'. Note that he says later that there are 'civil' sufarishies as well as 'military' sufarishies. Above pp. 116-17, 119.

sujjee mattee: sajji matti: 'subcarbonate of soda'. SDO, p. 45.

sussoor: susar: father-in-law; the word is a term of abuse and is replaced by various euphemisms. Cf. salah. WG, p. 793; CRAG, p. 248.

suttee: sati: 'a virtuous wife', especially one 'who consummates a life of duty by burning herself on the funeral pyre of her husband'. WG, pp. 754–5.

Syud: sa'id, sayid, saiyid: designation of a Muslim claiming descent from Husain, grandson of Muhummad. WG, p. 725.

talao: tal, talao: a lake or tank. CRAG, p. 267.

tallookdars: taluk, taluq: implies connection or dependency; in Oudh this was used of an estate that was a dependency within the kingdom; elsewhere the term was used to denote a dependent part of a zamindar's estate. The taluqdar was the holder of a taluq. WG, pp. 797–8.

tamarind: tree, *Tamarindus Indica*, cultivated for acid pulp of pods. HJ, pp. 894–5.

tatties: see khus, above.

tazeeas: ta'ziya, tazia: expression of sympathy, the mourning of the Shi'i for Husain and Hasan. The tabut or copy of the tomb at Kerbala which is carried in procession at Muhurrum (q.v.) is also popularly called ta'ziya, but ta'ziya properly means the passion play itself. *Encyclopaedia of Islam*, vol. iv, pp. 711–12; WG, p. 825; HJ, p. 904.

tehseel, tuhseel: tahsil: the collection of the public revenues, especially from land. WG, p. 801.

tehseeldars, tuhseeldars: tahsildar: the collector of the public revenues from one or more parganas. WG, p. 801.

telinga: term used in the eighteenth century as a synonym for sipahi (q.v.); it arose because the sipahis first came from 'Telinga country',

Index

Index

Index

Index

Index

Index

Index

Index

Index

Index

Index

050291

ST. MARY'S COLLEGE OF MARYLAND
ST. MARY'S CITY, MARYLAND